Interplay

Fifth Edition

Interplay

The Process of
Interpersonal Communication

Ronald B. Adler
Santa Barbara City College

Lawrence B. Rosenfeld
University of North Carolina at Chapel Hill

Neil Towne
Grossmont College

Harcourt Brace Jovanovich College Publishers

Fort Worth   Philadelphia   San Diego   New York   Orlando   Austin   San Antonio
Toronto   Montreal   London   Sydney   Tokyo

Publisher	Ted Buchholz
Acquisitions Editor	Janet Wilhite
Senior Project Editor	Dawn Youngblood
Production Manager	Tad Gaither
Manager of Art & Design	Guy Jacobs
Text Designer	Janet Bollow

Library of Congress Cataloging-in-Publication Data

Adler, Ronald B. (Ronald Brian), 1946–
    Interplay: the process of interpersonal
communication/Ronald B. Adler, Lawrence B.
Rosenfeld, Neil Towne.—5th ed.
      p.   cm.
    Includes bibliographical references and index.
    ISBN: 0–03–055493–4
    1. Interpersonal communication.   I. Rosenfeld,
Lawrence B.   II. Towne, Neil, 1928–   .
III. Title.
    BF637.C45A33   1992
    302.2—dc20   91–23943
                           CIP

ISBN: 0-03-055493-4

Requests for permission to make copies of any part of
the work should be mailed to: Permissions Department,
Harcourt Brace Jovanovich, Publishers, 8th Floor,
Orlando, Florida 32887

Address editorial correspondence to: 301 Commerce
Street, Suite 3700, Fort Worth, TX 76102

Address orders to: 6277 Sea Harbor Drive, Orlando, FL
32887   1-800-782-4479, or 1-800-433-0001 (in Florida)

Copyright information on page 410

Printed in the United States of America

2 3 4 5   0 4 3   9 8 7 6 5 4

Preface

This fifth edition of *Interplay* aims at striking a balance between consistency and change. It retains all the characteristics that have been well received by professors and students in the past. The writing style aims at being clear and readable, based on the belief that even the most important ideas can be presented in a straight-forward way. The focus is still on showing how theories and research relate to behavior in every-day settings, so that readers who ask "so what?" will always find an answer. Boxed "Student Reflections" throughout the book provide first-person accounts of how material in the text operates in situations that will be familiar to readers of every age and background. A variety of quotations, journalistic excerpts, photographs, cartoons, and poetry that illustrate concepts in a way that pure academic prose can't do continues to make *Interplay* accessible for the students.

This new edition of *Interplay* continues to offer guidelines for developing communication skills along with providing a comprehensive first look at theory and research in interpersonal communication. Our concept of communication competence reflects the current thinking that behavioral flexibility is an essential ingredient of effectiveness. We avoid simplistic prescriptions that suggest there is a single right way of communicating in every situation. For example, the discussion of empathic listening in Chapter 7 reinforces the value of using a wide range of listening styles. An expanded section in Chapter 9 discusses how "white lies" and equivocation can serve as ethical alternatives to complete self-disclosure. New material in Chapter 10 presents a range of compliance gaining strategies and offers suggestions on choosing the most effective, ethical approach for a given situation.

In this era of increasing diversity, the important topic of culture has received special emphasis throughout this edition of *Interplay*. Chapter 2 describes how culture affects the self-concept, and consequently communication behavior. Treatment of cultural influences on perception in Chapter 3 has been expanded. Chapter 5 describes new research showing how language shapes world view. The discussion of cultural variables in nonverbal communication has been expanded in Chapter 6. Material on how relationships vary from one culture to another has been added to Chapter 8, and Chapter 9 shows that self-disclosure has a cultural dimension.

Gender-related variables also are covered thoroughly in this edition. For example, Chapter 4 contains a new section on the role of gender in emotional expressiveness and sensitivity to others' emotional messages. Chapter 5 cites new research on the similarities and differences between male and female language use. A new section on gender and friendship has been introduced in Chapter 8.

In addition to these topics, coverage of a variety of important subjects has been expanded throughout the book. For example, Chapter 1 contains new information on the relationship between impersonal and interpersonal communication. Material in Chapter 5 on abstract language has been expanded to show that absolute precision and complete understanding aren't always desirable, and a new section on "I" language emphasizes how speaking for one's self can lead to more responsible thinking and smoother relationships. The model of listening in Chapter 7 has been expanded to reinforce the transactional nature of communication as more than a verbal ping-pong game in which speakers take turns sending and receiving messages. Material on defensive communication in Chapter 10 now contains a discussion of face maintenance. Chapter 11 places greater emphasis on the relational nature of conflicts, showing that how they are managed depends at least as much on the interaction between communicators as on the individual styles of each person.

Several new pedagogical features in this edition of *Interplay* should improve learning. Both brief and detailed tables of contents provide an overview of the book. Each chapter opens with an indication of key terms, as well as lists of both cognitive and behavioral objectives. The key terms are boldfaced and defined on first text mention. Chapters end with summaries that review important ideas. A complete glossary defines all the key terms introduced in the text. Throughout the book readers will encounter "teasers"—boxed questions that will encourage them to try the activities at the end of each chapter.

Along with the text itself, a variety of ancillary materials should make learning more efficient and effective.

- An Instructor's Manual by Mary Bozik provides a wide range of teaching and testing activities.
- The videotape "Interpersonal Communication in Action" by David Hudson and Sharon Ratliffe illustrates how communication skills look and sound in everyday life.
- Computerized programs help instructors create exams quickly and easily, leaving more time for working directly with students.

Changes like these don't happen in a vacuum. We are grateful for the suggestions from reviewers around the country who reviewed the manuscript for this edition of *Interplay:* Dr. Leonard Barchak, McNeese State University; Nan Peck, Northern Virginia Community College, Annondale; Thurman Knight, Anoka Ramsey Community College, Minnesota; Eric Eisenberg, University of Southern California; Carolyn Stephens, Concordia University, Wisconsin; Dr. Michael Schliessmann, South Dakota State University; Dr. Lynn Phelps, Ohio University; Dr. Vince Bloom, California State University, Fresno; David Natharius, California State University, Fresno; and Dr. Dirk Scheerhorn, University of Arizona.

We also continue to value the contributions of colleagues whose suggestions were helpful in past editions of *Interplay:* Ruth P. Anderson, North Carolina State University; Donald Berg, Southeast Missouri State University; Robert J. Dretz, Olympia College; George O. Enell, California State University at Fullerton; Leslye Evans, Iowa Western Community College; Mary C. Forestieri, Lane Community College; Barbara E. Gordon, Louisiana State University; Debra Grodin, University of Kentucky; Martha J. Haun, University of Houston; Kenneth Howard, University of Houston; Virginia T. Katz, University of Minnesota at Duluth; Anntarie Lanita Simms, Trenton State University; Dickie Spurgeon, Southern Illinois University at Edwardsville; and Eleanor Tucker, Grossmont College.

We also offer our thanks to the team of publishing professionals who helped us shape this edition from start to finish: Robin Adler, Buddy Barkalow, Janet Bollow, Mary Pat Donlon, Tad Gaither, Guy Jacobs, Charles Naylor, Leon Unruh, Janet Wilhite, and Dawn Youngblood.

Brief Contents

Detailed Contents

Part IV

Relational Dimensions of Interpersonal Communication

Interplay

Part One

Introduction

Interpersonal Process

Chapter 1
Interpersonal Process

After studying the material in this chapter

You should understand

1. The needs that effective communication can satisfy.

2. The differences between linear, interactive, and transactional communication models.

3. Situational and qualitative definitions of interpersonal communication.

4. The characteristics of competent communication.

You should be able to

1. Identify the important needs you attempt to satisfy by communicating.

2. Demonstrate how the transactional communication model applies to your interpersonal communication.

3. Describe the degrees to which your communication is impersonal and interpersonal, and describe the consequences of this combination.

4. Identify situations in which you communicate competently.

Key Terms

Channel
Cognitive complexity
Communication
Communication competence
Content message
Decoding
Encode
Environment

External noise
Feedback
Impersonal communication
Interactive communication model
Interpersonal communication
Linear communication model
Message
Noise

Physiological noise
Psychological noise
Receiver
Relational message
Self-monitoring
Sender
Transactional communication
    model

Everyone communicates. Students and professors, parents and children, employers and employees, friends, strangers, and enemies—all communicate. We have been communicating with others from the first weeks of life and will keep on doing so until we die.

Why study an activity you've done your entire life? There are three reasons: First, studying interpersonal communication will give you a new look at a familiar topic. For instance, in a few pages you will find that some people can go years—even lifetimes—without communicating in a truly interpersonal manner. In this sense, exploring human communication is rather like studying anatomy or botany—everyday objects and processes take on new meaning.

A second reason for studying the subject has to do with the staggering amount of time we spend communicating. In research at the University of Cincinnati, Rudolph Verderber and his associates (1976) measured the amount of time a sample of college students spent on various activities. The researchers found that their subjects spent an average of over 61 percent of their waking time engaged in some form of communication. Whatever the occupation, the results would not be too different.

There is a third, more compelling reason for studying interpersonal communication. To put it bluntly, none of us communicate as effectively as we could. Our friendships, jobs, and studies suffer because we fail to express ourselves well and to understand others accurately. If you pause now and make a mental list of communication problems you have encountered, you'll see that, no matter how successful your relationships, there is plenty of room for improvement in your everyday life. The information that follows will help you improve the way you communicate with some of the people who matter most to you.

Why We Communicate

Research demonstrating the importance of communication has been around longer than you might think. Frederick II, emperor of Germany from 1196 to 1250, was called *stupor mundi*—"wonder of the world"—by his admiring subjects. Along with his administrative and military talents, Frederick was a leading scientist of his time. A medieval historian described one of his interesting, if inhumane, experiments:

> He bade foster mothers and nurses to suckle the children, to bathe and wash them, but in no way to prattle with them, for he wanted to learn whether they would speak the Hebrew language, which was the oldest, or Greek, or Latin, or Arabic, or perhaps the language of their parents, of whom they had been born. But he labored in vain because all the children died. For they could not live without the petting and joyful faces and loving words of their foster mothers. (Ross and McLaughlin 1949: 366)

Fortunately, contemporary researchers have found less-dramatic ways to illustrate the importance of communication. In one study of

I see communication as a huge umbrella that covers and affects all that goes on between human beings. Once a human being has arrived on this earth, communication is the largest single factor determining what kinds of relationships he makes with others and what happens to him in the world about him. How he manages his survival, how he develops intimacy, how productive he is, how he makes sense, how he connects with his own divinity—all are largely dependent on his communication skills.

VIRGINIA SATIR

isolation, five subjects were paid to remain alone in a locked room. One lasted for eight days. Three held out for two days, one commenting, "Never again." The fifth subject lasted only two hours (Schachter 1959: 9–10).

You might question the value of experiments like these, arguing that solitude would be a welcome relief from the irritations of everyday life. It's true that all of us need solitude, often more than we get. On the other hand, each of us has a point beyond which we do not want to be alone. Beyond this point solitude changes from a pleasurable to a painful condition. In other words, we all need people. We all need to communicate.

PHYSICAL NEEDS

Communication is so important that it is necessary for physical health. A recent study suggests that a lack of social relationships rivals dangers including cigarette smoking, high blood pressure, and high blood lipid count, obesity, and lack of physical activity (House 1988). In his excellent anthology *Bridges, Not Walls,* John Stewart (1990: 5–6) cites research showing a wide range of medical hazards that result from a lack or breakdown of close relationships. For instance:

> Socially isolated people are two to three times more likely to die prematurely than are those with strong social ties. The type of relationship doesn't seem to matter: marriage, friendship, and religious and community ties all seem to increase longevity.
>
> Divorced men (before age 70) die from heart disease, cancer, and strokes at double the rate of married men. Three times as many die from hypertension; 5 times as many commit suicide; 7 times as many die from cirrhosis of the liver; and 10 times as many die from tuberculosis.
>
> The rate of all types of cancer is as much as five times higher for divorced men and women, compared to their single counterparts.
>
> Poor communication can contribute to coronary disease. One Swedish study examined 32 pairs of

identical twins. One sibling in each pair had heart disease, whereas the other was healthy. The researchers found that the obesity, smoking habits, and cholesterol levels of the healthy and sick twins did not differ significantly. Among the significant differences, however, were "poor childhood and adult interpersonal relationships," the ability to resolve conflicts, and the degree of emotional support given by others.

> The likelihood of death increases when a close relative dies. In one Welsh village, citizens who had lost a close relative died within one year at a rate more than five times greater than those who had not suffered from a relative's death.

Such research demonstrates the importance of satisfying personal relationships. Remember: Not everyone needs the same amount of contact, and the quality of communication is almost certainly as important as the quantity. The important point here is that personal communication is essential for our well-being. In other words, "people who need people" aren't "the luckiest people in the world" . . . they're the *only* people!

EGO NEEDS

Communication does more than enable us to survive. It is the *only* way we learn who we are. As you'll read in Chapter 2, our sense of identity comes from the way we interact with other people. Are we smart or stupid, attractive or ugly, skillful or inept? The answers to these questions don't come from looking in the mirror. We decide who we are based on how others react to us.

Deprived of communication with others, we would have no sense of identity. Stewart (p. 8) cites the case of the famous "Wild Boy of Aveyron," who spent his early childhood without any apparent human contact. The boy was discovered in January 1800 while digging for vegetables in a French village garden. He showed no behaviors one would expect in a social human being. The boy could not speak but uttered only weird cries. More significant than this absence of social skills was his lack of any identity as a human being. As author Roger Shattuck (1980: 37) put it, "The boy had no human sense of being in the world. He had no sense of himself as a person related to other persons." Only after the influence of a loving "mother" did the boy begin to behave—and, we can imagine, think of himself—as a human.

Like the boy of Aveyron, each of us enters the world with little or no sense of identity. We gain an idea of who we are from the way others define us. As Chapter 2 explains, the messages we receive in early childhood are the strongest, but the influence of others continues throughout life.

SOCIAL NEEDS

Besides helping define who we are, communication is the way we relate socially with others. Based on the work of earlier theorists, Rebecca Rubin and her associates (1988) identified six social needs we satisfy by communicating: *pleasure* (e.g., "because it's fun," "to have a good time"); *affection* (e.g., "to help others," "to let others know I care"); *inclusion* (e.g., "because I need someone to talk to or be with," "because it makes me less lonely"); *escape* (e.g., "to put off doing something I should be doing"); *relaxation* (e.g., because it allows me to unwind); and *control* ("because I want someone to do something for me," "to get something I don't have").

These social needs aren't equally important for all people at all times. For example, as age increases, communicating for pleasure and escape decreases, while communicating for affection increases. Education also influences our social goals for communicating. As education increases, communicating for inclusion becomes less common and communicating for control becomes a higher priority. Communica-

Every man, experiencing as he does his own solitariness and aloneness, longs for union with another.

ROLLO MAY
Love and Will

tion satisfaction was connected most strongly to the goals of pleasure, affection, inclusion, and relaxation.

PRACTICAL NEEDS

We shouldn't overlook the everyday, important functions communication serves. Communication is the tool that lets us tell the hairstylist to take just a little off the sides, the doctor where it hurts, and the plumber that the broken pipe needs attention *now!* Communication is the means of learning important information in school. In fact, college success is highly related to communication skill (Rubin and Graham 1988). It is the method you use to convince a prospective employer that you're the best candidate for a job, and it is the way to persuade the boss you deserve a raise. The list of common but critical jobs performed by communicating goes on and on, and it's worth noticing that the inability to express yourself clearly and effectively in every one of the above examples can prevent you from achieving your goal.

Psychologist Abraham Maslow (1968) suggested that human needs fall into five categories, each of which must be satisfied before we concern ourselves with the next one. As you read on, think about the ways in which communication is often necessary to satisfy each need. The most basic needs are *physical*: sufficient air, water, food, and rest, and the ability to reproduce as a species. The second category of

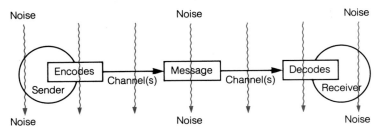

Figure 1–1   Linear communication model

Maslow's needs involves *safety:* protection from threats to our well-being. Beyond physical and safety concerns are the *social* needs we have mentioned already. Beyond them, Maslow suggests that each of us has the need for *self-esteem:* the desire to believe that we are worthwhile, valuable people. The final category of needs involves *self-actualization:* the desire to develop our potential to the maximum, to become the best person we can be.

The Communication Process

So far we have used the word "communication" as if its meaning were perfectly clear. In fact, the process of communication isn't as simple as it might seem.

A LINEAR VIEW

As recently as forty years ago, researchers viewed communication as something one person "does" to another (Shannon and Weaver 1949). In this view, communication is like giving an injection: A **sender encodes** ideas and feelings into some sort of **message** and then injects them by means of a **channel** (speech, writing, and so on) into a **receiver** (see Figure 1–1). If the message can get through any interference— termed **"noise"** in scientific jargon—communication has been successful.

Three types of noise can disrupt communication—external, physiological, and psychological. **External noise** includes those factors outside the receiver that make it difficult to hear, as well as many other kinds of distractions. For instance, too much cigarette smoke in a crowded room might make it hard for you to pay attention to another person, and sitting in the rear of an auditorium might make a speaker's remarks unclear. External noise can disrupt communication almost anywhere in our model—in the sender, channel, message, or receiver. **Physiological noise** involves biological factors in the receiver that interfere with accurate reception: hearing loss, illness, and so on.

This **linear communication model** does provide some useful information. For instance, it highlights how different channels can affect the way a receiver responds to a message. Should you say, "I love you" in person? Over the phone? By renting space on a billboard? By sending flowers and a card? With a singing telegram? Each channel does have its differences.

Psychological noise refers to forces within the sender and receiver that make them less likely to communicate effectively. For instance, a woman who hears the word "gal" may become so irritated that she has trouble listening objectively to the rest of a speaker's message. Likewise, an insecure employee may interpret a minor suggestion the boss makes as ridicule or criticism.

"I guess that's the message and I'm the medium."

Drawing by Weber; © 1989 The New Yorker Magazine, Inc.

But the linear model, despite its advantages, inaccurately suggests that communication flows in one direction, from sender to receiver. Although some types of messages (printed and broadcast messages, for example) do flow in a one-way, linear manner, most types of communication—especially the interpersonal variety—are two-way exchanges. To put it differently, the linear view ignores the fact that receivers *react* to messages by sending other messages of their own.

Consider, for instance, the significance of a friend's yawn as you describe your romantic woes. Or imagine the blush you may see as you tell one of your raunchier jokes to a new acquaintance. Nonverbal behaviors like these show that most face-to-face communication is a two-way affair. The discernible response of a receiver to a sender's message is called **feedback**. Not all feedback is nonverbal, of course. Sometimes it is oral, as when you ask an instructor questions about an upcoming test or volunteer your opinion of a friend's new haircut. In other cases it is written, as when you answer the questions on a midterm exam or respond to a letter from a faraway friend.

AN INTERACTIVE VIEW

When we add the element of feedback to our model, communication looks less like giving a linguistic injection than like playing a verbal and nonverbal tennis game in which messages pass back and forth between the parties (see Figure 1–2).

A quick glance at the **interactive communication model** in Figure 1–2 suggests that after a period of interaction, the mental images of the sender and receiver ought to match. If they do, we can say that an act of successful communication has occurred. However, your personal experience shows that misunderstandings

Student Reflection

Noise

I feel like writing to Dear Abby. My boss at work is a great guy, but he has terrible breath. Everytime he bends over my desk to talk about something, all I can think about is not gagging or running for the door. Sometimes I have no idea what he's saying to me. I've had fantasies of writing him an anonymous note or sticking a bottle of mouthwash in his desk. I know something has to happen: I'm not doing a good job, and he doesn't know why.

often occur between sender and receiver. Your constructive suggestion is taken as criticism; your friendly joke is taken as an insult; your hints are missed entirely. Such misunderstandings often occur because senders and receivers occupy different environments. In communication terminology, **environment** refers not only to a physical location, but also to the personal history that participants bring to a conversation. Although they have some experiences in common, they each see the situation in a unique way. Consider just some of the factors that might contribute to different environments:

A might be well rested and B exhausted;

A might be rich and B poor;

A might be rushed and B have nowhere to go;

A might have lived a long, eventful life and B might be young and inexperienced; and

A might be passionately concerned with the subject and B indifferent to it.

Notice that in Figure 1–2 the environments of A and B overlap. This intersecting area represents the background and knowledge that the communicators have in common. The size of this overlap varies between two people according to the topic of communication: In some areas it may be rather large, whereas on other subjects it may be extremely small. It is impossible to acquire all the background of another person, but the kind of careful listening described in Chapter 7 can boost the environmental overlap that leads to more accurate, satisfying communication.

Even with the addition of feedback and environment, the model in Figure 1–2 isn't completely satisfactory. Notice that it portrays communication as a static activity, suggesting that there are discrete "acts" of communication beginning and ending at identifiable times, and that a sender's message causes some effect in a receiver. Furthermore, it suggests that at any given moment a person is either sending or receiving.

A TRANSACTIONAL VIEW

None of these models is, in fact, valid for most types of communication. The activity of communicating is usually neither linear nor interactive, but *transactional.* There are several ways in which a transactional perspective differs from the more simplistic ones we've already discussed.

What do communication models tell you about your relationships with others? To find out, follow the directions in Activity 1 on page 25.

First, the **transactional communication model** reveals that communicators usually send and receive messages simultaneously, so

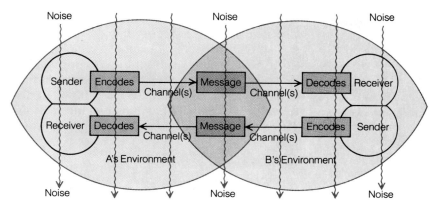

Figure 1–2   Interactive communication model

that the images of sender and receiver in Figure 1–2 should not be separated as if a person were doing only one or the other, but rather superimposed and redefined as "participants" (Rogers and Kincaid 1981; see Figure 1–3). At a given moment we are capable of receiving, **decoding,** and responding to another person's behavior, while at the same time that other person is receiving and responding to ours. Consider, for example, what might occur when you and a housemate negotiate how to handle household

chores. As soon as you begin to hear (receive) the words sent by your partner "I want to talk about cleaning the bathroom . . . ," you grimace and clench your jaw (sending a nonverbal message of your own while receiving the verbal one). This reaction leads your partner to interrupt himself, defensively sending a new message: "Now wait a minute . . . ."

Besides illustrating the simultaneous nature of face-to-face interaction, this example shows that it's difficult to isolate a single discrete "act"

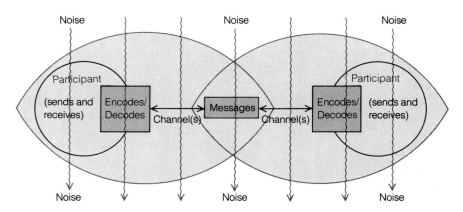

Figure 1–3   Transactional communication model

Sometimes she thought the trouble was, she and Leon were too well acquainted. The most innocent remark could call up such a string of associations, so many past slights and insults never quite settled or forgotten, merely smoothed over. They could no longer have a single uncomplicated feeling about each other.

ANNE TYLER
Morgan's Passing

of communication from the events that precede and follow it. Your partner's comment about cleaning the bathroom (and the way it was presented) probably grew from exchanges you had in the past. Likewise, the way you'll act toward each another in the future depends on the outcome of this conversation.

As communication researcher Steve Duck (1990: 5) put it, "relationships are best conceived . . . as unfinished business." By now you can see that a transactional model of communication should be more like a motion picture film than a gallery of still photographs. Although Figure 1–3 does a fair job of picturing the phenomenon we call communication, an animated version in which the environments, communicators, and messages constantly change would be an even better way of capturing the process. You can also see that communication is not something that people do *to* one another, but a process in which they create a relationship by interacting *with* each other.

Now we can summarize the definition of communication we have been developing. **Communication** is a *continuous, transactional process* involving *participants* who occupy different but overlapping *environments* and create a relationship by *simultaneously sending and receiving messages*, many of which are distorted by external, physical, and psychological *noise*.

Interpersonal and Impersonal Communication Defined

So far we have talked about the communication process without specifically discussing interpersonal communication. What is it? What distinguishes it from other types of interaction? There are many ways to answer this question

How much of your communication is interpersonal? How much is impersonal? Is this combination satisfying? To answer these questions, see Activity 2 on page 26.

(see, for example, Capella 1987). We will describe two of these ways. As you read the following description, think about the extent of your interpersonal communication.

INTERPERSONAL COMMUNICATION DEFINED

One way to define **interpersonal communication** is by looking at the number of people involved. In this sense, we could define interpersonal communication as any interaction between two people, usually face to face. Using this approach, a salesclerk and customer, or a police officer ticketing a speeding driver would be examples of interpersonal acts, whereas a teacher and class or authors such as we and a reader like you would not be.

You can probably sense that there's something wrong with this definition. Some exchanges between two people—salespeople and their customers or bureaucrats and the public, for example, don't seem personal in any sense of the word. In fact, after unsatisfying transactions like these we commonly remark, "I might as well have been talking to a machine." Conversely, some "public" kinds of communication seem quite personal. Teachers, religious ministers, and entertainers often establish a

"If you want to talk, why don't you call up a radio talk-show?"

personal relationship with their audiences. We certainly hope this book has at least some personal flavor.

If the number of people doesn't make communication personal, perhaps the setting in which communication occurs makes the difference. Could it be that lovers and families communicate interpersonally, while people at work or at school relate in a less personal way? Again, your experience probably shows that this distinction isn't accurate. Some families don't even deal with one another in a civilized manner, let alone a personal one. And many people in potentially impersonal settings build strong relationships.

If neither the number of people nor the setting makes communication interpersonal, what does? When we talk about interpersonal communication in this book, we're referring to the *quality* of interaction between individuals. In the next pages we'll explain the qualities that

distinguish interpersonal and **impersonal communication**.

Uniqueness   No two interpersonal relationships are alike, and the communication patterns reflect these differences.

The unique quality of interpersonal communication often takes the form of distinctive rules that evolve between the people. In one relationship you might exchange good-natured insults, while in another you are careful never to offend your partner. Likewise, you might handle conflicts with one friend or family member by expressing disagreements as soon as they arise; whereas the unwritten rule in another relationship is to withhold resentments until they build up and then clear the air periodically.

Unlike the distinctive quality of interpersonal relationships, impersonal ones are governed by the kind of standardized rules that Miss Manners describes: "Say 'please' and 'thank you'.'" "Shake hands when meeting for the first time." "Be careful about using profanity." Rules like these aren't phony; they are just standard forms to follow until we've created our own interpersonal conventions.

Even language patterns reflect the difference between unique, interpersonal relationships and more common impersonal ones. In less personal relationships we tend to stereotype the other person by using labels: "Anglo," "woman," "liberal," and so on. Such labels may be accurate as far as they go, but they hardly describe everything that is important about the other person. On the other hand, it's almost impossible to use one or two labels to describe someone you know interpersonally. "She's not *just* a police officer," you want to say. Or "Sure, he's against abortions, but there's more . . . ."

Irreplaceability Because interpersonal relationships are unique, they can't be replaced. This explains one reason why we usually feel so sad when a close friendship or love affair cools down. We know that no matter how many other relationships fill our lives, none of them will ever be quite like the one that just ended. People in less personal relationships are much easier to replace. It doesn't matter much which airlines reservation clerk or fast food attendant you deal with as long as the job gets done. The same principle applies in situations that *seem* more personal: If all you're looking for in a roommate is someone who will keep the place clean and share expenses, then there are lots of good candidates.

Interdependence In interpersonal relationships the fate of the people is connected. You might be able to brush off the anger, affection, excitement, or depression of someone you're not involved with interpersonally, but in an interpersonal relationship the other's life affects you. Sometimes the interdependence that comes

with a close relationship is a pleasure, as when you get a lift from a friend's successes. At other times being closely involved is a burden, as when a family member's moodiness makes your life miserable. In either case, interdependence is a fact of life in personal relationships.

Disclosure Another yardstick of interpersonal relationships is the amount of personal information the people share with one another. In impersonal relationships we don't reveal much about ourselves, but in interpersonal ones we feel more comfortable sharing our thoughts and feelings. This doesn't mean that all interpersonal relationships are warm and caring, or that all self-disclosure is positive. It's possible to reveal negative, personal information: "I'm really mad at you . . . ."

Intrinsic Rewards In impersonal communication we seek payoffs that have little to do with the people involved. For instance, when you advertise your used car, you deal with potential buyers in order to make a sale, not to make friends. Likewise, most people enroll in a college class to learn the subject matter and get academic credit, not to make friends with the professor. They would be satisfied with any competent instructor. Unlike these examples, communication in interpersonal relationships is its own reward. It doesn't matter *what* you talk about; developing the relationship is what's important.

Because interpersonal communication is characterized by the qualities of uniqueness, irreplaceability, interdependence, disclosure, and intrinsic rewards, it forms a small fraction of our interaction. The majority of our communication is relatively impersonal. We chat pleasantly with shopkeepers or fellow passengers on the bus or plane; we discuss the weather or current events with most classmates and neighbors; we deal with coworkers and teachers in a polite way, but considering the number of people we communicate with, interpersonal relationships are by far in the minority.

The rarity of interpersonal relationships isn't necessarily unfortunate. Most of us don't have the time or energy to create personal relationships with everyone we encounter. In fact, the scarcity of interpersonal communication contributes to their value. Like precious jewels and one-of-a-kind artwork, interpersonal relationships are special because of their scarcity.

INTERPERSONAL AND IMPERSONAL COMMUNICATION: A MATTER OF BALANCE

Now that you understand the differences between interpersonal and impersonal communication, we need to ask some important questions. Is interpersonal communication better than the impersonal variety? Is more interpersonal communication the goal?

Most relationships aren't either interpersonal *or* impersonal. Rather, they fall somewhere between these two extremes. Consider your own communication and you'll find that there is often a personal element in even the most impersonal situations. You might appreciate the unique sense of humor of a grocery checker or spend a few moments sharing private thoughts with the person cutting your hair. And even the most tyrannical, demanding, by-the-book boss might show an occasional flash of humanity.

Just as there's a personal element in many impersonal settings, there is also an impersonal side to our relationships with the people we care most about. There are occasions when we don't want to be personal: when we're distracted, tired, or busy, or just not interested. In fact, interpersonal communication is rather like rich food—it's fine in moderation, but too much can make you uncomfortable.

It's tempting to view relationships as fitting

Student Reflection

Interpersonal Communication Is Not Always Possible

I used to worry because my fiancé and I didn't always feel loving, or even interested in one another. Oh, we have our moments that resemble a Hollywood romance, but a lot of the time we're too tired, busy with other things to act and feel completely interested in one another. Now I realize that nobody can act completely interpersonal all of the time. I bet even Romeo and Juliet had their boring moments. I just wish Shakespeare and all those other writers would have made that point more clear.

---

somewhere on a continuum with "interpersonal" at one end and "impersonal" at the other. In reality, virtually every relationship contains both types of interaction in varying degrees. Professor Yanan Ju at the University of North Carolina has suggested that the combination of these two dimensions can be plotted on a graph, as illustrated in Figure 1–4. Some relationships are almost exclusively impersonal. You might, for example, attend a professor's lectures for an entire semester without discussing anything beyond the subject matter of the course. Only an occasional nonverbal exchange or brief remark might introduce a personal element into the otherwise formal teacher-student relationship. Other relationships contain a more equal blend of impersonal and interpersonal communication. For instance you might share some personal feelings with a neighbor about your love

Student Reflection

Friendship Affects Physical Condition

Almost everybody knows about the "runner's high" that you get from exercising. Well, I get a "friendship high." For the first time this year I have been blessed with a group of friends who really like me, and who I feel completely comfortable with. If I'm tired or frustrated from work or school, more often than not spending time with them will leave me feeling much better—not just emotionally, but physically too. Being with my friends gives me the same kind of relaxed, calm feeling I get after a long run or a workout at the gym. Now I can understand why people with strong relationships live longer.

of gardening or of pets, and spend an equal amount of time talking about more humdrum topics such as trash pickup and collecting each others' mail when you are away from home. At the other end of the spectrum, a couple who is head over heels in love would probably devote most of their conversation (when they bother to talk at all) to sharing their feelings for one another, and spend barely any time talking about the rest of the world. Even then, however, communication isn't totally unique and interpersonal. The lovers might occasionally act in stereotypically male or female roles rather than responding to one another as unique individuals. In this sense, the communication—even about love—is somewhat impersonal.

The blend of personal and interpersonal communication can shift in various stages of a relationship. The communication between young lovers who talk only about their feelings may change as their relationship develops, so that several years later their communication has become more routine and ritualized, and the percentage of time they spend on personal, relational issues drops and the conversation about less intimate topics increases. Chapter 8 discusses how communication changes as relationships pass through various stages, and Chapter 9 describes various theories of self-disclosure. As you read this information, you will see even more clearly that, while interpersonal communication can make life worth living, it isn't possible or desirable all the time.

Communication Principles

Before exploring the elements of interpersonal communication in the following chapters, we need to take a look at what communication is and what it isn't, at what it can and can't do. We begin by identifying several axioms of interpersonal communication.

How do the communication principles described on these pages operate in your life? What differences do they make? You can begin to answer these questions by completing Activity 3 on page 26.

COMMUNICATION CAN BE INTENTIONAL OR UNINTENTIONAL

Some communication is clearly deliberate: You probably plan your words carefully before asking the boss for a raise or offering constructive criticism, for example. Some scholars (e.g., Motley 1990) argue that only intentional messages like these qualify as communication. Others, however, suggest that even unintentional

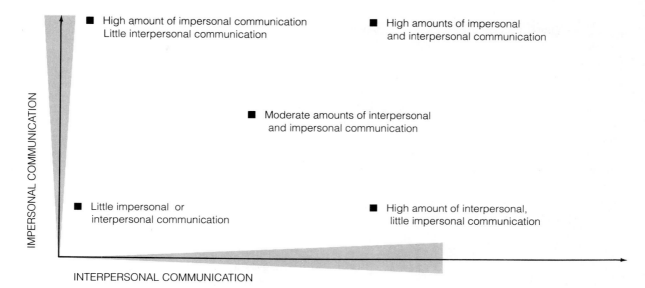

Figure 1–4   **A two dimensional model of impersonal and interpersonal communication**

behavior is communicative. Suppose, for instance, that a friend overhears you muttering complaints to yourself. Even though you didn't intend for her to hear your remarks, they certainly did carry a message. In addition to these slips of the tongue, we unintentionally send many nonverbal messages. You might not be aware of your sour expression, impatient shifting, or sigh or boredom, but others view them nonetheless.

ALL BEHAVIOR HAS THE POTENTIAL TO COMMUNICATE

Because both deliberate and unintentional behavior sends a message, many theorists (e.g., Bavelas 1990) argue that it is impossible not to communicate. Whatever you do—whether you speak or remain silent, confront or avoid, act emotional or keep a poker face—you provide information to others about your thoughts and feelings. In this sense we are like transmitters that can't be shut off.

Of course, people who decode your message may not interpret it accurately. They might take your kidding seriously or underestimate your feelings, for example. The message that you intend to convey may not even resemble the one others infer from your actions. This explains why the best way to boost understanding is to approach communication from what Glen Stamp and Mark Knapp (1990) have called an *interaction perspective*, in which the people involved discuss their intentions and their interpretations of one another until they have negotiated a shared meaning. The perception-checking skills you learn in Chapter 3 and the listening skills introduced in Chapter 7 will give you tools to make sure that the meaning of messages you send and receive are understandable to both you and others.

ALL MESSAGES HAVE A CONTENT AND A RELATIONAL DIMENSION

Virtually every verbal statement has a **content** dimension, the information it explicitly conveys: "Please pass the salt," "Not now, I'm tired," "You forgot to buy a quart of milk." In addition to this sort of obvious content, all messages also have a **relational** component (Watzlawick et al. 1967: 51–52), which expresses how you feel about the other person: whether you like or dislike the other person, feel in control or subordinate, feel comfortable or anxious, and so on. For instance, consider how many different relational messages you could communicate by simply saying "Thanks a lot" in different ways.

Sometimes the content dimension of a message is all that matters. For example, you may not care how the directory assistance operator feels about you as long as you get the phone number you're seeking. In truly interpersonal contexts, however, the relational dimension of a message is often more important than the content under discussion. This fact explains why disputes over apparently trivial subjects become so important. In such cases we're not really arguing over whose turn it is to take out the trash or whether to play tennis or swim. Instead, we're disputing the nature of the relationship. Who's in control? How important are we to each other? Chapter 10 explores several key relational issues in detail.

COMMUNICATION IS IRREVERSIBLE

We sometimes wish that we could back up in time, erasing words or acts and replacing them with better alternatives. Unfortunately, such reversal is impossible. Sometimes further explanation can clear up another's confusion or an apology can mollify another's hurt feelings; but other times no amount of explanation can erase the impression you have created. Despite the warnings judges issue in jury trials, it's impossible to "unreceive" a message. Words said and deeds done are irretrievable.

COMMUNICATION IS UNREPEATABLE

Because communication is an ongoing process, an event cannot be repeated. The friendly smile that worked so well meeting a stranger last week may not succeed with the person you encounter tomorrow: It may feel stale and artificial to you the second time around, or it may be wrong for the new person or occasion. Even with the same person, it's impossible to re-create an event. Why? Because both you and the other have changed. You've both lived longer. The behavior isn't original. Your feelings about each other may have changed. You need not constantly invent new ways to act around familiar people, but you should realize that the "same" words and behavior are different each time they are spoken or performed. Chapter 8 will alert you to the stages through which a relationship progresses.

Communication Misconceptions

Now that we have spent some time describing what communication is, we need to identify some things it is not (McCroskey and Wheeless 1976: 3–10). Avoiding these common misconceptions can save you a great deal of personal trouble.

MORE COMMUNICATION IS NOT ALWAYS BETTER

While not communicating enough can cause problems, *too much* talking can also be a mistake. Sometimes excessive communication is simply unproductive, as when two people "talk a problem to death," going over the same ground again and again without making progress. There are other times when talking too much actually aggravates a problem. We've all had the experience of "talking ourselves into a hole"—making a bad situation worse by pursuing it too far. As McCroskey and Wheeless put it, "More and more negative communication merely leads to more and more negative results" (p. 5).

Student Reflection

Content and Relational Messages

When I was growing up my brothers and I could always tell what kind of mood our father was in when he came home. We would ask him, "How was your day?" and he would always say "fine." But the <u>way</u> he said it—the sound of his voice and the expression on his face— told us instantly whether the rest of the evening would be fun, whether we should steer clear of him, or whether he would fall asleep on the living room floor after dinner. Dad never talked about his feelings towards himself or us, but he didn't have to—we could read him like a book.

"Let's just make that last remark of Don's an outtake, shall we?"

Drawing by Stevenson, copyright © 1983 the New Yorker Magazine, Inc.

Student Reflection

When Communication Is No Help

My next door neighbor is insane. He works on his truck way past midnight (with the radio turned all the way up), he screams at his wife, and for fun he teases his dog until it barks like crazy. I looked over all the communication techniques in this book and decided I'd use them to explain very rationally why I hoped he would keep the noise down.

I do think I delivered my little speech quite well: I wouldn't change anything if I had it to do over. But approaching him just made things worse. Now he's even louder, and he just snarls at me when I say hello. I can't decide whether to move, get earplugs, or call the police. But I do know that no amount of communicating is going to change this guy.

There are even times when *no* communication is the best course. Any good salesperson will testify that it's often best to stop talking and let the customer think about the product, and when two people are angry and hurt, they may say things they don't mean and will later regret. In such cases it's probably best to spend time cooling off, thinking about what to say and how to say it. Chapter 4 will help you decide when and how to share feelings.

COMMUNICATION WILL NOT SOLVE ALL PROBLEMS

Sometimes even the best-planned, best-timed communication won't solve a problem. Imagine, for example, that you ask an instructor to explain why you received a poor grade on a project you believe deserved top marks. The professor clearly outlines the reasons why you received the low grade, and sticks to that position after listening thoughtfully to your protests. Has communication solved the problem? Hardly.

Sometimes clear communication is even the *cause* of problems. Suppose, for example, that a friend asks you for an honest opinion of the $200 outfit he has just bought. Your clear and sincere answer, "I think it makes you look fat," might do more harm than good. Deciding when and how to self-disclose isn't always easy. See Chapter 9 for suggestions.

COMMUNICATION IS NOT A NATURAL ABILITY

Most people assume that communication is an aptitude that people develop without the need for training—rather like breathing. Although nearly everyone does manage to function passably without much formal communication training, most people operate at a level of effectiveness far below their potential. In fact, communication skills are rather like athletic ability. Even the most inept of us can learn to be more effective with training and practice.

Communication Competence

"What does it take to communicate better?" is probably the most important question you ask as you read this book. Answering it has been one of the leading challenges for communication scholars. While all the answers aren't in yet, research has identified a great deal of important and useful information about communication competence.

The first fact is that skillful communication can boost success and satisfaction. For example, married couples who were identified as

Miss Manners believes that the secret of an unhappy marriage is communication.

JUDITH MARTIN
Miss Manners' Guide to Excruciatingly Correct Behavior

---

effective communicators reported happier relationships than less skillful husbands and wives (Kirchler 1988). Communication skill is just as important in school. The grade point averages of college students were related positively to their communication competence (Rubin and Graham 1988). In "getting acquainted" situations, communication competence played a major role in whether a person was judged physically attractive, socially desirable, and good at the task of getting acquainted (Duran and Kelly 1988). Evidence also shows that those who speak well are more likely to be involved in community organizations and to be politically active (Vangelisti and Daly 1989). There's little question that the same principle holds in other contexts such as work, friendships, and family: Communication skill is an important ingredient of success.

COMMUNICATION COMPETENCE DEFINED

Most communication experts agree that **communication competence** is the ability to get what you are seeking from others in a manner that maintains the relationship on terms that are acceptable to both you and the other person. This definition may seem vague on one hand and wordy on the other, but a closer look shows that it suggests several important elements of communication competence.

There Is No Single "Ideal" or "Effective" Way to Communicate Your own experience shows that a variety of communication styles can be effective. Some very successful communicators are serious while others use humor; some are gregarious while others are more quiet; and some are more straightforward while others hint diplomatically. Just as there are many kinds of beautiful music or art, there are many kinds of competent communication. Furthermore, a type of communication that is competent in one setting might be a colossal blunder in another. The joking insults you routinely trade with one friend might offend a sensitive family member, and last Saturday night's romantic approach would probably be out of place at work on Monday morning. This means that there can be no surefire list of rules or tips that will guarantee your success as a communicator.

The value of flexibility in communication was illustrated by a study exploring how people handle embarrassing predicaments (Metts and Cupach 1989). Respondents described how they chose a coping strategy to fit the kind of embarrassing event. For example, excuses were most popular when a mistake was made ("I thought somebody else had invited you to the party"), while humor and attempts to repair the damage were preferred reactions to accidents: "Oh well, you needed your socks washed anyhow. Let me clean up that spilled drink"). Justifications that minimized the seriousness of the offense were a preferred response when the communicator deliberately performed an inappropriate act. ("I didn't realize she was so sensitive when I made the joke. She'll probably forget about it").

Flexibility is especially important when members of different cultures meet. Some communication skills seem to be universal (Ruben 1989). Every culture has rules that require speakers to behave appropriately, for example. But the definition of what kind of communication is appropriate in a given situation varies considerably from one culture to another. For example, belching after a meal is considered a compliment to the host in many Middle Eastern countries, while it would hardly be judged polite closer to home. Some cultural standards of appropriateness are more subtle: People in Japanese and Korean cultures tend to seek more information about a stranger's background than Americans and many Europeans (Gudykunst 1983).

Competence Is Situational   Because competent behavior varies so much from one situation and person to another, it's a mistake to think that communication competence is a trait that a person either possesses or lacks. It's more accurate to talk about *degrees* or *areas* of competence. You and the people you know are probably quite competent in some areas and less so in others. You might deal quite skillfully with peers, for example, while feeling clumsy interacting with people much older or younger, wealthier or poorer, more or less attractive than yourself. In fact, your competence with one person may vary from situation to situation. This means that it's an overgeneralization to say in a moment of distress, "I'm a terrible communicator!" when it's more accurate to say, "I didn't handle this situation very well, but I'm better in others."

Competence Has a Relational Dimension Since our definition of competent communication includes the satisfaction of both parties, we can judge a person's competence only by looking at how well the needs of the other people involved are satisfied. In this sense, communication is rather like most types of dancing. A brilliant, talented dancer who can't move smoothly with a partner lacks an important ingredient in skill. After all, interpersonal communication can occur only *with* others.

Competence Can Be Learned   Communication competence isn't an inborn characteristic like

hair color or height. Fortunately, it is a set of skills that anyone can learn. Sometimes competence is studied systematically—for instance, in communication classes. Even a modest amount of training can produce dramatic results. After only 30 minutes of instruction, one set group of observers became significantly more effective in detecting deception in interviews (deTurck and Miller 1990). Even without systematic training it's possible to develop communication skills through the processes of trial-and-error and observation. We learn from our own successes and failures, as well as from observing other models—both positive and negative. A recent study revealed that the passage of time does lead to improved communication skill: College students' communication competence increases over their undergraduate studies (Rubin et al. 1990).

CHARACTERISTICS OF COMPETENT COMMUNICATION

Despite the fact that competent communication varies from one situation to another, scholars have identified several common denominators that characterize effective communication in most contexts.

How competent are you as a communicator? Find out by asking the people who know you best. For details, see Activity 4 on page 26.

A Large Repertoire of Skills   As we've already seen, good communicators don't use the same approach in every situation. They know that sometimes it's best to be blunt and sometimes tactful, that there is a time to speak up and a time to be quiet. They understand that it's sometimes best to be serious and sometimes playful. In other words, the chances of behaving competently increase with the number of options you have about how to communicate. Just as a golfer has a wide range of clubs to use for various situations, a competent communicator has a large array of behaviors from which to choose.

Adaptability Having a large repertoire of possible behaviors is one ingredient of competent communication, but scholars have recognized that you have to be able to choose the *right* one for a particular situation (see, for example, Bochner and Kelly 1974; Spitzberg and Hurt 1987). Rod Hart and others (1972, 1980) have termed the ability to choose the right approach for a situation *rhetorical sensitivity.* As we've already said, an approach that works well at one time might be disastrous somewhere else. Effective communication means choosing the right response for the situation.

Ability to Perform Skillfully Once you have chosen the appropriate way to communicate you have to perform that behavior effectively. In communication, as in other activities, practice is the key to skillful performance.

Knowing how you want *to communicate is one thing, but being able to* perform *skillfully is another. You can gain practice in more effective communication by using the technique of behavior rehearsal. To learn more, see Activity 5 on page 26.*

Involvement Not surprisingly, effective communication occurs when the people care about one another and the topic at hand (Cegala et al. 1982). Rod Hart suggests that this involvement has several dimensions (adapted here from Knapp 1984: 342–43). It includes commitment to the other person and the relationship, concern about the message being discussed, and a desire to make the relationship clearly useful.

Student Reflection

Flexibility and Communication Competence

I'll call this "A Tale of Two Craigs." My first friend—I'll call him Craig M.—is hilarious. He has a joke for every occasion, and he never hesitates to tell them. Almost everything he says is funny, but sometimes his humor gets annoying. When I'm busy or serious, for example, or when I'm mad at him, I don't appreciate the kidding. But Craig M. doesn't pick up on my hints—he just keeps on joking away.

My other friend, Craig P., can also be funny. But he knows when to cut back on the humor. If he sees I'm not in the mood, he'll either talk normally or ask what's wrong or just back off. Craig M. may be much more fun at parties, but for the long haul Craig P. is the guy I appreciate.

Notice that these characteristics involve two themes. The first is *commitment.* Good communicators care about the other person, about the subject, and about being understood. The second theme is *profitability.* The most effective communication produces good results for everyone involved.

Empathy/Perspective Taking People have the best chance of developing an effective message when they understand the other person's point of view (Delia and Clark 1977; Delia, et al. 1979; Redmond 1985). And since others aren't always good at expressing their thoughts and feelings clearly, the ability to imagine how an issue

instance, imagine that a longtime friend seems to be angry with you. One possible explanation is that your friend is offended by something you've done. Another possibility is that something has happened in another part of your friend's life that is upsetting. Or perhaps nothing at all is wrong and you're just being overly sensitive. Researchers argue that a large number of constructs for interpreting the behavior of others increases the chances of acting in ways that will produce good results (O'Keefe and Sypher 1981).

Self-Monitoring   Psychologists use the term **self-monitoring** to describe the process of paying close attention to one's behavior and using these observations to shape the way one behaves. Self-monitors are able to detach a part of their consciousness to observe their behavior from a detached viewpoint, making observations like

"I'm making a fool out of myself."

"I'd better speak up now."

"This approach is working well. I'll keep it up."

It's no surprise that self-monitoring increases one's effectiveness as a communicator (Sypher and Sypher 1983). The ability mentally to ask the question "How am I doing?" and to change your behavior if the answer isn't positive is a tremendous asset for communicators. Low self-monitors blunder through life, sometimes succeeding and sometimes failing, without the detachment to understand why.

How does your behavior as an interpersonal communicator measure up against the standards of competence described in this chapter? Like most people, you will probably find some areas of your life that are very satisfying and others that you would like to change. As you read on in *Interplay*, realize that the information in each chapter offers advice that can help your communication become more productive and rewarding.

might look from the other's point of view is an important skill. The value of taking the other's perspective suggests one reason why listening is so important. Not only does it help us understand others, it gives us information to develop strategies about how best to influence them.

Cognitive Complexity   **Cognitive complexity** is the ability to construct a variety of different frameworks for viewing an issue. Cognitive complexity is an ingredient of communication competence because it allows us to make sense of people using a variety of frameworks. For

Summary

Communication is important for a variety of reasons. Besides satisfying practical needs, meaningful communication contributes to physical health, plays a major role in defining our identity, and forms the basis for our social relationships.

Early theorists viewed communication as a linear process in which senders aimed messages at passive receivers. This linear model was refined into an interactive one, which pictured communication as an exchange of messages between senders and receivers. More recently, communication has been described as an ongoing, transactional process in which individuals simultaneously send and receive, so that the meaning of a particular message is influenced by the history of the relationship and the experiences of the participants.

Interpersonal communication is best defined by the quality of interaction and not the number of people or the setting in which they meet. Interpersonal relationships are unique, irreplaceable, interdependent, scarce, and intrinsically rewarding. Even the strongest relationships are not completely interpersonal: They all have their more superficial, mechanical moments.

A variety of principles help explain the communication process. Messages can be intentional or unintentional. They almost always have both a content and a relational dimension. Once expressed, messages cannot be withdrawn. Finally, communication is unrepeatable.

In order to understand the communication process, it is important to recognize and avoid several common misconceptions. Despite the value of self-expression, more communication is not always better. In fact, there are occasions when more communication can increase problems. Even at its best, communication is not a panacea that will solve every problem. Effective communication is not a natural ability. While some people have greater aptitude at communicating, everyone can learn to interact with others more effectively.

Communication competence is the ability to get desired results from others in a manner that maintains the relationship on terms that are acceptable to both parties. There is no single ideal way to communicate: Flexibility and adaptability are characteristics of competent communicators, as are skill at performing behaviors, involvement with others, the ability to view issues from the other's point of view, cognitive complexity, and self-monitoring.

Activities

1. What percent of time do you spend communicating? Conduct an informal study to answer this question by keeping a one-day log of your activities. Based on your findings, answer the following questions:

   a. What percentage of your waking time is spent speaking and listening to others?

   b. Using the explanation on pages 12–16, describe what percentage of your entire communication is truly interpersonal.

c. How satisfied are you with your findings? How would you like to change your everyday communication?

2. Choose an everyday situation to illustrate the three communication models described in this chapter.
   a. Begin by illustrating the situation with the linear model.
   b. Next, add the elements contained in the interactive model and describe how this change more accurately describes the situation.
   c. Finally, represent the situation using the transactional model and explain how it represents the situation more completely and accurately.

3. You can see how the communication principles described on pages 16–19 apply in your life by recalling the following incidents:
   a. You unintentionally behaved in a way that sent a significant relational message.
   b. You sent a message that you later regretted. Despite your attempts, you discovered that it was impossible to withdraw the message.
   c. Despite your best efforts, you were unable to recreate a situation that had occurred in the past.

4. How competent are you as a communicator? You can begin to answer this question by interviewing someone who knows you well: a family member, friend, or fellow worker, for example.
   a. Describe the characteristics of competent communicators outlined on pages 22–24 of this chapter. Be sure your interviewee understands each of them.
   b. Ask your interviewee to rate you on each of the observable qualities. (It won't be possible for others to evaluate internal characteristics, such as cognitive complexity and self-monitoring.) Be sure this evaluation reflects your communication in a variety of situations: It's likely you aren't uniformly competent—or incompetent—in all of them.
   c. If your rating is not high in one or more areas, discuss with your partner how you could raise it.
   d. Consider whether another person might rate you differently. Why might this happen?

5. Knowing how you want to communicate isn't the same as being able to perform competently. The technique of behavior rehearsal provides a way to improve a particular communication skill before you use it in real life. Behavior rehearsal consists of four steps:
   a. Define your goal. Begin by identifying the way you want to behave.
   b. Break the goal into the behaviors it involves. Most goals are made up of several verbal and nonverbal parts. You may be able to identify these parts by thinking about them yourself, by observing others, by reading about them, or by asking others for advice.
   c. Practice each behavior before using it in real life. You can practice a new behavior by rehearsing it with others before you put it into action. Another approach is to picture yourself behaving in new ways. This mental image can boost effectiveness.
   d. Try out the behavior in real life. You can increase the odds of success if you follow two pieces of advice when trying out new communication behaviors. Work on only one sub-skill at a time, and start with easy situations. Don't expect yourself suddenly to behave flawlessly in the most challenging situations. Begin by practicing your new skills in situations in which you have a chance of success.

Readings

Barnlund, D. C. "A Transactional Model of Communication." In *Language Behavior: A Book of Readings in Communication*, J. Akin, A. Goldberg, G. Myers, and J. Stewart, eds. The Hague: Mouton, 1970.

Bavelas, J.B. "Behaving and Communicating: A Reply to Motley." *Western Journal of Speech Communication* 54 (1990): 593–602.

Bell, R. A., and J. A. Daly. "Some Communicator Correlates of Loneliness." *Southern States Communication Journal* 50 (1985):121–42.

Bochner, A. P., and C. W. Kelly. "Interpersonal Competence: Rationale, Philosophy, and Implementation of a Conceptual Framework." *Speech Teacher* 23 (1974): 270–301.

Capella, J. N. "Interpersonal Communication: Definitions and Fundamental Questions." In *Handbook of Communication Science*, C. R. Berger and S. H. Chaffee, eds. Beverly Hills, CA: Sage, 1987.

Cegala, D. J., G. T. Savage, C. C. Brunner, and A. B. Conrad. "An Elaboration of the Meaning of Interaction Involvement: Toward the Development of a Theoretical Concept." *Communication Monographs* 49 (1982): 229–48.

Cupah, W. R., and B. H. Spitzberg. "Trait Versus State: A Comparison of Dispositional and Situational Measures of Interpersonal Communication Competence." *Western Journal of Speech Communication* 47 (1983): 364–79.

Dance, F. E. X. "Toward a Theory of Human Communication." In *Human Communication Theory: Original Essays*, F. E. X. Dance, ed. New York: Holt, Rinehart and Winston, 1957.

*Dance, F. E. X. "The 'Concept' of Communication." *Journal of Communication* 20 (1970): 201–10.

Delia, J., and R. A. Clark. "Cognitive Complexity, Social Perception, and Listener-Adapted Communication in Six-, Eight-, Ten-, and Twelve-Year-Old Boys." *Communication Monographs* 44 (1977): 326–45.

Delia, J., S. Kline, and B. Burleson. "The Development of Persuasive Communication Strategies in Kindergarten through Twelfth-Graders." *Communication Monographs* 46 (1979): 241–56.

de Turck, M. A., and G. R. Miller. "Training Observers to Detect Deception: Effects of Self-Monitoring and Rehearsal." *Human Communication Research* 16 (1990): 603–20.

Duck, S. "Relationships as Unfinished Business: Out of the Frying Pan and into the 1990s." *Journal of Social and Personal Relationships* 7 (1990): 5–28.

Duran, R. L., and L. Kelly. "The Influence of Communicative Competence on Perceived Task, Social, and Physical Attraction." *Communication Quarterly* 36 (1988): 41–49.

Feingold, P. Toward a Paradigm of Effective Communication: An Empirical Study of Perceived Communicative Effectiveness. Doctoral dissertation, Purdue University, 1976.

Gudykunst, W. B. "Uncertainty Reduction and Predictability of Behavior in Low- and High-Context Cultures: An Exploratory Study." *Communication Quarterly* 31 (1983): 49–55.

Hart, R. P., and D. M. Burks. "Rhetorical Sensitivity and Social Interaction." *Speech Monographs* 39 (1972): 75–91.

Hart, R. P., R. E. Carlson, and W. F. Eadie. "Attitudes Toward Communication and the Assessment of Rhetorical Sensitivity." *Communication Monographs* 47 (1980): 1–22.

*Holtzman, P. D., and D. Ecroyd. *Communication Concepts and Models*. Skokie, IL: National Textbook, 1976.

House, J. "People Who Need People." *Psychology Today* 22 (November 1988): 8.

Kirchler, E. "Marital Happiness and Interaction in Everyday Surroundings: A Time-Sample Diary Approach for Couples." *Journal of Social and Personal Relationships* 5 (1988): 375–382.

*Knapp, M. L. *Interpersonal Communication and Human Relationships*. Boston: Allyn and Bacon, 1984.

McCroskey, J. C., and L. Wheeless. *Introduction to Human Communication*. Boston: Allyn and Bacon, 1976.

Maslow, A. H. *Toward a Psychology of Being.* New York: Van Nostrand Reinhold, 1968.

Metts, S. and W.R. Cupach, "Situational Influence on the Use of Remedial Strategies in Embarrassing Predicaments," *Communication Monographs* 56 (1989): 151–162.

*Miller, G. R. "On Defining Communication: Another Stab." *Journal of Communication* 16 (1966): 88–98.

*Miller, G. R. "The Current Status of Theory and Research in Interpersonal Communication." *Human Communication Research* 4 (Winter 1978): 164–78.

Motley, M. T. "On Whether One Can(not) Communicate: An Examination via Traditional Communication Postulates," *Western Journal of Speech Communication* 54 (1990): 1–20.

O'Keefe, D. J., and H. E. Sypher. "Cognitive Complexity Measures and the Relationship of Cognitive Complexity to Communication." *Human Communication Research* 8 (1981): 72–92.

Parks, M. R. "Interpersonal Communication and the Quest for Personal Competence." In *Handbook of Interpersonal Communication*. Beverly Hills, CA: Sage, 1985.

Phillips, G., and N. Metzger. *Intimate Communication*. Boston: Allyn and Bacon, 1976.

Redmond, M. V. "The Relationship between Perceived Communication Competence and Perceived Empathy." *Communication Monographs* 52 (1985): 377–82.

Richmond, V. P., and J. C. McCroskey. *Communication: Apprehension, Avoidance, and Effectiveness.* Scottsdale, AZ: Gorsuch Scarisbrick, 1985.

Rogers, E. M., and D. L. Kincaid. *Communication Networks.* New York: Free Press, 1981.

Ross, J. B., and M. M. McLaughlin, eds. *A Portable Medieval Reader.* New York: Viking, 1949.

Ruben, B. D. "The Study of Cross-Cultural Competence: Traditions and Contemporary Issues." *International Journal of Intercultural Relationships* 13 (1989): 229–40.

Rubin, R. B., and E. E. Graham, "Communication Correlates of College Success: An Exploratory Investigation," *Communication Education* 37 (1988): 14–27.

Rubin, R. B., E. E. Graham, and J. T. Mignerey, "A Longitudinal Study of College Students' Communication Competence," *Communication Education* 39 (1990): 1–14.

Rubin, R. B., E. M. Perse, and C. A. Barbato, "Conceptualization and Measurement of Interpersonal Communication Motives." *Human Communication Research* 14 (1988): 602–28.

Schachter, S. *The Psychology of Affiliation.* Stanford, CA: Stanford University Press, 1959.

Schutz, W. *The Interpersonal Underworld.* Palo Alto, CA: Science and Behavior Books, 1966.

Shannon, C. E., and W. Weaver. *The Mathematical Theory of Communication.* Urbana: University of Illinois Press, 1949.

Shattuck, R. *The Forbidden Experiment: The Story of the Wild Boy of Aveyron.* New York: Farrar, Straus & Giroux, 1980.

Spitzberg, B. H., and W. R. Cupah. *Interpersonal Communication Competence.* Beverly Hills, CA: Sage, 1984.

Spitzberg, B. H., and H. T. Hurt. "The Measurement of Interpersonal Skills in Instructional Contexts." *Communication Education* 36 (1987): 28–45.

Stamp, G. H., and M. L. Knapp, "The Construct of Intent in Interpersonal Communication." *Quarterly Journal of Speech* 76 (1990): 282–99.

*Stewart, J., ed. *Bridges, Not Walls: A Book About Interpersonal Communication,* 4th ed. New York: Random House, 1986.

*Stewart, J., and G. D'Angelo. *Together: Communicating Interpersonally,* 3d ed. New York: Random House, 1988.

Sypher, B. D., and H. E. Sypher. "Perceptions of Communication Ability: Self-Monitoring in an Organizational Setting." *Personality and Social Psychology Bulletin* 9 (1983): 297–304.

Vangelisti, A. L., and J. A. Daly, "Correlates of Speaking Skills in the United States: A National Assessment." *Communication Education* 38 (1989): 132–143.

Van Maanen, J. "On the Understanding of Interpersonal Relations." In *Essays in Interpersonal Dynamics*, W. Bennis, J. Van Maanen, E. H. Schein, and F. I. Steele, eds., Homewood, IL: Dorsey, 1978.

Verderber, R., A. Elder, and E. Weiler. "A Study of Communication Time Usage Among College Students." Unpublished study, University of Cincinnati, 1976.

Watzlawick, P., J. Beavin, and D. D. Jackson. *Pragmatics of Human Communication*. New York: W. W. Norton, 1967.

Weinstein, E. A. "The Development of Interpersonal Competence." In *Handbook of Socialization Theory and Research*, D. A. Goslin, ed. Chicago: Rand McNally, 1969.

*Items identified by an asterisk are recommended as especially useful follow-ups.

Part Two

Intrapersonal Foundations

Self-Concept

Chapter 2
Self-Concept

After studying the material in this chapter

You should understand

1. How to define self-concept.

2. How the self-concept develops.

3. The relationship between self-concept, personality, and communication.

4. The multidimensional, subjective, culture-based, resistant nature of the self-concept.

5. The role of self-fulfilling prophecies in shaping self-concept and influencing communication.

6. How people can change their self-concepts.

You should be able to identify

1. The key elements of your own self-concept.

2. The most important forces that have shaped your self-concept.

3. The influence you have on shaping the self-concept of others.

4. The differences between your perceived, desired, and presenting selves.

5. The elements of your perceived self that may be inaccurately favorable or unfavorable.

6. Any self-fulfilling prophecies that you impose on yourself or on others, and that others impose on you.

7. Steps you can take to change undesirable elements of your self-concept.

Key Terms

Cognitive conservatism
Desired Self
Face
Facework
Perceived Self

Personality
Presenting self
Reference groups
Reflected appraisal

Self-concept
Self-fulfilling prophecy
Significant other
Social comparison

Who are you?

Before reading on, take a few minutes to answer this question by trying the following simple exercise. First, make a list of the ten words or phrases that describe the most important features of who you are. Some of the items on your list may involve social roles: student, son or daughter, employee, and so on. Or you could define yourself through physical characteristics: fat, skinny, tall, short, beautiful, ugly. You may focus on your intellectual characteristics: smart, stupid, curious, inquisitive. Perhaps you can best define yourself in terms of moods, feelings, or attitudes: optimistic, critical, energetic. Or you could consider your social characteristics: outgoing, shy, defensive. You may see yourself in terms of belief systems: pacifist, Christian, vegetarian, libertarian. Finally, you could focus on particular skills (or lack of them): swimmer, artist, carpenter. In any case, choose ten words or phrases that best describe you and write them down.

Next, choose the one item from your list that is the most fundamental to who you are and copy it on another sheet of paper. Then pick the second-most fundamental item and record it as number two on your new list. Continue ranking the ten items until you have reorganized them all.

Now comes the most interesting part of the experience: Find a place where you won't be disturbed and close your eyes. Take a few moments to relax and then create a mental image of yourself. Try to paint a picture that not only captures your physical characteristics, but also reflects the attitudes, aptitudes, feelings, and/or beliefs included on your list. Take plenty of time to create this image.

Now recall (or peek at) your second list, noticing the item you ranked as number ten—the one least essential to your identity. Keeping your mental image in focus, imagine that this item suddenly disappeared from your person-

ality or physical makeup. Try to visualize how you would be different without that tenth item. How would it affect the way you act? The way you feel? The way others behave toward you? Was it easy to give up that item? Do you like yourself more or less without it? Take a few minutes with your eyes closed to answer these questions.

Without regaining the item you've just given up, continue your fantasy by removing item number nine. What difference does its absence make for you?

Slowly, at your own pace, continue the process by jettisoning one item at a time until you have given them all up. Notice what happens at each step of the process. After you've gone through your entire list, reclaim the items one by one until you are back to where you started.

How do you feel after trying this exercise? Most people find the experience a powerful one. They say that it clarifies how each of the items selected is fundamental to their identity. Many people say that they gain a clear picture of the parts of themselves they value and the parts with which they are unhappy.

Self-Concept Defined

What you've accomplished by creating this list is to begin describing your **self-concept:** a relatively stable set of perceptions you hold of yourself. One way to understand the self-concept is to imagine a special mirror that not only reflects physical features, but also allows you to view other aspects of yourself—emotional states, talents, likes, dislikes, values, roles, and so on. The reflection in that mirror would be your self-concept.

You probably recognize that the self-concept list you recorded is only a partial one. To make the description of yourself complete, you'd have to keep adding items until your list ran into

Children Learn What They Live

If a child lives with criticism he learns to condemn.

If a child lives with hostility he learns to fight.

If a child lives with ridicule he learns to be shy.

If a child lives with shame he learns to feel guilty.

If a child lives with tolerance he learns to be patient.

If a child lives with encouragement he learns confidence.

If a child lives with praise he learns to appreciate.

If a child lives with fairness he learns justice.

If a child lives with security he learns to have faith.

If a child lives with approval he learns to like himself.

If a child lives with acceptance and friendship he learns to find love in the world.

DOROTHY LAW NOLTE

hundreds of words. Take a moment now to explore some of the many parts of your self-concept simply by responding to the question "Who am I?" over and over again. Add these responses to the list you have already started. Your list will demonstrate the fact that the self-concept contains many dimensions (Marsh and Holmes 1990). Physical appearance (attractive, unusual) and skills (athletic, clumsy), social talents (gregarious, shy), roles (parent, student), intellectual traits (smart, intuitive), and emotional states (happy, confused)—all these and more comprise your self-concept.

Of course, not every item on your self-concept list is equally important. For example, the most significant part of one person's self-concept might consist of social roles, whereas for another it might be physical appearance, health, friendships, accomplishments, or skills.

How the Self-Concept Develops

Researchers generally agree that the self-concept does not exist at birth (Fitts 1971). An infant lying in a crib has no notion of self, no notion—even if verbal language were miraculously made available—of how to answer the question at the beginning of this chapter. Consider what it would be like to have no idea of your characteristic moods, physical appearance, social traits, talents, intellectual capacity, beliefs, or important roles. If you can imagine this experience—*blankness*—you can start to understand how the world appears to someone with no sense of self. Of course, you have to take one step further and *not know* you do not have any notion of self.

What forces have shaped your self-concept, making you the person you are today? Take a few moments to find out by completing Activity 1 on page 60.

Soon after birth the infant begins to differentiate among the things in the environment: familiar and unfamiliar faces, the sounds that mean food, the noises that frighten, the cat who jumps in the crib, the sister who tickles—each becomes a separate part of the world. Recognition of distinctions in the environment probably precedes recognition of the self.

You are a very important person—a "significant other" to some people in your life. You can explore just how influential you are in shaping others' self-concepts by turning to page 60 and completing Activity 2.

At about six or seven months, the child begins to recognize "self" as distinct from surroundings. If you've ever watched children at this age, you've probably marveled at how they can stare with great fascination at a foot, hand, and other body parts that float into view, almost as if they were strange objects belonging to someone else. Then the connection is made, almost as if the child were realizing, "The hand is *me*," "The foot is *me*." These first revelations form the child's earliest concept of self. At this early stage, the self-concept is almost exclusively physical, involving the child's basic realization of existing and of possessing certain body parts over which some control is exerted.

As the child develops, this rudimentary sense of identity expands into a much more complete and sophisticated picture that resembles the self-concept of adults. This evolution is almost totally a product of social interaction. Two complementary theories describe how interaction shapes the way individuals view themselves: reflected appraisal and social comparison (Rosenberg 1979).

REFLECTED APPRAISAL

Before reading on, try the following exercise: Either by yourself or aloud with a partner, recall someone you know or once knew who helped enhance your self-concept by acting in a way that made you feel accepted, worthwhile, important, appreciated, or loved. This person needn't have played a crucial role in your life, as long as the role was positive. Often one's self-concept is shaped by many tiny nudges as well as a few giant events. For instance, you might recall a childhood neighbor who took a special interest in you or a grandparent who never criticized or questioned your youthful foolishness.

After thinking about this supportive person, recall someone who acted in either a big or small way to diminish your self-esteem. Teachers, for instance, recall students who yawn in the middle of their classes. (The students may be tired, but it's difficult for teachers not to think that they are doing a poor, boring job.)

Student Reflection

The Power of Reflected Appraisal

I don't want to sound too sorry for myself, but I think a lot of my feelings of low self-esteem came from my parents. As I grew up, my mom and dad seemed to focus more on the negative than on the positive. If I would clean up my room six days out of seven, they would only mention the day I forgot. They would spend a few seconds saying "good work" for high grades and then talk for a half hour about the C I almost always got in math. They paid more attention to the way my friends and I dressed or the music we listened to (which they often didn't like) than to the fact that I hung around with good people and always told them the truth.

As I grew into my teens, I started to protect myself by paying less attention to my parents. I decided that if I was going to like myself, I needed to hang around people who also like me. The sad part is that I know my mom and dad <u>love</u> me. They just don't seem to <u>like</u> me very much.

After thinking about these two types of people, you should begin to see that everyone's self-concept is shaped by **reflected appraisal:** perceptions of the judgments of those around them. To the extent that you have received supportive messages, you have learned to appreciate and value yourself. To the degree that you have received critical signals, you are likely to feel less valuable, lovable, and capable. Thus, the

It is thus with most of us; we are what other people say we are. We know ourselves chiefly by hearsay.

ERIC HOFFER

self-concept you described in your list can be seen as a product of the messages you've received throughout your life.

Social scientists use the term **significant other** to describe a person whose evaluations are especially influential. A look at the people you recalled in the previous paragraphs will reveal that the evaluations of a few especially important people can have long-range effects. A teacher from long ago, a special friend or relative, or even a barely known acquaintance whom you respected can all leave an imprint on

2-10   © 1986 Universal Press Syndicate

Copyright © 1973 Universal Press Syndicate.

how you view yourself. To see the importance of significant others, ask yourself how you arrived at your opinion of yourself as a student...as a person attractive to others...as a competent worker...and you will see that these self-evaluations were probably influenced by the way others regarded you.

The family is the first place we receive messages from significant others. It provides us with our first feelings of adequacy and inadequacy, acceptance and rejection. Even before children can speak, people are making evaluations of them. The earliest months of life are full of messages that shape the self-concept. The amount of time parents allow their children to cry before attending to their needs communicates nonverbally to the children over a period of time just how important they are to the parents. The parental method of handling infants speaks volumes: Do they affectionately play with the child, joggling her gently and holding her close, or do they treat her like so much baggage, changing diapers or carrying out feeding and bathing in a brusque, businesslike manner? Does the tone of voice with which they speak to the child show love and enjoyment or disappointment and irritation?

In a review of self-concept literature, William Fitts (1971) focuses on parental influence on self-concept formation. Parents with healthy self-concepts tend to have children with healthy self-concepts, and parents with poor, negative, or deviant self-concepts tend to have children who view themselves in primarily negative ways. Interestingly, if one parent has a good self-concept and the other a poor self-concept, the child is most likely to choose the parent with the more positive self-concept as a model. If neither parent has a strong self-concept, it is likely that the child will seek an adult outside the family with whom to identify.

In families in which one parent has a strong, positive self-concept, the child is usually

Man wishes to be confirmed in his being by man, and wishes to have a presence in the being of the other.... Secretly and bashfully he watches for a Yes which allows him to be and which can come to him only from one human person to another.

MARTIN BUBER

provided with a secure environment in the form of love and attention. A child brought up in such an environment is able to face the world as a secure, confident person. If both parents have strong, positive self-concepts, then the effect is even more pronounced.

Later in life the influence of reflected appraisals is less powerful (McCall 1987). The evaluations of others still influence beliefs about the self in some areas, such as physical attractiveness and popularity. In other areas, however, the looking glass of the self-concept has become distorted, so that it shapes the input of others to conform with our existing beliefs. For example, if your self-concept includes the element "poor student," you may respond to a high grade by thinking, "I was just lucky" or "The professor must be an easy grader."

You might argue that not every part of your self-concept is shaped by others, that there are certain objective facts recognizable by self-observation alone. After all, nobody needs to tell you whether you are taller than others, speak with an accent, have curly hair, and so on. These facts are obvious.

Indeed, some features of the self *are* immediately apparent. But the *significance* we attach to them—that is, the rank we assign them in the hierarchy of our list and the interpretation we give them—depends greatly on the opinions of others. After all, many of your features are read-

ily observable, yet you don't find them important at all because nobody has regarded them as significant.

Recently we heard a woman in her eighties describing her youth. "When I was young," she declared, "we didn't worry about weight. Some people were skinny and others were plump, and we pretty much accepted the bodies God gave us." In those days it's unlikely that weight would have found its way onto the self-concept list you constructed because it wasn't considered significant. Compare the modern attitude: It's seldom that you pick up a popular magazine or visit a bookstore without reading about the latest diet fads, and TV ads are filled with scenes of slender, happy people. As a result you'll rarely find a person who doesn't complain about the need to "lose a few pounds."

Obviously such concern has a lot to do with the attention paid to slimness these days. Furthermore, the interpretation of characteristics such as weight depends on the way people important to us regard them. We generally see fat as undesirable because others tell us it is. In a society in which obesity is the ideal (and there are such societies), a person regarded as extremely heavy would be admired. In the same way, the significance of being single or married, solitary or sociable, aggressive or passive, depends on the interpretation society attaches to such traits. Thus, the importance of a given characteristic in your self-concept reflects the significance you see others attach to it.

Every person needs recognition. It is expressed cogently by the lad who says, "Mother, let's play darts. I'll throw the darts and you say 'Wonderful.'"

M. DALE BAUGHMAN

SOCIAL COMPARISON

So far we have looked at the way others' messages shape your self-concept. In addition to these messages, each of us forms our self-image by the process of **social comparison:** evaluating ourselves in terms of how we compare with others.

Two types of social comparison need highlighting. In the first, we decide whether we are *superior or inferior* by comparing ourselves to others. Are we attractive or ugly? A success or failure? Intelligent or stupid? It depends on whom we measure ourselves against.

You might feel just ordinary or inferior in terms of talent, friendships, or attractiveness if you compare yourself with an inappropriate reference group. You'll probably never be as beautiful as a Hollywood star, as agile as a professional athlete, or as wealthy as a millionaire. When you consider the matter logically, these facts don't mean you're worthless. Nonetheless, many people judge themselves against unreasonable standards and suffer accordingly. You'll read more about how to avoid placing perfectionistic demands on yourself in Chapter 3.

A child's life is like a piece of paper on which every passerby leaves a mark.

CHINESE PROVERB

In addition to feelings of superiority and inferiority, social comparison provides a way to decide if we are the *same as or different from* others. Research by psychologists William McGuire and Alice Padawer-Singer (1976) revealed that children were more likely to focus on characteristics like birthplace, ethnic background, height, weight, or other physical features when those traits were different from the majority of their classmates. This principle of distinctiveness illustrates the power of social comparison to shape identity. A child who is interested in ballet and who lives in a setting where such preferences are regarded as weird will start to accept this label if there is no support from others. Likewise, adults who want to improve the quality of their relationships but are surrounded by friends and family who don't recognize or acknowledge the importance of these matters will think of themselves as oddballs. Thus, it's easy to recognize that the **reference groups** against which we compare ourselves play an important role in shaping our view of ourselves.

What reference groups play a role in shaping your self-concept? How do they affect your feelings about yourself and your communication? You can find out by completing Activity 3 on page 60.

Using reference groups to determine whether we are different from others can get tricky because those others don't always reveal how they really think and feel. Many students in interpersonal communication classes, for example, discover that others share occasional feelings of social uncertainty that they thought were unusual. Thus, it's important to remember that people don't always *act* the way they *feel* and that you may not be as different as you think.

At first glance, social comparison theory seems rather deterministic. Besides being influ-

I have found the secret for eternal optimism. It's called *The Power of Negative Thinking.* All my life I've suffered from periods of depression because I got thinking about how much better a lot of people do things than I do. That's behind me now. Today I'm concentrating on the negative. When I do something badly, all I'm going to think about is the great number of people who probably would have done it even worse.

ANDY ROONEY

enced by how others see us, we are also shaped by how we measure up to others. At second glance, however, the concept of social comparison offers a way of reshaping an unsatisfying self-concept.

To some degree, we're in control of who is available for comparison. It's possible to seek out people with whom we compare favorably. This technique may bring to mind a search for a community of idiots in which you could appear as a genius, but there are healthier ways of changing your standards for comparison. For instance, you might decide that it's foolish constantly to compare your athletic prowess with professionals or campus stars, your looks with movie idols, and your intelligence with only Phi Beta Kappas. Once you place yourself alongside a truly representative sample, your self-concept may improve.

On the other hand, you can use social comparison to fool yourself. For instance, suppose you wanted to think of yourself as a tremendously effective communicator (many people do), even though others disagreed with this image. You could achieve your goal by choosing a best friend who was tongue-tied. If you chose to be a big fish in a small pond, you could hang around with extremely shy or ignorant people,

Student Reflection

The Dangers of Having a Personality

I used to think of myself as a shy person. It's true that I have a hard time getting to know new people, and that I enjoy spending quiet time with one or two friends more than going to a party full of strangers. But lately I've realized that I'm not <u>always</u> shy. When I'm with my family or at work or with my good friends I'm actually quite talkative. Somehow I feel better about myself if I don't use the word "shy" as a description.

and thereby assure yourself of seeming to be a "natural" leader.

Another way of using comparison to boost self-esteem unrealistically would be to argue that those who don't approve of you have worthless opinions, whereas others who think as you do have excellent judgment. Also, you could set up standards that only you and a few other people meet and thereby argue that you are a rare individual indeed. This may be somewhat illogical, but when a self-concept is at stake, who worries about logic?

The Self-Concept, Personality, and Communication

While the self-concept is an internal image we hold of ourselves, the personality is the view others have of us. We use the notion of **personality** to describe a relatively consistent set of traits people exhibit across a variety of situations (Steinfatt 1987). We use the notion of per-

sonality to characterize others as friendly or aloof, energetic or lazy, smart or stupid, and in literally thousands of other ways. In fact, one survey revealed almost 18,000 trait words in the English language that can be used to describe a personality (Allport and Odbert 1936). People seem to possess some innate personality traits. Psychologist Jerome Kagan (1984) reports that 10 percent of all children appear to be born with a biological disposition toward shyness. Babies who stop playing when a stranger enters the room, for example, are more likely than others to be reticent and introverted as adolescents. Likewise, Kagan found that another 10 percent of infants seem to be born with especially sociable dispositions. Research with twins also suggests that personality may be at least partially a matter of physical destiny (McCroskey and Richmond 1980). Biologically identical twins are much more similar in sociability than are fraternal twins. These similarities are apparent not only in infancy but also when the twins have grown to adulthood, and are noticeable even when the siblings have had different experiences.

How would you describe your personality as a communicator? Activity 4 on page 60 may show you that this personality unnecessarily lowers your self-esteem and keeps you from communicating effectively.

Despite its common use, the term *personality* is often an oversimplification. Much of our behavior isn't consistent. Rather, it varies from one situation to another. You may be quiet around strangers and gregarious with friends and family. You might be optimistic about your schoolwork or career and pessimistic about your romantic prospects. The term *easygoing* might describe your behavior at home, while you might be a fanatic at work. This kind of diversity is not only common; it's often desirable. The argumentative style you use with friends wouldn't be well received by the judge in traffic court when you appeal a citation. Likewise, the affectionate behavior you display with a romantic partner at home probably wouldn't be appropriate in public. As you read in Chapter 1, a wide range of behaviors is an important ingredient of communication competence. In this sense, a consistent personality can be more of a drawback than an asset—unless that personality is "flexible."

Even though the notion of personality can limit the ways we think and act, there are some fundamental differences between communicators who view themselves positively and those who feel more negative about themselves. Research reviewed by Mary Ann Scheirer and Robert Kraut (1979) shows a strong correlation between self-esteem and patterns of thought and action. A dramatic illustration of the effect of self-concept on communication comes from a comparison between kindergarten children with positive and negative self-concepts. Children with positive self-concepts generally exhibit a number of positive characteristics: They enter new situations fearlessly, make friends easily, and experiment with new materials without hesitation. They trust their teacher even when the teacher is a stranger, cooperate and follow rules, and largely control their own behavior. They are creative, imaginative, and free-thinking; talk freely and share experiences eagerly; and are independent and need minimal direction. Most important of all, they are happy.

Kindergarten children with negative self-concepts typically demonstrate opposite characteristics: They rarely show initiative, relying on others for direction and asking permission for almost everything. They seldom show spontaneity or enter new activities. They isolate themselves, talk very little, behave pos-

Student Reflection

The Self Is Multidimensional

I don't have just one presenting self. There are several "me's." I'm one kind of person with my friends (a joker, social), another kind with my family ("a good kid"), and still another with the people at work (serious). For a while I thought that I was being a phony, but I've realized that there are several sides to my personality, and with different people at different times, different sides show.

sessively with objects, make excessive demands, either withdraw or aggress, and act frustrated.

Although these behaviors refer to children about six years old, research with older children and adults finds similar patterns. Table 2–1 summarizes research describing how the level of self-esteem affects the communication behavior of adults.

Though it would be simplistic to divide the world into people with positive self-concepts and those with negative ones, the picture here is clear. The more positive we feel about ourselves, the more easily we will form and maintain interpersonal relationships, and the more rewarding those relationships will be.

Figure 2–1 shows the relationship between the self-concept and behavior. It illustrates how the self-concept both shapes much of our communication behavior and is affected by it. We can begin to examine the process by considering the self-concept you bring to an event. Suppose, for example, that one element of your self-concept is "nervous with authority figures,"

Table 2–1   Characteristics of Communicators with Positive and Negative Self-Esteem

Persons with Positive Self-Esteem	Persons with Negative Self-Esteem
1. Are likely to think well of others.	1. Are likely to disapprove of others.
2. Expect to be accepted by others.	2. Expect to be rejected by others.
3. Evaluate their own performance more favorably.	3. Evaluate their own performance less favorably.
4. Perform well when being watched: are not afraid of others' reactions.	4. Perform poorly when being watched: are sensitive to possible negative reactions.
5. Work harder for people who demand high standards of performance.	5. Work harder for undemanding, less critical people.
6. Are inclined to feel comfortable with others they view as superior in some way.	6. Feel threatened by people they view as superior in some way.
7. Are able to defend themselves against negative comments of others.	7. Have difficulty defending themselves against others' negative comments: are more easily influenced.

Reported by D. E. Hamachek, Encounters with Others: Interpersonal Relationships and You. New York, Holt, Rinehart and Winston, 1982.

That image probably comes from the evaluations of significant others in the past—perhaps teachers or former employers. If you view yourself as nervous with authority figures like these, you will probably behave in nervous ways when you encounter them in the future—in a teacher-student conference or a job interview. That nervous behavior is likely to influence the way others view your personality, which in turn will shape the way they respond to you—probably reinforcing the self-concept you brought to the event. Finally, the responses of others will affect the way you interpret future events: other job interviews, meetings with professors, and so on. This cycle illustrates the chicken-and-egg nature of the self-concept, which is shaped by significant others in the past, helps to govern your present behavior, and influences the way others view you.

Characteristics of the Self-Concept

Now that you have a better idea of how your self-concept has developed, we can take a closer look at some of its characteristics.

THE SELF-CONCEPT IS MULTIDIMENSIONAL

Just as the universe is composed of countless galaxies, each person's self-concept is a conglomeration of many beliefs. In fact, it is an oversimplification to talk about "the" self-concept as if each of us possessed only one. Morris Rosenberg (1979; Civikly 1982) describes three ways to view this construct: (1) how we view ourselves; (2) how we would like to view ourselves; and (3) how we present ourselves to others.

The first view—we can call it the **perceived self**—is quite complex. It contains your view of

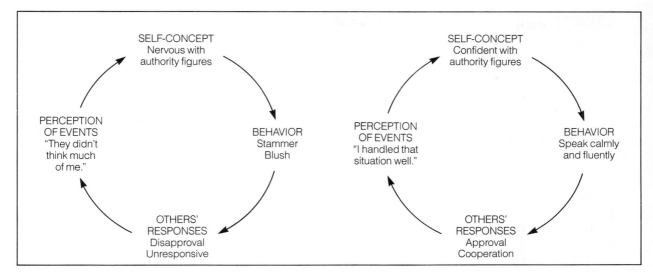

Figure 2–1   The self-concept and communication: a cyclic process. The interaction between the self-concept and communication with others can operate in both positive and negative ways.

your social status (including age, sex, socio-economic standing, and occupational position), social labels (such as "jock" or "parent"), past and present membership groups (religious, political, and ethnic), and "ego extensions" (material possessions with which you identify).

How satisfied are you with yourself? How much of your "real self" do you show to others? Explore these questions by completing Activity 5 on page 60.

The second view of self, the **desired self**, also contains a variety of elements. First there is the idealized image. Although this idealized image may be an unobtainable goal, research by Charles Pavitt (1989) shows that we use it to judge both our own and others' communication

competence. A second dimension of the self is the committed image, the one which you actually make efforts to obtain: degree, job, partner, and so on. Finally there is the moral image, which consists of all the messages you send about how you ought to think and act.

The third view of self, the **presenting self,** involves the image you want to project to the world. Social scientists often use the term **face** to describe the presenting self. The presenting self sometimes matches the perceived self. For instance, you might confess to the belief that you behaved admirably or made a fool of yourself last Saturday night. In other cases we present ourselves publicly in ways that more closely match the desired self, as when you know you behaved poorly but try to pass your behavior off as justified, or even virtuous ("I didn't file an income tax return because I

In a groping and tentative way, different selves may be rehearsed—the glamor girl, the caustic wit, the world-weary sophisticate, the dedicated revolutionary. Selves may be tried on or discarded like garments as adolescents attempt to convince others of their sophistication, cheerfulness, their allure, their intelligence.... When an adolescent—or anyone else—tries to achieve a certain goal, he does so not simply for the direct advantage it affords, but because it enables him to prove something about himself to himself. (pp. 48–49)

The self-concept is multidimensional in another way. It is an oversimplification to say that each of us possesses a single self-concept in the way we possess a single body. Many theorists argue that most people have flexible selves that vary from one situation to another (James 1892; Magnussen and Endler 1977; Mischel 1973). You might view yourself as smart and confident in some settings, for example, and feel ignorant and insecure in others. Research shows that communication behavior does, in fact, vary across situations (Hewes and Haight 1979). Despite this variation, many people believe—usually mistakenly—that they have stable personalities. In one study, researchers found that there was little behavioral difference between people who defined themselves as "shy" and those who chose the label "not shy" (Zimbardo 1977). In other words, both groups acknowledged reacting to some social situations with pounding heart, butterflies in the stomach, and blushing. Labeling made a significant difference: Whereas some subjects said, "I *am* shy," their more confident counterparts—who behaved in exactly the same manner—instead chose to say "I sometimes *act* shy."

It's easy to see that this second way of thinking leads to a much more satisfying—and in most cases a more realistic—self-appraisal. We'll have a great deal more to say about thinking and emotions in Chapter 4.

wanted to make a statement about the unconstitutional activities of the I.R.S.!"). The image you present to others can also fall somewhere between the perceived and ideal selves, as when you say, "Well, maybe I did act a *little* unfairly..."

Rosenberg notes that the presenting self is important throughout life, but it undergoes the greatest changes during adolescence:

"Oh, thank you, I only wish I felt as good as I look."

THE SELF-CONCEPT IS SUBJECTIVE

The way we view ourselves is often at odds with others' perceptions—and often with the observable facts. In one study (Myers 1980), a random sample of men were asked to rank themselves on their ability to get along with others. Defying mathematical laws, all subjects—every last one—put themselves in the top half of the population. Sixty percent rated themselves in the top 10 percent of the population, and an amazing 25 percent believed they were in the top 1 percent. In the same study, 70 percent of the men ranked the quality of their leadership in the top quarter of the population, whereas only 2 percent thought they were below average. Sixty percent said they were in the top quarter for athletic abilities, whereas only 6 percent viewed themselves as below average.

There are several reasons why some people have a self-concept that others would regard as unrealistically favorable. First, a self-estimation might be based on obsolete information. Perhaps your jokes used to be well received, or your grades were high, or your work was superior, and now the facts have changed. As you'll soon read, people are reluctant to give up a familiar self-image. This principle makes especially good sense when it's possible to avoid the unpleasant truth of the present by staying in the more desirable past.

A self-concept might also be excessively favorable due to distorted feedback from others. A boss may claim to be an excellent manager because assistants pour on false praise in order to keep their jobs. A child's inflated ego may be based on the praise of doting parents.

A third reason for holding an unrealistically high self-concept is that our society demands too much of its members. Much of the conditioning we receive in our early years implies that anything less than perfection is unsatisfactory, so that admitting mistakes is often seen as a sign of weakness. Instructors who fail to admit they don't know everything about a subject are afraid they will lose face with their colleagues and students. Couples whose relationships are beset by occasional problems don't want to admit that they have failed to achieve the "ideal" relationship they've seen portrayed in fiction. Parents who don't want to tell their children, "I'm sorry, I made a mistake," are afraid they'll lose the youngsters' respect.

If you try to represent yourself as a perfect communicator, then admitting your frailties becomes difficult. Such a confession becomes the equivalent of admitting one is a failure—and failure is not an element of most people's self-concept. Rather than label themselves failures, many people engage in self-deception, insisting to themselves and to others that their behavior is more admirable than the circumstances indicate. We'll have more to say about the reasons behind such behavior and its consequences when we discuss defense mechanisms in Chapter 10.

In contrast to the cases we've just described are the times when we view ourselves more *harshly* than the facts warrant. You may have known people, for instance, who insist that they are unattractive or incompetent in spite of your honest insistence to the contrary. In fact, you have probably experienced excessively negative self-evaluation yourself. Recall a time when you woke up with a case of the "uglies," convinced that you looked terrible. Remember how on such days you were unwilling to accept even the most sincere compliments from others, having already decided how wretched you appeared.

Many of us only fall into the trap of being overly critical occasionally, but others always have an unrealistically low self-concept.

Sidney Simon (1977), in his delightful book *Vulture: A Modern Allegory on the Art of Putting Oneself Down,* describes how we diminish our self-worth. Vultures have gained their unsavory reputation by swooping down on their victims and plucking away at their flesh—not a pretty sight. The psychological vulture Simon describes is just as unappealing. It waits for a self-put-down and then uses this moment of weakness to peck away at the self-esteem of its weakened victim. These psychological vultures, of course, are subjective: They are the unnecessary creations of their own victims.

There are two types of vulture attacks, one more subtle than the other: The most obvious kind occurs whenever we engage in an overt act of self-criticism. For example, a colleague of ours has a habit of bumping into things, which is not unusual. However, her response to such events is to exaggerate and overgeneralize them by criticizing herself: "I'm such a klutz!"

The more subtle kind of vulture attack occurs when we set unrealistic limitations on ourselves. Any statement that limits your capability to think or act within the limits of your potential invites another nibble at your self-esteem. "I couldn't say that to her!" "I could never give a speech!" "They'd never hire me for that job!" As soon as it senses such thoughts the vulture swoops down, claws extended, and carries off another chunk of self-esteem.

Simon suggests that we set ourselves up for vulture attacks in six areas: *physical* ("I'm too fat, thin, short, tall, clumsy"); *sexual* ("I'm unattractive to the opposite sex," "Nobody would want to go out with me"); *creative* ("I have no imagination," "I can't draw"); *family* ("I'm a disappointment to my parents," "I don't spend enough time with them"); *intelligence* ("I'm just dumb, I guess," "I'm no good in math"); and *relationships* ("Nobody would want me for a friend," "I'm too shy").

What are the reasons for such excessively negative self-evaluations? As with unrealistically high self-esteem, one source for an overabundance of self-put-downs is obsolete information. A string of past failures in school or with social relations can linger to haunt a communicator long after they have occurred, even though such events don't predict failure in the future. Similarly, we've known slender students who still think of themselves as fat and clear-complexioned people who still behave as if they were acne-ridden.

Distorted feedback can also create a self-image that is worse than a more objective observer would see. Having grown up around overly critical parents is one of the most common causes of a negative self-image. In other cases the remarks of cruel friends, uncaring teachers, excessively demanding employers, or even memorable strangers can have a lasting effect. As you read earlier, the impact of significant others and reference groups in forming a self-concept can be great.

Another cause for a strongly negative self-concept is the myth of perfection that is common in our society. From the time most of us learn to understand language, we are exposed to models who appear to be perfect at whatever they do. This myth is clearest when we examine the stories commonly told to children. In these stories the hero is wise, brave, talented, and victorious, whereas the villain is totally evil and doomed to failure. This kind of model is easy for a child to understand, but it hardly paints a realistic picture of the world. Unfortunately, many parents perpetuate the myth of perfection by refusing to admit that they are ever mistaken or unfair. Children, of course, accept this perfectionist facade for a long time, not

being in a position to dispute the wisdom of such powerful beings. From the behavior of the adults around them comes the clear message: "A well-adjusted, successful person has no faults."

Thus, children learn that in order to gain acceptance, they must pretend to "have it all together," even though they know they haven't. Given this naive belief that everyone else is perfect and the knowledge that you aren't, the self-concept will naturally suffer. We'll have a great deal to say about perfection and other irrational ideas, both in this chapter and in Chapter 8. In the meantime, don't get the mistaken impression that it's wrong to aim at perfection as an *ideal*. We're only suggesting that achieving this state is usually not possible, and to expect that you should do so will certainly lead to an unnecessarily low self-concept.

A final reason people often sell themselves short is also connected to social expectations. Curiously, the perfectionistic society to which we belong rewards those people who downplay the strengths we demand they possess (or pretend to possess). We term these people "modest" and find their behavior agreeable. On the other hand, we consider those who honestly appreciate their own strengths to be "braggarts" or "egotists," confusing them with the people who boast about accomplishments they do not possess. This convention leads most of us to talk freely about our shortcomings while downplaying our accomplishments. It's all right to proclaim that you're miserable if you have failed to do well on a project, but boastful to express your pride at a job well done. It's fine to remark that you feel unattractive, but egocentric to say that you think you look good.

After a while we begin to believe the types of statements we repeatedly make. The self-put-downs are viewed as modesty and become part of our self-concept, whereas the strengths and accomplishments go unmentioned and are forgotten. In the end we see ourselves as much worse than we are.

THE SELF IS INFLUENCED BY CULTURE

Although we seldom recognize the fact, our whole notion of the self is shaped by the culture in which we have been reared.

The most obvious feature of a culture is the language members use. If you live in a culture where everyone speaks the same tongue, then language will have little noticeable impact. But when your primary language is not the majority one, or when it is not prestigious, the sense of being a member of what social scientists call the "outgroup" is strong. At this point the speaker of a nondominant tongue can react in one of two ways: either to feel pressured to assimilate by speaking the "better" language, or to refuse to accommodate to the majority language and maintain loyalty to the ethnic tongue (Giles and Johnson 1987). In either case, the impact of language on the self-concept is powerful. On the one hand, the feeling is likely to be "I'm not as good as speakers of the native language," and on the other the belief is "there's

---

For men and women are not only themselves; they are also the region in which they were born, the city apartment or farm in which they learned to walk, the games they played as children, the old wives' tales they overheard, the food they ate, the schools they attended, the sports they followed, the poems they read, and the God they believed in.

W. SOMERSET MAUGHAM
The Razor's Edge

---

something unique and worth preserving in my language." A case study of Hispanic managers illustrates the dilemma of speaking a nondominant language (Banks 1987). The managers, employees in an Anglo-American organization, felt their feelings of Mexican identity threatened when they found that the road to advancement would be smoother if they de-emphasized their Spanish and adopted a more colloquial English style of speaking.

Cultures affect the self-concept in more subtle ways, too. Most Western cultures are highly individualistic, whereas traditional other cultures—most Asian ones, for example—are much more collective. When asked to identify themselves, Americans, Canadians, Australians, and Europeans would probably respond by giving their first name, surname, street, town, and country. Many Asians do it the other way around (Servaes 1989: 396). If you ask Hindus for their identity, they will give you their caste and village as well as their name. The Sanskrit formula for identifying oneself begins with lineage and goes on to state family, house, and ends with one's personal name (Bharati 1985).

These conventions for naming aren't just cultural curiosities: They reflect a very different way of viewing oneself. In collective cultures a person gains identity by belonging to a group. This means that the degree of interdependence among members of the society and its subgroups is much higher. Feelings of pride and self-worth are likely to be shaped not only by what the individual does, but by behavior of other members of the community. This linkage to others explains the traditional Japanese denial of self-importance—a strong contrast to the self-promotion that is common in individualistic Western cultures (Gudykunst and Ting-Toomey 1988: 83). Writer Pico Iyer captures the Japanese collective spirit, which is a vivid contrast to North American and European cultures:

In Japan, in fact, everything had been made level and uniform—even humanity. By one official count, 90 percent of the population regarded themselves as middle-class; in schools, it was not the outcasts who beat up the conformists, but vice versa. Every Japanese individual seemed to have the same goal as every other—to become like every other Japanese individual. The word for "different," I was told, was the same as the word for "wrong." And again and again in Japan, in contexts varying from the baseball stadium to the watercolor canvas, I heard the same unswerving, even maxim: "The nail that sticks out must be hammered down." (1988: 332)

This sort of cultural difference shows up in the level of comfort or anxiety people feel when communicating. In societies where the need to conform is great, there is a higher degree of communication apprehension. For example, as a group, residents of China, Korea, and Japan exhibit a higher degree of anxiety about speaking out than do members of individualistic cultures such as those of the United States and Australia (Klopf 1984). It's important to realize that different levels of communication apprehension don't mean that shyness is a "problem" in some cultures (Gudykunst and Ting-Toomey 1988: 145). In fact, just the opposite is true: In these societies reticence is valued. When the goal is to *avoid* being the nail that sticks out, it's logical to feel nervous when you make yourself appear different by calling attention to yourself. A self-concept that includes "assertive" behavior might make a Westerner feel proud, but in much of Asia it would more likely be cause for shame.

The difference between individualism and collectivism extends to the notion of **face-work**—the degree to which people act to preserve their own presenting image and the images of others. Stella Ting-Toomey (1988) has developed a theory that explains cultural differences in important norms, such as honesty and directness. She suggests that in individualistic Western cultures where there is a strong "I" orientation, the norm of speaking directly is honored; whereas in collectivistic cultures, where the main desire is to build connections between the self and others, indirect approaches that maintain harmony are considered more desirable. "I gotta be me" could be the motto of a Westerner, but "If I hurt you, I hurt myself" is closer to the Asian way of thinking.

A HEALTHY SELF-CONCEPT IS FLEXIBLE

People change. From moment to moment we aren't the same. We wake up in the morning in a jovial mood and turn grumpy before lunch. We find ourselves fascinated by a conversational topic one moment, then suddenly lose interest. One moment's anger often gives way to forgiveness the next. Health turns to illness and back to health. Alertness becomes fatigue, hunger becomes satiation, and confusion becomes clarity.

We also change from situation to situation. You might be a relaxed conversationalist with people you know but at a loss for words with strangers. You might be patient when explaining things on the job but have no tolerance for such explanations at home. You might be a wizard at solving mathematical problems but have a terribly difficult time putting your thoughts into words. We change over long stretches of time. We grow older, learn new facts, adopt new attitudes and philosophies, set and reach new goals, and find that others change their way of thinking and acting toward us.

The self-concept also tends to change over longer periods of time. Fitts (1971) summarizes an investigation that found that the degree to which a self-concept is positive *increases with age.* Measurements of the self-concepts of people 20, 30, 40, 50, 60, and 69 years old indicate that there is a steady increase in positive self-concept; generally, people feel better about themselves as they get older. Although the correlation is between self-concept and age, the real relationship is between self-concept and what happens as we get older. We gain more and more control over our lives; we gain the opportunity to structure situations to ensure that we will have good feelings about ourselves.

As we change in these and many other ways, our self-concept must also change in order to stay realistic. An accurate self-portrait today would not be exactly the same one we had a year ago or a few months ago or even yesterday. This does not mean that you change radically from day to day. The fundamental characteristics of your personality will stay the same for years, perhaps for a lifetime. It is likely, however, that in other important ways you are changing—physically, intellectually, emotionally, and spiritually.

THE SELF-CONCEPT RESISTS CHANGE

Although we change and a realistic self-concept should reflect this change, the tendency to resist revision of our self-perception is strong. When confronted with facts that contradict our self-perceptions, we tend to dispute the facts and cling to the outmoded self-image. This tendency to seek information that conforms to an existing self-concept has been labeled **cognitive conservatism** (Greenwald 1980). We are understandably reluctant to revise a favorable self-concept. If you were a thoughtful, romantic partner early in a relationship, it would be hard to admit that you might have become less considerate and attentive lately. Likewise, if you used to be a serious student, acknowledging that you have slacked off isn't easy.

Curiously, the tendency to cling to an outmoded self-perception holds even when the new image would be more favorable. We can recall literally scores of attractive, intelligent students who still view themselves as the gawky underachievers they were in the past. The tragedy of this sort of cognitive conservatism is obvious. People with unnecessarily low self-esteem can become their own worst enemies, denying themselves the validation they need and deserve to enjoy satisfying relationships.

Once the self is firmly rooted, only a powerful force can change it. At least four requirements must be met for an appraisal to be regarded as important (Gergen 1971): First of all, the person who offers a particular appraisal must be *someone we see as competent to offer it.* Parents satisfy this requirement extremely well because as young children we perceive that our parents know so much about us—more than we know about ourselves sometimes. Second, *the appraisal must be perceived as highly personal.* The more the other person seems to know about us and adapts what is being said to fit us, the more likely we are to accept judgments from this person. In addition, the appraisal must be *reasonable in light of what we believe about ourselves.* If an appraisal is similar to one we give ourselves, we will believe it; if it is somewhat dissimilar, we will probably still accept it; but if it is completely dissimilar, we will probably reject it.

Finally, appraisals that are *consistent* and *numerous* are more persuasive than those that contradict usual appraisals or those that only occur once. As long as only a *few* students yawn in class, a teacher can safely disregard them as a reflection on teaching ability. In like manner, you could safely disregard the appraisal of the angry date who tells you in no uncertain terms what kind of person behaves as you did. Of course, when you get a second or third similar appraisal in a short time, the evaluation becomes harder to ignore.

The Self-Fulfilling Prophecy

The self-concept is such a powerful force on the personality that it not only determines how you see yourself in the present, but can actually influence your future behavior and that of others. Such occurrences come about through a phenomenon called the self-fulfilling prophecy.

A **self-fulfilling prophecy** occurs when a person's expectation of an event makes the outcome more likely to happen than would otherwise have been true. Self-fulfilling prophecies occur all the time, although you might never have given them that label. For example,

- You expected to become nervous and botch a job interview and later did so.

- You anticipated having a good (or terrible) time at a social affair and your expectations came true.

- A teacher or boss explained a new task to you, saying that you probably wouldn't do well at first; you did not do well.

- A friend described someone you were about to meet, saying that you wouldn't like the person, which turned out to be correct.

In each of these cases, there is a good chance that the event happened because it was predicted. You needn't have botched the interview, the party might have been boring only because you helped make it so, you might have done better on the job if your boss hadn't spoken up, and you might have liked the new acquaintance if your friend hadn't given you preconceptions. In other words, what helped make each event take place as it did was your expectation of what would happen.

What self-fulfilling prophecies do you impose on yourself? What prophecies do you communicate to others? Turn to Activity 6 on page 61 to answer these questions.

There are two types of self-fulfilling prophecies. The first occurs when the expectations of one person govern another's actions. The classic example is a study Robert Rosenthal and Lenore Jacobson described in their book *Pygmalion in the Classroom* (1968):

> Twenty percent of the children in a certain elementary school were reported to their teachers as showing unusual potential for intellectual growth. The names of these 20 percent were drawn by means of a table of random numbers, which is to say that the names were drawn out of a hat. Eight months later these unusual or "magic" children showed significantly greater gains in IQ than did the remaining children who had not been singled out for the teachers' attention. The change in the teachers' expectations regarding the intellectual performance of these allegedly "special" children had led to an actual change in the intellectual performance of these randomly selected children.

In other words, some children may do better in school, not because they are more intelligent than their classmates, but because they learn that their teacher—a significant other—believes they can achieve.

Teachers usually convey their expectations in indirect, subtle ways. Rosenthal and DePaulo (1979) summarize the research in this area by describing four kinds of messages that label students as "special": *climate* (teachers are more supportive and confirming for certain students); *feedback* ("special" students get more positive and negative reactions than their classmates do); *input* (the "special" students get more material and material of a different nature than other children do); and *output* (teachers give some students more opportunities and more time to respond). The overall effect is clear: Students who are treated in a special way respond to their teachers' expectations.

To put this phenomenon in context with the self-concept, we can say that when a teacher communicates to a child the message "I think you're bright," the child accepts that evaluation and changes her self-concept to include that evaluation. Unfortunately, the same principle holds for students whose teachers send the message "I think you're stupid."

This type of self-fulfilling prophecy has been shown to be powerful in shaping the self-concept and behavior of people in a wide range of settings outside schools. Medical patients who unknowingly use placebos—injections of sterile water or doses of sugar pills that have no curative value—often respond just as favorably to treatment as people who actually receive an active drug. The patients believe they have taken a substance that will help them feel better, and this belief brings about a "cure." In psychotherapy Rosenthal and Jacobson describe several studies suggesting that patients who believe they will benefit from treatment do so, regardless of the type of treatment they receive. In the same vein, when a doctor believes a patient will improve, the patient may do so precisely because of this expectation, whereas

---

"If you think you can or can't you are right."

HENRY FORD

1.
2.
3.

BEWARE
OF THE
DOG

BEWARE
OF THE
DOG

another person for whom the physician has little hope often fails to recover. Apparently the patient's concept as being sick or well—as shaped by the doctor—plays an important role in determining the actual state of health.

In business the power of the self-fulfilling prophecy was proved as early as 1890. A new tabulating machine had just been installed at the U.S. Census Bureau in Washington, D.C. In order to use the machine, the bureau's staff had to learn a new set of skills that the machine's inventor believed to be quite difficult. He told the clerks that after some practice they could expect to punch about 550 cards per day; to process any more would jeopardize their psychological well-being. Sure enough, after two weeks the clerks were processing the anticipated number of cards, and reported feelings of stress if they attempted to move any faster.

Some time later an additional group of clerks was hired to operate the same machines. These workers knew nothing of the devices, and no one had told them about the upper limit of production. After only three days the new employees were each punching over 2,000 cards per day with no ill effects. Again, the self-fulfill-

Student Reflection

Self-Fulfilling Prophecies

In high school I hated my public speaking class. I used to be so afraid of giving a speech that my throat would close up and I would literally croak. Now I can see that expecting to get nervous made my anxiety even worse, and almost guaranteed that I would have an anxiety attack. I'll be taking a speech class next semester, and I am determined not to set myself up by expecting to fail. If I can find a way to predict that I'll do okay, then maybe I can create a self-fulfilling prophecy that helps me do better instead of worse.

ing prophecy seemed to be in operation. The original workers believed themselves capable of punching only 550 cards and behaved accordingly, whereas the new clerks had no limiting expectations as part of their self-concepts and so behaved more productively.

The self-fulfilling prophecy operates in families as well. If parents tell children for a long enough time that they can't do anything right, each child's self-concept will soon incorporate the idea, and each will fail at many tasks. On the other hand, if children are told that they are capable or lovable or kind, there is a much greater chance of their behaving accordingly.

Our beliefs are so important to us that we will do anything to keep them intact. One way we protect them is by claiming that an exception to our belief is "the exception that proves the rule." For example, in our organization consulting work, we have heard male executives argue that "women don't make good managers." When presented with evidence that gender is not a determinant of good managerial behavior, the usual response is "Oh, sure, but those women behaved like men!"

The prophecies that others impose contribute to a person's self-concept. The statement "You'll never understand algebra" leads to the belief "I'm a mathematical idiot," and the message "We asked you to do the job because we know it will be outstanding" helps shape the belief "I'm a talented and competent person."

Once established, a person's self-concept leads to a second type of self-fulfilling prophecy—one in which the expectations we hold about ourselves influence our own behavior. Like the botched job interview and the unpleasant party mentioned at the beginning of this section, there are many times when an event that needn't occur happens because you expect it to. In sports you've probably psyched yourself into playing either better or worse than usual; the only explanation for your unusual performance was your attitude. You've probably faced an audience at one time or another with a fearful attitude and forgotten your remarks, not because you were unprepared, but because you said to yourself, "I know I'll blow it."

Certainly you've had the experience of waking up in a grouchy mood and saying to yourself, "This will be a bad day." Once you decided, you acted in ways that made it come true. If you approached a class expecting to be bored, you most probably did lose interest, due partly to a lack of attention on your part. If you avoided the company of others because you expected that they had nothing to offer, your suspicions would have been confirmed—nothing exciting or new did happen to you. On the other hand, if you had approached the same day with the idea that it could be good, it probably would have been good. Smile at people, and they'll probably smile back. Enter a class determined to learn something, and you probably will—even if it's how not to instruct students! Approach many people with the idea that some of them will be good to know, and you'll most likely make some new friends. In such cases your attitude has a great deal to do with how you see yourself and how others will see you.

The self-fulfilling prophecy is an important force in interpersonal communication, but we don't want to suggest that it explains *all* behavior. There are certainly times when the expectation of an event's outcome won't bring about that outcome. Believing you'll do well in a job interview when you're clearly not qualified for the position is unrealistic. In the same way, there will probably be people and situations you won't enjoy, no matter what your expectations. To connect the self-fulfilling prophecy with the "power of positive thinking" is an over-simplification.

In other cases your expectations will be borne out because you're a good predictor, and not because of the self-fulfilling prophecy. For example, when children do not do well in school, it may be wrong to blame a parent or teacher, even though the behavior did match their expectations. In the same way, some workers excel and others fail, some patients recover and others don't, all according to our predictions but not *because* of them.

Keeping these qualifications in mind, we should recognize the tremendous influence that self-fulfilling prophecies have on our lives. To a great extent we are what we believe we are. In this sense we and those around us constantly create our self-concepts and our "selves."

Changing Your Self-Concept

You've probably begun to realize that it is possible to change an unsatisfying self-concept. In the next sections we'll discuss some methods for accomplishing such a change.

There is an old joke about a man who was asked if he could play a violin and answered, "I don't know. I've never tried." This is psychologically a very wise reply. Those who have never tried to play a violin really do not know whether they can or not. Those who say too early in life and too firmly, "No, I'm not at all musical," shut themselves off prematurely from whole areas of life that might have proved rewarding. In each of us there are unknown possibilities, undiscovered potentialities—and one big advantage of having an open self-concept rather than a rigid one is that we shall continue to expose ourselves to new experiences and therefore we shall continue to discover more and more about ourselves as we grow older.

S. I. HAYAKAWA

HAVE REALISTIC EXPECTATIONS

It's important to realize that some of your dissatisfaction might come from expecting too much of yourself. If you demand that you handle every act of communication perfectly, you're bound to be disappointed. Nobody is able to handle every conflict productively, to be totally relaxed and skillful in conversations, always to ask perceptive questions, or to be 100 percent helpful when others have problems. Expecting yourself to reach such unrealistic goals is to doom yourself to unhappiness at the start.

Sometimes it's easy to be hard on yourself because everyone around you seems to be handling themselves so much better than you. It's important to realize that much of what seems like confidence and skill in others is a front to hide uncertainty. They may be suffering from the same self-imposed demands for perfection that you place on yourself.

Are you unhappy with parts of your self-concept? Would you like to change them? If so, turn to Activity 7 on page 61 for suggestions.

Even when others seem more competent than you, it's important to judge yourself in terms of your own growth, and not against the behavior of others. Rather than feeling miserable because you're not as talented as an expert, realize that you probably are a better, wiser, or more skillful person than you used to be and that this growth is a legitimate source of satisfaction. Perfection is fine as an ideal, but you're being unfair to yourself if you actually expect to reach it.

HAVE A REALISTIC PERCEPTION OF YOURSELF

One source of a poor self-concept is inaccurate self-perception. As you've already read, such unrealistic pictures sometimes come from being overly harsh on yourself, believing that you're worse than the facts indicate. Of course, it would be foolish to deny that you could be a better person than you are, but it's also important to recognize your strengths. A periodic session of "bragging"—acknowledging the parts of yourself with which you're pleased and the ways you've grown—is often a good way to put your strengths and shortcomings into perspective.

An unrealistically poor self-concept can also come from the inaccurate feedback of others. Perhaps you are in an environment where you receive an excessive number of negative messages, many of which are undeserved, and a minimum of encouragement. We've known many women, for example, who have returned to college after many years spent in homemaking where they received virtually no recognition for their intellectual strengths. It's amazing that these women have the courage to come to college at all, their self-concepts are so negative; but they do come, and most are thrilled to find that they are much brighter and more competent intellectually than they suspected. In the same way, workers with overly critical supervisors, children with cruel "friends," and students with unsupportive teachers are all prone to suffering from low self-concepts due to excessively negative feedback.

If you fall into this category, it's important to put into perspective the unrealistic evaluations you receive, and then to seek out more supportive people who will acknowledge your assets as well as point out your shortcomings. Doing so is often a quick and sure boost to the self-concept.

HAVE THE WILL TO CHANGE

Often we say we want to change, but aren't willing to do the necessary work. In such cases the responsibility for not growing rests squarely on your shoulders. Often we maintain an unrealistic self-concept by claiming that we "can't" be the person we'd like to be, when in fact we're simply not willing to do what's required. You *can* change in many ways, if only you are willing to put out the effort.

HAVE THE SKILL TO CHANGE

Trying is often not enough. There are times when you would change if you knew how to do so.

First, you can seek advice—from books such as this one, the suggested readings at the end of each chapter, and other printed sources. You can also get advice from instructors, counselors, and other experts, as well as from friends. Of course, not all the advice you receive will be useful, but if you read widely and talk to enough people, you have a good chance of learning the things you want to know.

A second method of learning how to change is to observe models—people who handle themselves in the ways you would like to master. It's often been said that people learn more from models than in any other way, and by taking advantage of this principle you will find that the world is full of teachers who can show you how to communicate more successfully. Become a careful observer. Watch what people you admire do and say, not so that you can copy them, but so that you can adapt their behavior to fit your own personal style.

At this point you might be overwhelmed by the difficulty of changing the way you think about yourself and the way you act. Remember, we never said that this process would be easy (although it sometimes is). But even when change is difficult, it's possible if you are serious. You don't need to be perfect, but you *can* improve your self-concept and, as a result, your communication—*if you choose to.*

"YOU'RE A VERY FINE FELLOW!"

ECHO POINT

© Gahan Wilson.

Student Reflection

The Will to Change

Last year I lost about fifteen pounds and started to shape up by going to the gym. This was quite a change for me after being a flabby weakling most of my life. It wasn't always easy to exercise or say no to a second helping of mashed potatoes, but the results were worth the effort.

Now I see that changing the way I communicate will take the same kind of discipline. Being open to criticism instead of getting defensive and listening instead of arguing won't be easy. But if I stick to it and take one day at a time, I can shape up my attitude the same way I shaped up my body.

Summary

The self-concept is a relatively stable set of perceptions that individuals have of themselves. The self-concept consists of three dimensions: the perceived, desired, and presenting selves. In some cases these three dimensions are closely integrated, while in others they are quite different. Each person's self-concept is shaped early in life and is modified later by the reflected appraisal of others, as well as by social comparison with reference groups.

Whereas the self-concept is an internal image we have of ourselves, the personality is the view others hold of us. The relationship between self-concept, behavior, personality, and perception is circular: The self-concept shapes the way we communicate, which in turn affects the judgments others make of our personality. Their reactions in turn influence our perception of events, either reinforcing or changing our self-concept.

The self-concept has several important characteristics. It is multidimensional: In most cases there are actually several "selves," each with different attributes. The self is also subjective. The beliefs we have about ourselves may be strong, but they are usually distorted either positively or negatively. Although the self-concept is resistant to change, a healthy self usually evolves over time. In many respects we are not the same people we used to be, and the self-concept should reflect this evolution. Finally, the self-concept is shaped in part by the culture in which the person was raised. Even the notions of selfhood and individuality are different in non-Western cultures.

Self-fulfilling prophecies are predictions that make an outcome more likely to occur. In some self-fulfilling prophecies we make predictions about our own behavior, while in others our expectations influence the way others think or act. In either case, these predictions can produce either constructive or unsatisfying results.

Changing one's self-concept is not easy, but it is possible. Some important considerations are beginning with a realistic perception of oneself instead of being overly critical, having realistic expectations about how much change is possible, being determined to invest the necessary effort in changing, and learning the skills necessary to change.

Activities

1. You can appreciate the power of others to shape your self-concept by identifying an important part of your self-concept. The element may be positive (e.g., "intelligent," "good athlete") or negative (e.g., "unattractive," "selfish"). Recall a single message from a significant other that played an important role in shaping this part of your self-concept.

2. Interview someone with whom you have an important interpersonal relationship: a friend, family member or romantic partner, for example. Ask that person to describe what effect you have on his or her self-concept. Focus on your specific behaviors: individual occasions where you said or did something that affected your partner's self-concept.

3. What reference groups do you use to define your self-concept? What is the effect of using these groups as a basis for judging yourself? How might you view yourself differently if you used other reference groups as a basis for comparison?

4. Pick three terms that describe your personality as a communicator. Do these terms describe you in all situations, or are they sometimes inaccurate? If you have different "personalities" in different situations, describe them. Finally, consider how defining yourself as having a single personality affects the way you behave. How might you think, feel, and act differently if you had a less consistent, all-encompassing view of your personality?

5. What are the most important differences among your perceived, desired, and presenting selves? In what way are the three selves similar? How do these differences influence your self-concept? How might your feelings and behavior change if you were to bring the three selves into closer alignment?

6. Describe two incidents in which self-fulfilling prophecies you have imposed on yourself have affected your communication. Explain how each of these predictions shaped your behavior, and describe how you might have behaved differently if you had made a different prediction. Next, describe two incidents in which you imposed self-fulfilling prophecies on others. What effect did your prediction have on these peoples' actions?

7. Identify one communication-related part of your self-concept you would like to change. Use the guidelines on pages 57–59 to describe how you could make that change.
   a. Decide if your expectations for change are realistic. Don't expect to become a new person: becoming a *better* one should be enough.
   b. Recognize your strengths as well as your shortcomings. You may not be as bad as you think you are!
   c. Decide whether you are willing to make the necessary effort to change. Good intentions are an important start, but hard work is also necessary.
   d. Make sure you understand how you want to behave. Consult books, experts, and observe models to get a clear idea of your new goals and how to achieve them.

Readings

Allport, G. W., and H. W. Odbert, "Trait Names, a Psychological Study." *Psychological Monographs* 47 (1936).

Asher, J. "Born to Be Shy?" *Psychology Today* 21 (1987): 56–64.

Banks, S. P. "Achieving 'Unmarkedness' in Organizational Discourse: A Praxis Perspective on Ethnolinguistic Identity." *Journal of Language and Social Psychology* 6 (1982): 171–90.

Bharti, A. "The Self in Hindu Thought and Action." In *Culture and Self: Asian and Western Perspectives*. New York: Tavistock, 1985.

Civikly, J. M. "Self-Concept, Significant Others, and Classroom Communication." In *Communication in the Classroom*, L. Barker, ed. Urbana: University of Illinois Press, 1982.

Felson, R. B. "Communication Barriers and the Reflected Appraisal Process." *Social Psychology Quarterly* 43 (1980): 223–33.

Felson, R. B. "Reflected Appraisal and the Development of Self." *Social Psychology Quarterly* 48 (1985): 71–78.

*Fitts, W. H. *The Self-Concept and Self-Actualization*. Nashville, TN: Counselor Recordings and Tests, 1971.

*Gergen, K. J. *The Concept of Self*. New York: Holt, Rinehart and Winston, 1971.

Gergen, K. J. "The Healthy, Happy Human Being Wears Many Masks." *Psychology Today* 5 (May 1972): 31–35, 64–66.

Giles, H., and P. Johnson, "Ethnolinguistic Identity Theory: A Social Psychological Approach to Language Maintenance." *International Journal of Sociology of Language* 68 (1987): 69–99.

Greenwald, A. G. "The Totalitarian Ego: Fabrication and Revision of Personal History," *American Psychologist* 35 (1980): 603–18.

Greenwald, A. G., and A. R. Pratkanis. "The Self." In *Handbook of Social Cognition*, R. S. Wyer and T. K. Srull, eds. Hillsdale, NJ: Lawrence Erlbaum, 1984.

Gudykunst, W. B., and S. Ting-Toomey, *Culture and Interpersonal Communication*. Newbury Park, CA: Sage, 1988.

Hamachek, D. *Encounters with the Self*. Fort Worth, TX: Holt, Rinehart and Winston, 1987.

Harré, R. "The Social Construction of Selves." In *Self and Identity: Psychological Perspectives,* K. Yardley and T. Honess, eds. London: Wiley, 1987.

Hewes, D. E., and L. Haight. "The Cross-Situational Consistency of Communicative Behaviors: A Preliminary Investigation." *Communication Research* 6 (1979): 243–70.

Iyer, P. *Video Night in Katmandu.* New York: Knopf, 1988.

James, W. *Psychology: The Briefer Course.* New York: Henry Holt, 1892.

Kagan, J. *The Nature of the Child.* New York: Basic Books, 1984.

Klopf, D. "Cross-Cultural Apprehension Research: A Summary of Pacific Basin Studies." In *Avoiding Communication: Shyness, Reticence, and Communication Apprehension,* J. Daly and J. McCroskey, eds. Beverly Hills, CA: Sage, 1984.

Marsh, H. W., and I. M. Holmes, "Multidimensional Self-Concepts: Construct Validation of Responses by Children." *American Educational Research Journal* 27 (1990): 89–117.

McCall, G. J. "The Self-Concept and Interpersonal Communication." In *Interpersonal Processes: New Directions in Communication Research,* M. E. Roloff and G. R. Miller, eds., Beverly Hills, CA: Sage, 1987.

McCroskey, J. C., and V. P. Richmond. *The Quiet Ones: Communication Apprehension and Shyness.* Dubuque, IA: Gorsuch Scarisbrick, 1980.

McGuire, W. J., and A. Padawer-Singer, "Trait Salience in the Spontaneous Self-Concept," *Journal of Personality and Social Psychology* 33 (1976): 743–54.

Magnussen, D., and N. Endler. *Personality at the Crossroads.* New York: Wiley, 1977.

Mischel, W. "Toward a Cognitive Social Learning Reconceptualization of Personality." *Psychological Review* 80 (1973): 252–83.

Myers, D. "The Inflated Self." *Psychology Today* 14 (May 1980): 16.

Pavitt, C. "Biases in the Recall of Communicators' Behaviors." *Communication Reports* 2 (1989): 9–15.

*Rosenberg, M. *Conceiving the Self.* New York: Basic Books, 1979.

Rosenthal, R., and L. Jacobson, *Pygmalion in the Classroom,* New York: Holt, Rinehart and Winston, 1968.

*Rosenthal, R., and B. M. DePaulo. "Expectancies, Discrepancies, and Courtesies in Nonverbal Communication." *Western Journal of Speech Communication* 43 (1979): 76–95.

Scheirer, M., and R. E. Kraut. "Increasing Educational Achievement via Self-Concept Change." *Review of Educational Research* 49 (Winter 1979); 131–50.

Servaes, J. "Cultural Identity and Modes of Communication," in *Communication Yearbook* 12, J. A. Andersen, ed. Newbury Park, CA: Sage, 1989.

Simon, S. B. *Vulture: A Modern Allegory on the Art of Putting Oneself Down.* Niles, IL; Argus Communications, 1977.

Steinfatt, T. M. "Personality and Communication: Classical Approaches" In *Personality and Interpersonal Communication,* J. C. McCroskey and J. A. Daly, eds. Newbury Park, CA: Sage, 1987.

Ting-Toomey, S. "A Face-Negotiation Theory." In *Theory in Interpersonal Communication,* Y. Kim and W. Gudykunst, eds, Newbury Park, CA: Sage, 1988.

Zimbardo, P. *Shyness.* Reading, MA: Addison-Wesley, 1977.

---

*Items identified by an asterisk are recommended as especially useful follow-ups.

Perception

Chapter 3
Perception

After studying the material in this chapter

You should understand

1. How the processes of selection, organization, and interpretation operate in human perception.

2. How physiological factors influence interpersonal perception.

3. How cultural factors influence interpersonal perception.

4. How social roles influence interpersonal perception.

5. How the self-concept influences interpersonal perception.

6. Common psychological factors that distort interpersonal perception.

7. The nature of interpersonal empathy.

You should be able to

1. Describe the physiological, cultural, social, and psychological influences that have shaped your perception of important people and events.

2. Describe your interpersonal conflicts from other people's points of view, showing how and why those others view events so differently.

3. Use perception checking to clarify your understanding of another person's point of view.

Key Terms

Androgyny
Empathy
Interpretation
Organization
Perception checking
Punctuation
Selection
Sex role
Sympathy

"Look at it my way . . ."
"Put yourself in my shoes . . ."
"If you really knew how I felt, . . ."
"YOU DON'T UNDERSTAND ME!"
Such statements reflect one of the most common barriers to effective, satisfying communication. We talk to (or at) one another until we're hoarse and exhausted; yet we still don't really understand each other. We're left feeling isolated and alone, despairing that our words don't seem able to convey the depth and complexity of what we think and feel. Something more seems necessary.

We've often fantasized about what that "something more" might be. Sometimes our image of the ideal understanding-promoter takes the shape of a device with two chairs. The users would seat themselves and place electrically connected metallic caps on their heads. When the switch was thrown, each person would instantly experience the other's world. Each would see through the other's eyes, possess the other's memories, and in all other ways know how it felt to be the other person.

You can imagine how misunderstandings would disappear and tolerance would increase once everyone used this invention. It's hard to harbor dislike once you've been inside another person's skin.

Our miracle chair doesn't exist, so this chapter will have to attempt the same goal. We'll explore the subject of *social cognition,* the cognitive processes that we use to categorize and explain human behavior in relationships. We'll discuss the many ways in which each of us experiences the world uniquely, and try to help you transcend the egocentric viewpoint that each of us usually occupies.

The Perception Process

We will begin our study of social cognition by looking at how the perception process operates.

The first point to realize is that we do not take notice of every stimulus that is available to us. William James made this point poetically when he said, "To the infant the world is just a big, blooming, buzzing confusion." Newborn children certainly are overwhelmed with an overload of new sensations, and they spend the first years of life learning which stimuli are meaningful and important.

Even as adults we are faced with more stimuli than we can manage. It would be impossible to focus on every word, noise, sight, or other sensation, so we find ways of screening out stimuli that seem unimportant and making sense of the remainder. The perception process occurs in three steps.

SELECTION

Because we are exposed to more input than we can possibly manage, the first step in perceiving is the **selection** of data to which we will attend. There are several factors that cause us to notice some messages and ignore others. Generally speaking, we pay attention to behavior that is *salient*—that jumps out at us being out of the ordinary.

How do selection, organization, and interpretation operate in everyday life to create differing perceptions? See for yourself by trying Activity 1 on page 89.

Stimuli that are *intense* often attract our attention. Something (or someone) that is louder, larger, or brighter stands out. This attraction explains why—other things being equal—we're more likely to remember extremely tall or short people, and why someone who laughs or talks loudly attracts more attention (not always favorable) than do quiet people.

Stimuli that are *repetitious* also attract attention. Just as a quiet but steadily dripping faucet can dominate your awareness, messages we hear again and again become noticeable.

Attention also is related to *contrast* or *change* in stimulation. Unchanging things or people become less and less noteworthy, until some change reminds us of them. This principle explains why we sometimes come to take wonderful people for granted, and why we appreciate them only when they stop being so wonderful or go away.

A final factor that influences selection involves *motives.* Just as a hungry person looks for a restaurant or a tardy one glances at clocks, someone looking for romance notices potential partners.

ORGANIZATION

After selecting information from the environment, we must arrange it in some meaningful way in order to make sense of the world. We call this **organization.** The raw sense data we perceive can be organized in more than one way. For instance, consider the picture of the boxes in Figure 3–1. How many ways can you view the figure? Most people have a hard time finding more than one perspective, although Figure 3–2 shows that there are four ways to view the image.

Like these boxes, we create ways of organizing all the information we select from the environment. We do this by using *perceptual schema,* cognitive frameworks that allow us to organize the raw data we have selected.

Steve Duck (1976) has described four types of

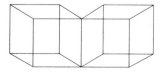

Figure 3–1

schemata that help us classify others. *Physical constructs* classify people according to their appearance: beautiful or ugly, fat or thin, young or old, and so on. *Role constructs* use social position: student, attorney, wife, and so on. *Interaction constructs* focus on social behavior: friendly, helpful, aloof, and sarcastic, for example. The final organizing scheme uses *psychological constructs:* generous, nervous, insecure, and so on.

These schemata are useful in two ways: First, they allow us to form impressions of others. Imagine that you've just met a new person in class or at a party. Without these constructs, you would have no way to answer the question "What's this person like?" Once you have classified others using various perceptual constructs, they become a useful way to predict future behavior. If you've classified a professor, for example, as "friendly," you'll handle questions or problems one way; if your analysis is "mean," your behavior will probably be quite different.

The kinds of constructs we use strongly affect the way we relate to others. Young children usually don't classify people according to their skin color. They are just as likely to identify an Anglo, black, or Asian by age, size, or personality. As they become more socialized, however, they learn that one common organizing principle in today's society is ethnicity, and their perceptions of others change. What constructs do you use to classify the people you encounter in your life? Consider how your relationship might change if you used different schema.

Another form of organization involves the way we identify the causes and effects in interaction. Watzlawick, Beavin, and Jackson (1967: 56) term this process **punctuation,** and illustrate it by describing a running quarrel between a husband and wife. The husband accuses the wife of being a nag, while she complains that he is withdrawing from her. Figure 3–3 describes this cycle.

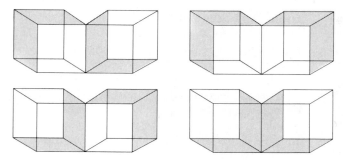

Figure 3–2

Notice that the order in which each partner punctuates this cycle affects how the dispute looks. The husband begins by blaming the wife: "I withdraw because you nag." The wife organizes the situation differently, starting with the husband: "I nag because you withdraw." Once the cycle gets rolling, it is impossible to say which accusation is accurate. The answer depends on how the sequence is punctuated.

Anyone who has seen two children argue about "who started it" can understand that haggling over causes and effects isn't likely to solve a conflict. In fact, the kind of finger pointing that goes along with assigning blame will probably make matters worse. Rather than argue about whose punctuation of an event is correct, it's far more productive to recognize that a dispute can look different to each person, and then move on to the more important question, "What can we do to make things better?"

INTERPRETATION

Once our perceptual constructs are in place, we selectively perceive and make sense of behaviors in ways that fit them.

Interpretation plays a role in virtually every interpersonal act. Is the person who smiles at you across a crowded room interested in romance or simply being polite? Is a friend's

kidding a sign of affection or irritation? Should you take an invitation to "drop by anytime" literally or not?

There are several factors that cause us to interpret an event one way or another. The first is *relational satisfaction*. The behavior that seems positive when you are happy with a partner might seem completely different when the

Figure 3–3   The way a communication sequence is punctuated affects its perceived meaning. Which comes first, the nagging or the withdrawing?

Student Reflection

Punctuation and Conflict

At age eighteen it's important for me to begin having my own life, separate from my family. This is hard for my parents to accept. They still want to know what I'm doing and thinking. Where am I going? Who will I be with? Do I know what I'm doing? The more they push, the more I draw away. This has become a real problem for all of us.

After reading this chapter I see that we've been punctuating things differently. To me it's been "The more my parents push, the more I want to draw away." To them it's been "The more you draw away, the more we push to stay in your life."

We need to break this circle. I think that if I tell my mom and dad more about my life <u>before</u> they ask, they'll push less. And my parents have to understand that if they stop <u>asking</u> me to share my life with them, it will be easier for me to give them what they want.

relationship isn't satisfying (Bradbury 1990; Manusov 1990). For example, unhappy spouses are more likely than happy ones to make negative interpretations of their mates' behaviors. To see how this principle operates, recall the husband-wife quarrel we discussed earlier. Suppose the wife suggests that they get away for a weekend vacation. If the marriage has been troubled, the husband might interpret his wife's idea as more nagging ("You never pay attention to me") and the fight will continue. If the relationship is solid, he is more likely to view the suggestion as a bid for a romantic getaway. It wasn't the event that shaped the interpretation, but the way the husband interpreted it.

A second factor that influences interpretations is *past experience*. What meanings have similar events held? If, for instance, you've been gouged by landlords in the past, you might be skeptical about an apartment manager's assurances that careful housekeeping will assure the refund of your cleaning deposit.

Assumptions about human behavior also influence interpretations. "People do as little work as possible." "In spite of their mistakes, people generally do the best they can." Such beliefs shape the way you interpret another's actions.

Expectations are another factor that shape our interpretations. If you imagine your boss is unhappy with you, you'll probably feel threatened by a request to "see me in my office Monday morning." On the other hand, if you imagine that your work will be rewarded, your weekend will be filled with pleasant anticipation.

Knowledge of others affects the way we interpret their actions. If you know a friend has just been jilted by a lover or fired from a job, you'll interpret his aloof behavior differently than if you were unaware of what happened. If you know an instructor is rude to all students, then you won't be likely to take her remarks personally.

Finally, *personal moods* affect interpretations. When you're feeling insecure, the world is a different place than when you're confident. The same goes for happiness and sadness or any other opposing emotions. The way we feel determines how we'll interpret events.

Sometimes an emotional state isn't just temporary. Some people can be classified as chronically apprehensive about communicating. This

For the most part we do not see first and then define; we define first and then see.

WALTER LIPPMANN

sort of apprehension can distort perceptions. For example, men in one study who were high in communication apprehension viewed women with whom they spoke as less physically attractive, less trustworthy, and less satisfying to interact with than did other men who were more confident (Ayers 1989). This research suggests how an apprehensive communicator's distorted interpretations could short-circuit the development of satisfying relationships. He might think about a potential companion, "She's not *that* good looking, and I probably wouldn't have much fun if I did get to know her, so why bother?" It's easy to see how this attitude could lead to an unsatisfying self-fulfilling prophecy.

Although we have talked about selection, organization and interpretation separately, the three phases of perception can occur in differing sequences. For example, a parent or baby-sitter's past interpretations (such as "Jason is a troublemaker") can influence future selections (his behavior becomes especially noticeable) and the organization of events (when there's a fight, the assumption is that Jason started it). As with all communication, perception is an ongoing process in which it is hard to pin down beginnings and endings.

I strive automatically to bring the world into harmony with my own nature.

GEORGE BERNARD SHAW

Influences on Perception

How we select, organize, and interpret data about others is influenced by a variety of factors. Some of our perceptual judgments are affected by physiology, others by cultural and social factors, and still others by psychological factors.

PHYSIOLOGICAL INFLUENCES

Visit a large camera store and you'll be confronted by an impressive array of equipment: everything from cheap pocket models to sophisticated systems including lenses, filters, tripods, and timers. Some cameras can photograph miniature items at close range, and others can capture distant objects clearly. With the right film, it's even possible to take pictures of objects invisible to the unaided eye. There's only one world "out there," but different equipment allows us to see different parts of it. In the same way, each person's perceptual equipment gives a different image of the world. Sometimes these pictures are so unalike that it seems as if we're not talking about the same events at all.

The Senses   The differences in how each of us sees, hears, tastes, touches, and smells stimuli can affect interpersonal relationships. Consider the following everyday situations:

"Turn down that radio! It's going to make me go deaf."
"It's not too loud. If I turn it down, it will be impossible to hear it."

"It's freezing in here."
"Are you kidding? We'll suffocate if you turn up the heat!"

"Why don't you pass that truck? The highway is clear for half a mile."
"I can't see that far, and I'm not going to get us killed."

These disputes aren't just over matters of opinion. The sensory data we receive is dif-

Student Reflection

Physiology and Perception

I've always thought my four-year-old nephew's artwork of humans with pig noses were cute, but I just realized why he draws faces that way. When you're only three feet tall, you look up at adults. From that angle, people *do* look like they have pig noses!

ferent. Differences in vision and hearing are the easiest to recognize, but other gaps also exist. There is evidence that identical foods taste different to various individuals (Bartoshuk 1980). Odors that please some people repel others (Montcrieff 1966). Likewise, temperature variations that leave some of us uncomfortable are inconsequential to others. Remembering these differences won't eliminate them but will remind us that other people's preferences aren't crazy, just different.

The same event can appear as completely different realities due to a whole range of physiological, social, and cultural factors. Learn just how different perceptions can be by following the instructions in Activity 2 on page 89.

Age   Older people view the world differently than younger ones because of a greater scope and number of experiences. Developmental differences also shape perceptions. Swiss psychologist Jean Piaget (1952) described a series of stages that children pass through on their way to adulthood. According to Piaget, younger children are incapable of performing mental feats that are natural to the rest of us. Until they approach the age of seven, for example, they aren't able to take another person's point of view. This fact helps explain why youngsters often seem egocentric, selfish, and uncooperative. A parent's exasperated plea "Can't you see I'm too tired to play?" just won't make sense to a four-year-old full of energy, who imagines that everyone else must feel the same.

Health   Recall the last time you came down with a cold, flu, or some other ailment. Do you remember how different you felt? You probably had much less energy. It's likely that you felt less sociable, and that your thinking was slower than usual. Such changes have a strong impact on how you relate to others. It's good to realize that someone else may be behaving differently because of illness. In the same way, it's important to let others know when you feel ill, so they can give you the understanding you need.

Fatigue   Just as illness can affect your relationships, so can excessive fatigue. Again it's important to recognize that you or someone else may behave differently when fatigued. Trying to deal with important issues at such times can get you into trouble.

Hunger   Our digestive system often rules our behavior. One experiment demonstrated this fact (McClelland and Atkinson 1948). Subjects were denied food for up to fourteen hours. During this time they were asked to describe what they saw projected on a screen at very low light levels. In truth, no image at all was projected. Despite this fact, the subjects did report seeing objects. As their hunger grew, the number of food-related observations increased.

Our own experience confirms the fact that we often grow grumpy when hungry, and sleepy

SALLY FORTH
by Greg Howard

after stuffing ourselves. These facts suggest that conducting important business at the wrong time in our biological cycle can create interpersonal problems.

Biological Cycles   Are you a "morning person" or a "night person"? Most of us can answer this question pretty easily, and there's a good physiological reason why. Each of us has a daily cycle in which all sorts of changes constantly occur, including variations in body temperature, sexual drive, alertness, tolerance to stress, and mood (Luce 1971). Most of these changes are due to hormonal cycles. For instance, adrenal hormones, which affect feelings of stress, are secreted at higher rates during some hours. In the same manner, the male and female sex hormones enter our systems at variable rates. We often aren't conscious of these changes, but they surely govern the way we relate toward each other. Once we're aware that our own daily cycles and those of others govern our feelings and behavior, it becomes possible to run our lives so that we deal with important issues at the most effective times.

For some women, the menstrual cycle plays an important role in shaping feelings and thus affects communication. But women aren't the only ones whose communication is affected by periodic changes in mood. Many men, too, go through recognizable mood cycles, but theirs aren't marked by obvious physical changes. These men, sometimes unaware, seem to go through biologically regulated periods of good spirits followed by equally predictable times of depression (Ramey 1972). The average length of this cycle is about five weeks, although in some cases it's as short as sixteen days or as long as two months. However long it may be, this cycle of ups and downs is quite regular.

Although neither men nor women can change these emotional cycles, simply learning to expect them can be a big help in improving communication. When you understand that a bad mood is predictable from physiological causes, you can plan for it. You'll know that every few weeks your patience will be shorter, and you'll be less likely to blame your bad moods on innocent bystanders. The people around you can also learn to expect your periodic lows. If they can attribute them to biology, maybe they won't get angry at you.

Student Reflection

Culture Shapes Our Judgments of Others

I was born and raised in Brooklyn. After high school I moved out here to California to live with my cousin. I had plenty of friends back home, but it's harder to fit in out here. To me everybody seems like they're half dead—they talk slowly and don't seem to care about much of anything. My cousin tells me I come across as the classic aggressive New Yorker who wants to butt in and argue about everything. Back home I was normal, but here I look like a freak. I guess what's normal in one place is abnormal somewhere else.

CULTURAL INFLUENCES

Culture plays a major role in shaping our perceptions of the world and its inhabitants. This fact was demonstrated in studies exploring the domination of vision in one eye over the other (Bagby 1957). Researchers used a binocular-like device that projects different images to each eye. The subjects were twelve United States natives and twelve Mexicans. Each was presented with ten pairs of photographs, each pair containing one picture from United States culture (e.g., a baseball game) and one from Mexican culture (e.g., a bullfight). After viewing each pair of images, the subjects reported what they saw. The results clearly illustrated the power of culture to influence perceptions: Subjects had a strong tendency to see the image from their own background.

Cultural selection, organization, and interpretation exert a powerful influence on the way we view others' communication. Even beliefs about the very value of talk differ from one culture to another (Wiemann et al. 1986). Western cultures view talk as desirable and use it for social purposes as well as to perform tasks. Silence has a negative value in these cultures. It is likely to be interpreted as lack of interest, unwillingness to communicate, hostility, anxiety, shyness, or a sign of interpersonal incompatibility. Westerners are uncomfortable with silence, which they find embarrassing and awkward.

On the other hand, Asian cultures perceive talk quite differently. For thousands of years, Asian cultures have discouraged the expressions of thoughts and feelings. Silence is valued, as Taoist sayings indicate: "In much talk there is great weariness," or "One who speaks does not know; one who knows does not speak." Unlike Westerners who are uncomfortable with silence, Japanese and Chinese believe that remaining quiet is the proper state when there is nothing to be said. To Easterners a talkative person is often considered a show-off or insincere.

It's easy to see how these different views of speech and silence can lead to communication problems when people from different cultures meet. Both the talkative Westerner and the silent Asian are behaving in ways they believe are proper; yet each views the other with disapproval and mistrust. Only when they recognize the different standards of behavior can they adapt to one another, or at least understand and respect their differences.

In Middle Eastern countries, personal odors play an important role in interpersonal relationships. Arabs consistently breathe on people when they talk. As anthropologist Edward Hall (1969: 160) explains:

cathy®   **by Cathy Guisewite**

© 1986, Universal Press Syndicate.

To smell one's friend is not only nice, but desirable, for to deny him your breath is to act ashamed. Americans, on the other hand, trained as they are not to breathe in people's faces, automatically communicate shame in trying to be polite. Who would expect that when our highest diplomats are putting on their best manners they are also communicating shame? Yet this is what occurs constantly, because diplomacy is not only "eyeball to eyeball" but breath to breath.

Perceptual differences don't just occur between residents of different countries. Within a single national culture, regional and ethnic differences can create very different realities. In a fascinating series of studies, Peter Andersen, Myron Lustig, and Janis Anderson (1987, 1988) discovered that climate and geographic latitude were remarkably accurate predictors of communication predispositions. People living in southern latitudes of the United States are more socially isolated, less tolerant of ambiguity, higher in self-esteem, more likely to touch others, and are more likely to verbalize their thoughts and feelings. This sort of finding helps explain why communicators who travel from one part of a country to another find that their old patterns of communicating don't work as well in their new location. A southerner whose relatively talkative, high-touch style seemed completely normal at home might be viewed as pushy and aggressive in a new northern home.

Geography, of course, isn't the only factor that shapes perception. The gap between cultures often extends beyond dissimilar norms to a wide range of different experiences and feelings. One of the clearest examples of these differing perceptions is the gap between white and black people in the United States. Even among people of goodwill, the life experiences of the two races may be impossible to understand fully.

John Howard Griffin (1959) found one way to bridge the gulf that separates whites and blacks. Realizing the impossibility of truly understanding the black experience by reading and talking about it, he went one step further: Through a series of treatments that included doses of skin-darkening drugs, he transformed himself into a black man—or at least a man with black skin. Then he traveled through the southern United

---

When I meet someone from another culture, I behave in the way that is natural to me, while the other behaves in the way that is natural to him or her. The only problem is that our "natural" ways do not coincide.

RAYMONDE CARROLL

States to get in touch with what it truly meant to be black in this country. He was treated like a black, and eventually, to his own surprise, found himself responding to white people's demands as if he were black. The insults, the prejudice, sickened him.

This experiment took place in the Deep South of 1959, and times have certainly changed since then. To what extent is the world still a different place to contemporary whites and blacks? How about other groups—Hispanics, Asians, Native Americans, old people, and women? Do you ever find yourself prejudging or being prejudged before getting acquainted with someone from a different sector of society?

Perhaps by sharing the personal experiences of others in your group, you can gain a more personal insight into how people from different cultures view life in your community, not only in terms of discrimination, but also in terms of values, behavioral norms, and political and economic issues. How would life be different if you were of a different race or religion, social or economic class? See if you can imagine this.

SOCIAL INFLUENCES

Almost from the time we are born, each of us is indirectly taught a whole set of roles we're expected to play. In one sense this collection of prescribed parts is necessary because it enables a society to function smoothly and provides the security that comes from knowing what's expected of you. In another way, having roles defined in advance can lead to wide gaps in understanding. When roles become unquestioned and rigid, people tend to see the world from their own viewpoint, having no experiences to show them how other people view it. Naturally, in such a situation communication suffers.

Sex Roles In every society one of the most important factors in determining roles is sex. How should a woman act? What kinds of behavior define being a man? Until recently most of us never questioned the answers our society gave to these questions of **sex role.** Boys are made of "snips and snails and puppy-dog tails" and grow up to be the breadwinners of families; little girls are "sugar and spice and everything nice," and their mothers are irrational, intuitive, and temperamental.

While research on male and female behavior does offer some support for such stereotypes (e.g., Rosenthal and DePaulo 1979; Rosenfeld and Fowler 1976; Fowler and Rosenfeld 1979), other studies show that men and women communicate in very similar ways (e.g., Donnell and

Table 3–1   Bem's Sex Types

	Male	Female
Masculine	Masculine males	Masculine females
Feminine	Feminine males	Feminine females
Androgynous	Androgynous males	Androgynous females
Undifferentiated	Undifferentiated males	Undifferentiated females

Hall 1980; Montgomery and Norton 1981). This mixed bag of similarities and differences between male and female behavior can be explained by the work of Sandra Bem (1974), who expanded the traditional male-female dichotomy. Bem reasoned that masculinity and femininity are not opposite poles of a single continuum, but rather two separate sets of behavior. With this view, an individual can be masculine, feminine, or exhibit both types of characteristics. The male-female dichotomy, then, is replaced with four psychological sex types, including masculine, feminine, androgynous (masculine and feminine traits are seen in **androgyny**), and undifferentiated (neither masculine nor feminine). Combining the four psychological sex types with the traditional physiological sex types, we arrive at the eight categories listed in Table 3–1.

In a series of studies designed to test whether psychological sex was a better predictor of behavior than anatomical sex, Bem (1974, 1975, 1976; Bem and Lenney 1976) observed the responses of psychological sex types to a variety of situations that called for independence, nurturance, and performance on sex-typed and non-sex-typed tasks. She found that only androgynous subjects (those who rate high on both masculine and feminine traits) display a high level of masculine independence as well as a high level of feminine nurturance. In general, research by Bem and others supports the conclusion that androgynous individuals are less restricted in their behaviors and are better able to adapt to situations that require characteristics presumed of men *or* women. This flexibility, this sex role transcendence, may be the hallmark of mental health.

Masculine males and feminine females, the sex-typed individuals who most likely come to mind when we think of the words "male" and "female," experience more personality development problems, more marital problems, and

more problem-solving difficulties than do androgynous males and females. Traditional sex role stereotypes describe masculine males and feminine females fairly well.

What does this discussion of sexual stereotypes and attitudes have to do with perception

I have noticed
that men
somewhere around forty
tend to come in from the field
with a sigh
and removing their coat in the hall
call into the kitchen
   you were right
   grace
   it ain't out there
   just like you've always said
and she
with the children gone at last
breathless
puts her hat on her head
   the hell it ain't
coming and going
they pass
in the doorway

RIC MASTEN

and communication? A great deal. Each one of the eight psychological sex types, including the stereotyped masculine males and feminine females, perceives interpersonal relationships differently. For example, masculine males probably see their interpersonal relationships as opportunities for competitive interaction, as opportunities to win something. Feminine females probably see their interpersonal relationships as opportunities to be nurturing, to express their feelings and emotions. Androgynous males and females, on the other hand, probably differ little in their perceptions of their interpersonal relationships.

Androgynous individuals probably see their relationships as opportunities to behave in a variety of ways, depending on the nature of the relationships themselves, the context in which a particular relationship takes place, and the myriad other variables affecting what might constitute appropriate behavior. These variables are usually ignored by the sex-typed masculine males and feminine females, who have a smaller repertoire of behavior.

Occupational Roles   The kind of work we do also governs our view of the world. Imagine five people taking a walk through the park. One, a botanist, is fascinated by the variety of trees and plants. The zoologist is on the lookout for interesting animals. The third, a meteorologist, keeps an eye on the sky, noticing changes in the weather. The fourth, a psychologist, is totally unaware of the goings-on of nature, concentrating instead on the interaction among the people in the park. The fifth, a pickpocket, quickly takes advantage of the others' absorption to collect their wallets. There are two lessons in this little story: The first, of course, is to watch your wallet carefully. The second is that our occupational roles frequently govern our perceptions.

Even within the same occupational setting, the different roles of participants can affect their experience. Consider a typical college classroom, for example: The experiences of the instructor and students are often quite dissimilar. Having dedicated a large part of their lives to their work, most professors see their subject matter—whether French literature, physics, or speech communication—as vitally important. Students who are taking the course to satisfy a general education requirement may view the subject as one of many obstacles standing between them and a degree, or as a chance to meet new people.

Another difference centers on the amount of knowledge people possess. To an instructor who has taught the course many times, the material probably seems extremely simple; but to students encountering it for the first time, it may seem strange and confusing. Toward the end of a semester or quarter, the instructor might be pressing onward hurriedly to cover all the course material, while the students are fatigued from their studies and ready to move more slowly. We don't need to spell out the interpersonal strains and stresses that come from such differing perceptions.

The most dramatic illustration of how occupational roles shape perception occurred in the early 1970s. Stanford psychologist Philip Zimbardo (1971) recruited a group of middle-class, well-educated young men, all white except for one Asian. He randomly chose eleven to serve as "guards" in a mock prison set up in the basement of Stanford's psychology building. He issued the guards uniforms, handcuffs, whis-

"Sure it's beautiful, but I can't help thinking about all the interstellar dust out there."

American Scientist, © Reprinted by permission.

Student Reflection

Occupational Roles and Perception

I work in the emergency room of our county hospital. Every day I see people who are very sick and have terrible injuries. I've seen more people than I care to remember die. When I come home and my six-year-old son complains about a scraped knee or a splinter, it's hard for me to feel very sympathetic. On days when I've cared for people who are barely alive, I want to say to him, "Quit whining. There's nothing wrong with you!" I have to remember that the standards I use at work just aren't fair at home.

tles, and billy clubs. The remaining ten subjects became "prisoners" and were placed in rooms with metal bars, bucket toilets, and cots.

Zimbardo let the guards establish their own rules for the experiment. The rules were tough: no talking during meals and rest periods and after lights out. They took head counts at 2:30 A.M. Troublemakers received short rations.

Faced with these conditions, the prisoners began to resist. Some barricaded their doors with beds. Others went on hunger strikes. Several ripped off their identifying number tags. The guards reacted to the rebellion by clamping down hard on protesters. Some turned sadistic, physically and verbally abusing the prisoners. They threw prisoners into solitary confinement. Others forced prisoners to call each other names and clean out toilets with their bare hands.

Within a short time the experiment had become reality for both prisoners and guards. Several inmates experienced stomach cramps and lapsed into uncontrollable weeping. Others suffered from headaches, and one broke out in a head-to-toe rash after his request for early "parole" was denied by the guards.

The experiment was scheduled to go on for two weeks, but after six days Zimbardo realized that what had started as a simulation had become too intense. "I knew by then that they were thinking like prisoners and not like people," he said. "If we were able to demonstrate that pathological behavior could be produced in so short a time, think of what damage is being done in 'real' prisons. . . ."

This dramatic exercise, in which twenty-one well-educated, middle-class citizens turned almost overnight into sadistic bullies and demoralized victims, tells us that how we think is a function of our roles in society. It seems that *what* we are is determined largely by society's designation of *who* we are.

Mood   Our emotional state strongly influences how we view people and events, and therefore how we communicate. An experiment using hypnotism dramatically demonstrated this fact (Lebua and Lucas 1945). Each subject was shown the same series of six pictures, each time having been put in a different mood. The descriptions of the pictures differed radically, depending on the emotional state of the subject. For example, these are descriptions by one subject in various emotional states while describing a picture of people digging in a swampy area:

Happy mood   "It looks like fun, reminds me of summer. That's what life is for, working out in the open, really living—digging in the dirt, planting, watching things grow."

Anxious mood   "They're going to get hurt or cut. There should be someone older there who knows what to do in case of an accident. I wonder how deep the water is."

Critical mood   "Pretty horrible land. There ought to be something more useful for kids of that age to do instead of digging in that stuff. It's filthy and dirty and good for nothing."

Such evidence shows that our judgments often say more about our own attitudes than about the other people involved. Research shows that couples in unsatisfying relationships are more likely than satisfied partners to blame one another when things go wrong (Fincham and Beach 1988; Fincham, et al. 1987). They are also more likely to believe that their partners are selfish and have negative intentions.

Although there's a strong relationship between mood and happiness, it's not clear which comes first: the perceptual outlook or the amount of relational satisfaction. There is some evidence that perception leads to satisfaction rather than the opposite order (Fletcher et al. 1987). In other words, the attitude/expectation we bring to a situation shapes our level of happiness or unhappiness. Of course, once started this process can create a spiral. If you're happy about your relationship, you will be more likely to interpret your partner's behavior in a charitable way. This, in turn, can lead to greater happiness. Of course, the same process can work in the opposite direction. One remedy to serious distortions—and unnecessary conflicts—is to monitor your own moods. If you're aware of being especially critical or sensitive, you can avoid overreacting to others.

Self-Concept   A final factor that influences perception is the self-concept. Extensive research shows that a person with positive self-esteem is

likely to think well of others, whereas someone with negative self-esteem is likely to have a poor opinion of others (see, for example, Baron 1974). Your own experience may bear out this fact: Persons with negative self-esteem are often cynical and quick to ascribe the worst possible motives to others, whereas those who feel good about themselves are disposed to think favorably about the people they encounter. As one writer put it, "What we find 'out there' is what we put there with our unconscious projections. When we think we are looking out a window, it may be, more often than we realize, that we are really gazing into a looking glass."

Besides distorting the facts about others, our self-concepts also lead us to distorted views of ourselves. We already hinted at this fact when we explained in Chapter 2 that the self-concept is not objective. "It wasn't my fault," you might be tempted to say, knowing deep inside that you were responsible. "I look horrible," you might think as you look into the mirror, despite the fact that everyone around you sincerely insists you look terrific.

Such distortions usually revolve around the desire to maintain a self-concept that has been threatened. Recall that in Chapter 2 we described the tendency to maintain a presenting self-image, which is often an idealized form of the person we privately believe ourselves to be. If you want to view yourself as a good student or musician, for example, then an instructor who gives you a poor grade or a critic who doesn't appreciate your music *must* be wrong, and you'll find evidence to show it. If you want to think of yourself as a good worker or parent, then you'll find explanations for the problems in your job or family which shift the responsibility away from you. Of course, the same principle works for people with excessively negative self-images: They'll go out of their way to explain any information that's favorable to them in terms that show they really are incompetent or undesirable.

Common Tendencies in Perception

Physiology, social and cultural roles, and self-concept aren't the only factors that affect our perceptions of others. A large body of research has revealed several tendencies that often affect the judgments we make (see Hamachek 1982: 29–30).

Being influenced by what is most obvious is understandable. As you read earlier, we select stimuli from our environment that are noticeable; that is, intense, repetitious, unusual, or otherwise attention-grabbing. The problem is that the most obvious factor is not necessarily the only cause—or the most significant one—of an event. For example:

- When two children (or adults, for that matter) fight, it may be a mistake to blame the one who lashes out first. Perhaps the other one was at least equally responsible, teasing or refusing to cooperate.

- You might complain about an acquaintance whose malicious gossiping or arguing has become a bother, forgetting that by putting up with that kind of behavior you have been at least partially responsible.

- You might blame an unhappy work situation on the boss, overlooking other factors beyond her control such as a change in the economy, the policy of higher management, or demands of customers or other workers.

These examples show that it is important to take time to gather all the facts.

Labeling people according to our first impressions is an inevitable part of the perception process. Such labels are a way of making interpretations. "She seems cheerful." "He seems sincere." "They sound awfully conceited."

If they're accurate, impressions can be useful ways of deciding how to respond best to people in the future. Problems arise, however, when the labels we attach are inaccurate; for once we form an opinion of someone, we tend to hang onto it and make any conflicting information fit our image.

Suppose, for instance, you mention the name of your new neighbor to a friend. "Oh, I know him," your friend replies. "He seems nice at first, but it's all an act." Perhaps this appraisal is off base. The neighbor may have changed since your friend knew him, or perhaps your friend's judgment is simply unfair. Whether the judgment is accurate or not, once you accept your friend's evaluation, it will probably influence the way you respond to the neighbor. You'll look for examples of the insincerity you've heard about . . . and you'll probably find them. Even if the neighbor were a saint, you would be likely to interpret his behavior in ways that fit your expectations. "He *seems* nice," you might think, "but it's probably just a front." Of course, this sort of suspicion can create a self-fulfilling prophecy, transforming a genuinely nice person into an undesirable neighbor.

What perceptual errors do you commit? What are the consequences? Answer these questions by completing Activity 3 on page 89.

Given the almost unavoidable tendency to form first impressions, the best advice we can give is to keep an open mind and be willing to change your opinion as events prove you mistaken.

WE ASSUME OTHERS ARE LIKE US

People commonly imagine others possess the same attitudes and motives that they do. For example, research shows that people with negative self-esteem imagine that others view them unfavorably, whereas people who like themselves imagine that others like them, too (King 1979: 152). Likewise, people with hard-driving "Type A" personalities rate everyone else higher on Type A characteristics than do less intense

Type B's (DiPilato et al. 1988). The frequently mistaken assumption that others' views are similar to our own applies in a wide range of situations. For example:

- You've heard a slightly raunchy joke that you found funny. You might assume that it won't offend a friend. It does.

- You've been bothered by an instructor's tendency to get off the subject during lectures. If you were a professor, you'd want to know if you were creating problems for your students; so you decide that your instructor will probably be grateful for some constructive criticism. Unfortunately, you're wrong.

- You lost your temper with a friend a week ago and said some things you regret. In fact, if someone said those things to you, you would consider the relationship was finished. Imagining that your friend feels the same way, you avoid making contact. In fact, your friend feels that he was partly responsible and has avoided you because he thinks you're the one who wants to end things.

These examples show that others don't always think or feel the way we do and that assuming similarities can lead to problems. Sometimes you can find out the other person's real position by asking directly, sometimes by checking with others, and sometimes by making an educated guess after you've thought the matter out. All these alternatives are better than simply assuming everyone would react the way you do.

WE FAVOR NEGATIVE IMPRESSIONS

What do you think about Harvey? He's handsome, hardworking, intelligent, and honest. He's also conceited.

Did the last quality make a difference in your evaluation? If it did, you're not alone. Research shows that when people are aware of both the positive and negative characteristics of another, they tend to be more influenced by the undesirable traits (Kellerman 1989). In one study, for example, researchers found that job interviewers were likely to reject candidates who revealed negative information even when the total amount of information was highly positive (Regan and Totten 1975).

Sometimes this attitude makes sense. If the negative quality clearly outweighs any positive ones, you'd be foolish to ignore it. A surgeon with shaky hands and a teacher who hates children, for example, would be unsuitable for their jobs, whatever their other virtues. But much of the time it's a bad idea to pay excessive attention to negative qualities and overlook good ones. Some people make this mistake when screening potential friends or dates. They find some who are too outgoing or too reserved, others who aren't intelligent enough, and still others who have a strange sense of humor. Of course, it's important to find people you truly enjoy, but expecting perfection can leave you lonely.

WE BLAME INNOCENT VICTIMS

The blame we assign for misfortune depends on who the victims are. When others suffer, we often blame the problem on their personal qualities. On the other hand, when we're the victims, we find explanations outside ourselves. Consider a few examples:

- When *they* botch a job, we think they weren't listening well or trying hard enough; when *we* make the mistake, the problem was unclear directions or not enough time.

- When *he* lashes out angrily, we say he's being moody or too sensitive; when *we* blow off steam, it's because of the pressure we've been under.

- When *she* gets caught speeding, we say she should have been more careful; when *we* get the

ticket, we deny we were driving too fast or say, "Everybody does it."

There are at least two explanations for this kind of behavior. Because most of us want other people to approve of us, we defend ourselves by finding explanations for our own problems that make us look good. Basically we're saying, "It's not *my* fault." Also, putting others down can be a cheap way to boost our own self-esteem; we are stating, in effect, "I'm better than they are."

We don't always fall into the kind of perceptual tendencies described in this section. Sometimes, for instance, people *are* responsible for their misfortunes, and our problems are not our fault. Likewise, the most obvious interpretation of a situation may be the correct one. Nonetheless, a large amount of research has proven again and again that our perceptions of others are often distorted in the ways we have described. The moral, then, is clear: Don't assume that your first judgment of a person is accurate.

Perception Checking

With the likelihood for perceptual errors so great, it's easy to see how a communicator can leap to the wrong conclusion and make inaccurate assumptions. Consider the defense-arousing potential of incorrect accusations like these:

"Why are you mad at me?" (Who said you were?)

"What's the matter with you?" (Who said anything was the matter?)

"Come on now. Tell the truth." (Who said you were lying?)

Even if interpretations like these are correct, dogmatic mind-reading statements are likely to generate defensiveness. The skill of **perception**

checking provides a better way to share your interpretations. A complete perception check has three parts:

- a description of the behavior you noticed;

- two possible interpretations of the behavior;

- a request for clarification about how to interpret the behavior.

How good are you at using perception checking in everyday situations? Sharpen your skill by following the directions for Activity 4 on page 89.

Perception checks for the preceding three examples would look like this:

> "When you stomped out of the room and slammed the door" (behavior), "I wasn't sure whether you were mad at me" (first interpretation) "or just in a hurry" (second interpretation). "How *did* you feel?" (request for clarification).
>
> "You haven't laughed much in the last couple of days" (behavior). "It makes me wonder whether something's bothering you" (first interpretation) "or whether you're just being quiet" (second interpretation). "What's up?" (request for clarification).
>
> "You said you really liked the job I did" (behavior), "but there was something about your voice that made me think you may not like it" (first interpretation). "Maybe it's just my imagination, though" (second interpretation). "How do you really feel?" (request for clarification).

Perception checking is a tool for helping us understand others accurately instead of assuming that our first interpretation is correct. Because its goal is mutual understanding, perception checking is a cooperative approach to communication. Besides leading to more accurate perceptions, it signals an attitude of respect and concern for the other party, saying in effect, "I know I'm not qualified to judge you without some help."

Sometimes an effective perception check won't need all of the parts listed above to be effective:

> "You haven't dropped by lately. Is anything the matter?" (single interpretation combined with request for clarification).
>
> "I can't tell whether you're kidding me about being cheap or if you're serious" (behavior combined with interpretations). "Are you mad at me?"
>
> "Are you *sure* you don't mind driving? I can use a ride if it's no trouble, but I don't want to take you out of your way" (no need to describe behavior).

Empathy in Interpersonal Relationships

After reading this far, you can see how difficult it is to gain an accurate impression of others. Despite the challenges that perceptual errors pose, understanding others is arguably the most important ingredient of satisfying interpersonal communication.

EMPATHY DEFINED

The ability to recreate another person's perspective, to experience the world from the other's point of view, is called **empathy.** As we'll use the term here, empathy involves three dimensions (Stiff et al. 1988). On one level, empathy involves *perspective taking*—the ability to take on the viewpoint of another person. This understanding requires a suspension of judgment, so that for the moment you set aside your own opinions and take on those of the other person. Besides cognitive understanding, empathy also has an *affective* dimension—what social scientists term *emotional contagion*. In everyday language, emotional contagion means that we experience the same feelings that others have. We know their fear, joy, sadness, and so on. A third ingredient of empathy is a genuine *concern* for the welfare of the other person. Not

*"Operator, I'd like to make a person-to-person call, and
I'd like to reverse the roles."*

Drawing by Stevens, © 1990, The New York Magazine, Inc.

only do we think and feel as others do, but we have a genuine concern for their well-being.

The linguistic roots of the word "empathy" shed light on the word's meaning. *Empathy* is derived from two Greek words that mean "feeling (in)side," which suggests that empathy is *experiencing* the other's perception—in effect, becoming that person temporarily. This kind of understanding is very different from **sympathy.** The Greek roots for *sympathy* mean "feeling with." As this definition implies, when you feel sympathetic you stand beside the other person. You feel compassion, but you do not share the other person's emotions. Despite your concern, sympathy involves less identification than does empathy. When you sympathize, the confusion, joy, or pain belongs to another. When you

empathize, the experience becomes your own, at least for the moment.

How empathic are you? You can get an idea by asking someone who knows you well. See Activity 5 on page 90 for more details.

The roots of empathic ability can run deep. Research suggests that the ability to empathize may be shaped by heredity (Adler 1990). Studies of identical and fraternal twins indicate that identical female twins are more similar to one another in their ability to empathize than are fraternal twins. Interestingly, there seems to be no difference between males. Although empathy may have a biological basis, environment can still play an important role. For example, parents who are sensitive to their children's feelings tend to have children who also reach out to others.

The impact of truly empathizing with another person is powerful, as actor Dustin Hoffman learned when he played the role of a female in the movie *Tootsie*. During the film's production Hoffman participated in several screen tests to assess his progress. Leslie Bennetts (1983) of the *New York Times* news service described Hoffman's experience:

> At one screen test, he—as Dorothy Michaels, the soap opera star he plays in the film—was improvising in front of the camera when he was asked whether he thought he would ever have children.
>
> In her soft southern voice, Dorothy said no, she said she thought she wouldn't be having children. Her interrogator persisted: Why not? "I think it's a little late in the day for that," said Dorothy—and, suddenly overwhelmed, she burst into tears.
>
> "I felt so terrible that I would never have that experience," says Hoffman, his voice still filled with wonderment. . . . I've been acting . . . nearly 30 years . . . and I've never had a moment like that before in my life."

The role had a powerful impact on Hoffman, opening the way for intensive self-examination. He began to explore the issues raised by the film: What does it mean to be a woman? What barriers do our gender and attractiveness create?

His experiences as Dorothy Michaels gave Hoffman other insights. In altering his physical experience, Hoffman had to come to grips with the fact that, though he might convincingly portray a woman, he could never turn himself into a pretty one. "The next step was outrage over how he was treated by men; while Hoffman freely admits that he, as a man, has been guilty of the same sin, he was devastated that his homeliness as a woman rendered him next to invisible to many men."

As Dorothy, Hoffman encountered men who would meet "her," say hello, and "immediately start looking over my shoulder trying to find an attractive woman! I could feel that number printed on me, that I was a four, or maybe a six. And I would get very hostile: I wanted to get even with them. But I also realized I wouldn't ask myself out: If I looked the way I looked as Dorothy, I wouldn't come up to myself at a party."

A friend is visiting your city for the first time and he wants to gain a general view of the city. You take him first to the north end where there is a tall tower with a view commanding the whole area. Then you take him to a similar spot at the south end. At that point your friend exclaims with great amazement, "How very strange! The city looks quite different from here!" Now, what is your reaction? Something of shock, for you rightly assume that every normal adult understands that things in physical space look different from differing points of view. You probably conclude that your friend is, to say the least, a bit unbalanced and in need of psychiatric attention.

Now, the really strange thing is that what every normal person understands by himself as far as things in *physical* space are concerned, most people do not understand, and even do not want to understand, as far as phenomena in *social* space are concerned. And any attempt to explain the relativity of social perspectives, and its full implications, usually meets with strong psychological resistance.

GUSTAV ICHNEISER
Appearances and Realities

Total empathy is impossible to achieve. Completely understanding another person's point of view is simply too difficult a task for humans since their backgrounds are so different and their communication skills are limited. Nonetheless, it is useful to strive for total empathy, and to measure the success of interpersonal relationships by how closely we approach it.

THE VALUE OF EMPATHY

As you read in Chapter 1, the ability to empathize is so important that it is generally considered to be one ingredient of communicative competence. Empathy serves several functions in relationships of all types (adapted from Redmond 1986: 22).

Value for the Target of Empathy   The person whose thoughts and feelings are being understood profits in several ways.

1. **Increased self-esteem**   Usually others respond to your point of view with judgments such as: "That's right . . ." or "No, it's not that way at all . . ." An empathic response is different: It suggests the listener is willing to accept you as you are, without any evaluations. It's flattering to find that someone is interested enough in your position to hear you out without passing judgment.

2. **Comfort**   The act of being understood can be tremendously reassuring, whether or not the other person's insights offer any other help. When others empathize, a common thought is "I'm not alone."

3. **Increased trust**   Since judgments and indifference are the most common responses to statements, trust in others is likely to grow when they suspend judgments and simply try to understand you.

Value for the Empathizer   For the person who is empathizing, the ability to recreate another person's experience has numerous advantages. In fact, the payoffs for the empathizer can be even greater than for the recipient.

1. **Altruism**   Since empathizing has so many advantages for the recipient, the empathizer can feel good about helping another person.

The belief that one's own view of reality is the only reality is the most dangerous of all delusions.

PAUL WATZLAWICK

---

2. **Explanation and Clarification** Understanding another's point of view is likely to boost your own knowledge. Even if you disagree with that person's position, spending some time understanding it is likely to provide useful information. Why *is* your friend angry at you? What *do* members of the other sex want? Empathizing helps answer questions like these.

3. **Relational development** Projecting yourself into another person's shoes will probably make that person seem less strange or different. As a result, the gap between you and the other is likely to narrow and the relationship to grow. Bingham and Wiemann (1984) found, for instance, that there is a high correlation between perceived empathy and the level of intimacy in a relationship. The more people feel they understand one another and are understood in return, the closer they feel to one another.

4. **Prediction** Knowing other people's points of view allows you to make better predictions about how they are likely to behave in the future.

5. **Influence** Empathizing with others provides clues about how to approach them in ways that will change their attitudes. Knowing how your professor feels about you in particular or students in general should help you adapt your behavior to get the results you seek.

Desirable as it is, too much empathy can lead to burnout. Studies focusing on human service workers at a psychiatric hospital showed that a high degree of responsiveness to the needs of others led to several symptoms of burnout: depersonalization of the person being helped, emotional exhaustion, reduced feelings of personal accomplishment and, ultimately, in less emotional commitment to the needy person (Miller et al. 1988). This evidence doesn't mean that empathizing is a guaranteed path to burnout. Rather, it suggests that, in addition to being concerned for others, it's necessary to take care of your own needs as well.

REQUIREMENTS FOR EMPATHY

Empathy may be valuable, but it isn't always easy. In fact, research shows that it's hardest to empathize with people who are different from us radically: in age, sex, socioeconomic status, intelligence, and so forth (Cronkhite 1976: 82). In order to make such perceptual leaps, you need to develop several skills and attitudes.

Open-mindedness Perhaps the most important characteristic of an empathic person is the ability and disposition to be open-minded—to set aside for the moment beliefs, attitudes, and values and consider those of the other person. Open-mindedness is especially difficult when the other person's position is radically different from your own. The temptation is to think (and sometimes say): "That's crazy!" "How can you believe that?" or "I'd do it this way..."

Being open-minded is often difficult because people confuse *understanding* another's position with *accepting* it. They are quite different matters. To understand why a friend disagrees

---

The test of a first-rate intelligence is the ability to hold two opposed ideas in mind at the same time and still retain the ability to function.

F. SCOTT FITZGERALD

with you, for example, doesn't mean you have to give up your position and accept hers.

Imagination   Being open-minded often isn't enough to allow empathy. You also need enough imagination to be able to picture another person's background and thoughts. A happily married or single person needs imagination to empathize with the problems of a friend considering divorce. A young person needs it to empathize with a parent facing retirement. A teacher needs it to understand the problems facing students, just as students can't be empathic without trying to imagine how their instructor feels.

Making the effort to put oneself in another's position can produce impressive results. In one study (Regan and Totten 1975), college students were asked to list their impressions of people either shown in a videotaped discussion or described in a short story. Half of the students were instructed to empathize with the people as much as possible, and the other half were not given any instructions about empathizing. The results were impressive: The students who did not practice empathy were prone to explain a person's behavior in terms of personality characteristics. For example, they might have explained a cruel statement by saying the speaker was mean, or they might have attributed a divorce to the partners' lack of understanding. The empathic students, on the other hand, were more aware of possible elements in the situation that might have contributed to the reaction. For instance, they might have explained a person's unkind behavior in terms of job pressures or personal difficulties instead of simply labeling that person as mean. In other words, practicing empathy seems to make people more tolerant.

Commitment   Because empathizing is often difficult, a third necessary quality is a sincere desire to understand another person. Listening to unfamiliar, often confusing information takes time and isn't always fun. If you aim to be empathic, be willing to face the challenge.

By now you can see the tremendous challenges that face us when we want to understand one another. Physiological distortion, psychological interference, social and cultural conditioning—not to mention the problems of language we will discuss in the next chapter—all insulate us from our fellow human beings. But the news isn't all bad: With a combination of determination and skill, we can do a better job of bridging the gulf of understanding that separates us and, as a result, enjoy more satisfying interpersonal relationships.

Summary

Many communication challenges arise because of differing perceptions. The process of interpersonal perception is a complex one, and a variety of factors cause each person's view of reality to vary.

Perception involves three phases: selection, organization, and interpretation. Because communication is a process, these phases may occur simultaneously or in any order. A number of influences can affect how we select, organize and interpret others' behavior. Physiological factors include age, health, fatigue, hunger, and biological cycles. Cultural influences also shape how we recognize and make sense of others' words and actions. Finally, social influences, such as sex roles and occupational roles play an important role in the way we view those with whom we interact.

Our perceptions are often affected by common perceptual tendencies. We are often influenced by obvious stimuli, even if they are not the most important factors. We cling to first impressions, even if they are mistaken. We assume others are similar to us. We favor negative impressions over positive ones. Finally, we are more likely to blame others than ourselves for misfortunes.

One way to verify the accuracy of interpretations is through perception checking. Instead of jumping to conclusions, communicators who check their perceptions describe the behavior they noticed, offer two equally plausible interpretations, and ask for clarification by their partner.

Empathy is the ability to experience the world from another person's perspective. There are three dimensions to empathy: perspective taking, emotional involvement, and concern for the other person. Empathy has benefits for both the empathizer and the recipient. Some evidence suggests that there may be hereditary influences on the ability to empathize, but that ability can be developed with practice. Requirements for empathy include open-mindedness, imagination, and commitment.

Activities

1. Choose one of the following situations and describe how it could be perceived differently by two people. Be sure to include the steps of selection, organization, and interpretation.
   a. A customer complains to a salesperson about poor service in a busy store.
   b. A parent and teenager argue about the proper time for returning home after a Saturday night date.
   c. A quiet student feels pressured when called upon by an instructor to speak up in class.
   d. A woman and a man argue about whether to increase balance in the workplace by making special efforts to hire employees from underrepresented groups.

2. Either individually or in a group, describe how the same event could be experienced differently by three people whose perceptions were influenced by the following factors:
   a. Physiological influences (age, sensory factors, health, etc.)
   b. Cultural influences
   c. Social influences (sex roles, occupational roles, self-concept, etc.)

3. Pages 80–82 of your text outline several common perceptual tendencies. Describe instances in which you committed each of them, and explain the consequences of each one. Which of these perceptual tendencies are you most prone to make, and what are the potential results of making it? How can you avoid these tendencies in the future?

4. Improve your perception checking ability by developing complete perception checking statements for each of the following situations. Be sure your statements include a description of the behavior, two equally plausible interpretations, and a request for verification.
   a. You made what you thought was an excellent suggestion to your boss. He or she said, "I'll get back to you about that right away." It's been three weeks, and you haven't received a response yet.
   b. You haven't received the usual weekly phone call from your family in over a month. Last time you spoke, you had an argument about where to spend the holidays.

c. One of your oldest and best friends with whom you have shared the problems of your life for years has recently changed when around you. The formerly casual hugs have become longer and stronger, and the occasions where you "accidently" brush up against one another have become more frequent.

d. One of your friends hasn't returned your last few phone calls, and when you saw him or her downtown, he or she glanced your way and then hurried away.

5. How empathic are you? Find out by sharing your perception of how a friend, family member, fellow worker, or student experiences an event. After your discussion, ask your partner how accurate your perception seems in the following terms:

a. perspective taking: your ability to see the issue as the other person does.

b. emotional contagion: your ability to share the other person's emotional experience.

c. concern: The degree to which you seem to genuinely care about the other person's well-being.

Readings

Adler, T. "Even Babies Empathize, Scientists Find; But Why?" *APA Monitor* 21 (June 1990): 9.

*Alpero, M., M. Lawrence, and D. Wolsk. *Sensory Processes*. Belmont, CA: Brooks/Cole, 1967.

Andersen, P., M. Lustig, and J. Andersen. "Regional Patterns of Communication in the United States: Empirical Tests." Paper presented at the annual convention of the Speech Communication Association, New Orleans, 1988.

Andersen, P., M. Lustig, and J. Andersen, "Changes in Latitude, Changes in Attitude: The Relationship Between Climate, Latitude, and Interpersonal Communication Predispositions." Paper presented at the annual convention of the Speech Communication Association, Boston, 1987.

Ayers, J. "The Impact of Communication Apprehension and Interaction Structure on Initial Interactions," *Communication Monographs* 56 (1989): 75–88.

Bagby, J. W. "A Cross-Cultural Study of Perceptual Predominance in Binocular Rivalry." *Journal of Abnormal and Social Psychology* 54 (1957): 331–34.

*Baird, J. E., Jr. "Sex Differences in Group Communication: A Review of Relevant Research." *Quarterly Journal of Speech* 62 (1976): 179–92.

Bardwick, J. M., and E. Douvan. "Ambivalence: The Socialization of Women." In *Women in Sexist Society*, V. Gornick and B. Moran, eds. New York: Basic Books, 1971.

Baron, P. "Self-Esteem, Ingratiation, and Evaluation of Unknown Others." *Journal of Personality and Social Psychology* 30 (1974): 104–9.

Bartoshuk, L. "Separate Worlds of Taste." *Psychology Today* 14 (September 1980): 48–63.

Bem, S. L. "The Measurement of Psychological Androgyny." *Journal of Consulting and Clinical Psychology* 42 (1974): 155–62.

*Bem, S. L. "Probing the Promise of Androgyny." In *Beyond Sex-Role Stereotypes: Readings Toward a Psychology of Androgyny*, A. G. Kaplan and J. P. Bean, eds. Boston: Little, Brown, 1976.

Bem, S. L. "Sex Role Adaptability: One Consequence of Psychological Androgyny." *Journal of Personality and Social Psychology* 31 (1975): 634–43.

Bem, S. L., and E. Lenney. "Sex-Typing and the Avoidance of Cross-Sex Behavior." *Journal of Personality and Social Psychology* 33 (1976): 48–54.

Bennetts, L. "Hoffman: Role as Woman Shattering." *Chapel Hill Newspaper* (January 16, 1983): 17E, 19E.

Bingham, S., and J. Wiemann. "Perceived Empathy as a Link Between Perceived Communication Competence and Interpersonal Intimacy." Paper presented at the annual meeting of the Central States Speech Association Meeting, 1984.

Bradbury, T. N., and Fincham, F. D. "Attributions in Marriage: Review and Critique." *Psychological Bulletin* 107 (1990): 3–33.

Canary, D. J., and B. H. Spitzberg. "Attribution Biases and Associations Between Conflict Strategies and Competence Outcomes." *Communication Monographs* 75 (1990): 139–151.

Cline, M. "The Influence of Social Context on the Perception of Faces." *Journal of Personality* 25 (1956): 142–58.

*Condon, J., and F. S. Yousef. *Introduction to Intercultural Communication.* Indianapolis: Bobbs-Merrill, 1975.

Cronkhite, G. *Communication and Awareness.* Menlo Park, CA: Cummings, 1976.

Di Pilato, M., S. G. West, and G. M. Chartier. "Person Perception of Type As and Type Bs: A Round Robin Analysis." *Journal of Social and Personal Relationships* 5 (1988): 263–366.

Donnell, S., and J. Hall. *Men and Women as Managers: A Significant Case of No Significant Differences.* The Woodlands, TX: Telometrics International, 1980.

Duck, S. "Interpersonal Communication in Developing Acquaintances." In *Explorations in Interpersonal Communication,* G. R. Miller, ed. Beverly Hills, CA: Sage, 1976.

*Eisenberg, N., and J. Strayer, eds. *Empathy and Its Development.* New York: Cambridge University Press, 1987.

Fincham, F. D., S. R. H. Beach, and G. Nelson, "Attribution Processes in Distressed and Nondistressed Couples 5: Real versus Hypothetical Events." *Cognitive Therapy and Research* 12 (1988): 505–14.

Fincham, F. D., S. R. H. Beach, and G. Nelson, "Attribution Processes in Distressed and Nondistressed Couples 3: Causal and Responsibility Attributions for Spouse Behavior. *Cognitive Therapy and Research* 11 (1987): 71–86.

Fletcher, G. J. O., F. D. Fincham, L. Cramer, and N. Heron. "The Role of Attributions in the Development of Dating Relationships." *Journal of Personality and Social Psychology* 53 (1987): 481–89.

Fowler, G. D., and L. B. Rosenfeld. "Sex Differences and Democratic Leadership Behavior." *Southern Speech Communication Journal* 45 (1979): 69–78.

*Goss, B. *The Psychology of Human Communication.* Prospect Heights, IL: Waveland, 1988.

Greenblatt, L., J. E. Hasenauer, and V. S. Freimuth. "Psychological Sex Type and Androgyny in the Study of Communication Variables: Self-Disclosure and Communication Apprehension." *Human Communication Research* 6 (1981): 117–29.

*Griffin, J. H. *Black Like Me.* Boston: Houghton Mifflin, 1959.

Hall, E. T. *The Hidden Dimension.* New York: Doubleday Anchor, 1969.

Hamachek, D. E. *Encounters with Others: Interpersonal Relationships and You.* New York: Holt, Rinehart and Winston, 1982.

Harrison, R. "Nonverbal Behavior: An Approach to Human Communication." In *Approaches to Human Communication,* R. Budd and B. Ruben, eds. New York: Spartan Books, 1972.

Horn, J. "Conversation Breakdowns: As Different as Black and White." *Psychology Today* 8 (May 1974): 30.

Kellerman, K. "The Negativity Effect in Interaction: It's All in Your Point of View." *Human Communication Research* 16 (1989): 147–83.

King, R. G. *Fundamentals of Human Communication.* New York: Macmillan, 1979.

LaFrance, M., and C. Mayo. "A Review of Nonverbal Behaviors of Women and Men." *Western Journal of Speech Communication* 43 (1979): 96–107.

Lebua, C., and C. Lucas. "The Effects of Attitudes on Descriptions of Pictures." *Journal of Experimental Psychology* 35 (1945): 517–24.

Luce, G. G. *Body Time.* New York: Pantheon Books, 1971.

McLelland, D. C., and J. W. Atkinson. "The Projective Expression of Needs: I. The Effect of Different Intensities of the Hunger Drive on Perception." *Journal of Psychology* 25 (1948): 205–22.

Manusov, V. "An Application of Attribution Principles to Nonverbal Behavior in Romantic Dyads." *Communication Monographs* 57 (1990): 104–18.

Miller, K. I., J. B. Stiff, and B. H. Ellis, "Communication and Empathy as Precursors to Burnout among Human Service Workers," *Communication Monographs* 55 (1988): 250–65.

Montcrieff, R. W. *Odour Preferences.* New York: Wiley, 1966.

Montgomery, B. M., and R. W. Norton. "Sex Differences and Similarities in Communicator Style." *Communication Monographs* 48 (1981): 121–32.

Piaget, J. *The Origins of Intelligence in Children.* New York: International Universities Press, 1952.

Planap, S. "Relational Schemata: A Test of Alternative Forms of Relational Knowledge as Guides to Communication." *Human Communication Research* 12 (1985): 3–29.

Ramey, E. "Men's Cycles." *Ms.* (Spring 1972): 10–14.

Redmond, M. V. "An Inclusive Conceptualization of Empathy." Paper presented at the annual meeting of the Speech Communication Association, Chicago, 1986.

Regan, D. T., and J. Totten. "Empathy and Attribution: Turning Observers into Actors." *Journal of Personality and Social Psychology* 35 (1975): 850–56.

Ringwald, B., R. D. Mann, R. Rosenwein, and W. J. McKeachie. "Conflict and Style in the College Classroom." *Psychology Today* 4 (1971): 45–47, 76, 78–79.

*Rosenfeld, L. B., J. M. Civikly, and J. R. Herron. "Anatomical Sex, Psychological Sex, and Self-Disclosure." In *Self-Disclosure,* G. J. Chelune, ed. San Francisco: Jossey-Bass, 1979.

*Rosenthal, R., and B. M. DePaulo. "Expectancies, Discrepancies, and Courtesies in Nonverbal Communication." *Western Journal of Speech Communication* 43 (1979): 76–95.

Rosenfeld, L. B., and G. D. Fowler. "Personality, Sex, and Leadership Style." *Communication Monographs* 43 (1976): 320–24.

*Schneider, D. J., A. H. Hastrof, and P. C. Ellsworth. *Person Perception,* 2d ed. Reading, MA: Addison-Wesley, 1979.

Schneider, R. A. "The Sense of Smell and Human Sexuality." *Medical Aspects of Human Sexuality* 5 (1971): 156–68.

Sillars, A. J. "Attribution and Communication: Are People 'Naive Scientists' or Just Naive?" In *Social Cognition and Communication.* M. E. Roloff and C. R. Berger, eds. Beverly Hills, CA: Sage, 1982.

Stiff, J. B., J. P. Dillard, L. Somera, H. Kim, and C. Sleight, "Empathy, Communication, and Prosocial Behavior," *Communication Monographs* 55 (1988): 198–213.

Trenholm, S., and T. Rose. "The Compliant Communicator: Teacher Perceptions of Appropriate Classroom Behavior." *Western Journal of Speech Communication* 45 (1981): 13–26.

Watzlawick, P., J. Beavin, and D. D. Jackson. *Pragmatics of Human Communication.* New York: W. W. Norton, 1967.

Wiemann, J. M., V. Chase, and H. Giles. "Beliefs about Talk and Science in a Cultural Context." Paper presented at the annual meeting of the Speech Communication Association, Chicago, 1986.

Zimbardo, P. G. *The Psychological Power and Pathology of Imprisonment.* Statement prepared for the U.S. House of Representatives Committee on the Judiciary, Subcommittee No. 3, Robert Kastemeyer, Chairman. Unpublished manuscript. Stanford University, 1971.

---

*Items identified by an asterisk are recommended as especially useful follow-ups.

Emotions

Chapter 4
Emotions

After studying the material in this chapter

You should understand

1. The four components of emotion.

2. The factors that influence the expression of emotion in contemporary society.

3. The influence of gender on emotional expressiveness and sensitivity.

4. The benefits of expressing emotions appropriately.

5. The characteristics of facilitative and debilitative emotions.

6. The relationship between activating events, thoughts, and emotions.

7. Seven fallacies that result in unnecessary, debilitative emotions.

8. The steps in the rational-emotive approach to coping with debilitative feelings.

You should be able to

1. Observe the physical and cognitive manifestations of some emotions you experience.

2. Label your own emotions accurately.

3. Identify the degree to which you express your emotions and the consequences of this level of expression.

4. Realize which of your emotions are facilitative and which are debilitative.

5. Identify the fallacious beliefs that have led you to experience some debilitative emotions.

6. In a specific situation, apply the rational-emotive approach to managing your debilitative emotions.

7. Determine the appropriate circumstances and methods for expressing some emotion you have not disclosed.

Key Terms

Debilitative emotions
Facilitative emotions
Fallacy of approval
Fallacy of catastrophic
  expectations

Fallacy of causation
Fallacy of helplessness
Fallacy of overgeneralization
Fallacy of perfection

Fallacy of shoulds
Mixed emotions
Primary emotions
Self-talk

At one time or another, you've probably imagined how different life would be if you became disabled in some way. The thought of becoming blind, deaf, or immobile is certainly frightening, and though a bit morbid, it can remind you to appreciate the faculties you do have. Now, have you ever considered how life would be if you somehow lost your ability to experience emotions?

Although life without feelings wouldn't be as dramatic or crippling as other disabilities, its effects would be profound. An emotionless world would be free of boredom, frustration, fear, and loneliness. But the cost of such a pain-free existence would be the loss of emotions like joy, pride, and love. Few of us would be willing to make that sort of trade-off.

Feelings play a fundamental role in interpersonal relationships. As Ellen Berscheid (1987: 79) points out, truly important communication almost always has a strong emotional component. Because emotions are such an important part of human communication, we will take a close look at them in this chapter. We'll explore exactly what feelings are, discuss the ways they are handled in contemporary society, and see how recognizing and expressing them can improve relationships. We'll explore a method for coping with troublesome, debilitating feelings that can inhibit rather than help your communication. And finally, we'll look at some guidelines that should give you a clearer idea of when and how to express your emotions effectively.

What Are Emotions?

Suppose that a visitor from another planet asked you to explain emotions. What would you say? You might start by saying that emotions are things that we feel. This definition doesn't say much, because you would probably describe feelings as being synonymous with emotions.

Social scientists who study the role of feelings generally agree that there are several components to our emotions (see, for example, Pfeiffer and Wong 1989).

PHYSIOLOGICAL CHANGES

When a person experiences strong emotions, many bodily changes occur. For example, the physical aspects of fear include an increased heartbeat, a rise in blood pressure, an increase in adrenalin secretions, an increase in blood sugar, a slowing of digestion, and a dilation of the pupils. Loneliness increases physiological stress, impairs body functioning, and creates feelings of physical discomfort (Gerstein and Tesser 1987). Some of these changes offer a significant clue to our emotions once we become aware of them. For instance, one woman we know began focusing on her internal messages and learned that every time she returned to the city from a vacation she felt an empty feeling in the pit of her stomach. From what she'd already learned about herself, she knew that this sensation always accompanied things she dreaded. Then she realized she was much happier in the country.

Another friend of ours had always appeared easygoing and agreeable, even in the most frustrating circumstances. After focusing on internal messages, he discovered his mild behavior contrasted strongly with the tense muscles and headaches that he got during trying times. This new awareness led him to realize that he did indeed experience frustration and anger—and that he somehow needed to deal with these feelings if he was going to feel truly comfortable.

NONVERBAL MANIFESTATIONS

A quick comparison between the emotionless Spock of *Star Trek* and full-blooded humans

"What the hell was *that*? Something just swept over me—like
contentment or something."

Drawing by Weber; © 1981 The New Yorker Magazine, Inc.

tells us that feelings show up in many nonverbal behaviors. Postures, gestures, facial expression, body positioning, and distance all provide clues suggesting our emotional state.

One of the first social scientists to explore the relationship between emotion and behavior was Charles Darwin. In 1872 Darwin published *The Expression of Emotion in Man and Animals*, which asserted that humans and certain other creatures seemed to behave in similar ways when enraged. Later researchers confirmed the premise that among humans, at least, the most basic emotional expressions are universal. A. G. Gitter and his colleagues (1972) found that peo-

ple from a variety of cultures all agreed on the facial expressions that indicate emotions such as fear, sadness, happiness, and pain. Chapter 6 discusses the value of observing nonverbal messages as clues to emotion.

COGNITIVE INTERPRETATIONS

The physiological aspects of fear, such as a racing heart, perspiration, tense muscles, and a boost in blood pressure, are surprisingly similar to the physical changes that accompany excitement, joy, and other emotions. In other words, from measuring the physical condition of someone experiencing a strong emotion, it would be difficult to determine whether the person was trembling with fear or quivering with excitement. The recognition that the bodily components of most emotions are similar led some psychologists (see Schachter and Singer 1962; Valins 1966) to conclude that the experience of fright, joy, or anger comes primarily from the *label* that we give to the same physical symptoms. If the cause of the physiological changes is unexplained, the person experiencing them uses situational cues—presumed relevant to the physiological arousal—to make a decision about the cause. An emotional state, therefore, is the product of an unexplained physiological arousal plus relevant situational cues. This cognitive explanation of emotion has been labeled *attribution theory*. Psychologist Philip Zimbardo (1977) offers a good example of attribution in action:

> I notice I'm perspiring while lecturing. From that I infer I am feeling nervous. If it occurs often, I might even label myself a "nervous person." Once I have the label, the next question I must answer is "Why am I nervous?" Then I start to search for an appropriate explanation. I might notice some students leaving the room, or being inattentive. I am nervous because I'm not giving a good lecture. That makes me nervous. How do I know it's not good? Because I'm boring my audience. I am nervous because I am a boring lecturer and I want to be a good lecturer. I feel inadequate. Maybe I should open a delicatessen instead. Just then a student says, "It's hot in here. I'm perspiring and it makes it tough to concentrate on your lecture." Instantly, I'm no longer "nervous" or "boring."

In his book *Shyness*, Zimbardo (1977) discusses the consequences of making inaccurate or exaggerated attributions. In a survey of more than 5,000 subjects, over 80 percent described themselves as having been shy at some time in their lives, while more than 40 percent considered themselves presently shy. Most significantly, the "not shy" people behaved in virtually the *same* way as their shy counterparts. They would blush, perspire, and feel their hearts pounding in certain social situations. The biggest difference between the two groups seemed to be the label with which they described themselves. This difference is significant. Someone who notices the symptoms we've described and thinks, "I'm such a shy person!" will most likely feel more uncomfortable and communicate less effectively than a person with the same symptoms who thinks, "Well, I'm a bit shaky here, but that's to be expected."

VERBAL EXPRESSION

The fourth component of emotion is verbal expression. As Gerard Egan (1977) points out, there are several ways to express a feeling verbally. The first is through single words like those in Table 4–1: I'm angry, excited, depressed, curious, and so on. Many people are limited to these single-word expressions and suffer from impoverished emotional vocabularies. They have a hard time describing more than a few basic feelings, such as "good" or "bad," "terrible" or "great."

Another way of expressing feelings verbally is to use descriptive words or phrases: "I feel all jumbled up," "I'm on top of the world," and so on. As long as such terms aren't too obscure—for example, "I feel somnolent"—they can effectively express your emotional state.

The ability to express emotions verbally is crucial to effective communication. For example, notice the difference between the comments in each pair:

> "When you kiss me and nibble on my ear, I think you want to make love."

> "When you kiss me and nibble on my ear, I think you want to make love and I feel excited (or disgusted)."

Table 4–1   Descriptions of Emotional States

affectionate	evil	judgmental	self-reliant
afraid	excited	lively	sexy
alarmed	exhilarated	lonely	shallow
alienated	fatalistic	loving	shy
alone	fearful	masculine	silly
angry	feminine	masked	sincere
anxious	flirtatious	masochistic	sinful
apathetic	friendly	melancholy	sluggish
attractive	frigid	misunderstood	soft
awkward	frustrated	needy	sorry
beaten	generous	old	stubborn
beautiful	genuine	optimistic	stupid
bewildered	gentle	out of control	superior
brave	giddy	overcontrolled	supported
calm	glad	paranoid	supportive
caring	grateful	passionate	suspicious
closed	grudging	peaceful	sympathetic
comfortable	guilty	persecuted	tender
committed	gutless	pessimistic	terrified
compassionate	happy	phony	threatened
competent	hateful	pitiful	tolerant
concerned	hopeful	playful	torn
confident	hopeless	pleased	touchy
confused	hostile	possessive	triumphant
contented	humorous	preoccupied	two-faced
cowardly	hurt	prejudiced	ugly
cruel	hyperactive	pressured	unsure
curious	impatient	protective	understanding
cut off	immobilized	proud	unresponsive
defeated	impatient	quiet	useless
defensive	inadequate	rejected	vindictive
dejected	incompetent	remorseful	violent
dependent	indecisive	repelled	weary
depressed	inferior	repulsive	weepy
desperate	inhibited	restrained	wishy-washy
disappointed	insecure	reverent	youthful
eager	insincere	sad	zany
easygoing	involved	sadistic	zealous
embarrassed	isolated	secure	zesty
envious	jealous	seductive	zippy
evasive	joyful	self-pitying	zonked

"Ever since we had our fight, I've been avoiding you."

"Ever since we had our fight, I've been avoiding you because I've been so embarrassed (or so angry)."

Many people think they're expressing their feelings clearly, when in fact their statements are emotionally counterfeit. For instance, it may sound emotionally revealing to say, "I feel like going to a show," or "I feel we've been seeing too much of each other." Neither of these statements actually exhibits emotional content. In the first sentence, the word "feel" really represents an intention: "I *want* to go to a show." In the second sentence, the "feeling" is really a thought: "I *think* we've been seeing too much of each other." The absence of emotion in each case becomes recognizable when you add a word with genuine feeling to the sentence. For instance, "I'm *bored* and I want to go to a show," or "I think we've been seeing too much of each other and I feel *confined.*"

What emotions play the biggest role in your life? How clearly do you communicate them? Find out by following the directions in Activity 1 on page 120.

Student Reflection

Socialization and Emotional Expressiveness

Working in the college day-care center has showed me how important it is to teach people the right and wrong way to deal with their emotions.

When children start coming to the center as two-year-olds, they have no control over their feelings. When they're mad they scream, hit, or even bite anyone who gets in their way. We teach them that it's okay to <u>feel</u> angry, but that they need to <u>act</u> in more acceptable ways.

By the time they leave us for kindergarten most of the kids are good at expressing anger verbally. Just yesterday I heard one of our four-year-olds tell a playmate, "Austin, I don't like it when you push me. Stop it!"

It's too bad some adults don't behave as well as our kids!

Emotions in Contemporary Society

As these examples suggest, the clarity and range of emotional expression in today's society are low. Many of the limitations on the communication of emotions come from general social conventions. Another factor that governs emotional expression is gender.

SOCIAL CONVENTIONS

Count the number of genuine emotional expressions you hear over a two- or three-day period. You'll probably discover that emotional expressions are rare. People are generally comfortable making statements of fact and often delight in expressing their opinion, but they rarely disclose how they feel.

Not surprisingly, the emotions that people *do* share directly are usually positive. Communicators are reluctant to send messages that embarrass or threaten the "face" of others (Shimanoff 1988). Historians Carol and Peter Stearns (1986) offer a detailed description of the ways contemporary society discourages expressions of anger. Compared to past centuries, Americans today strive to suppress this "unpleasant" emotion in almost every context including child-raising, on the job, and in personal relationships. Research supports this analysis. One study of married couples revealed that the partners shared complimentary feelings (e.g., "I love you") or face-saving ones ("I'm sorry I yelled at you") (Shimanoff 1985). They also willingly disclosed both positive and negative feelings about absent third parties ("I like Fred," "I'm uncomfortable around Gloria"). On the other hand, the husbands and wives rarely verbalized face-threatening feelings ("I'm disappointed in you") or hostility ("I'm mad at you").

Why do people fail to express the full range of their feelings? There are several reasons. First, society discourages the expression of most feelings. From the time children are old enough to understand language, they learn that the range of acceptable emotions is limited. We are told: "Don't get angry at your brother"; "That isn't funny"; "There's no reason to feel bad"; "Don't get so excited!" Each of these messages denies its recipient the right to experience a certain feeling. Anger isn't legitimate, and neither is fear. There's something wrong with finding certain situations humorous. Feeling bad is considered silly. Excitement isn't desirable, so keep your emotions under control. Repeated often enough, the underlying instruction comes through loud and clear—only a narrow range of emotions is acceptable to share or experience.

In addition, the actions of most adults create a model suggesting that grownups shouldn't express too many feelings. Expressions of affection are fine within limits: A hug and kiss for Mom is all right, but a young man should shake hands with Dad. Affection toward friends becomes less and less frequent as we grow older, so that even a simple statement such as "I like you" is seldom heard between adults.

Second, expression of emotions is further limited by the requirements of many social roles. Salespeople are taught always to smile at customers, no matter how obnoxious. Teachers are portrayed as paragons of rationality, supposedly representing their field of expertise and instructing their students with total impartiality. Students are rewarded for asking "acceptable" questions and otherwise being submissive creatures.

Furthermore, stereotyped sex roles discourage people from freely expressing certain emotions. The stereotype states that men don't cry and are rational creatures. They must be strong, emotionally and physically. Aggressiveness is a virtue ("the Marine Corps builds men"). Women, on the other hand, are often socialized in a manner that allows them to express their emotions by crying. The stereotype states that women should be irrational and intuitive. A certain amount of female determination and assertiveness is appealing, but when faced with a man's resistance they ought to defer (Pearson 1991).

The third reason people fail to express their emotions is the result of all these restrictions: Many of us lose the ability to recognize emotions and to feel deeply. As a muscle withers away when it is unused, so our capacity to recognize and act on certain emotions diminishes. It's hard to cry after spending a lifetime fulfilling the role society expects of a man, even when the tears are inside. After years of denying your anger, the ability to recognize that feeling takes real effort. For someone who has never acknowledged love for friends, accepting the emotion can be difficult indeed.

The fourth and final reason concerns the fear of self-disclosure we will explore in Chapter 9. In a society that discourages the expression of feelings, emotional self-disclosure can be risky. For a parent, boss, or teacher whose life has been built on the presumption of confidence and certainty, it may be frightening to say, "I'm sorry, I was wrong." A person who has made a life's work out of not relying on others has a hard time saying, "I'm lonesome. I want your friendship."

Moreover, a person who musters up the courage to share such feelings still risks suffering unpleasant consequences. Others might misunderstand: An expression of affection might be construed as a romantic come-on, and a confession of uncertainty might appear to be a sign of weakness. Another risk is that emotional honesty might make others feel uncomfortable. Finally, there's always a chance that emotional candor could be used against you, either out of cruelty or thoughtlessness.

GENDER AND EMOTIONS

There is no apparent difference between the way men and women experience emotions (Tavris and Wade 1984). The range and intensity of emotions both sexes feel are the same. Both men and women are as likely to feel nervous in unfamiliar social situations; both get equally angry during conflicts or when treated badly; both feel a sense of grief and loss when relationships break up; and both are embarrassed when they make public mistakes.

Do you reveal your feelings in an important relationship, or do you keep them to yourself? What are the consequences of your emotional expressiveness? Answer this question by trying Activity 2 on page 120.

Despite the similarity of how we *feel* emotions, there are significant differences in the way women and men *express* those feelings in many situations (Wade and Tavris 1987: 339; Bowers et al. 1985). Research on emotional expression suggests that there is at least some truth in the cultural stereotype of the unexpressive male and the more demonstrative

Student Reflection
Living with Gender Differences in Emotional Expressiveness

When it comes to emotions my boyfriend fits the male stereotype. I used to worry because he almost never says "I love you," and I thought that meant he didn't care for me.

Now I realize that Rob does care, but he just doesn't talk about it much. I've learned to look for more subtle ways to know how he feels about me: whether he'll skip an afternoon of basketball so we can be together, or whether he'll hold my hand when we're walking in public.

Sure, I wish he was more romantic. But I've learned that words aren't the only way to say "I love you." I guess men are like icebergs: Most of their feelings are hidden below the surface.

female. As a group, women are more likely than men to express feelings of vulnerability including fear, sadness, loneliness, and embarrassment. Men rarely express these sentiments, especially to their male friends, although they may open up to the woman they love. On the other hand, men are less bashful about revealing their strengths and positive emotions. Men are also more likely to use aggressive means to express anger, fear, or hurt pride.

Differences between the sexes also exist in the sensitivity to others' emotions. Psychologist Robert Rosenthal and his colleagues developed the Profile of Nonverbal Sensitivity (PONS) test to measure the ability to recognize emotions that are expressed in the facial expressions, movements, and vocal cues of others. Women consistently score slightly higher on this test than men (Hall 1978).

Of course, these gender differences are statistical averages, and many men and women don't fit these profiles. Furthermore, gender isn't the *only* variable that affects emotional sensitivity. Another factor is the sex of the other person: People generally are better at recognizing emotions of members of the same sex. Familiarity with the other person also leads to greater sensitivity. For example, dating and married couples are significantly better at recognizing each others' emotional cues than are strangers. A third factor is the difference in power between the two people. People who are less powerful learn—probably from necessity—to read the more powerful person's signals. One experiment revealed that "women's intuition" should be relabeled "subordinate's intuition." In opposite sex twosomes, the less powerful person—regardless of sex—was better at interpreting the leader's nonverbal signal than vice versa (Snodgrass 1985).

Benefits of Expressing Emotions Appropriately

In light of all the social conditioning and personal risks that discourage us from expressing feelings, it's understandable why so many people are emotionally uncommunicative. Let's look at the benefits that can flow from sharing feelings appropriately.

PHYSICAL HEALTH

Sharing emotions is healthy. In fact, keeping your feelings pent up can lead to psychosomatic illnesses. We're not referring to hypochondria, in which people believe they are ill but aren't, or malingering, in which they pretend to be sick. A psychosomatic disease is real: It does not differ from an organically induced illness. What distinguishes a psychosomatic illness is its psychological basis. The pain comes from a physical condition, but the problem has its origins in some aspect of the person's psychological functioning. Psychosomatic problems can grow out of the chronic stress that results when unexpressive people don't share their feelings. The physiological changes that accompany strong emotions (digestion slows, heartbeat increases, adrenalin is secreted, and respiration grows quicker) are short-lived for people who can express their feelings, whereas those who fail to act on these impulses develop a continuous state of physiological tension. Such tension damages the digestive tract, lungs, circulatory system, muscles, joints, and the body's immune system. It even hastens the process of aging (McQuade and Aikman 1974).

Coronary problems also are related to emotional inexpressiveness. In a study of men and women in their 20s and 30s, researchers found that male "repressors"—people who act happy but have trouble acknowledging their troublesome emotions—averaged a whopping 40 points higher on a cholesterol scale than people who are more honest with themselves and others about experiencing anxiety (Chollar 1989).

Other studies report a similar connection between the inability to communicate emotions well and coronary problems. Over a five-year period Flanders Dunbar (1947) studied a random sample of 1,600 cardiovascular patients at Columbia Presbyterian Medical Center in New York City. She found that four out of five patients shared common emotional charac-

Student Reflection

Finding the Courage to Express Emotions

As a rock climber I've learned to face my fear and still keep going. If I backed off when I was afraid, I'd never get off the ground.

I just realized that I need to have the same kind of courage in my relationships. If I want to get anywhere with important people—my fiancée, my boss, my friends—I need to speak up. This is scary for me, but since I've recognized that most kinds of accomplishments are frightening, I find it easier to take the plunge.

Of course, in rock climbing and personal relationships you can get hurt by taking foolish risks. But in both cases staying comfortable isn't the answer. Like the old saying goes, nothing ventured, nothing gained.

teristics, many of which were representative of either nonassertive or aggressive communicators. In fact, most of the patients were argumentative, had trouble expressing their feelings, and kept people at a distance. McQuade and Aikman (1974) describe other characteristics of cardiovascular sufferers: They are easily upset but unable to handle upsetting situations, eager to please but longing to rebel, and alternately passive and irritable.

Evidence also suggests that nonassertive people are prone to yet another physical problem. The immunological system, which protects the body against infection, apparently functions less effectively when a person is under

I believe that courage is all too often mistakenly seen as the absence of fear. If you descend by rope from a cliff and are not fearful to some degree, you are either crazy or unaware. Courage is seeing your fear in a realistic perspective, defining it, considering the alternatives and choosing to function in spite of risk.

LEONARD ZUNIN

stress. The body doesn't always respond quickly enough to infection; and sometimes the body even responds incorrectly, as in the case of allergic reactions. Stress has even been diagnosed as one cause of the common cold. Stress or anxiety alone is not sufficient to cause a disorder; a source of infection must also be present. However, as research by Swiss physiologist Hans Selye (1956) suggests, persons subjected to stress have an increased chance of contracting infectious disease. Selye states, "If a microbe is in or around us all the time and yet causes no disease until we are exposed to stress, what is the cause of our illness, the microbe or the stress?"

Men have a higher incidence of stress-related ailments such as ulcers, and there may be a link between these ailments and stereotypical male nonexpressiveness. "Why Men Don't Cry" (1984), a report on the work of biochemist William Frey, points out tears from crying (not the kind associated with peeling onions) contain certain chemicals that build up in the body during stress. Crying rids the body of these chemicals and reduces the level of stress. Men, who cry about one-fifth as much as women, may be adversely affecting their health.

All this talk about psychosomatic illness is not intended to suggest that nonassertion or nonexpressiveness automatically leads to ulcers and heart trouble, or perhaps worse. Obviously, many shy or aggressive people never suffer from such ailments and many assertive people do. There are also many other sources of stress in our society: financial pressures, the problems of people we care for, pollution, crime, and the nagging threat of war, to name a few. Nonetheless, an increasing amount of evidence suggests that the person who is not fully expressive increases the risk of developing physical disabilities. Just as nonsmokers are less likely to contract lung cancer than their pack-a-day counterparts, skillful communicators have a better chance of living a healthy life.

INCREASED INTIMACY

Beyond the physiological benefits, another advantage of expressing emotions is the chance of reaching greater intimacy with others. While intimacy isn't necessary or even desirable in every relationship, it is a state most of us seek with a small number of important people. While close relationships don't require a constant exchange of emotions, it is necessary for the partners to keep in touch with one another's important feelings—both about one another and about other parts of their lives. Without this sort of emotional intimacy, the relationship becomes emotionally barren. It may have practical value, but it isn't likely to satisfy the deeper need for affiliation that most of us desire.

A note of caution: Sharing every emotion you experience is not always wise. When deciding whether to express a feeling that is difficult for you or another person to handle, read the guidelines for self-disclosure in Chapter 9.

CONFLICT RESOLUTION

Although expressing feelings can sometimes lead to trouble, the consequences of not sharing them can be just as bad. When people don't

The greatest discovery of my generation is that human beings can alter their lives by altering their attitudes of mind.

WILLIAM JAMES

communicate, boring marriages don't change, friendships continue in hurtful patterns, and job conditions stay unpleasant. How long can such destructive patterns go on? Surely there comes a time when it's necessary either to share emotions or to give up on the relationship. Moreover, research on conflict resolution conducted by David Johnson (1971) and others suggests that the skillful expression of emotions actually increases the quality of problem solving. After all, unresolved feelings can create obstacles that keep individuals and groups from dealing most effectively with their problems. On the other hand, once the participants in a conflict have expressed their feelings, they're in a position to resolve the problems that led to them. Chapter 11 introduces several methods for handling interpersonal conflicts constructively.

Coping with Debilitative Feelings: A Cognitive Approach

At this point you may think that experiencing and expressing emotions is always beneficial. Actually, this position is extreme: Some feelings do little good for anyone. For instance, feeling dejected can sometimes provide a foundation upon which to grow ("I'm so miserable now that I must do something to change"). Often, however, depression prevents people from acting effectively. The same point can be made about rage, terror, and jealousy: Most of the time these emotions do little to promote personal well-being or to improve relationships.

DEBILITATIVE VS. FACILITATIVE EMOTIONS

We need to make a distinction between **facilitative emotions,** which contribute to effective functioning, and **debilitative emotions,** which hinder or prevent effective performance. The difference isn't one of quality so much as degree. For instance, a certain amount of anger or irritation can be constructive, since it often stimulates a person to improve the unsatisfying conditions. Rage, on the other hand, usually makes matters worse. The same is true for fear. A little bit of nervousness before an important athletic contest or job interview may boost you just enough to improve your performance (mellow athletes or actors usually don't do well). Total terror is something else. One big difference, then, between facilitative and debilitative emotions is their *intensity*.

As Gerald Kranzler (1974) points out, intense feelings of fear or rage cause trouble in two ways: First, the strong emotions keep you from thinking clearly. We've seen students in public speaking classes whose fear is so great that they can't even remember their name, let alone the subject of their speech. Second, intense feelings lead to an urge to act, to do *something, anything* to make the problem go away. Because a person who feels so strongly doesn't think clearly, the resulting action may cause more trouble. At one time or another, we've all lashed out in anger, saying words we later regretted. A look at almost any newspaper provides a grim illustration of the injury and death that can follow from the physical assaults of intensely angry people.

There is nothing good or bad but thinking makes it so.

SHAKESPEARE
Hamlet

> No one can make you feel inferior unless you agree to it.
>
> ELEANOR ROOSEVELT

A second characteristic of debilitative feelings is their extended *duration*. Feeling depressed for a while after the breakup of a relationship or the loss of a job is natural. Spending the rest of one's life grieving over the loss accomplishes nothing. In the same way, staying angry at someone for a wrong inflicted long ago can be just as punishing to the grudge holder as to the wrongdoer.

Research by psychologist Andrew Ortony has revealed that an emotional response may last as short as five seconds, although most last more than an hour (Adler 1990). The average duration of an emotion was about 40 hours—much longer than researchers had previously suspected. This means that the flash of anger a friend shows today might be a hangover from yesterday's outburst. Realizing this fact can help you avoid defensiveness, since it suggests that you aren't necessarily the target of the anger.

It's no surprise that the importance of a triggering event affects the length of time an emotion lasts. We feel the pain of a major humiliation longer than a minor embarrassment, for example. But Ortony's research suggests that important events don't always result in more intense emotions. The end of a love affair might leave you in despair, but a dull depression could also be the result.

THINKING AND FEELING

Our goal, then, is to find a method for getting rid of debilitative feelings while remaining sensitive to the more facilitative emotions. Fortunately, such a method was developed by cognitive psychologists such as Aaron Beck (1976) and Albert Ellis (1977). The method is based on the idea that the key to changing feelings is to change unproductive thinking. Let's see how it works.

For most people, emotions seem to have a life of their own. People wish they could feel calm when approaching strangers, yet their voices quiver. They try to appear confident when asking for a raise, but their eyes twitch nervously. Many people would say that the strangers or the boss *make* them feel nervous, just as they would say that a bee sting causes them to feel pain. They connect physical and emotional discomfort in the way pictured in Table 4–2. When looking at emotions in this way, people may believe they have little control over how they feel. The causal relationship between physical pain and emotional discomfort (or pleasure) isn't, however, as great as it seems. Cognitive psychologists and therapists argue that it is not *events*, such as meeting strangers or being jilted by a lover, that cause people to feel poorly, but rather the *beliefs they hold* about these events.

Ellis tells a story that clarifies this point. Imagine yourself walking by a friend's house and seeing your friend come to a window and call you a string of vile names. (You supply the friend and the names.) Under the circumstances, it's likely that you would feel hurt and upset. Now imagine that instead of walking by the house, you were passing a mental institution when the same friend, who was obviously a patient there, shouted the same offensive names at you. In this case, your reaction would probably be quite different; most likely, you'd feel sadness and pity.

In this story the activating event—being called names—was the same in both cases, yet the emotional consequences were very different. The reason for different feelings has to do with the pattern of thinking in each case. In the first instance you would most likely think that your friend was angry with you and that you must have done something terrible to deserve such a response. In the second case you would probably assume that your friend had experienced some psychological difficulty, so you would probably feel sympathetic.

This example illustrates that people's *interpretations* of events determine their feelings. Therefore, a more accurate model for emotions would look like Table 4–3, on page 108.

The key, then, to understanding and changing feelings lies in the pattern of thought, which manifests itself through **self-talk** (Braiker 1989). To understand how self-talk works, pay attention to the part of you that, like a little voice, whispers in your ear. Take a moment now and listen to what the voice is saying.

Did you hear the voice? It was quite possibly saying, "What little voice? I don't hear any voices!" This little voice talks to you almost constantly:

"Better pick up a loaf of bread on the way home."
"I wonder when he's going to stop talking."
"It's sure cold today!"
"Are there two or four cups in a quart?"

"We are our language," it is often said; but our real language, our real identity, lies in an inner speech, in that ceaseless stream and generation of meaning that constitutes the individual mind. It is through inner speech that the child develops his own concepts and meanings; it through inner speech that he achieves his own identity; it is through inner speech, finally, that he constructs his own world.

OLIVER SACKS, M. D.
Seeing Voices

Table 4–2 Stimulus-Response Model of Physical and Emotional Reactions

Activating Event	Consequences
bee sting ⟶	physical pain
meeting strangers ⟶	nervous feelings

At work or at play, while reading the paper or brushing our teeth, we all tend to think. This thinking voice rarely stops. It may fall silent for a while when you're running, riding a bike, or meditating, but most of the time it rattles on.

IRRATIONAL BELIEFS

This process of self-talk is essential to understanding debilitative feelings. Ellis suggests that many debilitative feelings come from accepting a number of irrational beliefs—we'll call them fallacies here—that lead to illogical conclusions, and, in turn, to debilitating feelings.

The Fallacy of Perfection People who accept the **fallacy of perfection** believe that a worthwhile communicator should be able to handle any situation with complete confidence and skill. Although such a standard of perfection can serve as a goal and a source of inspiration (rather like making a hole in one for a golfer), it's totally unrealistic to expect that you can reach or maintain this level of behavior. The truth is, people simply aren't perfect. Perhaps the myth of the perfect communicator comes from believing too strongly in novels, TV, or films. In these media perfect characters are often depicted, such as the perfect mate or child, the totally controlled and gregarious host, and the incredibly competent professional. Although these fabrications are certainly appealing, real people will inevitably come up short compared to them.

Table 4–3   Cognitive Model of Emotional Reactions

Activating Event	Thought or Belief	Consequences
being called names $\longrightarrow$	"I've done something wrong." $\longrightarrow$	hurt, upset
being called names $\longrightarrow$	"My friend must be sick." $\longrightarrow$	pity, sympathy

People who believe that it's desirable and possible to be a perfect communicator come to think that people won't appreciate them if they are imperfect. Admitting mistakes, saying "I don't know," or sharing feelings of uncertainty or discomfort thus seem to be social defects. Given the desire to be valued and appreciated, these people are tempted at least to try to *appear* perfect. They assemble a variety of social masks, hoping that if they can fool others into thinking that they are perfect, perhaps they'll find acceptance. The costs of such deception are high. If others ever detect that this veneer of confidence is false, the person hiding behind it is considered a phony. Even if the facade goes undetected, the performance consumes a great deal of psychological energy and diminishes the rewards of approval.

David Burns, in "The Perfectionist's Script for Self-Defeat" (1980), delineates the costs and benefits of perfectionism. The list of benefits, especially lasting ones, is nonexistent because early successes rarely are maintained; the list of costs is a long one, including impaired health, troubled relationships, painful mood swings, anxiety, and decreased productivity (which is ironic since the perfectionist's goal is often higher productivity). The fear of failure, of being less than perfect, often causes the perfectionist to avoid risks, take the safe routes, and engage in safe relationships. The perfectionist sets high goals (out of fear of being second-rate), fears rejection for being less than perfect, becomes upset over making a mistake, and keeps pushing harder to do better in the future.

The irony for these people is that their efforts are unnecessary. Research by Eliot Aronson (1972) and others suggests that the people we regard most favorably are those who are competent but not perfect. Why? First, many people understand that the acts of would-be perfectionists are a desperate struggle. It's obviously easier to like someone who is not trying to deceive you than someone who is. Second, most people become uncomfortable around a person regarded as perfect. Knowing they don't measure up to certain standards, most people are tempted to admire this superhuman only from a distance.

Not only can subscribing to the myth of perfection keep others from liking you, it also acts as a force to diminish self-esteem. How can you like yourself when you don't measure up to your own standards? You become more liberated each time you comfortably accept the idea that you are not perfect. For example: Like everyone else, you sometimes have a hard time expressing yourself. Like everyone else, you make mistakes

I never was what you would call a fancy skater— and while I seldom actually fell, it might have been more impressive if I had. A good resounding fall is no disgrace. It is the fantastic writhing to avoid a fall which destroys any illusion of being a gentleman. How like life that is, after all!

ROBERT BENCHLEY

from time to time, and there is no reason to hide it. You are honestly doing the best you can to realize your potential, to become the best person you can be.

The Fallacy of Approval Another mistaken belief is based on the idea that it is vital—not just desirable—to obtain everyone's approval. Communicators who subscribe to the **fallacy of approval** go to incredible lengths to seek acceptance from people who are significant to them, even to the extent of sacrificing their own principles and happiness. Adherence to this irrational myth can lead to some ludicrous situations, such as feeling nervous because people you really don't like seem to disapprove of you, or feeling apologetic when you are not at fault, or feeling embarrassed after behaving unnaturally to gain another's approval.

The myth of acceptance is irrational. It implies that some people are more respectable and more likable because they go out of their way to please others. Often this implication simply isn't true. How respectable are people who have compromised important values simply to gain acceptance? Are people highly thought of who repeatedly deny their own needs as a means of buying approval? Genuine affection and respect are hardly due such characters. In addition, striving for universal acceptance is irrational because it is simply not possible. Sooner or later a conflict of expectations is bound to occur. One person approves of a certain kind of behavior, whereas another approves only the opposite course of action.

Don't misunderstand: Abandoning the fallacy of approval does not mean living a life of selfishness. It's still important to consider the needs of others. It's also pleasant—one might even say necessary—to strive for the respect of certain people. The point is that the price is too high when people must abandon their needs and principles in order to gain this acceptance.

ZIGGY copyright 1974 Ziggy and Friends, Inc.
Distributed by Universal Press Syndicate.

The Fallacy of Should One huge source of unhappiness is the inability to distinguish between what *is* and what *should be,* or the **fallacy of should.** For instance, imagine a person who is full of complaints about the world:

"There should be no rain on weekends."
"People ought to live forever."
"Money should grow on trees."
"We should all be able to fly."

Beliefs such as these are obviously foolish. However pleasant such wishing may be, insisting that the unchangeable should be altered won't affect reality one bit. Yet many people torture themselves by engaging in this sort of irrational thinking: They confuse "is" with "ought." They say and think:

"That guy should drive better."
"She shouldn't be so inconsiderate."
"They ought to be more friendly."
"You should work harder."

A man said to the universe:
"Sir, I exist!"
"However," replied the universe,
"The fact has not created in me
A sense of obligation."

STEPHEN CRANE

In each of these cases, the person *prefers* that people behave differently. Wishing that things were better is perfectly legitimate, and trying to change them is, of course, a good idea; but it is unreasonable for people to *insist* that the world operate just as they want it to. Parents wish their children were always considerate and neat. Teachers wish that their students were totally fascinated with their subjects and willing to study diligently. Consumers wish that inflation weren't such a problem. As the old saying goes, those wishes and a dime (now more like a dollar) will get you a cup of coffee.

Becoming obsessed with shoulds yields three bad consequences: First, this obsession leads to unnecessary unhappiness. People who are constantly dreaming about the ideal are seldom satisfied with what they have. For instance, partners in a marriage who focus on the ways in which their mate could be more considerate, sexy, or intelligent have a hard time appreciating the strengths that drew them together in the first place.

Second, the obsession keeps you from changing unsatisfying conditions. One instructor, for example, constantly complains about the problems at the university: The quality of teaching should be improved, pay ought to be higher, the facilities should be upgraded, and so on. This person could be using the same energy to improve such conditions. Of course, not all problems have solutions; but when they do,

complaining is rarely very productive. As one college administrator puts it, "Rather than complain about the cards you are dealt, play the hand well."

Finally, this obsession tends to build a defensive climate in others. Imagine living around someone who insisted that people be more punctual, work harder, or refrain from using certain language. This kind of carping is obviously irritating. It's much easier to be around people who comment without preaching.

The Fallacy of Overgeneralization   The **fallacy of overgeneralization** occurs when a person bases a belief on a limited amount of evidence. Consider the following statements:

"I'm so stupid! I can't understand how to do my income tax."

"Some friend I am! I forgot my best friend's birthday."

In these cases people have focused on a single shortcoming as if it represented everything. Sometimes people forget that despite their difficulties, they have solved tough problems, and that although they can be forgetful, they're often caring and thoughtful.

A second, related category of overgeneralization occurs when we exaggerate shortcomings:

"You *never* listen to me."
"You're *always* late."
"I can't think of *anything*"

Upon closer examination, such absolute statements are almost always false and usually lead to discouragement or anger. It's better to replace overgeneralizations with more accurate messages:

"You often don't listen to me."
"You've been late three times this week."
"I haven't had any ideas I like today."

The Fallacy of Causation   People who live their lives in accordance with the **fallacy of causation** believe they should do nothing that can hurt or in any way inconvenience others because it will cause them to feel a particular way. For example, you might visit friends or family out of a sense of obligation rather than a genuine desire to see them because, you believe, not to visit them will hurt their feelings. Did you ever avoid objecting to behavior that you found troublesome because you didn't want to cause anger? You may, on occasion, have pretended to be attentive—even though you were running late for an appointment and in a rush—because you didn't want a person to feel embarrassed for "holding you up." Then there were the times when you substituted praise for more honest negative responses in order to avoid *causing* hurt.

A reluctance to speak out in such situations often results from assuming that one person can cause another's emotions—that you hurt, confuse, or anger others. Actually, the assumption is seldom correct. A person doesn't *cause* feelings in others; rather, others *respond* to your behavior with feelings of their own. Your behavior is, at most, an *invitation* to the other person, who can respond in a variety of ways, including not at all. Consider how strange it sounds to suggest that people *make* others fall in love with them. Such a statement simply doesn't make sense. It would be more correct to say that people first act in one way or another; then others may or may not fall in love as a result of these actions. In the same way, it's incorrect to say that people *make* others angry, upset, even happy. Behavior that upsets or pleases one person might not bring any reaction from another. More accurately, people's responses are determined as much by their own psychological makeup as by others' behavior.

Restricting communication because of the myth of causation can produce three damaging consequences: First, people often will fail to meet your needs. There's little likelihood that people will change their behavior unless they know that it affects you in a negative way.

Second, when you don't complain about troublesome behavior, your resentment is likely to remain and build up. Although this reaction is illogical, as your feelings have never been known, it is still nearly inevitable.

Third, once your deceptiveness is discovered, others may find it difficult to determine when you are genuinely upset. Even your most fervent assurances become suspect, since others can never be sure when you are concealing resentments.

The Fallacy of Helplessness   The **fallacy of helplessness** suggests that satisfaction in life is determined by forces beyond our control. People with this outlook continuously see themselves as victims:

> "There's no way a woman can get ahead in this society. It's a man's world, and the best thing I can do is to accept it."

> "I was born with a shy personality. I'd like to be more outgoing, but there's nothing I can do about that."

> "I can't tell my boss that she is putting too many demands on me. If I did, I might lose my job."

The error in such statements becomes apparent once a person realizes that few paths are completely closed. Most "can't" statements can, in fact, more correctly be rephrased in one of two ways:

The first is to say that you *won't* act in a certain way, that you *choose* not to do so. For instance, you may choose not to stand up for your rights or to follow unwanted requests, but it is usually inaccurate to claim that some outside force keeps you from doing so. The other way to rephrase a "can't" is to say that you *don't*

know how to do something. Examples of such a situation include not knowing how to complain in a way that reduces defensiveness, or not being aware of how to conduct a conversation. Many difficulties a person claims can't be solved do have solutions: The task is to discover those solutions and to work diligently at applying them.

When viewed in this light, many "can'ts" are really rationalizations to justify an unwillingness to change. Research supports the dangers of helpless thinking (Marangoni and Ickes 1989). Lonely people tend to attribute their poor interpersonal relationships to uncontrollable causes. "It's beyond my control," they think. For example, lonely people are more negative than nonlonely ones about ever finding a mate. Also, they expect their relational partners to reject them. Notice the self-fulfilling prophecy in this

attitude: Believing that your relational prospects are dim can lead you to act in ways that make you an unattractive prospect. Once you persuade yourself that there's no hope, it's easy to give up trying. On the other hand, acknowledging that there is a way to change—even though it may be difficult—puts the responsibility for the predicament on your shoulders. Knowing that you can move closer to your goals makes it difficult to complain about the present. You can become a better communicator.

The Fallacy of Catastrophic Expectations Some fearful people operate on the assumption that if something bad can happen, it probably will, or the **fallacy of catastrophic expectations**—a position similar to Murphy's Law. These statements are typical of such an attitude:

"If I invite them to the party, they probably won't want to come."

"If I speak up in order to try to resolve a conflict, things will probably get worse."

"If I apply for the job I want, I probably won't be hired."

"If I tell them how I really feel, they'll probably laugh at me."

It's undoubtedly naive blithely to assume that all of your interactions with others will succeed, but it's equally wrong to assume they will fail. One consequence of this attitude is that you'll be less likely to be expressive at important times. To carry the concept to its logical extreme, imagine people who fear *everything:* How could they live their lives? They wouldn't step outside in the morning to see what kind of day it was for fear they'd be struck by lightning or a falling airplane. They wouldn't drive a car for fear of a collision. They wouldn't engage in any exercise for fear the strain might cause a heart attack. Do these examples seem ridiculous? Consider if you have ever withdrawn from communicating because you were afraid of unlikely consequences. A certain amount of prudence is wise, but carrying caution too far can lead to a life of lost opportunities.

What irrational fallacies operate in your life? Does your irrational thinking interfere with satisfying communication? Explore these questions by completing Activities 3 and 4 on page 120.

Even when one acts in spite of catastrophic fantasies, problems occur. One way to escape from the myth of catastrophic failure is to reassess the consequences that would follow if you failed in your efforts to communicate. Failing in a given situation usually isn't as bad as it seems.

What if people do laugh? Suppose you don't get the job? What if others do get angry at certain remarks? Are these matters really that serious?

Sharing Feelings: When and How?

Now that we've talked about how to deal with debilitative emotions, the question remains: What is the best way to share facilitative feelings with others? It's obvious that indiscriminately sharing every feeling of boredom, fear, affection, irritation, and so on, would often cause trouble. On the other hand, we can clearly strike a better balance between denying or downplaying feelings on the one hand and totally cutting loose with them on the other. The suggestions that follow are some guidelines on when and how to express emotions. They will give you the best chances for improving your relationships.

RECOGNIZE YOUR FEELINGS

It's an obvious but important fact that you can share your feelings best when you're aware of what they are. Some people are quite sensitive to their emotional state, while others pay more attention to factual, logical information when making decisions (Booth-Butterfield and Booth-Butterfield 1990). As you've already read, there are a number of ways in which feelings can become evident. Physiological changes can clearly indicate emotions. Monitoring your nonverbal behaviors (facial expression, voice tone, posture, and so on) is another excellent way to keep in touch with your feelings (see Chapter 6). You can also recognize your feelings by monitoring your self-talk as well as the verbal messages you send to others. It's not far from the verbal statement "I hate this!" to the realization "I'm angry (or bored, or nervous, or embarrassed)." Any way you recognize your feelings,

Student Reflection

Multiple Emotions

From time to time I have tremendous arguments with my parents about religion and dating. They believe that I should only go out with people from our faith, and I'm not willing to put those kinds of limits on my life.

I used to get extremely upset after these fights. How could I be so angry at the people who mean so much to me? It was very disturbing. Lately I've realized that there's nothing strange about loving people <u>and</u> being mad at them. We still have our arguments, but they feel less threatening.

the same point applies: It's important to know how you feel in order to tell others about your feelings.

SHARE MULTIPLE EMOTIONS

Many times the feeling we express isn't the only one we're experiencing. Consider the case of Heidi and Mike at a party. The subject of self-defense has come up, and in front of their friends, Heidi recounts the time Mike drunkenly picked a fight in a bar, only to receive a sound beating from a rather short, elderly, pudgy customer. Later, in private, Mike confronts Heidi angrily, "How could you? That was a rotten thing to say. I'm furious at you." Mike's anger may be justified, but he failed to share with Heidi the emotion that preceded and in fact was responsible for his anger, namely the embarrassment he felt when a secret he hoped to keep private was exposed to others. If he had shared this primary feeling, Heidi could have understood his rage and responded in a more constructive way. Anger often isn't the primary emotion, although it's the one we may express. In addition to embarrassment, it's often preceded by confusion, disappointment, frustration, or sadness. In each of these cases it's important to share the primary feeling as well as the anger that follows.

According to Carol Tavris (1982), most emotions aren't "pure," but combinations that reflect the complex structure of most of our problems and our lives. Jealousy, for example, can be viewed as a combination of several different emotions: distress, anger, disgust, contempt, fear, and even shame (Bush et al. 1988). Likewise, loneliness can include feelings of

cathy®   **by Cathy Guisewite**

anger toward self and others, estrangement, and depression (Mikulincer and Segal 1990). Some situations stir up a whole array of separate emotions. For example, parents are likely to feel a combination of anger and worry when a teenager returns home from a date three hours late. Joy and guilt are a common combination among those working to establish independence from their families. Ventilating only one component of the mix as Mike did, expressing his anger without so much as a nod to his embarrassment, emphasizes that emotion to the exclusion of the others. In this circumstance, according to Tavris, "You aren't ventilating the anger; you're practicing it" (p. 32). Indeed, Mike may just convince himself that anger is *all* he feels.

Robert Plutchik (1980) developed the "emotion wheel" pictured in Figure 4–1 to illustrate the distinction between eight **primary emotions** (placed inside the perimeter of the wheel) and eight **mixed emotions,** based on combinations of the primary emotions (placed outside the wheel). Whether or not you agree with the way Plutchik orders emotions, the emotion wheel suggests that many feelings should be described with more than a single term. To say that you feel "glad" a friend called to make peace after an argument probably doesn't tell the whole story. Other emotions you're probably experiencing (and might want to share) could include relief, embarrassment (that you didn't call first), gratitude, and nervousness. Such complexity explains why so many

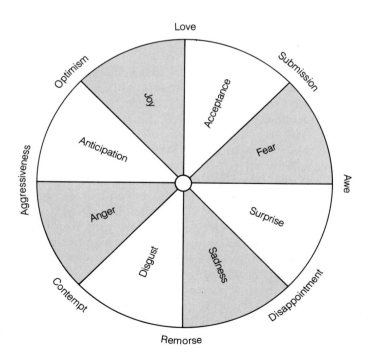

Figure 4–1   The emotion wheel: primary and mixed emotions

scholars have compared emotions to colors: Some are primary and some are secondary, and all appear in an almost infinite range of shades.

Another way emotions are like colors is in their intensity. A primary emotion can range from its mildest to its most intense state. Some people fail to communicate clearly because they understate their emotions, failing to let others know how strongly they feel. To say you're "annoyed" when a friend breaks an important promise, for example, would probably be an understatement. In other cases, people chronically overstate the strength of their feelings. To them, everything is "wonderful" or "terrible." The problem with such exaggeration is that they have no words left to describe a truly intense emotion adequately. If chocolate chip cookies from the local bakery are "fantastic," how does it feel to fall in love?

DISTINGUISH FEELING FROM ACTING

When children are infants, they often go through long spells of late-night crying. Most parents experience moments in the wee hours of the morning when they are so tired that they feel like abandoning the screaming infant. Needless to say, they rarely follow through on this impulse.

Of course, most of us would like to be the kind of people who are totally patient, accepting, and rational, but we're not. Although we don't always want to act on our immediate feelings, we also don't want to ignore them so that they'll build up inside and eventually consume us. For this reason we feel best when we can express what's happening, and then decide whether or not we'll act on it.

For instance, it may be appropriate to acknowledge nervousness in some new situations, even though you might not choose to show it. Likewise, you can acknowledge attraction to certain men or women even though you

might not choose to act on these feelings. It's possible to get in touch with the boredom you sometimes experience in meetings and classes, even though you'll most likely resist falling asleep or walking out. In other words, just because you feel a certain way doesn't mean you must always act it out.

This distinction is extremely important, for it can liberate you from the fear that acknowledging and sharing a feeling will commit you to some disastrous course of action. If, for instance, you say to a friend, "I feel so angry that I could punch you in the nose," it becomes possible to explore exactly why you feel so furious and then to resolve the problem that led to the anger. Pretending that nothing is the matter, on the other hand, will do nothing to diminish resentful feelings, which can go on to contaminate a relationship.

ACCEPT RESPONSIBILITY FOR YOUR FEELINGS

Although you often experience a feeling in response to the behavior of others, it's important to understand that others don't *cause* your feelings. In other words, people don't make you sad, happy, and so on; *you* are responsible for the way you react. Look at it this way: It's obvious that people are more easily upset on some days than on others. Little things that usually don't bother you can suddenly bring on a burst of emotion. Therefore it isn't the things or people themselves that determine your reactions, but rather how you feel at a given time. If, for example, you're especially harassed due to the press of unfinished work, you may react angrily to a personal joke a friend has made. Was the friend responsible for this upset? No, it's more correct to say that the pressure of work—something within you—set off the anger. The same principle holds true for other emotions: Unrequited love doesn't break our hearts; we allow ourselves to feel hurt, or rather,

we simply are hurt. A large dose of alcohol doesn't make us sad or happy; those emotions are already within us.

Wayne Dyer (1976: 171), outlining his positive measures for dealing with debilitative emotions and irrational beliefs, includes accepting responsibility. He argues that we need to remind ourselves that it is not what others do that bothers us, but our *reactions* to it.

> Decide that any and all unhappiness that you choose will never be the result of someone else, but rather that it will be the result of you and your own behavior. Remind yourself constantly that any externally caused unhappiness reinforces your own slavery, since it assumes that you have no control over yourself or them, but they have control over you.

It's important to make sure that language reflects the fact of self-responsibility for feel-ings. Instead of "You're making me angry," say, "I'm getting angry." Instead of "You hurt my feelings," say, "I feel hurt when you do that." People don't make us like or dislike them, and pretending that they do denies the responsibility each of us has for our own emotions.

CHOOSE THE BEST TIME AND PLACE

When you do choose to share your feelings with another person, it's important to pick a time and place that's appropriate. Often the first flush of a strong feeling is not the best time to speak out. If you're awakened by the racket caused by a noisy neighbor, by storming over to complain you might say things you'll regret later. In such a case it's probably wiser to wait until you have thought out carefully how you might express your feelings. If your goals

Student Reflection

Timing Is Everything

I can't believe what I did the other day! I had been reminding our thirteen-year-old to clean up his room all week so the house would look good when the family arrived for a weekend visit.

When I got home from work last Friday (after a very tough day) and the job still wasn't done, I blew up in front of three of his friends. I scolded my son, using all the usual parental lines like "What's the matter with you . . . ?"

My anger was justified, but there was no excuse for embarrassing him in front of his friends. The scene is over now, but I'm sure the other boys think I'm a shrew. It takes a lot of self-control to wait for the right moment to deliver an emotional message.

include maintaining a relationship with the other person or gaining some kind of cooperation, expressing your feelings at the wrong time or in the wrong place *might* feel good for a moment, but the lasting effects may be costly.

Even after you've waited for the first flush of feeling to subside, it's still important to choose the time that's best suited to the message. Being rushed, tired, or disturbed by some other matter are all good reasons for postponing the sharing of a feeling. Often, dealing with emotions can take a great amount of time and effort, and fatigue or distraction will make it difficult to devote enough energy to follow through on the

matter you've started. In the same manner, before sharing, you ought to be sure that the recipient of your message is ready to listen.

SPEAK CLEARLY AND UNAMBIGUOUSLY

Out of confusion or discomfort we sometimes express emotions in an unclear way. Sometimes this entails using many words where one will do better. For example, "Uh, I guess what I'm trying to say is that I was pretty upset when I waited for you on the corner where we agreed to meet at 1:30 and you didn't show up until 3:00," would be better stated as, "I was angry when you were an hour and a half late." One key to making emotions clear is to realize that you most often can summarize a feeling in a few words. In the same way, a little thought can probably provide brief reasons for feeling a certain way.

Another way we express a feeling unclearly is by discounting or qualifying it: "I'm a *little* unhappy"; "I'm *pretty* excited"; "I'm *sort of* confused." Of course, not all emotions are strong—we do experience degrees of sadness and joy—but some communicators have a tendency to discount almost every feeling.

Should you share your emotions with the important people in your life, or should you keep your feelings to yourself? Answer this important question by completing Activity 5 on page 120.

An emotion can also be expressed unclearly when it is sent in a code. This coding most often happens when the sender is uncomfortable about sharing the feeling in question. Some codes are verbal, as when the sender hints at the message. For example, an indirect way to say "I'm lonesome" might be, "I guess there isn't much happening this weekend, so if you're not busy why don't you drop by?" This indirect code has its advantages: It allows the sender to avoid self-disclosure by expressing an unhappy feeling, and it also serves as a safeguard against the chance of being rejected outright. On the other hand, such a message is so indirect that the chances of the real feeling being recognized are reduced. For this reason people who send coded messages stand less of a chance of having their emotions understood and their needs met.

Finally, you express yourself most unambiguously when you make it clear that your feeling is centered on a specific set of circumstances, rather than the whole relationship. Instead of saying "I resent you," say "I resent you when you don't keep your promises." Rather than "I'm bored with you," say "I'm bored when

you talk about money." Be aware that, in the course of knowing anyone, you're bound to feel positive at some times and negative at others. By limiting comments to the specific situation, you can express a feeling directly without jeopardizing the relationship.

Emotions are a powerful force in human affairs. They account for the best moments in our lives and for some of the most difficult ones. This chapter has shown that emotions are like many natural forces: Though powerful, they can be managed. The challenge for effective communicators is to acknowledge the power of emotions and take every possible step to use them to improve interpersonal relationships.

Summary

Emotions are an often overlooked but essential element in interpersonal relationships. There are four components to most emotions: physiological changes, nonverbal behavior, cognitive interpretations, and verbal expression.

Expressing emotions appropriately can lead to a variety of benefits including physical health, greater intimacy, and better resolutions of conflicts. Despite these benefits, the degree of emotional expressiveness in contemporary society is low. What few emotions people do communicate directly are positive: "Difficult" feelings like anger are expressed indirectly, if at all. Social conventions and roles discourage greater expression of feelings. Men, for example, are less likely than women to express emotions and less able to recognize them in others. As a consequence of emotional unexpressiveness, the ability to recognize many emotions declines. Even when people do recognize their feelings, fear of the consequences of revealing them often leads to nondisclosure.

Not all emotions are beneficial. Debilitative emotions can impair functioning and interfere with effective relationships. A rational-emotive approach can minimize unnecessarily debilitative feelings by enabling a person to identify and eliminate the illogical thinking that causes them.

A number of guidelines can help communicators decide when and how to express their feelings in a constructive way. Recognizing emotions, sharing multiple feelings, distinguishing feeling from acting, accepting responsibility for one's emotions, choosing the best time and place to share them, and speaking clearly and unambiguously can all contribute to more effective relationships.

Activities

1. You can discover your emotional range by reviewing the list of feelings in Table 4–1 on page 98. Use the information there to complete the following steps.
   a. Group the emotions into five categories reflecting how frequently you experience each one.
      1 = almost never 2 = rarely 3 = occasionally 4 = often 5 = almost constantly
   b. Pick the ten emotions that play the most important role in your interpersonal relationships and answer the following questions for each:
      What physiological changes occur when you experience this emotion?
      What nonverbal behaviors characterize your expression of this emotion?
      What thoughts occur to you as you experience this emotion?
      How do you express this emotion verbally?

2. Think of a relationship that plays an important role in your life. Identify the emotions you express in this relationship and the ones you do not reveal. Use the information in this chapter to analyze your reasons for disclosing some emotions and not others. Are you satisfied with the consequences of your present level of disclosure?

3. Identify the debilitative emotions that arise in one of your important interpersonal relationships. What is the self-talk that triggers each emotion? How rational is this self-talk? Dispute any irrational beliefs, and report on the effect this thinking has on your emotions and on your communication behavior in the relationship.

4. From your personal experience, identify examples of each irrational belief identified in this chapter. Which of the fallacies do you succumb to most often? What are the relational consequences of this thinking?

5. Choose a relationship with an important person in your life. The relationship needn't be highly personal. You might, for example, focus on an employer, a professor, or a neighbor. First, identify an emotion that you have not expressed to this person. Then use the information on pages 113–119 to determine whether you should reveal your feelings to this person.

Readings

Adler, R. B. *Confidence in Communication: A Guide to Assertive and Social Skills.* New York: Holt, Rinehart and Winston, 1977.

Adler, T. "Look at Duration, Depth in Research on Emotion." *APA Monitor* (October 1990): 10.

Aronson, E. *The Social Animal.* New York: Viking, 1972.

Beck, A. T. *Cognitive Therapy and the Emotional Disorders.* New York: International Universities Press, 1976.

Berscheid, E. "Emotion and Interpersonal Communication." In *Interpersonal Processes: New Directions in Communication Research,* M. E. Roloff and G. R. Miller, eds. Beverly Hills, CA: Sage, 1987.

Bienvenu, M. J., Sr. "Inventory of Anger Communication (IAC)." In *The 1976 Annual Handbook for Group Facilitators*, J. W. Pfeiffer and J. E. Jones, eds. La Jolla, CA: University Associates, 1976.

Booth-Butterfield, M. and S. Booth-Butterfield. "Conceptualism Affect as Information in Communication Production." Human Communication Research, 16 (1990): 451–476.

*Bowers, J. W., S. M. Metts, and W. T. Duncanson. "Emotion and Interpersonal Communication." In *Handbook of Interpersonal Communication*, M. L. Knapp and G. R. Miller, eds. Beverly Hills, CA: Sage, 1985.

Braiker, H. B. "The Power of Self-Talk." *Psychology Today* 23 (December 1989): 23–27.

Brown, B. B. *New Mind, New Body: Bio-Feedback—New Directions for the Mind.* New York: Harper & Row, 1979.

Burns, D. D. "The Perfectionist's Script for Self-Defeat." *Psychology Today* 14 (November 1980): 34–52.

Bush, C. R., J. P. Bush, and J. Jennings, "Effects of Jealousy Threats on Relationship Perceptions and Emotions." *Journal of Social and Personal Relationships* 5 (1988): 285–303.

Chollar, S, "Hidden Emotions, High Cholesterol." *Psychology Today* 23 (September 1989): 24.

Clanton, G., and L. G. Smith. *Jealousy.* Englewood Cliffs, NJ: Prentice-Hall, 1976.

Constantine, L. L. *Treating Relationships.* Lake Mills, IA: Graphic, 1976.

Corzine, W. L. *The Phenomenon of Jealousy: A Theoretical and Empirical Analysis.* New York: Macmillan, 1981.

Dunbar, F. *Mind and Body: Psychosomatic Medicine.* New York: Random House, 1947.

Dyer, W. W. *Your Erroneous Zones.* New York: Avon Books, 1976.

Egan, G. *You and Me: The Skills of Communicating and Relating to Others.* Monterey, CA: Brooks/Cole, 1977.

*Ellis, A., and R. Harper. *A New Guide to Rational Living.* North Hollywood, CA: Wilshire Books, 1977.

Gerstein, L. H., and A. Tesser, "Antecedents and Responses Associated with Loneliness," *Journal of Social and Personal Relationships* 4 (1987): 329–63.

Gitter, A. G., H. Block, and D. Mostofsky. "Race and Sex in the Perception of Emotion." *Journal of Social Issues* 170 (1972): 63–78.

Gudykunst, W. B., and S. Ting-Toomey, *Culture and Interpersonal Communication* Newbury Park, CA: Sage, 1988.

Hall, J. "Gender Effects in Decoding Nonverbal Cues." *Psychological Bulletin* 85 (1978): 845–57.

Johnson, D. "The Effects of Expressing Warmth and Anger upon the Actor and the Listener." *Journal of Counseling Psychology* 18 (1971): 571–78.

Jones, J. E., and A. G. Banet, Jr. "Dealing with Anger." In *The 1976 Annual Handbook for Group Facilitators*, J. W. Pfeiffer and J. E. Jones, eds. La Jolla, CA: University Associates, Inc., 1976.

Kelley, C. "Jealousy: A Proactive Approach." In *The 1980 Annual Handbook for Group Facilitators*, J. W. Pfeiffer and J. E. Jones, eds. La Jolla, CA: University Associates, Inc., 1980.

Kranzler, G. *You Can Change How You Feel: A Rational-Emotive Approach.* Eugene, OR: RETC Press, 1974.

Lazarus, A., and A. Fay. *I Can If I Want To.* New York: William Morrow, 1975.

Mace, D. R. "Two Faces of Jealousy." *McCall's* (April 1981): 58–63.

Marangoni, C., and W. Ickes. "Loneliness: A Theoretical Review with Implications for Measurement." *Journal of Social and Personal Relationships* 6, 1989: 93–128.

McQuade, A., and A. Aikman. *Stress: What It Is and What It Does to You.* New York: E. P. Dutton, 1974.

Mikulincer, M., and J. Segal, "A Multidimensional Analysis of the Experience of Loneliness." *Journal of Social and Personal Relationships* 7 (1990): 209–30.

Pearson, J. C. *Gender and Communication*, 2d ed. Dubuque, IA: Wm. C. Brown, 1991.

Pfeiffer, S. M., and P. P. Wong, "Multidimensional Jealousy." *Journal of Social and Personal Relationships* 6 (1989): 181–96.

Plutchik, R. *Emotion: A Psychoevolutionary Synthesis.* New York: Harper & Row, 1980.

Ray, L., and R. Tucker. "The Emotional Components of Jealousy: A Multivariate Investigation." Unpublished paper, Bowling Green State University, 1980.

Rosenthal, R., J. A. Hall, D. Archer, M. R. DiMatteo, and P. L. Rogers, "The PONS Test: Measuring Sensitivity to Nonverbal Cues." In *Nonverbal Communication*, S. Weitz, ed. 2nd ed. New York: Oxford University Press, 1979.

Sawrey, W. "An Experimental Investigation of the Role of Psychological Factors in the Production of Gastric Ulcers in Rats." *Journal of Comparative Physiological Psychology* 49 (1956): 457–61.

Schachter, S., and J. Singer. "Cognitive, Social and Physiological Determinants of Emotional State." *Psychological Review* 69 (1962): 379–99.

Selye, H. *The Stress of Life.* New York: McGraw-Hill, 1956.

Shimanoff, S. B. "Degree of Emotional Expressiveness as a Function of Face—Needs, Gender, and Interpersonal Relationship." *Communication Reports* 1 (1988): 43–53.

Shimanoff, S. B. "Rules Governing the Verbal Expression of Emotions Between Married Couples." *Western Journal of Speech Communication* 49 (1985): 149–65.

Snodgrass, S. E. "Women's Intuition: The Effect of Subordinate Role on Interpersonal Sensitivity." *Journal of Personality and Social Psychology* 49 (1985): 146–55.

Stearns, C. A., and P. Stearns, *Anger: The Struggle for Emotional Control in America's History.* Chicago: University of Chicago Press, 1986.

Tavris, C. "Anger Defused." *Psychology Today* 16 (November 1982): 25–35.

Tavris, C. *Anger: The Misunderstood Emotion.* New York: Simon and Schuster, 1983.

*Tavris, C. and C. Wade, *The Longest War: Sex Differences in Perspective*, 2d ed. San Diego: Harcourt Brace Jovanovich, 1984.

Timmons, F. R. "Research on College Dropouts. In *Psychological Stress in the Campus Community*, L. Bloom, ed. New York: Behavioral Publications, 1975.

Valins, S. "Cognitive Effects of False Heart-Rate Feedback." *Journal of Personality and Social Psychology* 4 (1966): 400–08.

"Why Men Don't Cry." *Science Digest* 92 (June 1984): 24.

Wolf, S. W. *The Stomach.* Oxford: Oxford University Press, 1965.

*Zimbardo, P. *Shyness: What It Is, What to Do About It.* Reading, MA: Addison-Wesley, 1977.

---

*Items identified by an asterisk are recommended as especially useful follow-ups.

Part Three

Creating and
Understanding Messages

Language

Chapter 5
Language

After studying the material in this chapter

You should understand

1. The symbolic nature of language.

2. That language is rule-governed.

3. That meanings are in people, not words.

4. The consequences of using various types of troublesome language.

5. The ways in which entire languages, and the choice of terminology and structure within a language, shape attitudes.

6. The ways in which language reflects the attitudes of a speaker.

7. The differences between male and female speech.

8. The relationship between language use and gender and sex roles.

You should be able to

1. Recognize cases in which you have ascribed meanings to words instead of people.

2. Identify the kinds of troublesome language described in this chapter and suggest more effective alternatives.

3. Clarify your personal problems, goals, appreciative messages, complaints, and requests with behavioral descriptions.

4. Identify the ways your language reflects your degree of credibility, status, and power.

5. Describe how linguistic messages have contributed to your present degree of self-esteem.

6. Notice how your language reflects your own sense of power, attraction to others, interest in topics, intimacy, and responsibility.

7. Identify the masculine and feminine characteristics of your speech.

Key Terms

"But" statement	Equivocal language	Pragmatic rules
"I" language	Euphemism	Relative language
"We" statement	Hedges	Semantic rules
"You" language	Hesitations	Static evaluation
Abstraction ladder	Intensifier	Syntactic rules
Disclaimer	Polite language form	Tag question
Emotive language	Powerless speech mannerisms	

"I don't know what you mean by 'glory,'" Alice said.

Humpty Dumpty smiled contemptuously. "Of course you don't—till I tell you. I meant 'there's a nice knock-down argument for you!'"

"But 'glory' doesn't mean 'a nice knock-down argument,'" Alice objected.

"When I use a word," Humpty Dumpty said, in a rather scornful tone, "it means just what I choose it to mean—neither more nor less."

"The question is," said Alice, "whether you can make words mean so many different things."

"The question is," said Humpty Dumpty, "which is to be master—that's all."

LEWIS CARROLL
Through the Looking Glass

Like Alice, at one time or another everyone has felt trapped in a linguistic wonderland. Words shift meanings until we don't know what others, or even we ourselves, are saying. Although language is an imperfect vessel with which to convey ideas, it also is a marvelous tool. On an everyday level, it allows us to carry on the normal activities that make a civilized life possible. Language is a foundation for our personal relationships, and it is a tool for understanding and expressing our spiritual nature. To appreciate the tremendous importance of language, imagine how impossible life would be without it. Most disabilities are troublesome, but not completely debilitating: We could survive without eyesight or hearing, and life would still be possible without a limb. But without the ability to use language, we would hardly be human—at least not in the usual sense of the word.

In this chapter we will explore the relationship between words and ideas. We will describe some important characteristics of language, and show how these characteristics affect our day-to-day communication. We will outline several types of troublesome language and show how to replace them with more effective kinds of speech. Finally, we will look at the power language has to shape and reflect our attitudes toward others.

The Nature of Language

We will begin our survey by looking at some features that characterize all languages. These features explain both why language is such a useful tool and why it can be so troublesome.

LANGUAGE IS SYMBOLIC

As you first read in Chapter 1, words are arbitrary symbols that have no meaning in themselves. The word "five," for example, is a kind of code that represents the number of fingers on your hand only because we agree that it does. As Bateson and Jackson (1964: 271) point out, "There is nothing particularly five-like in the number 'five.'" To a speaker of French, the symbol *"cinq"* would convey the same meaning; to a computer, the same value would be represented by the electronically coded symbol "00110101."

Even sign language, as "spoken" by most deaf people, is symbolic in nature and not the pantomime it might seem. Because this form of communication is symbolic and not literal, there are literally hundreds of different sign languages spoken around the world that have evolved independently whenever significant numbers of deaf people are in contact (Sacks 1989: 17). These distinct languages include American Sign Language, British Sign Language, French Sign Language, Danish Sign Language, Chinese Sign Language ... even Australian Aboriginal and Mayan sign languages.

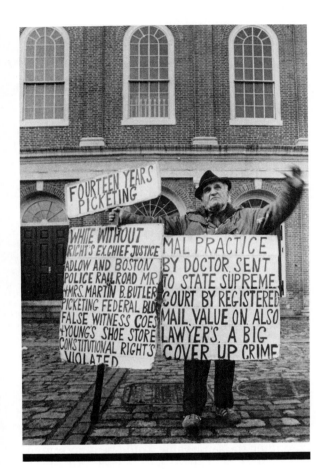

Despite the fact that symbols are arbitrary, people often act as if they had some meaning in themselves. S. I. Hayakawa (1964: 27) points out the vague sense we often have that foreign languages are rather odd, and that the speakers really ought to call things by their "right" names. To illustrate the mistaken belief that words are inherently connected to the things they label, Hayakawa describes the little boy who was reported to have said, "Pigs are called pigs because they are such dirty animals."

LANGUAGE IS RULE-GOVERNED

The only reason symbol-laden languages work at all is that people agree on how to use them. The linguistic agreements that make communication possible can be codified in rules. Languages contain two types of rules. **Syntactic rules** govern the way symbols can be arranged. For example, in English, syntactic rules require every word to contain at least one vowel and prohibit sentences such as "Have you the cookies brought?" which would be a perfectly acceptable arrangement in German. Although most of us aren't able to describe the syntactic rules that govern our language, it's easy to recognize their existence by noticing how odd a statement that violates them appears. Another look at sign languages spoken by the deaf shows the importance of syntactic rules. As Oliver Sacks (1989: 30) points out, true sign languages have their own syntax and grammar, which have a completely different character from any spoken or written language. It is not possible to transliterate a spoken tongue into sign word by word or phrase by phrase as we often can do when switching between two spoken languages—their structures are just too different. Most uninformed people believe that sign language is unspoken English or French, but in truth it is nothing of the sort.

What role do rules play in everyday conversations? See Activity 1 on page 155 to find out.

Semantic rules also govern our use of language. Whereas syntax deals with structure, semantics governs meaning. Semantic rules reflect the ways in which speakers of a language respond to a particular symbol. Semantic rules are what make it possible for us to agree that "bikes" are for riding and "books" are for reading; and they help us know whom we will encounter when we use rooms marked "men" and "women." Without semantic rules, communication would be impossible: Each of us would use symbols in unique ways, unintelligible to others.

Semantic rules help us understand the meaning of individual words, but they often don't explain how language operates in everyday life. Consider the statement "Let's get together tomorrow." The semantic meaning of the words in this sentence is clear enough, yet as the selec-

"WHEN I SAY 'RUNNED', YOU KNOW I MEAN 'RAN'. LET'S NOT QUIBBLE."

tion from Miss Manners on page 140 shows, the statement could be taken in several ways: It could be a request ("I hope we can get together"), a polite command ("I want to see you"), an empty cliché ("I don't really mean it"). We learn to distinguish the accurate meanings of such speech acts through **pragmatic rules** (see Trenholm 1986: 85–96). These rules—usually understood by all players in the language game—help us understand the speaker's intention. For example, the relationship between the communicators plays a large role in defining many statements. Our example, "I want to see you," is likely to mean one thing when uttered by your boss, and another entirely when it comes from your lover. Likewise, the situation in which the statement is made plays a role. Saying "I want to see you" at the office will probably have a different meaning than the same words uttered at a cocktail party. Of course, the nonverbal behaviors that accompany a statement also help explain its meaning. Even gender and cultural background help qualify the meaning of a statement. For instance, one study revealed that men of Chinese and Japanese ancestry produced messages with more intensity than did their female counterparts, while there were no significant differences between the messages of Caucasian men and women (Miller et al. 1987). Such findings make it clear that simply understanding a speaker's words isn't enough to explain what a statement means.

MEANINGS ARE IN PEOPLE, NOT IN WORDS

If the semantic rules of language were more precise, and if everyone followed those rules, we would suffer from fewer misunderstandings. You respond to a "while you were out" note and spend a full day trying to reach Barbara, only to find you called the wrong Barbara. You have an hour-long argument about "feminism" with a friend, only to discover that you were using the term in very different ways.

These problems occur because people attach different meanings to the same word or words. Ogden and Richards (1923) illustrated this point graphically in their well-known "triangle of meaning" (see Figure 5–1). This model shows that there is only an indirect relationship—indicated by a broken line—between a word and the thing or idea it claims to represent.

Misunderstandings often occur because meanings are in people, and not in words. You can begin to recognize how these misunderstandings operate in your life by trying Activity 2 on page 156.

The Ogden and Richards model is oversimplified since not all words refer to physical "things," or referents. For instance, some referents are abstract ideas (like "love"), while others (like "angry" or "exciting") aren't even nouns. Despite these shortcomings, the triangle of meaning is useful, since it clearly demonstrates that meanings are in people, not in words.

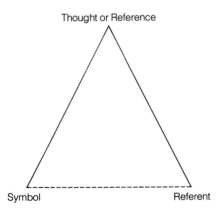

Figure 5–1   Ogden and Richards' triangle of meaning

Overcoming Troublesome Language

After reading this far, you may be thinking that effective communication is hopeless. If no two people speak the same language, what hope is there for understanding one another fully? The semantic barriers that block understanding are certainly great, but they can be overcome to a great extent. By recognizing the kinds of problems we face when using language, you can speak and listen in ways that boost the odds of communicating accurately.

AVOID EQUIVOCAL LANGUAGE

The most obvious semantic misunderstandings involve **equivocal language**—words that have

more than one commonly accepted definition. Some equivocal misunderstandings are amusing, as the following newspaper headlines found by Gyles Brandreth (1982: 222–23) illustrate:

Man Found Dead in Graveyard

Local Man has Longest Horns in Texas

Massive Organ Draws a Crowd

20-Year Friendship Ends at the Altar

Other equivocal misunderstandings are trivial. Recently we ate dinner at a Mexican restaurant and ordered a "tostada with beans." Instead of being served a beef tostada with beans on the side, we were surprised to see the waiter bring us a plate containing a tostada *filled* with beans. As with most equivocal misunderstandings, hindsight showed that the phrase "tostada with beans" has two equally correct meanings.

"I love you" [is] a statement that can be expressed in so many varied ways. It may be a stage song, repeated daily without any meaning, or a barely audible murmur, full of surrender. Sometimes it means: *I desire you* or *I want you sexually.* It may mean: *I hope you love me* or *I hope that I will be able to love you.* Often it means: *It may be that a love relationship can develop between us* or even *I hate you.* Often it is a wish for emotional exchange: *I want your admiration in exchange for mine* or *I give my love in exchange for some passion* or *I want to feel cozy and at home with you* or *I admire some of your qualities.* A declaration of love is mostly a request: *I desire you* or *I want you to gratify me,* or *I want your protection* or *I want to be intimate with you or I want to exploit your loveliness.*

Sometimes it is the need for security and tenderness, for parental treatment. It may mean: *My self-love goes out to you.* But it may also express submissiveness: *Please take me as I am,* or *I feel guilty about you, I want, through you, to correct the mistakes I have made in human relations.* It may be self-sacrifice and a masochistic wish for dependency. However, it may also be a full affirmation of the other, taking the responsibility for mutual exchange of feelings. It may be a weak feeling of friendliness, it may be the scarcely even whispered expression of ecstasy. "I love you,"—wish, desire, submission, conquest; it is never the word itself that tells the real meaning here.

J. A. M. MEERLOO
Conversation and Communication

Other equivocal misunderstandings can be more serious. A nurse gave one of her patients a scare when she told him that he "wouldn't be needing" his robe, books, and shaving materials anymore. The patient became quiet and moody. When the nurse inquired about the odd behavior, she discovered that the poor man had interpreted her statement to mean he was going to die soon. In fact, the nurse meant he would be going home shortly.

Some equivocal misunderstandings can go on for a lifetime. Consider the word "love." J. A. Lee (1973) points out that people commonly use that term in six very different ways: *eros* (romantic love), *ludus* (game-playing love), *storge* (friendship love), *mania* (possessive, dependent love), *pragma* (logical love), and *agape* (all-giving, selfless love). Imagine the conflicts that would occur between a couple who sincerely pledged their love to one another, each with a different kind of love in mind. "If you really love me, why are you acting like this?" we can imagine them asking one another—never realizing that they each view the relationship differently.

Vigilance is the best way to avoid equivocal misunderstandings. Whenever you face a term that has the remotest chance of being interpreted in more than one way, take the time to clarify its meaning: "I hate that idea. Well, I don't really *hate* it, but there are a couple of reasons why I think it won't work . . . ."

BEWARE OF STATIC EVALUATION

"Mark is a nervous guy." "Karen is short-tempered." "You can always count on Wes." Statements that contain or imply a **static evaluation**—the word "is" leads to the mistaken assumption that people are consistent and unchanging—clearly an incorrect belief. Instead of labeling Mark as permanently and totally nervous, it would probably be more

> Notice the difference between what happens when a man says to himself, "I have failed three times," and what happens when he says, "I am a failure."
>
> S. I. HAYAKAWA

accurate to outline the situations in which he behaves nervously. The same goes for Karen, Wes, and the rest of us: We are more changeable than the way static, everyday language describes us.

Edward Sagarian (1976) writes about an unconscious language habit that imposes a static view of others. Why is it, he asks, that we say "He *has* a cold," but say "He *is* a convict" or a genius, a slow learner, or any other set of behaviors that are also not necessarily permanent? Sagarian argues that such linguistic labeling leads us to typecast others, and in some cases forces them to perpetuate behaviors that could be changed.

Describing John as "boring" (you can substitute "friendly," "immature," or many other adjectives) is less correct than saying, "The John I encountered yesterday seemed to me to be . . . ." The second type of statement describes the way someone behaved at one point; the first categorizes him as if he had always been that way.

Alfred Korzybski (1933) suggested the linguistic device of dating to reduce static evaluation. He suggested adding a subscript whenever appropriate to show the transitory nature of many objects and behaviors. For example, a teacher might write as an evaluation of a student: "Susan$_{May\ 12}$ had difficulty cooperating with her classmates." Although the actual device of subscripting is awkward in writing and impractical in conversation, the idea it rep-

resents can still be used. Instead of saying, "I'm shy," a more accurate statement might be "I haven't approached any new people since I moved here." The first statement implies that your shyness is an unchangeable trait, rather like your height, while the second one suggests that you are capable of changing.

DISTINGUISH FACTS FROM INFERENCES

We can make statements about things we observe as well as about things we do not observe. The problem is that the grammar of

our language does not distinguish between the two. "She is driving a Mercedes" is *grammatically* equivalent to "She is seething with rage," yet the first sentence is a matter of fact, whereas the second is inferential. We can directly observe the car and her driving it, but we cannot directly observe her seething rage. Any statement we make about rage is based on a few observations and conclusions we draw from them.

Arguments often result when we label our inferences as facts:

A: Why are you mad at me?

B: I'm not mad at you. Why have you been so insecure lately?

A: I'm not insecure. It's just that you've been so critical.

B: What do you mean, "critical"? I haven't been critical. . . .

Instead of trying to read the other person's mind, a far better course is to identify the observable behaviors (facts) that have caught your attention and to describe the interpretations (inferences) that you have drawn from them. After describing this train of thought, ask the other person to comment on the accuracy of your interpretation:

> "When you didn't return my phone call (fact), I got the idea that you're mad at me (inference). Are you?" (question)

> "You've been asking me whether I still love you a lot lately (fact), and that makes me think you're feeling insecure (inference). Is that right?" (question)

USE EMOTIVE WORDS WITH CAUTION

Emotive language seems to describe something but really announces the speaker's atti-tude toward it. If you approve of a friend's roundabout approach to a difficult subject, you might call her "tactful"; if you don't like it, you might accuse her of "beating around the bush." Whether the approach is good or bad is more a matter of opinion than of fact, although this difference is obscured by emotive language.

It's easy to use emotive language without even knowing that you are editorializing instead of describing people, ideas, objects, and events. Raise your consciousness about how emotive language operates by trying Activity 3 on page 156.

You can appreciate how emotive words are really editorial statements when you consider these examples:

If You Approve, Say	If You Disapprove, Say
thrifty	cheap
traditional	old-fashioned
extrovert	loudmouth
cautious	coward
progressive	radical
information	propaganda
military victory	massacre
eccentric	crazy

Using emotive labels can have ugly consequences. Although experimental subjects who heard a derogatory label used against a member of a minority group expressed annoyance at this sort of slur, the negative emotional terms did have an impact (Giles and Franklyn-Stokes 1989: 125; Kirkland et al. 1987). Not only did the unwitting subjects rate the minority individual's competence lower when that person performed poorly, but they also found fault with others who associated socially with the minority person—even members of the subject's own ethnic group.

The best way to avoid arguments involving emotive words is to describe the person, thing, or idea you are discussing in neutral terms, and to label your opinions as such. Instead of saying, "I wish you'd quit making those sexist remarks," say "I really don't like it when you call us 'girls' instead of 'women'." Not only are nonemotive statements more accurate, they have a much better chance of being well received by others.

EXPLAIN RELATIVE WORDS

Relative language gains meaning by comparison. For example, do you attend a large or small school? This depends on what you compare it to. Alongside a campus such as the University of Michigan, with over 30,000 students, your school may look small; but compared with a smaller institution, it may seem quite large. Relative words such as "fast" and "slow," "smart" and "stupid," "short" and "long," are clearly defined only through comparison.

Using relative terms without explaining them can lead to communication problems. Have you ever responded to someone's question about the weather by saying it was warm, only to find out the person thought it was cold? Have you followed a friend's advice and gone to a "cheap" restaurant, only to find that it was twice as expensive as you expected? Have classes you heard were "easy" turned out to be hard? The problem in each case resulted from failing to link the relative word to a more measurable term.

USE EUPHEMISMS SPARINGLY

Euphemisms (from the Greek word meaning "to use words of good omen") are pleasant terms substituted for blunt ones. Euphemisms soften the impact of information that might be unpleasant. Unfortunately, this pulling of lin-

Student Reflection
Word Choice and Attitude

I've taken two communication classes this year, and they were completely different. I just figured out a big reason why. In one class my professor used language that made it sound as if communication had nothing to do with us. He would always refer to "people" or "communicators" as if they were from another planet, or at least another species. One day he announced that his lecture topic would be "How men and women speak when they are together." If men and women are they, who are we?

My other professor talked about how we communicate. "Does watching violence on television make us more aggressive?" she would ask. "Do movies teach us how to be husbands or wives or parents?" The two different ways of using language seemed trivial at first, but now I can see that they said a lot about how each professor approached the course.

guistic punches often obscures the accuracy of a message.

There are certainly cases where tactless honesty can be brutal: "What do I think of your new hair style? I think it's ugly!" or "How do I feel about the relationship? I can hardly wait to get away from you!" At the same time, being too indirect can leave others wondering where you stand: "What an original haircut," or "We could grow closer than we are now." When choosing how to broach difficult subjects, the challenge is to be as kind as possible without sacrificing

We use higher-level abstractions all the time. For instance, rather than saying "Thanks for washing the dishes," "Thanks for vacuuming the rug," "Thanks for making the bed," it's easier to say "Thanks for cleaning up." In such everyday situations, abstractions are a useful kind of verbal shorthand.

At other times the vagueness of abstractions allows us to avoid confrontations by deliberately being unclear (Eisenberg 1984; Eisenberg and Witten 1987). Suppose, for example, your boss is enthusiastic about a new approach to doing business that you think is a terrible idea. Telling the truth might seem too risky; but lying—saying "I think it's a great idea"—wouldn't feel right either. In situations like this an abstract answer can hint at your true belief without a direct confrontation: "I don't know . . . It's sure unusual . . . It *might* work." The same sort of abstract language can help you avoid embarrassing friends who ask for your opinion with questions like "What do you think of my new haircut?" An abstract response like "It's really different!" may be easier for you to deliver—and for your friend to receive—than the clear, brutal truth: "It's really ugly!" Chapter 9 will have more to say about abstract equivocations as an alternative to complete self-disclosure on the one hand and lies on the other.

Although vagueness does have its uses, highly abstract language can cause four types of problems. The first is stereotyping. Imagine someone who has had one bad experience and, as a result, blames an entire group: "Marriage counselors are worthless," "Californians are all flaky," or "Men are no good." Overly abstract expressions like these can cause people to *think* in generalities, ignoring uniqueness. As you learned in Chapter 2, expecting people to act a certain way can become a self-fulfilling prophecy. If you expect the worst of people, you have a good chance of getting it.

Besides narrowing your own options, excessively abstract language can also confuse oth-

either your integrity or the clarity of your message. (The guidelines for self-disclosure outlined in Chapter 9 will help you.)

CHOOSE THE PROPER LEVEL OF ABSTRACTION

High-level abstractions are convenient ways of generalizing about similarities between several objects, people, ideas, or events. Figure 5–2 is an **abstraction ladder** that shows how to describe the same phenomenon at various levels of abstraction.

ers. Telling the hairstylist "not too short" or "more casual" might produce the look you want, or it might lead to an unpleasant surprise.

Coming down the abstraction ladder can help you communicate more effectively and get what you seek from others. To learn how behavioral language can be so useful, try Activity 4 on page 156.

Overly abstract explanations can also cause problems of a more serious nature. Imagine the frustration that could come from these vague complaints:

A: We never do anything that's fun anymore.
B: What do you mean?
A: We used to do lots of unusual things, but now it's the same old stuff, over and over.
B: But last week we went on that camping trip, and tomorrow we're going to that party where we'll meet all sorts of new people. Those are new things.
A: That's not what I mean. I'm talking about *really* unusual stuff.
B: *(becoming confused and a little impatient)* Like what? Taking hard drugs or going over Niagara Falls in a barrel?
A: Don't be stupid. All I'm saying is that we're in a rut. We should be living more exciting lives.
B: Well, I don't know what you want.

Overly abstract language also leads to confusing directions:

Professor: I hope you'll do a thorough job on this paper.
Student: When you say thorough, how long should it be?
P: Long enough to cover the topic thoroughly.
S: How many sources should I look at when I'm researching it?
P: You should use several—enough to show me that you've really explored the subject.
S: And what style should I use to write it?
P: One that's scholarly but not too formal.
S: Arrgh!!!

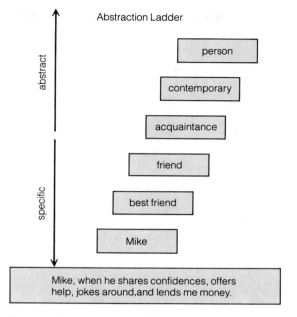

Figure 5–2   Abstraction ladder

From p. 374 *Understanding Human Behavior* 6/e James J. McConnell Holt, 1989

Even appreciation can suffer from being expressed in overly abstract terms. Psychologists have established that behaviors that are reinforced will recur with increased frequency. Your statements of appreciation will encourage others to keep acting in ways you like; but if they don't know just what it is that you appreciate, the chances of their repeating that behavior are lessened. There's a big difference between "I appreciate your being so nice" and "I appreciate the way you spent time talking to me when I was upset."

Overly abstract language can leave you unclear even about your own thoughts. At one time or another we've all felt dissatisfied with ourselves and others. Often these dissatisfactions show up as thoughts such as "I've got to get better organized" or "She's been acting strangely lately." Sometimes abstract statements such as these are shorthand for specific behaviors that

cathy   by Cathy Guisewite

we can identify easily; but in other cases we'd have a hard time explaining what we'd have to do to get organized or what the strange behavior is. Without clear ideas of these concepts it's hard to begin changing matters. Instead, we tend to go around in mental circles, feeling vaguely dissatisfied without knowing exactly what is wrong or how to improve it.

You can make your language—and your thinking—less abstract and more clear by learning to make *behavioral descriptions* of your problems, goals, appreciations, complaints, and requests. We use the word *behavioral* because such descriptions move down the abstraction ladder to describe the specific, observable objects and actions we're thinking about. Table 5–1 shows how behavioral descriptions are much more clear and effective than vague, abstract statements.

Language Shapes Our World

Language not only clarifies or obscures meaning. In some cases the language we use actually shapes our attitudes—even our entire view of the world.

CULTURAL PERSPECTIVE

Sometimes cultural differences in the use of language can produce amusing results. The "I'm a Pepper" commercial that worked so well in the United States to advertise the Dr Pepper soft drink caused problems in England, where the word *pepper* is slang for prostitution (Hamilton 1990: 8).

On a more serious and fundamental level, anthropologists have long known that the culture people live in shapes their perceptions of reality. Social scientists have found that cultural perspective is at least partially shaped by the language that members of that culture speak (Giles and Franklyn-Stokes 1989). For

Words do not label things already there. Words are like the knife of the carver: They free the idea, the thing, from the general formlessness of the outside. As a man speaks, not only is his language in a state of birth, but also the very thing about which he is talking.

EDMUND CARPENTER

Table 5–1   Abstract and Behavioral Descriptions

	Abstract Description	Behavioral Description			Remarks
		Who is involved	*In what circumstances*	*Specific behaviors*	
Problem	I'm no good at meeting strangers.	People I'd like to date.	At parties and in school.	I think, "They'd never want to date me." Also, I don't originate conversations.	Behavioral description more clearly identifies thoughts and behaviors to change.
Goal	I'd like to be more assertive.	Telephone and door-to-door solicitors.	When I don't want the product or can't afford it.	Instead of apologizing, I want to keep saying "I'm not interested" until they go away.	Behavioral description clearly outlines how to act; abstract description doesn't.
Appreciation	"You've been a great boss."	(no clarification necessary)	When I've needed to change my schedule because of school exams or assignments.	"You've rearranged my hours cheerfully."	Give both abstract and behavioral descriptions for best results.
Complaint	"I don't like some of the instructors around here."	Professors A and B.	In class when students ask questions the professors think are stupid.	They either answer in a sarcastic voice (you might demonstrate) or accuse us of not studying hard enough.	If talking to A or B, use only behavioral description. With others, use both abstract and behavioral descriptions.
Request	"Quit bothering me!"	You and your friends, X and Y.	When I'm studying for exams.	"Instead of asking me over and over to party with you, I wish you'd accept my comment that I need to study tonight."	Behavioral description will reduce defensiveness and make it clear that you don't *always* want to be left alone.

"Why did she ask me how I feel if she didn't want to hear about what I've been through?"

I'm not going to address him as 'dear' or sign myself 'Yours truly' or 'Sincerely' when he's certainly not dear to me and I'm not truly or sincerely or any other way his."

"They told me I could stay with them any time I'm in town, and when I wrote them about next weekend, they said they already had plans and didn't offer to cancel them."

Naturally patient and tolerant, not to say saintly, Miss Manners nonetheless grows testy with people who make such arguments. She cannot believe that they honestly don't understand what a conventional phrase is. They think they want to strip these remarks of their usefulness and then laugh at their nakedness. What a nasty urge that is.

However, it does occasionally happen that an expression of that sort can change its meaning somewhat, or that it could have more than one meaning, depending on how and by whom it is said. Here, therefore, is a short glossary of social idioms:

How do you do? How are you? Both of these mean *Hello.* The correct question, when you want to know how someone's digestion or divorce is getting along is *Tell me, how have you really been?*

Call me. This can mean *Don't bother me now—let's discuss it on office time.* or *I would accept if you asked me out* or *I can't discuss this here* or *Don't go so fast.*

I'll call you. This has opposite meanings, and you have to judge by the delivery. One is *Let's start something* and the other is *Don't call me.*

Let's have lunch. Among social acquaintances, this means *If you ever have nothing to do on a day I have nothing to do, let's get together.* Among business acquaintances, it means *If you have something useful to say to me I'll listen.*

Let's have dinner. Among social acquaintances, it means *Let's advance this friendship.* Among business acquaintances it means *Let's turn this into a friendship.*

Please stop by some time and see me. Said to someone who lives in the same area, it means *Call me if you'd like to visit me.* Genuine dropping in disappeared with the telephone, so if you want to encourage that, you have to say *I'm always home in the mornings. Don't bother to call; just drop by.*

Please come and stay with me. Said to someone from another area, this means *I would consider extending an invitation at your convenience if it coincides with my convenience.*

We must get together. Watch out here, because there are several similar expressions. This one means *I like you but I'm too busy now to take on more friendships.*

We really must see more of each other. One of the tricky ones, this actually means *I can't take the time to see you.*

We really must do this more often. Another variation. This one is really *This was surprisingly enjoyable, but it's still going to happen infrequently.*

Yours truly, Yours sincerely. The first is business, the second distant social. Both mean *Well, I guess that's all I've got to say so I'll close now.*

Is all that clear? Oh, one last thing. People who say *I only say what I really mean,* really mean, *I am about to insult you.*

JUDITH MARTIN
Miss Manners' Guide to
Excruciatingly Correct Behavior

example, bilingual speakers seem to think differently when they change languages. In one study, French Americans were asked to interpret a series of pictures. When they spoke in French, their descriptions were far more romantic and emotional than when they used English to describe the same kind of images. Likewise, when students in Hong Kong were asked to complete a values test, they expressed more traditional Chinese values when they answered in Cantonese than when they spoke English. In Israel, both Arab and Jewish students saw bigger distinctions between their group and "outsiders" when using their native language than when they spoke in English, a neutral tongue. Examples like these show the power of language to shape cultural identity . . . sometimes for better, and sometimes for worse.

Does the world look different when described in other languages? You can begin to answer this question by trying Activity 5 on page 156.

Linguistic influences start early in life. English-speaking parents often label the mischievous pranks of their children as "bad," implying that there is something immoral about acting wild. "Be good!" they are inclined to say. On the other hand, French adults are more likely to say *"Sois sage!"*—"Be wise." The linguistic implication is that misbehaving is an act of foolishness. Swedes would correct the same action with the words *"Var snell!"*—"Be friendly, be kind." By contrast, German adults use the command *"Sei artig!"*—literally "Be of your own kind"—in other words, get back in step, conform to your role as a child (Sinclair 1954).

Student Reflection

Language and World View

Because my parents speak Japanese fluently, they talk to each other in that language. My mom took a few courses in the local high school, and so she speaks English better than my father. This affects intimacy in our family in a unique way. Because my older brother can understand Japanese better than the rest of us, he and Dad are much closer to each other. My dad tells us he can tell our brother how he really feels. He thinks in Japanese and feels funny trying to find the right English words. As a result, my younger brother and I are closer to our mom, and my older brother is closer to our dad. This is frustrating when I want to get close to my dad. I wind up doing it through my mom, who explains what I really mean and feel—in Japanese!

IMPRESSION FORMATION

It isn't necessary to study German, Swedish, French, or Nootka to see how language shapes perception. Research shows that the way speakers of English express a message—perhaps more than the message itself—shapes the impression others form of them.

Credibility   Scholarly speaking is a good example of how speech style influences perception. We refer to what has been called the Dr. Fox hypothesis (Cory 1980): "An apparently legitimate speaker who utters an unintelligible mes-

In one way, titles are a form of psychic compensation, and if too many titles are distributed, the currency is depreciated. But a title is also a tool. If our salesman is a vice-president and yours is a sales rep, and both are in a waiting room, guess who gets in first and gets the most attention.

If you find you can't get applicants for menial jobs, maybe your titles are obsolete. Nobody today can admit . . . that he's a clerk or a busboy. One airline improved a bad situation by changing "ramp service clerk" to "ramp service engineer." A restaurant cured a chronic busboy shortage by changing the title to "logistics engineer."

ROBERT TOWNSEND
Up the Organization

---

sage will be judged competent by an audience in the speaker's area of apparent expertise." The Dr. Fox hypothesis got its name from one Dr. Myron L. Fox, who delivered a talk followed by a half-hour discussion on "Mathematical Game Theory as Applied to Physical Education." The audience included psychiatrists, psychologists, social workers, and educators. Questionnaires collected after the session revealed that these educated listeners found the lecture clear and stimulating.

Despite his warm reception by this learned audience, Fox was a complete fraud. He was a professional actor whom researchers had coached to deliver a lecture of double-talk—a patchwork of information from a *Scientific American* article mixed with jokes, non sequiturs, contradictory statements, and meaningless references to unrelated topics. When wrapped in a linguistic package of high-level professional jargon, however, the meaningless

gobbledygook was judged as important information. In other words, Fox's credibility came more from his style of speaking than from the ideas he expressed.

The same principle seems to hold for academic writing (Armstrong 1980). A group of thirty-two management professors rated material according to its complexity rather than its content. When a message about consumer behavior was loaded with unnecessary words and long, complex sentences, the academics rated it highly. When the same message was translated into more readable English, with shorter words and clearer sentences, the professors judged the same research as less competent.

The way in which a message is delivered can even mean the difference between freedom and imprisonment. Experimental subjects judged criminal defendants less guilty, more attractive, and more authoritative when their replies to an attorney's questions were free of **hesitations** and **hedges** ("sort of," "kind of," and so on). When the same responses contained hedges and hesitations, raters were less sympathetic to the answers (Hosman and Wright 1987).

Language creates an impression of us—for better or worse. You can see how linguistic impression formation operates by completing Activity 6 on page 156.

Status In the stage classic *My Fair Lady*, Professor Henry Higgins transformed Eliza Doolittle from a lowly flower girl into a high-society woman by replacing her cockney accent with an upper-crust speaking style. The power of speech to influence status is a real-life fact. In 1971 British researcher Howard Giles conducted experiments that conclusively demonstrated (if any proof was necessary) that in Britain, judgments of attractiveness and status are strongly

influenced by style of speech. Other research by social psychologists in North America shows that the same principle applies in the New World (see Giles and Poseland 1975). For example, speakers of Black English have shorter job interviews and receive fewer job offers than applicants who speak standard English (Terrell and Terrell 1983).

Power Communication researchers have identified a number of language patterns that add to or detract from a speaker's power to influence others. In a study of courtroom speech, Bonnie Erickson and her colleagues (1978) identified several **powerless speech mannerisms** (see Table 5–2). Experimental subjects who heard testimony containing these powerless forms judged the speakers less credible and the positions they advocated less acceptable than when the same testimony was presented without the

powerless elements. Further research has showed that just one type of powerless speech mannerism is enough to make a person appear less authoritative or socially attractive (Hosman 1989). Although powerful speech may help attorneys win cases, it can work against plaintiffs and defendants, who are sometimes viewed by experimental jurors as being more blameworthy—probably because they appear to have more control over their lives than less powerful speakers, whom juries would be inclined to see as victims (Bradac et al. 1981). Bradac and Mulac (1984b) conclude that outside the jury setting, people who use the powerless language forms in Table 5–2 are perceived as powerless and ineffective.

Racism and Sexism The language used to describe gender or ethnicity can shape the way both speaker and hearers view the people being

Table 5–2 Examples of Powerless Language

Hedges	"I'm *kinda* disappointed…" "I *think* we should…" "I *guess* I'd like to…"
Hesitations	"*Uh,* can I have a minute of your time?" "*Well,* we could try this idea…" "I wish you would—*er*—try to be on time."
Intensifiers	"I *really* do think that…" "I'm not *very* hungry."
Polite Forms	"Excuse me, *sir*…"
Tag Questions	"It's about time we got started, *isn't it*?" "*Don't you think* we should give it another try?"
Disclaimers	"*I probably shouldn't say this, but*…" "*I'm not really sure, but*…"

described. Racist and sexist language greatly affects the self-concepts of the people discriminated against (Pearson 1991). An article in *The New York Times Magazine* by Casey Miller and Kate Swift (1972) points out some of the aspects of our language that discriminate against women, suggesting women are of lower status than men. Miller and Swift write that, except for words referring to females by definition, such as "mother" and "actress," English defines many nonsexual concepts as male. The underlying assumption is that people in general are men. Also, words associated with males have positive connotations, such as "aggressive," "confident," "forceful," "strong," and "tough"; whereas words related to females are fewer and often have less positive connotations, such as "fickle," "frivolous," "jolly," and "timid" (Heilbrun 1976).

Differences in definitions of the terms "woman" and "man" in the *Oxford English Dictionary* indicate discriminatory treatment. The definition of "woman" is an adult female being, a female servant, a lady-love or mistress, and a wife. "Man" is defined as a human being, the human creature regarded abstractly, an adult male endowed with manly qualities, and a person of importance or position (O'Donnell 1973).

Sexism even extends to the language of the deaf (Pearson 1991). American Sign Language divides the head into two areas: Above the center is used to represent words such as "he," "him," "father," and so on; whereas below the center is used to represent "she," "her," and "mother." In general, the area closest to the brain is used for masculine referents and the area closest to the mouth is used for feminine referents. For example, an intelligent woman is signed as "thinks like a man," a secretary is "a girl who writes," and the president is a "respected man." In general, sign language portrays women as expressive and men as rational.

Any language expressing stereotyped sexual attitudes or assuming the superiority of one sex over another is sexist, so adding feminine endings to nonsexual words, such as "poetess" for female poet, is as sexist as "separate but equal" is racist.

While sexist language usually defines the world as made up of superior men and inferior women, racist language usually defines it as composed of superior whites and other inferior racial groups. Words and images associated with "white" are usually positive, whether it's

A change in language can transform our appreciation of the cosmos.

BENJAMIN LEE WHORF

the hero-cowboy in white clothing or connotations of white as "pure," "clean," "honorable," "innocent," "bright," and "shiny." The words and images associated with black are often negative, a concept that reaches from the black hat of the villain cowboy and the black cat that causes bad luck to phrases like "black market," "blackball," "blacklist," and "Black Tuesday" (the day the stock market crashed).

To the extent that our language is both sexist and racist, our view of the world is affected. For example, men are given more opportunity than women to see themselves as "good," and in the same way whites are given more opportunity than blacks. Language shapes the self-concepts of those it labels in such a way that members of the linguistically slighted group see themselves as inferior.

Many linguistic changes beginning in the late 1960s aimed at teaching speakers and writers a new vocabulary in order to change the destructive connotations that accompany many of our words. For example, "Black is beautiful" was an effort to reduce perceived status differences between blacks and whites.

Changes in writing style were also designed to counter the sexual prejudices inherent in language, particularly eliminating the constant use of "he" and introducing various methods either to eliminate reference to a particular sex, or to make reference to both sexes (Miller and Swift 1972). Words that use "man" generically to refer to humanity at large often pose problems, but only to the unimaginative. Consider the following substitutions: "mankind" may be replaced with "humanity," "human beings," "human race," and "people"; "man-made" may be replaced with "artificial," "manufactured," and "synthetic"; "manpower" may be replaced with "labor," "workers," and "workforce"; and "manhood" may be replaced with "adulthood."

In the same way, "Congressmen" are "members of Congress;" "firemen" are "fire fighters;" "chairmen" are "presiding officers," "leaders," and "chairs;" "foremen" are "supervisors;" "policemen" and "policewomen" are both "police officers;" and "stewardesses" and "stewards" are both "flight attendants."

Throughout this book we have used a number of techniques for avoiding sexist language: switching to the sexually neutral plural (they); occasionally using the passive voice to eliminate sexed pronouns; carefully balancing individual masculine and feminine pronouns in illustrative material; and even doing total rewrites to delete conceptual sexual bias.

Language Reflects Our Attitudes

Besides shaping perceptions, language often reflects the attitudes of a speaker. Feelings of attraction, control, commitment, responsibility—all these and more are reflected in the way we speak.

IDENTITY

The label we choose for ourselves and encourage others to use says a great deal about who we think we are and how we want others to view us. For many people, changes in age lead to changes in names. The diminutive that seemed to fit as a child doesn't fit as well in adolescence or adulthood. Thus, Vinnie may become Vince, and Danny may insist on being called Dan or Daniel. It still may be fine for close friends to use diminutives, but not others. The shift to more formal, adult names may not be as pronounced for some women: It's not uncommon to meet an adult Betsy or Susie. But when being taken seriously is the goal in this world where women are all too often treated with less respect than they deserve, having a serious name can be an asset. A male president of the United States may have been elected without changing his name from Jimmy to James, but it's hard to imagine a female public figure who would risk being called Cindy or Babs. Contemporary female officeholders prove the point: Names like Patty Schroeder or Jeannie Kirkpatrick just don't sound right.

Women in Western society face a conscious choice about how to identify themselves when they marry. They may follow the tradition of taking their husband's last name, hyphenate their own name and their husband's, or keep their birth name. A fascinating study by Karen Foss and Belle Edson (1989) revealed that a woman's choice is likely to reveal a great deal about herself and her relationship with her husband. Surveys revealed that women who have taken their husband's names place the most importance on relationships, with social expectations of how they should behave second, and issues of self coming last. By contrast, women who kept their birth names put their personal concerns ahead of relationships and social expectations. Women with hyphenated names fall somewhere between the other groups, valuing self and relationships equally.

POWER

We already saw how the use of certain language lessens a speaker's ability to influence others (see Table 5–2, page 138). The use of "powerful" or "powerless" language also reflects the speaker's own sense of control over others. Notice the difference in the perceived control in the following examples:

> Excuse me, sir. I hate to say this, but I...uh...I guess I won't be able to turn in the assignment on time. I had a personal emergency and...well...it was just impossible to finish it by today. I'll have it in your mailbox on Monday, OK?

> I won't be able to turn in the assignment on time. I had a personal emergency and it was impossible to finish it by today. I'll have it in your mailbox on Monday.

Whether or not the professor finds the excuse acceptable, it's clear that the second speaker feels confident, whereas the first one is apologetic and uncertain. The first statement is a classic example of what has come to be called "one-down" communication.

Some relationships are characterized by complementary communication, in which one partner uses consistently powerful language, while the other responds with powerless speech. A demanding boss and compliant employees or the stereotypically tyrannical husband and submissive wife are examples of complementary relationships. In symmetrical relationships, the power is distributed more evenly between the partners: Both may use equally powerful or powerless speech. The locus of power isn't constant: As relationships pass through different stages, the distribution of power shifts, and so do the speech patterns of the partners (Fisher and Drecksel 1983). You can test this principle for yourself. Recall situations where you were feeling especially vulnerable, uncertain, confused, or powerless. Did your language include the characteristics listed in Table 5–2? Did these characteristics disappear when you felt more safe, confident, or powerful? What factors led to these changes? The subject being discussed? Your feelings about yourself at the moment? The way the other person was treating you?

Simply counting the number of powerful or powerless statements won't always reveal who has the most control in a relationship. Social rules often mask the real distribution of power. A boss who wants to be pleasant might say to a secretary, "Would you mind retyping this letter?" In truth, both boss and secretary know this is an order and not a request, but the questioning form makes the medicine less bitter (Bradac 1983: 155). Therefore, a knowledge of the context and the personalities of two speakers is necessary before it's safe to make any assumptions about who controls whom.

ATTRACTION AND INTEREST

Social customs discourage us from expressing like or dislike in many situations. Only a clod would respond to the question "What do you think of the cake I baked for you?" by saying "It's terrible." Bashful or cautious suitors might not admit their attraction to a potential partner. Even when people are reluctant to speak out candidly, the language they use can suggest their degree of interest and attraction toward a person, an object, or an idea. Morton Wiener and Albert Mehrabian (1968) outline a number of linguistic clues that reveal these attitudes.

Demonstrative Pronoun Choice   Although several pronouns can correctly refer to a person, some are more positive than others. Consider the difference between saying, "These people want our help" and the equally accurate "Those people want our help." Most people would probably conclude that the first speaker is more sympathetic than the second. In the same way, speakers sound more positive when they say, "Here's Tom" than if they say, "There's Tom." The difference in such cases is one of grammatical *distance*. People generally suggest attraction by indicating closeness and dislike by linguistically removing themselves from the object of their conversation.

Sequential Placement   Another way to signify attitude is to place positive items earlier in a sequence. For example, notice the difference between discussing "Jack and Jill" and referring to "Jill and Jack." Likewise, consider how people respond to questions about courses they are taking or friends they intend to invite to an upcoming party. In many cases the first person or subject mentioned is more important or better liked than subsequent ones. (Of course, sequential placement isn't always significant. You may put "toilet bowl cleaner" at the top of your shopping list simply because it's closer to the market door than champagne.) Wiener and Mehrabian point out an interesting example of the sequencing principle that often occurs in psychotherapy, where the patient mentions a certain subject first, not because it is most important, but because it's the easiest one to discuss. Even here the same principle applies: Positive subjects often precede negative ones.

Negation   People usually express liking in a direct, positive manner while they use more indirect, negative language with less favorable subjects. Imagine, for instance, that you ask a friend's opinion about a book, movie, or restaurant. Consider the difference between the responses "It was good" and "It wasn't bad." In the same way, the positive "I'd like to get together with you" may be a stronger indication of liking than the more negative "Why don't we get together?"

Duration   The length of time people spend discussing a person or subject can also be a strong indicator of attraction either to the subject or to the person with whom they're talking. If you ask a new acquaintance about work and receive the brief response "I'm a brain surgeon" with nothing more, you would probably suspect either that the subject was a sensitive one or that this person wasn't interested in you. Of course, there may be other reasons for short answers, such as preoccupation, but one good yardstick for measuring liking is the time others spend communicating with us.

Intimacy   Beyond simple interest and liking, language can also reflect the degree of intimacy between two partners. The most obvious indications are terms of affection or endearment. In romantic relationships, labels such as "honey" or "babe" suggest a new degree of intimacy. Even nonromantic friends often begin to use special labels for each other as their relationship becomes stronger: "OK, buddy"; "See you later, amigo." Friends, lovers, and family members also create "personal idioms" that are unique to their relationship (Hopper et al. 1981). The pet names children often use for their grandparents are a clear example. J. Berris- ford Worthington may be the terror of the boardroom, but to his loving grandchildren he's "Baba." At a party you might introduce an old friend as "Barbara," but to your circle of friends she's "Babs."

The language partners use when problems arise also reveals their degree of intimacy. Research shows that partners who are strongly committed to a relationship tend to use emo- tional appeals and personal rejection when arguing their case, whereas less intimate cou- ples tend to rely on more logical arguments (Fitzpatrick and Winke 1979). Partners also use linguistic devices to smooth over disputes (Krueger 1982). One such device is blaming the problem on forces external to the self and the

---

"My hand is doing this movement . . . "

"Is *it* doing the movement?"

"I am moving my hand like this . . . and now the thought comes to me that . . . "

"The thought 'comes' to you?"

"I have the thought."

"You *have* it?"

"*I think.* Yes. I think that I use 'it' very much, and I am glad that by noticing it I can bring it all back to me."

"Bring it back?"

"*Bring myself back.* I feel thankful for this."

"*This?*"

"Your idea about the 'it.'"

"My idea?"

"I feel thankful towards you."

CLAUDIO NARANJO

---

relationship: "I know I've been touchy lately. It's nothing you've done: Work has been frantic lately." Other cohesiveness-building devices in conversation include balanced turn-taking, fre- quent topic shifting, and frequent interrupting during mutual affirmation:

"You've sure been a good sport about . . . "

"I know you don't want to be selfish, and . . . "

"I'm glad you're so understanding. I wish I could . . . "

RESPONSIBILITY

Besides indicating liking or interest, language can also reflect a speaker's unconscious will- ingness to take responsibility for statements, as the following categories show.

The "It" Statement   Notice the difference be- tween the sentences of each set:

"It bothers me when you're late."

"I'm worried when you're late."

"It's nice to see you."

"I'm glad to see you."

"It's a boring class."

"I'm bored in the class."

"It" statements externalize the subject of the conversation. The subject is neither the person talking nor the one listening, but some "it" that is never really identified. Whenever people hear the word "it" used this way, they should ask themselves what "it" refers to. They inevitably find that the speaker uses "it" to avoid clearly identifying to whom the thought or feeling belongs.

The "You" Statement   The word "you" also allows the speaker to disown comments that might be difficult to express:

"You get frightened" instead of "I get frightened..."

"You wonder..." instead of "I wonder..."

"You start to think..." instead of "I'm starting to think..."

The "We" Statement   The word "we" can sometimes bring people together by pointing out their common beliefs. But in other cases the **"we" statement** becomes a device for diffusing the speaker's responsibility by referring to a nebulous collection of people who don't really exist. Like "it" and "you," "we" often really means "I." "We all believe..." means "I believe...," and "We ought to..." means "I want to...." (You might notice that this text uses a lot of "we's." Do you find your beliefs included enough to justify the use of this word?)

Questions   In the manner of "you" statements, questions often pass responsibility to the other person. They can also be used as a form of flattery ("Where did you get that lovely tie?"), or as a replacement of "I" statements (the most common). Some therapists argue that there are very few *real* questions; most questions hide some statement that the person does not want to make, possibly out of fear.

"What are we having for dinner?" may hide the statement "I want to eat out," or "I want to get a pizza."

"How many textbooks are assigned in that class?" may hide the statement "I'm afraid to get into a class with too much reading."

"Are you doing anything tonight?" can be a less risky way of saying, "I want to go out with you tonight."

"Do you love me?" safely replaces the statement "I love you," which may be too embarrassing, too intimate, or too threatening for the person to say directly.

When you point one accusing finger at someone, three of your own fingers point back at you.

LOUIS NIZER

The "But" Statement   Statements that take the form X-but-Y can be quite confusing. A closer look at the **"but" statement** explains why. "But" has the effect of canceling the thought that precedes it:

"You're a really swell person, but I think we ought to stop seeing each other."

"You've done good work for us, but we're going to have to let you go."

"This paper has some good ideas, but I'm giving it a grade of D because it's late."

These "buts" often mask the speaker's real meaning behind more-pleasant-sounding ideas. A more accurate and less confusing way of expressing complex ideas is to replace "but" with "and." In this way you can express a mixture of attitudes without eliminating any of them.

"I" Language   Some statements imply that a complaint is the fault of the person being criticized:

"I wish you wouldn't be so critical!"

"You didn't keep your promise!"

"You're really crude sometimes!"

Statements like these are examples of **"you" language**—speech that expresses or implies a judgment of the other person. Despite its name, "you" language doesn't have to contain the pronoun "you," which is often implied rather than stated outright:

"That was a stupid joke!" ["Your jokes are stupid."]

"Don't be so critical!" ["You're too negative."]

"Mind your own business!" [You're too nosy."]

As Chapter 9 will explain in detail, an outright or implied "you" statement suggests that the speaker is qualified to judge the target—not a position that most people are willing to accept, even when the evaluation is correct.

What difference does "I" language make in interpersonal relationships? See for yourself by trying Activities 7 and 8 on page 156.

Fortunately there's a better way to express a complaint. **"I" language** shows that the speaker takes responsibility by describing his or her reaction to the other's behavior without making any judgments about its worth. A complete "I" statement has three parts. It describes (1) the other person's behavior, (2) your feelings, and (3) the consequences the other's behavior has for you:

"I get embarrassed [feeling] when you talk about my bad grades in front of our friends [behavior]. I'm afraid they'll think I'm stupid [consequence]."

"When you didn't pick me up on time this morning [behavior] I was late for class and I wound up getting chewed out by the professor [consequences]. That's why I got so mad [feeling]."

"I haven't been very affectionate [consequence] because you've hardly spent any time with me in the past few weeks [behavior]. I'm confused [feeling] about how you feel about me."

When the chances of being misunderstood or getting a defensive reaction are high, it's a good idea to include all three elements in your "I" message. In some cases, however, only one or two of them will get the job done:

"I went to a lot of trouble fixing this dinner, and now it's cold. Of course I'm mad!" [The behavior is obvious.]

"I'm worried because you haven't called me up." ["Worried" is both a feeling and a consequence.]

Even the best "I" statement won't work unless it's delivered in the right way. If your words are perfect but your tone of voice, facial expression, and posture all send "you" messages, a defensive response is likely to follow. The best way to make sure your actions match your words is to remind yourself before speaking that your goal is to explain how the other's behavior affects you—not to act like a judge and jury.

Gender and Language

So far we have discussed language use as if it were identical for both sexes. In many cases, however, there are significant differences between the way men and women speak.

CONTENT

While there is much variation within each gender, on the average men and women discuss a surprisingly different range of topics. The first research on conversational topics was conducted over 60 years ago (Landis and Burt 1924). Despite the changes in male and female roles since then, the results of recent studies are remarkably similar (Haas and Sherman 1982a, 1982b; Sherman and Haas 1984). In these surveys, women and men ranging in age from 17 to 80 described the range of topics each discussed with friends of the same sex. Certain subjects were common to both sexes: work, movies, and television proved to be frequent topics for both groups. Both men and women reserved discussions of sex and sexuality for members of the same gender. The differences between men and women were more striking than the similarities. Female friends spent much more time discussing relationship problems; family, health, and reproductive matters; weight; food; clothing; and men. Women also reported discussing other women frequently. Men, on the other hand, were more likely to discuss music, current events, sports, business, and other men. Both men and women were equally likely to discuss personal appearance, sex, and dating in same-sex conversations. True to one common stereotype, women were more likely to gossip about close friends and family (Lewin and Arluke 1985). By contrast, men spent more time gossiping about sports figures and media personalities. Women's gossip was no more derogatory than men's.

These differences can lead to frustration when men and women try to converse with one another. Sherman and Haas report that "trivial" is the word often used by both men and women to describe topics discussed by the opposite sex. "I want to talk about important things," a woman might say, "like how we're getting along. All he wants to do is talk about the news or what we'll do this weekend."

REASONS FOR COMMUNICATING

Men and women, at least in the United States, use language for different purposes. The contrast between male and female speech begins in childhood. Deborah Tannen (1989) summarizes a variety of studies showing that boys use talk to assert control over one another, while girls' conversations are more often aimed at maintaining social harmony. Transcripts of conversations between preschoolers aged two to five showed that girls are far more cooperative than boys (Sachs 1987). They preceded their proposals for action by saying "Let's," as in "Let's go find some" or "Let's turn back. Move these out first." By contrast, boys gave orders like "Lie down" or "Gimme your arm."

The difference between male and female uses of language continues into adulthood. In general, men value talks with friends for the freedom, playfulness, and camaraderie of the talks. When Sherman and Haas asked them what they liked best about their all-male talk, the most frequent answer was its ease. A common theme was appreciation of the practical value of conversation: new ways to solve problems about cars, taxes, and other everyday matters. Some men also mentioned enjoying the humor and rapid pace that characterized their all-male conversations.

Women, on the other hand, tended to look for different kinds of satisfaction when talking with

"Now that we've learned to talk, try to speak the same language."

By Herbert Goldberg; © 1970 by Saturday Review, Inc.

Consider the marriage of a man who has had most of his conversations with other men, to a woman who has had most of hers with other women. . . . He is used to fast-paced conversations that typically stay on the surface with respect to emotions, that often enable him to get practical tips or offer them to others and that are usually pragmatic or fun. She is used to conversations that, while practical and fun too, are also a major source of emotional support, self-understanding and the understanding of others. Becoming intimate with a man, the woman may finally start expressing her concerns to him as she might to a close friend. But she may find, to her dismay, that his responses are all wrong. Instead of making her feel better, he makes her feel worse. The problem is that he tends to be direct and practical, whereas what she wants more than anything else is an empathetic listener. Used to years of such responses from close friends, a woman is likely to be surprised and angered by her husband's immediate "Here's what ya do. . . ."

MARK SHERMAN AND ADELAIDE HAAS

their friends. The most common theme mentioned was a feeling of empathy or understanding—"To know you're not alone," as some put it, or "The feeling of sharing and being understood without a sexual connotation." Whereas men commonly described same-sex conversations as something they *liked,* females characterized their woman-to-woman talks as a kind of contact they *needed.*

The greater frequency of female conversations reflects their importance. Nearly 50 percent of the women surveyed said they called friends at least once a week just to talk, whereas less than half as many men did so. In fact, 40 percent of the men surveyed reported that they never called another man just to chat.

CONVERSATIONAL STYLE

Women and men behave differently in conversations than do men. (For summaries, see Giles and Street, 1985, and Kohn, 1988). For example, women ask more questions in mixed-sex conversations than do men—nearly three times as many, according to one study (Fishman 1978). Other research has revealed that in mixed-sex conversations men interrupt women far more than the other way around (Zimmerman and West 1975). Some theorists have argued that such differences cause women's speech to be less powerful and more emotional than men's (see, for example, Lakoff 1975). Research has supported these theories—at least in some cases. Even when clues about the speakers' sex were edited out, raters found clear differences between transcripts of male and female speech. In one study women's talk was judged more aesthetic, while men's talk was seen as more dynamic, aggressive, and strong. In another, male job applicants were rated more fluent, active, confident, and effective than females.

Other studies have revealed that men and women behave differently in different conversational settings. For example, in mixed-sex dyads men talk longer than women, while in same-sex situations women speak for a longer time. In larger groups men talk more, while in smaller settings women do more of the speaking. In same-sex conversations there are other differences between men and women: Females use more questions, justifiers, intensive adverbs, personal pronouns, and adverbials. Men use more directives, interruptions, and filler words to begin sentences (Mulac et al. 1988).

In light of these differences, it's easy to wonder how men and women manage to communicate with each other at all. One reason cross-sex conversations do run smoothly is that women accommodate to the topics men raise (Fishman 1978). Both men and women regard topics introduced by women as tentative, whereas topics that men bring up are more likely to be pursued. But women seem to grease the wheels of conversation by doing more work than men to maintain conversations. A complementary difference between men and women also promotes cross-sex conversations: Men are more likely to talk about themselves with women than with other men (Landis and Burt 1924); and since women are willing to adapt to this topic, conversations are likely to run smoothly, if one-sidedly.

NONGENDER VARIABLES

Despite the differences in the way men and women speak, the link between gender and language use isn't as clear-cut as it might seem. A large number of studies have found no significant difference between male and female speech in areas such as use of profanity (Mulac 1976), use of qualifiers such as "I guess" or "This is just my opinion" (Crosby et al. 1981), **tag questions** (Dubois and Crouch 1975), and vocal fluency (Silverman and Zimmer 1979). In one study of men and women engaging in naturally occurring conversations, there were more differences within members of each sex than between genders (Zahn 1989).

Some on-the-job research shows that male and female supervisors in similar positions behave the same way and are equally effective (Day and Stodgill 1972). Other studies, however, have found differences between the style of men and women (Baird and Bradley 1979). Female managers were rated as providing more information, putting more emphasis on happy interpersonal relationships, and being more encouraging, receptive to new ideas, concerned, and attentive. Male managers were rated as being more dominant, direct, and quick to challenge. The researchers concluded that "male and female managers [exerted] leadership in their own distinct fashions." They also argued that females may be superior managers because their verbal communication promotes more job satisfaction.

A growing body of research explains some of the apparent contradictions in similarities and differences between female and male speech: Factors other than gender influence language use. For example, social philosophy plays a role. Feminist wives talk longer than their husbands, while nonfeminist wives talk less. Orientation toward problem solving also plays a role in conversational style: Whether a speaker has a cooperative or competitive orientation has greater influence on interaction than gender (Fisher 1983).

The speaker's occupation also influences speaking style. For example, male day-care teachers' speech to their students resembles the language of female teachers more closely than it resembles the language of fathers at home (Gleason 1983). Overall, doctors interrupt their patients more often than the reverse, although male patients do interrupt female physicians more often than they do male physicians (Zimmerman and West 1975). A close study of trial transcripts showed that the speaker's experience on the witness stand and occupation had more to do with language use than did gender. The researcher concluded that "So-called women's language is neither characteristic of all women nor limited only to women" (O'Barr 1982). If women generally use "powerless" language, this fact probably reflects their social role in society at large. As the balance of power grows more equal between men and women, we can expect many linguistic differences to shrink.

SEX ROLES

Why is the research on gender differences so confusing? In some cases male and female speech seems identical, while other studies reveal important differences. As we've already said, one reason for the confusion is that other factors besides gender influence the way people speak: the setting in which conversation takes place, the expertise of the speakers, and their social roles (husband/wife, boss/employee, and so on). Also, female roles are changing so rapidly that many women simply don't use the conversational styles that characterized their older sisters and mothers. But in addition to these factors, another powerful force that influences the way individual men and women speak is their *sex role*. Recall the various sex-types described in Chapter 3 (pages 74–76): masculine, feminine, and androgynous. Remember that these sex-types don't necessarily line up neatly with gender. There are "masculine" females, "feminine" males, and androgynous communicators who combine traditionally masculine and feminine characteristics.

Research shows that linguistic differences are often a function of these sex roles more than the speaker's biological sex (male or female). Donald Ellis and Linda McCallister (1980) identified a series of experimental subjects by sex type: masculine, feminine, or androgynous. They then observed the language behavior of these subjects in group discussions to determine whether each psychological sex-type used a characteristic language pattern.

The results showed that language does, in fact, reflect psychological sex-type. One area in which this distinction became apparent was relational control. Whenever individuals interact, their messages have implications for how the power in their relationship will be distributed. Messages can express dominance ("one-up"), submissiveness ("one-down"), or equivalence (mutual identification). Ellis and McCallister found that the masculine sex-type subjects used significantly more dominance language than did either feminine or androgynous group members. Feminine members expressed slightly more submissive behaviors and more equivalence behaviors than the androgynous group members, and their submissiveness and equivalence were much greater than the masculine subjects.

The patterns of interaction between members of the same psychological sex-type were also revealing. Masculine subjects engaged in a pattern that the authors described as "competitive symmetry": A masculine sex-type would respond to another member's bid for control with a counterattempt to dominate the relationship, resulting in an almost continuous series of "one-up" interactions. Feminine sex-type subjects responded to another's bid for control unpredictably, using dominance, submission, and equivalence behaviors in an almost random fashion. Androgynous individuals behaved in a more predictable pattern: They most frequently met another's bid for dominance with a symmetrical attempt at control, but then moved quickly toward an equivalent relationship, sometimes acting deferentially during a transitional stage. Ellis and McCallister characterize this approach as more workable and efficient than either the sex-typical masculine or feminine styles.

As you read the foregoing information, it's important to realize that "masculinity" and "femininity" are culturally recognized sex roles, not necessarily gender related. For instance, at one time or another we have classified some speakers as "feminine men" or "masculine women." It is tempting to quarrel with Bem's use of the terms "masculine" and "feminine," arguing that these terms perpetuate stereotyping. Whatever descriptors you use, the overriding point remains: Language reflects a speaker's attitudes.

Language reflects attitudes. Language shapes attitudes. Language can clarify or obscure. Symbols stand for ideas, but not always the same ones. Our brief look at language shows that words and things aren't related in the straightforward way that we might assume. Because it's so difficult to understand each other's ideas through words, it's tempting to look for better alternatives. As you'll see in the next chapter, other ways of communicating do exist, but often we're faced with no other choice but to carry on with our often inadequate means of verbal expression. The best we can do is to proceed with caution, trying our best to understand each other and always realizing that the task is a difficult one.

Summary

Language is both a marvelous communication tool and the source of many interpersonal problems. Any language is a collection of symbols, governed by a variety of rules and used to convey messages between people. Because of its symbolic nature, language is not a precise vehicle: Meanings rest in people, and not in words themselves. Several types of troublesome language are unavoidable, and should be used with caution: equivocal terms, inferential statements, emotive words, relative terms, euphemisms, and highly abstract descriptions.

Language not only describes events, but also shapes our perceptions of them. The very language we speak imposes a unique world view that may differ from those of speakers of other tongues. Within a language, the choice of terms we use influence how people, events, objects, and ideas are perceived. Language also reflects our attitudes, showing our chosen identity, feelings of power, attraction to and interest in others, and willingness to accept responsibility for our thoughts and feelings.

The relationship between gender and language is a confusing one. There are many differences in the ways men and women speak: the content of their conversations varies, as do their reasons for communicating and their conversational style. Not all differences in language use can be accounted for by the speaker's gender, however. Occupation, social philosophy, and orientation toward problem-solving also influence the use of language, and psychological sex role can be more of an influence than biological sex.

Activities

1. For each of the following scenes, describe one syntactic, one semantic, and one pragmatic rule:
   a. Asking an acquaintance out for a first date.
   b. Declining an invitation to a party.
   c. Responding to a stranger who has just said "excuse me" after bumping into you in a crowd.

2. Recall an incident in which you were misunderstood. Explain how this event illustrated the principle "Meanings are in people, not words."

3. Get a better sense of how emotive language reflects the speaker's attitude instead of simply describing objects, ideas, or behavior by following philosopher Bertrand Russell's game of "conjugating irregular verbs." In this activity you show how three terms can be used to show very different opinions. Consider these sample "conjugations":

   I'm casual   We read love stories
   You're careless   You read erotic literature
   He's a slob   They read pornography

   Try a few conjugations of your own by completing each of the following statements:
   a. I'm tactful
   b. I'm conservative
   c. I'm quiet
   d. I'm relaxed
   e. I'm assertive

4. Translate the following into behavioral language:
   a. An abstract goal for improving your interpersonal communication (e.g., "be more assertive" or "stop being so sarcastic") into behavioral terms.
   b. A complaint you have with an other person (e.g. "selfish" or "insensitive").

   In both cases, describe the person or people involved, the circumstances in which the communication will takes place, and the precise behaviors involved. What difference will using the behavioral descriptions be likely to make in your relationships?

5. Interview someone who is fluent in more than one language. Ask that person to give you examples of ideas that change meaning when expressed from one language to the other or ideas that cannot be translated precisely from one language to the other.

6. Create two scenarios for an applicant interviewing for a job as a management intern at a local business. In the first scenario, the applicant should act in ways that lower his or her credibility, status, and power. In the second scene, the applicant should use language to enhance his or her credibility, status, and power.

7. You can develop your skill at delivering "I" messages by following these steps:
   a. Visualize situations in your life when you might have sent each of the following messages:
   "Your'e not telling me the truth!"
   "You only think of yourself!"
   "Don't be so touchy!"
   "Quit fooling around!"
   "You don't understand a word I'm saying!"
   b. Write alternatives to each statement using "I" language.

8. Think of three "you" statements you could make to people in your life. Transform each of these statements into "I" language and rehearse them with a classmate.

Readings

Armstrong, J. S. "Unintelligible Management Research and Academic Prestige." *Interfaces* 10 (1980): 80–86.

Baird, J. E., Jr., and P. H. Bradley. "Styles of Management and Communication." *Communication Monographs* 46 (1979): 101–11.

*Bate, B. *Communication and the Sexes*. New York: Harper & Row, 1988.

Bateson, G., and D. D. Jackson. "Some Varieties of Pathogenic Organization." *Disorders of Communication* 42 (Research Publications: Association for Research in Nervous and Mental Disease, 1964): 270–83.

Berger, C. R., and J. J. Bradac. *Language and Social Knowledge: The Social Psychology of Language.* London: Edward Arnold, 1982.

*Berryman, C. L., and J. R. Wilcox. "Attitudes Toward Male and Female Speech: Experiments on the Effects of Sex-Typical Language." *Western Journal of Speech Communication* 44 (1980): 50–59.

*Bradac, J. J. "The Language of Lovers, Flowers, and Friends: Communicating in Social and Personal Relationships." *Journal of Language and Social Psychology* 2 (1983): 141–62.

Bradac, J. J., M. R. Hemphill, and C. H. Tardy. "Language Style on Trial: Effects of 'Powerful' and 'Powerless' Speech upon Judgments of Victims and Villains." *Western Journal of Speech Communication* 45 (Fall 1981): 327–41.

Bradac, J. J., and A. Mulac. "Attributional Consequences of Powerful and Powerless Speech Styles in a Crisis-Intervention Context." *Journal of Language and Social Psychology* 3 (1984a): 1–19.

Bradac, J. J., and A. Mulac. "A Molecular View of Powerful and Powerless Speech Styles: Attributional Consequences of Specific Language Features and Communicator Intentions." *Communication Monographs* 51 (1984b): 307–19.

Brandreth, G. *More Joy of Lex.* New York: William Morrow, 1982.

Burgoon, M., J. P. Dillard, and N. E. Doran. "Friendly or Unfriendly Persuasion: The Effects of Violations of Expectations by Males and Females." *Human Communication Research* 10 (1983): 283–94.

Chase, S. *The Tyranny of Words.* New York: Harvest Books, 1938.

Clark, V. P., P. A. Eschholz, and A. F. Rosa, eds. *Language: Introductory Readings,* 2d ed. New York: St. Martin's, 1977.

*Condon, J. C. *Semantics and Communication,* 2d ed. New York: Macmillan, 1975.

Cory, C. T., ed. "Bafflegab Pays." *Psychology Today* 13 (May 1980): 12.

*Coupland, N., H. Giles, and J. M. Wiemann, *"Miscommunication" and Problematic Talk.* Newbury Park, CA: Sage, 1991.

Crosby, F., P. Jose, and W. Wong-McCarthy, "Gender, Androgony, and Conversational Assertiveness." In *Gender and Nonverbal Behavior,* C. Mayo and N. Henley, eds. New York: Springer-Verlag, 1981.

Davis, O. "The English Language Is My Enemy." In *Language: Concepts and Processes,* J. A. DeVito, ed. Englewood Cliffs, NJ: Prentice-Hall, 1973.

Day, D. R., and R. M. Stodgill. "Leader Behavior of Female Supervisors: A Comparative Study." *Personnel Psychology* 25 (1972): 353–60.

*Donohue, W. A., D. P. Cushman, and R. E. Nofsinger, Jr. "Creating and Confronting Social Order: A Comparison of Rules Perspectives." *Western Journal of Speech Communication* 44 (1980): 5–19.

Dubois, B., and I. Crouch. "The Question of Tag Questions in Women's Speech: They Don't Really Use More of Them, Do They?" *Language and Society* 4 (1975): 289–94.

*Eakins, B. W., and R. G. Eakins. *Sex Differences in Human Communication.* Boston: Houghton Mifflin, 1978.

Eisenberg, E. M. "Ambiguity as Strategy in Organizational Communication." *Communication Monographs* 51 (1984): 227–42.

Eisenberg, E. M., and M. G. Witten, "Reconsidering Openness in Organizational Communication." *Academy of Management Review* 12 (1987): 418–26.

Ellis, D. G., and L. McCallister. "Relational Control Sequences in Sex-Typed and Androgynous Groups." *Western Journal of Speech Communication* 44 (1980): 35–49.

Erickson, B., E. A. Lind, B. C. Johnson, and W. M. O'Barr. "Speech Style and Impression Formation in a Court Setting: The Effects of 'Powerful' and 'Powerless' Speech." *Journal of Experimental Social Psychology* 14 (1978): 266–79.

Fisher, B. A. "Differential Effects of Sexual Composition and Interactional Content on Interaction Patterns in Dyads." *Human Communication Research* 9 (1983): 225–38.

Fisher, B. A., and G. L. Drecksel. "A Cyclical Model of Developing Relationships: A Study of Relational Control Interaction." *Communication Monographs* 50 (1983): 66–78.

Fishman, P. "Interaction: The Work Women Do." *Social Problems* 25 (1978): 397–406.

Fitzpatrick, M. A., and J. Winke. "You Always Hurt the One You Love: Strategies and Tactics in Interpersonal Conflict." *Communication Quarterly* 27 (1979): 3–16.

Foss, K. A., and B. A. Edson, "What's in a Name? Accounts of Married Women's Name Choices." *Western Journal of Speech Communication* 53 (1989): 356–73.

Francis, W. N. "Word-Making: Some Sources of New Words." In *Language: Introductory Readings*, 2d ed., V. P. Clark, P. A. Eschholz, and A. F. Rosa, eds. New York: St. Martin's, 1977.

Giles, H., and A. Franklyn-Stokes. "Communicator Characteristics." In *Handbook of International and Intercultural Communication*, M. K. Asante and W. B. Gudykunst, eds. Newbury Park, CA: Sage, 1989.

Giles, H., and P. F. Poseland. *Speech Style and Social Evaluation*. New York: Academic Press, 1975.

*Giles, H., and R. L. Street, Jr. "Communication Characteristics and Behavior." In *Handbook of Interpersonal Communication*, M. L. Knapp and G. R. Miller, eds. Beverly Hills, CA: Sage, 1985.

Giles, H., and J. M. Wiemann. "Language, Social Comparison, and Power." In *Handbook of Communication Science*, C. R. Berger and S. H. Chaffee, eds. Beverly Hills, CA: Sage, 1987.

Gleason, J. B. "Men's Speech to Young Children." In *Language, Gender, and Society*, B. Thorne, ed. Rowley, MA: Newbury House, 1983.

Haas, A., and M. A. Sherman. "Conversational Topic as a Function of Role and Gender." *Psychological Reports* 51 (1982a): 453–54.

Haas, A., and M. A. Sherman. "Reported Topics of Conversation Among Same-Sex Adults." *Communication Quarterly* 30 (1982b): 332–42.

Hamilton, C. *Communicating for Results*. Belmont, CA: Wadsworth, 1990.

*Hayakawa, S. I. *Language in Thought and Action*. New York: Harcourt Brace Jovanovich, 1964.

Heilbrun, A. B. "Measurement of Masculine and Feminine Sex Role Identities as Independent Dimensions." *Journal of Consulting and Clinical Psychology* 44 (1976): 183–90.

Hopper, R., M. L. Knapp, and L. Scott. "Couples' Personal Idioms: Exploring Intimate Talk." *Journal of Communication* 31 (1981): 23–33.

Hosman, L. A. "The Evaluative Consequences of Hedges, Hesitations, and Intensifiers: Powerful and Powerless Speech Styles," *Human Communication Research* 15 (1989): 383–406.

Hosman, L. A., and J. W. Wright II. "The Effects of Hedges and Hesitations on Impression Formation in a Simulated Courtroom Context." *Western Journal of Speech Communication* 51 (1987): 173–88.

Kirkland, S. L., J. Greenberg, and T. Pysczynski, "Further Evidence of the Deleterious Effects of Overheard Derogatory Ethnic Labels: Derogation Beyond the Target." *Personality and Social Psychology Bulletin* 12 (1987): 216–27.

Kohn, A. "Girl Talk, Guy Talk." *Psychology Today* 22 (February 1988): 65–66.

Korzybski, A. *Science and Sanity*. Lancaster, PA: Science Press, 1933.

Krueger, D. "Marital Decision Making: A Language-Action Analysis." *Quarterly Journal of Speech* 68 (1982): 273–87.

Lakoff, R. *Language and Woman's Place*. New York: Harper Colophon Books, 1975.

Landis, M., and H. Burt. "A Study of Conversations." *Journal of Comparative Psychology* 4 (1924): 81–89.

Lee, J. A. *The Colors of Love: Exploration of the Ways of Loving*. Don Mills, Ontario: New Press, 1973.

Lewin, J., and A. Arluke. "An Exploratory Analysis of Sex Differences in Gossip." *Sex Roles* 12 (1985): 281–86.

Liska, J., E. W. Mechling, and S. Stathas. "Differences in Subjects' Perceptions and Believability Between Users of Deferential and Nondeferential Language." *Communication Quarterly* 29 (1981): 40–48.

Markel, N. N., J. F. Long, and T. J. Saine. "Sex Effects in Conversational Interaction: Another Look at Male Dominance." *Human Communication Research* 2 (1976): 356–64.

Martin, J. N., and R. T. Craig. "Selected Linguistic Sex Differences During Initial Social Interaction of Same-Sex and Mixed-Sex Dyads." *Western Journal of Speech Communication* 47 (1983): 16–28.

McLaughlin, M. L., M. J. Cody, M. L. Kane, and C. S. Robey. "Sex Differences in Story Receipt and Story Sequencing Behaviors in Dyadic Conversations." *Human Communication Research* 7 (1981): 99–116.

Miller, C. and K. Swift. "One Small Step for Genkind." *The New York Times Magazine* (April 16, 1972). Reprinted in *Language: Concepts and Processes*, J. A. DeVito, ed. Englewood Cliffs, NJ: Prentice-Hall, 1973.

Miller, C. and K. Swift. *Words and Women*. Garden City, NY: Anchor Press, 1976.

Miller, M. D., R. A. Reynolds, and R. E. Cambra. "The Influence of Gender and Culture on Language Intensity." *Communication Monographs* 54 (1987): 101–5.

Mulac, A. "Effects of Obscene Language upon Three Dimensions of Listener Attitude." *Communication Monographs* 43 (1976): 300–7.

Mulac, A., J. M. Wiemann, S. J. Widenmann, and T. W. Gibson, "Male/Female Language Differences and Effects in Same-Sex and Mixed-Sex Dyads: The Gender-Linked Language Effect," *Communication Monographs* 55 (1988): 315–35.

*Newman, E. *A Civil Tongue*. Indianapolis: Bobbs-Merrill, 1976.

O'Barr, W. M. *Linguistic Evidence: Language, Power, and Strategy in the Courtroom*. New York: Academic Press, 1982.

O'Donnell, H. S. "Sexism in Language." *Elementary English* 50 (1973): 1067–72.

Ogden, C. K., and I. A. Richards. *The Meaning of Meaning*. New York: Harcourt, Brace, 1923.

*Pearson, J. C. *Gender and Communication*. 2d Ed., Dubuque, IA: Wm. C. Brown, 1991.

Sachs, J. "Young Children's Language Use in Pretend Play." *Language, Gender and Sex in Comparative Perspective*, S. U. Philips, S. Steele, and C. Tanz, eds. Cambridge: Cambridge University Press, 1987.

Sacks, O. *Seeing Voices: A Journey into the World of the Deaf*. Berkeley: University of California Press, 1989.

Sagarian, E. "The High Cost of Wearing a Label." *Psychology Today* (March 1976): 25–27.

Sherman, M. A., and A. Haas. "Man to Man, Woman to Woman." *Psychology Today* 17 (June 1984): 72–73.

Shimanoff, S. B. "The Role of Gender in Linguistic References to Emotive States." *Communication Quarterly* 30 (1983): 174–79.

Silverman, E., and C. Zimmer. "The Fluency of Women's Speech." In *Papers in Southwest English IV: Proceedings of the Conference on the Sociology of the Languages of American Women*, B. Dubois and I. Crouch, eds. San Antonio, TX: Trinity University Press, 1979.

Sinclair, L. "A Word in Your Ear." In *Ways of Mankind*. Boston: Beacon Press, 1954.

*Tannen, D. *You Just Don't Understand: Women and Men in Conversation*. New York: William Morrow, 1989.

Terrell, S., and F. Terrell, "Effects of Speaking Black English upon Employment Opportunities," *ASHA Bulletin* 25 (1983): 27–35.

*Trenholm, S. *Human Communication Theory*. Englewood Cliffs, NJ: Prentice-Hall, 1986.

Whorf, B. L. *Language, Thought and Reality*, J. B. Carroll, ed. Cambridge, MA: M.I.T. Press, 1956.

Wiener, M., and A. Mehrabian. *A Language Within Language: Immediacy, a Channel in Verbal Communication*. New York: Appleton-Century-Crofts, 1968.

Wood, B. S. *Children and Communication: Verbal and Nonverbal Language Development*. Englewood Cliffs, NJ: Prentice-Hall, 1976.

Zahn, C. J. "The Bases for Differing Evaluations of Male and Female Speech: Evidence from Ratings of Transcribed Conversation," *Communication Monographs* 56 (1989): 59–74.

Zimmerman, D. H., and C. West. "Sex Roles, Interruptions, and Silences in Conversation." In *Language and Sex: Difference and Dominance*, B. Thorne and N. Henley, eds. Rowley, MA: Newbury House, 1975.

*Items identified by an asterisk are recommended as especially useful follow-ups.

Nonverbal Communication

Chapter 6
Nonverbal Communication

After studying the material in this chapter

You should understand

1. The five distinguishing characteristics of nonverbal communication.

2. The functions that nonverbal communication can serve.

3. The various types of nonverbal communication.

You should be able to

1. Describe your nonverbal behavior in any situation.

2. Identify nonverbal behavior that repeats, substitutes for, complements, accents, regulates, or contradicts a verbal message.

3. Analyze the attitudinal messages in examples of your own nonverbal behavior.

4. Share your interpretation of another's nonverbal behavior appropriately.

Key Terms

Accenting	Illustrators	Personal space
Chronemics	Intimate distance	Proxemics
Complementing	Kinesics	Public distance
Contradicting	Leakage	Regulating
Deception clues	Manipulators	Repeating
Disfluencies	Nonverbal communication	Social distance
Double messages	Paralanguage	Substituting
Emblems	Personal distance	Territory

People don't always say what they mean ... but their body gestures and movements tell the truth!

Will he ask you out? Is she encouraging you? Know what is really happening by understanding the secret language of body signals. You can:

Improve your sex life ...

Pick up your social life ...

Better your business life ...

Read Body Language *so that you can penetrate the personal secrets, both of intimates and total strangers ...*

Does her body say that she's a loose woman?

Does her body say that she's a phony?

Does her body say that she's a manipulator?

Does her body say that she's lonely?

Unless you've been trapped in a lead mine or doing fieldwork in the Amazon Basin, claims like these are probably familiar to you. Almost every drugstore, supermarket, and airport bookrack has its share of "body language" paperbacks. They promise that, for only a few dollars and with a fifth-grade reading ability, you can learn secrets that will change you from a fumbling social failure into a self-assured mindreader who can uncover a person's deepest secrets at a glance.

Claims like these aren't new. Eighteenth century Swiss physiognomist Johann Caspar Lavater claimed that the physical features of a forehead revealed characteristics of a personality (Lavater 1980). For example, a "retentive" forehead was the sign of "the most faithful, industrious, and justly discerning men on God's earth." Lavater claimed that a "French" forehead signified a "choleric" personality, the "firmness of which appears to boarder on harshness."

Observations like these, whether they are hundreds of years old or contemporary, are almost always exaggerations or fabrications. Don't misunderstand: There *is* a scientific body of knowledge about nonverbal communication, and it *has* provided many fascinating and valuable clues to human behavior. That's what this chapter is about. It's unlikely the next few pages will turn you instantly into a rich, sexy, charming communication superstar, but don't go away. Even without glamorous promises, a quick look at some facts about nonverbal communication shows that it's an important and valuable field to study.

Nonverbal Communication Defined

If *non* means "not" and *verbal* means "with words," then it seems logical that *nonverbal communication* would involve "communication without words." This definition is an oversimplification, however: It fails to distinguish between *vocal* communication (by mouth) and *verbal* communication (with words). As Table 6–1 shows, some nonverbal messages have a vocal element, whereas others do not. A better definition of **nonverbal communication** is "messages expressed by nonlinguistic means."

These nonlinguistic messages are important because what we *do* often conveys more meaning than what we *say*. Albert Mehrabian (1972), a psychologist working in the field of nonverbal behavior, claims that 93 percent of the emotional impact of a message comes from a nonverbal source, whereas only a paltry 7 percent is verbal. Anthropologist Ray Birdwhistell (1970) describes a 65–35 percent split between actions and words. Although we must not generalize too much from these figures (Hegstrom 1979), the point remains: Nonverbal communication contributes a great deal to shaping perceptions.

The power of nonverbal cues increases as we grow into adulthood. Children between the ages of six and twelve use a speaker's words to make

Table 6–1   Types of Communication

	Vocal Communication	Nonvocal Communication
Verbal Communication	Spoken Words	Written words
Nonverbal Communication	Tone of voice, sighs, screams, vocal qualities (loudness, pitch, and so on)	Gestures, movement, appearance, facial expression, and so on

Adapted from John Stewart and Gary D'Angelo, *Together: Communicating Interpersonally,* 2d ed. Reading, MA: Addison-Wesley, 1980: 22.

sense of a message (Pearson 1989: 73–74). But as adults, we rely more on nonverbal cues to form many impressions. For example, audiences put more emphasis on nonverbal cues than on words to decide whether speakers are honest (Hale and Stiff 1990; Stiff et al. 1990). They also use nonverbal behaviors to judge the character of speakers as well as their competence and composure; and differences in nonverbal behavior influence how much listeners are persuaded by a speaker (Burgoon et al. 1990).

You might ask how nonverbal communication can be so powerful. At first glance it seems as if meanings come from words. To answer this question, imagine that you've just arrived in a foreign country in which the inhabitants speak a language you don't understand. Visualize yourself on a crowded street, filled with many types of people, from the very rich to the very poor. In spite of these differences in wealth, there seems to be little social friction, with one exception. On one corner two people seem close to a fight. One man—he seems to be a shopkeeper—is furious at a customer, who seems to be complaining about an item he has just bought. Two police officers stroll by and obviously notice the commotion, but walk on unconcerned. Most of the pedestrians are in a great hurry, rushing off to who-knows-

where . . . all except one couple. They are oblivious to everything but each other, obviously in love.

Although you've never been here before, you feel comfortable because everyone seems friendly and polite. Shoppers murmur apologetically when they bump into you on the crowded sidewalks, and many people smile when your eyes meet theirs. In fact, you notice that one attractive stranger seems very friendly, and quite interested in you. In spite of the fact that you've been warned to watch out for shady characters, you know there's no danger here. "Why not?" you think. "It's a vacation." You smile back and both of you walk toward each other. . . .

Aside from being a pleasant daydream, this little experiment should have proved that it's possible to communicate without using words. With no knowledge of the language, you were able to make a number of assumptions about what was going on in that foreign country. You obtained a picture of the economic status of some of its inhabitants, observed some conflicts and speculated about their nature, noticed something about the law enforcement policy, formed impressions about the pace of life, and became acquainted with courtship practices. How did you do all this work? You tuned into the many nonverbal channels available: facial expressions, clothing, postures, gestures, vocal tones, and more. Of course, you don't have to travel abroad to recognize nonverbal messages, for they're present all the time. Because we're such a vocal society, we often ignore the other channels through which we all communicate; but they're always there.

Characteristics of Nonverbal Communication

The many types of nonverbal communication share some characteristics. Some of these characteristics are similar to verbal, linguistic means of communication; others are different.

NONVERBAL COMMUNICATION EXISTS

Our fantasy trip to the foreign country demonstrated that nonverbal messages exist. Even without talking, it's possible to get an idea about how others are feeling. In fact, you can often learn more about others by noticing what they do rather than what they say. Sometimes you might suspect people seem friendly, sometimes distant, sometimes tense, excited, bored, amused, or depressed. The point is that without any formal experience you can recognize and to some degree interpret messages that other people send nonverbally. In this chapter we want to sharpen the skills you already have, to give you a better grasp of the vocabulary of nonverbal language, and to show you how this understanding can help you know yourself and others better.

ALL BEHAVIOR HAS COMMUNICATIVE VALUE

Think back to a recent time you spent with another person. Suppose we asked you not to communicate any messages at all while with your partner. What would you have done? Closed your eyes? Withdrawn into a ball? Left the room? You can probably see that even these

behaviors communicate messages that mean you're avoiding contact.

Some people cannot speak and others are unable to hear. Is it possible not to communicate nonverbally? To answer this question, try Activity 1 on page 199.

Take a minute and try *not* communicating. Find a partner and spend some time trying not to disclose any messages to each other. What happened?

"I tell you, Mr. Arthur, this survey has no way of registering a nonverbal response!"

"That was unkind, darling. When their mouths turn up at the corners they want to be friends."
Used by permission of the estate of Michael ffolkes.

The impossibility of not communicating is extremely significant because it means that each of us is a kind of transmitter that cannot be shut off. No matter what we do, we send out messages that say something about ourselves. If, for instance, someone were observing you now, what nonverbal clues would they get about how you're feeling? Are you sitting forward or reclining back? Is your posture tense or relaxed? Are your eyes wide open, or do they keep closing? What does your facial expression communicate now? Can you make your face expressionless? Don't people with expressionless faces communicate something to you? Even uncontrollable behaviors can convey a message. You may not intend to show that you're embarrassed, but your blushing can still be a giveaway. Of course, not all behaviors (intentional or not) will be interpreted correctly: Your trembling hands might be taken as a sign of nervousness when you're really shivering from the cold. But whether or not your behavior is intentional, and whether it is interpreted accurately, all nonverbal behavior has the potential to create messages.

The fact that people are constantly displaying nonverbal behaviors is important because it means that we have an unending source of information available about ourselves and others. If you can tune into these signals, you will have clues about how others may be feeling and thinking, and the chances of responding better to their behavior can grow.

NONVERBAL MESSAGES ARE PRIMARILY ATTITUDINAL

Nonverbal communication is especially well suited to convey attitudes. It is less effective at conveying thoughts or ideas. You can test this assertion by seeing which of the following messages are easiest to express nonverbally:

1. "I'm tired."
2. "I'm in favor of capital punishment."
3. "I'm attracted to another person in the group."

Writer (to movie producer Sam Goldwyn): Mr. Goldwyn, I'm telling you a sensational story. I'm only asking for your opinion, and you fall asleep.

Goldwyn: Isn't sleeping an opinion?

---

4. "I think prayer in the schools should be allowed."
5. "I'm angry at someone in the room."

This experience shows that, short of charades, ideas don't lend themselves to nonverbal expressions nearly as well as attitudes. This explains why it's possible to understand the attitudes or feelings of others, even if you aren't able to understand the subject of their communication.

NONVERBAL COMMUNICATION IS AMBIGUOUS

Some words of caution before introducing you to a fourth feature of nonverbal communication: A great deal of ambiguity surrounds nonverbal behavior (Manusov 1990: 16). To understand what we mean, consider how you would interpret silence from your companion during an evening together. Consider all the possible meanings of this nonverbal behavior: warmth, anger, preoccupation, boredom, nervousness, thoughtfulness . . . the possibilities are many.

Not all nonverbal behavior is equally ambiguous. In laboratory settings, subjects are better at identifying positive facial expressions such as happiness, love, surprise, and interest than negative ones like fear, sadness, anger, and disgust (Druckmann et al. 1982: 52). In real life, however, spontaneous nonverbal expressions are so ambiguous that observers are unable to identify accurately what they mean (Motley and Camden 1988). Even apparently unambiguous

This couple has just learned that they won $1 million in the New Jersey state lottery.

emotions can be misinterpreted, however, as the photo above indicates. What do you imagine the couple is feeling? Grief? Anguish? Agony? After making a guess, check your skill by reading the accompanying caption.

Government authorities are often aware of the hazards of misinterpreting ambiguous nonverbal messages. White House experts recently updated the Washington-Moscow hot line that

---

"Boss," he said. "I've dozens of things to say to you. I've never loved anyone as much before. I've hundreds of things to say, but my tongue just can't manage them. So I'll dance them for you!"

NIKOS KAZANTZAKIS
Zorba the Greek

enables the United States and Soviet governments to communicate in times of crisis. Despite the available technology, experts rejected the idea of adding video and voice links because "in a crisis situation, we wouldn't want to leave room for mistaken interpretations or impressions that might be drawn from facial expressions or voice patterns" (*Newsweek* 1984).

The same kind of caution is wise when responding to nonverbal cues in more personal situations. Rather than jumping to conclusions about the meaning of a sigh, smile, slammed door, or yawn, it's far better to consider such messages as clues to be checked out: "When you yawned, I got the idea you might be tired of me. Is that right?" Popular advice on the subject notwithstanding, it's usually *not* possible to read a person like a book.

NONVERBAL COMMUNICATION IS CULTURE-BOUND

The significance of many nonverbal behaviors varies from one culture to another (Blonston 1985). The "A-OK" gesture made by joining thumb and forefinger to form a circle is a cheery affirmation to most Americans, but it has less positive meanings in other parts of the world (Ekman et al. 1984). In France and Belgium it means "You're worth zero." In Greece and Turkey it is a vulgar sexual invitation, usually meant as an insult. In light of such cross-cultural ambiguity, it's easy to imagine how an innocent tourist might wind up in serious trouble.

Less obvious cross-cultural differences can damage relationships without the people ever recognizing exactly what has gone wrong. Edward Hall (1969) points out that, whereas Americans are comfortable conducting business at a distance of roughly four feet, people from the Middle East stand much closer. It is easy to visualize the awkward advance and retreat pattern that might occur when two diplomats or businesspeople from these cultures meet. The Middle Easterner would probably keep moving forward to close the gap that feels so wide, while the American would continually back away. Both would feel uncomfortable, probably without knowing why.

Nonverbal communication may exist everywhere, but codes can differ from one culture to another. Discover some cultural differences by following the directions for Activity 2 on page 199.

Like distance, patterns of eye contact vary around the world (Kleinke et al. 1976; Watson 1970). A direct gaze is considered appropriate for speakers in Latin America, the Arab world, and southern Europe. On the other hand, Asians, Indians, Pakistanis, and northern Europeans gaze at a listener peripherally or not at all. In either case, deviations from the norm are likely to make a listener uncomfortable.

Differing cultural norms for nonverbal behavior make the potential for cross-cultural misunderstandings great. For example, many Anglo school teachers use quasi-questions that hint at the information they are seeking. An elementary school instructor might encourage the class to speak up by making an incorrect statement that demands refutation: "So twelve divided by four is six, right?" Most Anglo students would recognize this behavior as a way of testing their understanding. But this style of questioning is unfamiliar to many students raised in traditional black cultures, who aren't likely to respond until they are directly questioned by the instructor (Rubin 1986). Given this difference, it is easy to imagine how some teachers might view minority children as unresponsive or slow, when in fact they are simply following a different set of rules.

Despite these differences, many nonverbal behaviors are pan-cultural. Certain expressions have the same meanings around the world. Smiles and laughter are a universal signal of positive emotions, for example, while the same sour expressions convey displeasure in every culture (Weitz 1974). Charles Darwin (1872) believed that such expressions are the result of evolution, survival mechanisms that allowed early humans to convey emotional states before the development of language. The innateness of some facial expressions becomes even more clear when we examine the behavior of children born deaf and blind (Eibl-Eibesfeldt 1972). Despite a lack of social learning, these children display a broad range of expression. They smile, laugh, and cry in ways virtually identical to normal infants.

While nonverbal expressions like these may be universal, the way they are used varies widely around the world. In some cultures display rules discourage the overt demonstration of feelings like happiness or anger. In other cultures the same feelings are perfectly appropriate. Thus, a Japanese might appear much more controlled and placid than an Arab, when in fact their feelings might be identical.

The same principle operates closer to home among cocultures. For example Melanie Booth-Butterfield and Felicia Jordan (1988) found that black women in all-black groups were nonverbally more expressive and interrupted each other more than white women in all-white groups. This doesn't mean that black women always feel more intensely than their white counterparts. A more likely explanation is that the two groups follow different cultural rules. The researchers found that in racially mixed groups both black and white women moved closer to each others' style. This nonverbal convergence shows that skilled communicators can adapt their behavior when interacting with members of other cultures or cocultures in order to make the exchange more smooth and effective.

Student Reflection

Nonverbal Communication Varies from One Culture to Another

My parents are both from Mexico, and I was raised in a very traditional Mexican way. My current boyfriend's family is the first Anglo one I've spent very much time with, and their style is very different. When my relatives get together, the men usually go in one direction and the women in another. But in Steve's family everyone stays together much more. I was also surprised to see the men in Steve's family helping out so much by setting the table and even washing the dishes. Steve and his sister speak up when they disagree with their parents, so that his family argues a great deal. Sometimes the arguing is friendly and sometimes it is angry. At my home you would never see this! Sometimes I am a little uncomfortable in this culturally different family. I feel better when I remember that although the rules may be different the people are the same.

Differences Between Verbal and Nonverbal Communication

Nonverbal and verbal messages are both indispensable: It's hard to imagine how we could function without either one. Much of the value of these two ways of communicating come from their differences.

SINGLE VS. MULTIPLE CHANNELS

Most verbal messages—words, sentences, and paragraphs—reach us one at a time, rather like pearls on a string. In fact, it's physically impossible for a person to speak more than one word at a time. Unlike the spoken word, however, nonverbal messages don't arrive in such an orderly, sequential manner. Instead, they bombard us simultaneously from a multitude of channels. Consider the everyday act of meeting a person for the first time. On a verbal level there's relatively little information exchanged in the clichés that occupy the first few minutes of most conversations ("How's it going . . . " "Great weather we've been having . . . " "What's your major?"). But at the same moment the number of nonverbal messages available to you is overwhelming: the other person's facial expressions, postures, gestures; the clothing he or she wears,

---

It was terribly dangerous to let your thoughts wander when you were in any public place or within range of a telescreen. The smallest thing could give you away. A nervous tic, an unconscious look of anxiety, a habit of muttering to yourself—anything that carried with it the suggestion of abnormality, of having something to hide. In any case, to wear an improper expression on your face (to look incredulous when a victory was announced, for example) was itself a punishable offense. There was even a word for it in Newspeak: *facecrime*, it was called.

GEORGE ORWELL
Nineteen Eighty-four

---

the distance the person stands from you, and so on. In one way this multichannel onslaught of nonverbal messages is a boon, since it provides so many ways of learning about others. In another sense, however, the number of simultaneous messages is a problem, for it's difficult to recognize the overwhelming amount of nonverbal information we receive from others every moment.

DISCRETE VS. CONTINUOUS

Verbal messages—words, sentences, and paragraphs—form messages with clear beginnings and endings. In this sense we can judge whether or not others are communicating verbally by observing whether or not they are speaking or writing. Unlike the written and spoken word, however, nonverbal communication is continuous and never ending. As we've already said, nonverbal communication is a constant, unstoppable process. The postures, gestures, and other types of messages described in the following pages provide a constant flow of messages. Even the absence of a message (an unanswered letter or an unreturned phone call) is a message. As one communication expert said when referring to nonverbal communication, "Nothing never happens."

DELIBERATE VS. UNCONSCIOUS

While we usually think about what we want to say before speaking or writing, most nonverbal messages aren't deliberate. Of course we do pay attention to some of our nonverbal behavior: smiling when we want to convince others we're happy or making sure our handshake is firm to show that we're straightforward and decisive. But there are so many nonverbal channels that it's impossible to think about and control all of them. Thus, our slumping shoulders might contradict our smiles, and our sweating palms might cancel out all the self-confidence of our firm handshakes. The unconscious nature of most nonverbal behavior explains why it offers so many useful cues about how others are feeling.

CLEAR VS. AMBIGUOUS

While verbal communication can be confusing, we have already seen that most nonverbal cues are even more vague. Nonverbal messages aren't completely ambiguous, of course: It's probably accurate to guess that a frown signifies some sort of negative feeling and that a smile indicates a positive emotion. But we often need language to tell us why others feel as they do. Is the boss smiling because she likes your idea or because she finds it amusing but completely impractical? Does your instructor's frown indicate confusion with your remarks or disagreement? The best way to find out is to ask for a verbal clarification, not to depend on your reading of the nonverbal cues.

VERBAL VS. NONVERBAL IMPACT

When we are exposed to both verbal and nonverbal messages, research shows that we find the nonverbal signals much more powerful (summarized in Burgoon 1985). In a variety of settings (including job interviews, therapy sessions, first meetings), adults rely more on nonverbal messages than on words when interpreting the messages of others. Nonverbal cues are especially likely to carry weight when they contradict a speaker's words. In one series of experiments, friendly, neutral, and unfriendly verbal messages were paired with parallel nonverbal behaviors. Raters who judged the verbal and nonverbal messages separately found them equal in strength. But when the two messages were combined, the nonverbal statements carried as much as 12.5 times more weight than the verbal ones.

Functions of Nonverbal Communication

Although this chapter deals with nonverbal communication, don't get the idea that our words and actions are unrelated. Quite the opposite is true: Verbal and nonverbal communication are interconnected, although not always in the same way. Let's take a look at the various relationships between our words and other types of expression.

See for yourself how nonverbal communication can serve a variety of functions. Follow the directions in Activity 3 on page 200.

REPEATING

First, nonverbal behavior may be **repeating** a verbal message. If someone asked you for directions to the nearest drugstore, you could say, "Go north about two blocks," and then repeat your instructions nonverbally by pointing north. This kind of repetition is especially use-

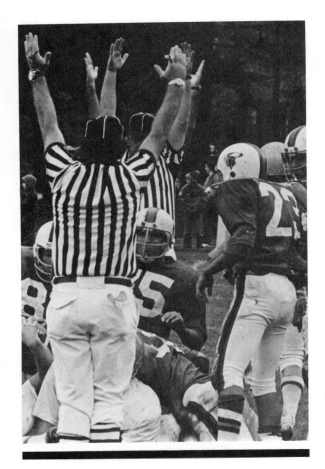

ful when we're describing an idea with a visual dimension, such as size, shape, or direction.

SUBSTITUTING

We can **substitute** nonverbal messages for verbal ones we communicate. For example, instead of saying, "Go north about two blocks," you could point north and add, "About two blocks." The usefulness of substitution goes far beyond simply describing physical ideas. For instance, the more you know someone, the easier it is to use nonverbal expressions as a kind of shorthand to substitute for words. When you see a familiar friend wearing a certain facial expression, it isn't necessary to ask, "What kind of day did you have?" In the same way, experience has probably shown you that certain kinds of looks, gestures, and other clues say far better than words, "I'm angry at you," or "I feel great."

Some nonverbal behaviors—called **emblems**—are culturally understood substitutes for verbal expressions. Nodding the head up and down is an accepted way of saying yes in most cultures. Likewise, a side-to-side head shake is a nonverbal way of saying no, and a shrug of the shoulders is commonly understood as meaning "I don't know" or "I'm not sure." Remember, however, that some emblems—like the "A-OK" sign we mentioned earlier—vary from one culture to another, and other nonverbal signs can be ambiguous even within a single culture. A wink, for example, might mean something entirely different to the person on the receiving end than it does to the winker.

Because of this potential ambiguity, it's often dangerous to substitute unspoken messages. Even with the people you know best, there's room for misunderstanding, and the potential for jumping to wrong conclusions increases the less you know the other person. Remember our warning: Nonverbal communication is ambiguous.

In the intercourse of social life, it is by little acts of watchful kindness recurring daily and hourly, by words, tones, gestures, looks, that affection is won and preserved.

GEORGE AUGUSTUS SALA

COMPLEMENTING AND ACCENTING

Whereas nonverbal emblems convey meaning independent of words, **illustrators** serve the functions of **complementing** and **accenting** verbal statements. Illustrators are behaviors that have no meaning of their own. Snapping your fingers, running your fingers through your hair, or pounding one fist into the other can accompany a positive statement in one instance and a negative one in others: The meaning of such gestures is specific to their context.

Emblems are used consciously; you roll your eyes and circle your finger around one ear to signal "He's crazy." Illustrators are usually unconscious (Ekman et al. 1984). We rarely plan the smiles and frowns, sighs and laughs, and all the other nonverbal behaviors that so richly complement and accent our words.

REGULATING

Nonverbal behaviors sometimes help control verbal interaction by **regulating** it. The best example of such regulation is the wide array of turn-taking signals in everyday conversation (Duncan 1972, 1974; Duncan and Fiske 1979). Research has shown that three nonverbal signals indicate a speaker has finished talking and is ready to yield to a listener: (1) changes in vocal intonation—a rising or falling in pitch at the end of a clause; (2) a drawl on the last syllable or the stressed syllable in a clause; (3) a drop in vocal pitch or loudness when speaking a common expression, such as "you know." You can see how these regulators work by observing almost any conversation.

Eye contact is another way of regulating verbal communication. Lack of visual contact is one way to signal turn taking, or even to exclude an unwanted person from a conversation. Speakers make surprisingly little eye contact during a conversation, but they commonly focus on another person when coming to the end of their turn. Children (and some socially insensitive adults) have not learned all the subtle signals of such turn taking. Through a rough series of trial and error (*very* rough in some homes), children finally learn how to "read" other people well enough to avoid interrupting behaviors.

CONTRADICTING

Finally, and often most significantly, nonverbal behavior can often *contradict* the spoken word.

Dr. Oliver Sacks tells the story in *The Man Who Mistook His Wife for a Hat,* a study of bizarre neurological disorders. As Dr. Sacks passed through a hospital aphasia ward, the patients were all roaring with laughter. The President was on the television screen, giving a serious speech. Why were they laughing?

Victims of global aphasia can no longer understand the meaning of words. But they remain extraordinarily sensitive to tone of voice, vocal color, body language. "Thus the feeling I sometimes have—which all of us who work closely with aphasiacs have—that one cannot lie to an aphasiac," Dr. Sacks explains.

"He cannot grasp your words, and so cannot be deceived by them; but what he grasps he grasps with infallible precision, namely the *expression* that goes with the words. . . . Thus it was the grimaces, the histrionisms, the false gestures and, above all, the false tones and cadences of the voice, which rang false for these wordless but immensely sensitive patients."

JACK ROSENTHAL
"The Ring of Untruth"

If you said, "Go north about two blocks" and pointed south, your nonverbal message would be **contradicting** what you said.

Although sending such incompatible messages might sound foolish at first, there are times when we deliberately do just that. One frequent use of **double messages** (as they're often called) is to send a message politely but clearly that might be difficult to handle if it were expressed in words. For instance, think of a time when you became bored with a conversation while your companion kept rambling on. At such a time the most straightforward statement would be "I'm tired of talking to you and want to go meet someone else." Although it might feel good to be so direct, this kind of honesty is impolite for anyone over five years of age.

Instead of being blunt, people frequently rely on nonverbal methods of sending the same message. While nodding politely and murmuring, "uh-huh" and "No kidding?" at the appropriate times, you can signal a desire to leave by looking around the room, turning slightly away from the speaker, or even making a point of yawning. In most cases such clues are enough to

---

I suppose it was something you said
That caused me to tighten
And pull away.
And when you asked,
"What is it?"
    I, of course, said,
"Nothing."
Whenever I say, "Nothing,"
You may be very certain there is something.
The something is a cold, hard lump of Nothing.

LOIS WYSE

---

end the conversation without the awkwardness of expressing outright what's going on.

Courtship is one area in which double messages abound. Even in these liberated times, the answer "no" to a romantic proposition may mean "yes." Of course, it may also really mean an emphatic "no." The success of many relationships has depended on the ability of one partner to figure out—mostly using nonverbal messages—when a double message is being sent, and when to take the words at face value.

Deception is perhaps the most interesting type of double message. Signals of deception (often called **leakage**) can occur in every type of nonverbal behavior. Some nonverbal channels are more revealing than others, however. Facial expressions are less revealing than body clues, probably because deceivers pay more attention to controlling their faces (Ekman and Friesen 1969). Even more useful is the voice, which offers a rich variety of leakage clues (DePaulo et al. 1980; Greene et al. 1985; Mehrabian 1971). In one experiment subjects who were encouraged to be deceitful made more speech errors, spoke for shorter periods of time, and had a lower rate of speech than others who were encouraged to express themselves honestly. Another study (Streeter et al. 1977) revealed that the vocal frequency of a liar's voice tends to be higher than that of a truth teller. Research also shows that deceivers delivering a prepared lie responded more quickly than truth tellers, mainly because there was less thinking involved (Greene et al. 1985). When unprepared, however, deceivers generally took longer than both prepared deceivers and truth tellers.

As this research shows, deceivers don't always broadcast cues that reveal their lies. Nonverbal evidence of lying is most likely to occur when the deceivers haven't had a chance to rehearse, when they feel strongly about the information being hidden, or when they feel anxious or guilty about their lies. Even when deception

Table 6–2   Circumstances in Which a Deceiver Leaks Nonverbal Clues to Deception

Leakage Most Likely	Leakage Least Likely
Wants to hide emotions being experienced at the moment.	Wants to hide information unrelated to emotions.
Feels strongly about the information being hidden.	Has no strong feelings about the information being hidden.
Feels apprehensive about the deception.	Feels confident about the deception.
Feels guilty about being deceptive.	Experiences little guilt about the deception.
Gets little enjoyment from being deceptive.	Enjoys the deception.
Needs to construct the message carefully while delivering it.	Knows the deceptive message well and has rehearsed it.

Based on material from "Mistakes When Deceiving" by Paul Ekman, in *The Clever Hans Phenomenon: Communication with Horses, Whales, Apes, and People,* Thomas A. Sebeok and Robert Rosenthal, eds. New York: New York Academy of Sciences, 1981: 269–78.

clues are abundant, they aren't necessarily direct signals of lying itself; rather, they may reflect the anxiety that some liars feel. Table 6–2 outlines some conditions under which liars are likely to betray themselves through nonverbal leakage.

Despite the nonverbal clues, it isn't always easy to detect deception. Sometimes the very suspicion that someone is lying can improve the deceiver's attempts to hide the truth. David Buller and his associates (1989) discovered that communicators who probe the messages of deceptive communicators are no better at detecting lies than those who don't investigate the truth of a message. The researchers speculate that deceivers who are questioned become more vigilant about revealing the truth, and that their greater caution results in a better coverup of deception cues.

Some people are better than others at uncovering deception. For example, younger people are better than older ones at uncovering lies (Lieberman et al. 1988). Women are consistently more accurate than men at detecting lying and what the underlying truth really is (McCornack and Parks 1990). The same research showed that as people become more intimate their accuracy in detecting lies declines. This is a surprising fact: Intuition suggests that we ought to be better at judging honesty as we become more familiar with others.

When one is pretending, the entire body revolts!

ANAIS NIN

"*I've had eye contact with women before, Marcia—but never like this.*"

Despite their overall accuracy at detecting lies, women are more inclined to fall for the deception of intimate partners than men.

Types of Nonverbal Communication

So far we've talked about the characteristics of nonverbal communication and the ways unspoken messages relate to our use of words. Now it's time to look at the many types of nonverbal communication.

FACE AND EYES

The face and eyes are probably the most noticeable parts of the body. However, the nonverbal messages from the face and eyes are not the easiest to read. The face is a tremendously complicated channel of expression to interpret for three reasons.

First, it's hard to describe the number and kind of expressions commonly produced by the face and eyes. For example, researchers have found that there are at least eight distinguishable positions of the eyebrows and forehead,

Fie, fie upon her!
There's language in her eyes, her cheek, her lip.
Nay, her foot speaks; her wanton spirits look out
at every joint and motive in her body.

WILLIAM SHAKESPEARE
Troilus and Cressida

eight more of the eyes and lids, and ten for the lower face (Ekman and Friesen 1975). When you multiply this complexity by the number of emotions we experience, you can see why it would be almost impossible to compile a dictionary of facial expressions and their corresponding emotions.

Facial expressions can also be difficult to read because they change with incredible speed. For example, slow-motion films have shown expressions fleeting across a subject's face in as short a time as one-fifth of a second. Also, it seems that different emotions show most clearly in different parts of the face: happiness and surprise in the eyes and lower face; anger in the lower face, brows, and forehead; fear and sadness in the eyes; and disgust in the lower face.

Finally, most people are reasonably successful at disguising or censoring undesired messages (O'Hair et al. 1981). In spite of this censoring, the rapid speed at which expressions can change, and the inability of senders to see their own faces and make sure they send the desired messages, means that each of us does convey a great deal of "true" information, whether we want to or not.

Two prominent researchers in this area, Paul Ekman and Wallace Friesen (1975), talk about three ways in which we falsify messages by controlling our facial expression. First, sometimes we hide a lack of feeling by *simulating* For

example, suppose someone tells you that a friend you know only casually was in a minor auto accident. You may not be particularly concerned by this news, but you feign an expression of upset because you feel the situation calls for it. The real feeling you had was closer to indifference, but you created the upset expression to meet the demands of the social situation.

At other times we avoid expressing an undesired emotion by *neutralizing* our expression. For example, suppose the doorbell chimes just as you get into the shower. You have to shut off the water, dry yourself, jump into a robe, and rush to the door before the person who rang walks off—all in about twenty seconds. Your expression as you race to the door is probably one of anger, or at least irritation. Just as you open the door you neutralize the expression, toning it down, covering the expression of the real feeling.

There's a big difference between observing nonverbal behaviors and interpreting their meaning. Explore the distinction by trying Activity 4 on page 200.

A third technique of falsifying involves *masking* a true emotion with one seemingly more appropriate. Boring classes may result in half-closed eyes, frequent yawns, and a dull, glazed-over expression, but they also give rise to a common mask for boredom: an "interested" face, one with wide-open eyes, a brow wrinkled to convey thought, and the expression of other more situation-appropriate responses.

The face is the mirror of the mind, and eyes without speaking confess the secrets of the heart.

ST. JEROME

The eyes themselves can send several kinds of messages. Gazes and glances are usually signals of the looker's interest. The *type* of interest can vary, however. Sometimes looking is a conversational turn-taking signal that says, "I'm finished talking. Now it's your turn." Gazing also is a good indicator of liking (Druckmann et al. 1982: 77–79). Sometimes eye contact *reflects* liking that already exists, and at other times it actually *creates* or *increases* liking—hence the expression "making eyes." Paradoxically, there are courtship games in which the players deliberately hide their liking by avoiding one another's eyes.

In other situations eye contact indicates interest, but not attraction or approval. A teacher who glares at a rowdy student or a police officer who "keeps an eye on" a suspect are both signaling their interest with their eyes.

Several studies show that a high degree of eye contact can influence verbal responses. In interviews where the questioner gazed intently while asking questions, subjects made more self-references and revealed more intimate information (Snow 1972; Ellsworth and Ross 1976). These findings have practical implications for information seekers of all types: If you want to get the most out of your conversation, keep your gaze focused on the other person.

Even the pupils of our eyes communicate. E. H. Hess and J. M. Polt (1960) measured the amount of pupil dilation while showing men and women various pictures. The results of the experiment were interesting: The pupils grow larger in proportion to the degree of interest a person has in an object. For example, men's pupils grew about 18 percent larger when looking at pictures of a naked woman, and the rate of dilation for women looking at a naked man's picture was 20 percent. The greatest increase in pupil size occurred when women looked at a picture of a mother and infant. A good salesper-

...the expression of a well-made man appears
not only in his face,
It is in his limbs and joints also, it is curiously in
the joints of his hip and wrists,
It is in his walk, the carriage of his neck, the flex
of his waist and knees, dress does not hide him...

WALT WHITMAN
Leaves of Grass

son can increase profits by being aware of pupil dilation. As Edward Hall (1969) describes, he was once in a Middle East bazaar, where an Arab merchant insisted that a customer looking at his jewelry buy a certain piece to which the shopper hadn't been paying much attention. The vendor had been watching the pupils of the buyer's eyes and had known what the buyer really wanted.

BODY MOVEMENT

Another way we communicate nonverbally is through the physical movement of our bodies: our posture, gestures, physical orientation to others, and so on. Social scientists use the term **kinesics** to describe the study of human body movements.

To appreciate the communicative value of kinesic messages, stop reading for a moment and notice how you're sitting. What does your position say nonverbally about how you feel? Are there any other people near you now? What messages do you get from their present posture? By paying attention to the postures of those around you, as well as to your own, you'll find another channel of nonverbal communication that reveals how people feel about themselves and others.

The English language indicates the deep links between posture and communication. English is full of expressions that tie emotional states with body postures:

"I won't take this lying down!"

"He can't stand on his own two feet."

"She has to carry a heavy burden."

"Take a load off your back."

"You're all wrapped up in yourself."

"Don't be so uptight!"

Such phrases show an awareness of posture, even if it's often unconscious. The main reason we miss most posture messages is that they aren't too obvious. It's seldom that people who feel weighed down by a problem hunch over dramatically. When we're bored, we usually don't lean back and slump enough to embarrass the person with whom we're bored. In interpreting posture, then, the key is to look for small changes that might be shadows of the way people feel.

Psychologist Albert Mehrabian (1972) has found that other postural keys to feelings are tension and relaxation. He says that we take relaxed postures in nonthreatening situations and tighten up when threatened. We can tell a good deal about how others feel simply by watching how tense or loose they seem to be. For example, he suggests that the degree of tenseness in business interactions can reveal status differences: The lower-status person is generally the more rigid and tense appearing, whereas the one with higher status is more relaxed. Often we picture a "chat" with the boss (or professor or judge) this way; we sit ramrod straight while our "superior" leans back in a chair.

The same principle applies to social situations. Often you'll see someone laughing and talking as if perfectly at home, with a posture

James Thurber.

that shouts nervousness. Some people never relax, and their posture shows it.

We use our entire body to communicate through postures, but we also express feelings with just one body part through gesturing. Like other forms of nonverbal communication, gestures can either reinforce or contradict a speaker's words. We've all seen the reinforcing power of certain body movements. For instance, imagine the gestures that would accompany the following statements:

"What can I do about it?"

"I can't stand it anymore!"

"Now let me tell you something!"

"Easy now. It'll be all right."

It was easy to envision what gestures should accompany each message, wasn't it? You can see what an important role these movements play by imagining a speaker expressing the same words without gesturing. Somehow the speaker would seem less involved or sincere. In fact, an absence of gestures is usually a good indication that the speaker may be feeling unenthusiastic about the subject being discussed.

Sometimes gestures are intentional—a cheery wave or thumbs up, for example. In other cases, however, our gestures are unconscious. Occasionally an unconscious gesture will consist of an unambiguous emblem, such as a shrug that clearly means "I don't know." Another revealing set of gestures is what psychiatrist Albert Scheflen (1965) calls "preening behaviors"—stroking or combing one's hair, glancing in a mirror, and rearranging one's clothing. Scheflen suggests that these behaviors signal some sort of interest in the other person: perhaps an unconscious sexual come-on or perhaps a sign of less intimate interest. More often, however, gestures are ambiguous. In addition to illustrators, another group of ambiguous gestures consists what we usually call *fidgeting*—movements in which one part of the body grooms, massages, rubs, holds, fidgets, pinches, picks, or otherwise manipulates another part. Social scientists call these behaviors **manipulators.** Social rules may discourage us from performing more manipulators in public, but people still do so without noticing.

Research reveals what common sense suggests—that increased use of manipulators is often a sign of discomfort (Ekman and Friesen 1974). But not *all* fidgeting signals uneasiness. People also are likely to use manipulators when relaxed. When they let their guard down (either alone or with friends), they will be more likely to fiddle with an earlobe, twirl a strand of hair, clean their fingernails. Whether or not the fidgeter is hiding something, observers are likely to interpret manipulators as a signal of dishonesty. Since not all fidgeters are liars, it's important not to jump to conclusions about the meaning of manipulations.

Actually, *too few* gestures may be as significant an indicator of double messages as *too many* (Ekman 1985). Lack of gesturing may signal a lack of interest, sadness, boredom, or low enthusiasm. Illustrators also decrease whenever someone is cautious about speaking. For these reasons, a careful observer will look for either an increase or a decrease in the usual level of gestures.

Gestures can produce a wide range of reactions in receivers (Druckmann et al. 1982: 71–72). In many situations, the right kinds of gesturing can increase persuasiveness. Increasing hand and arm movements, a leaning forward, fidgeting less, and keeping limbs open all make a speaker more effective at influencing others. Even more interesting is the fact that persuasiveness increases when one person mirrors another's movements. When persuader and audience are reasonably similar, reciprocating the other person's gestures has a positive effect, whereas acting in a contrary manner is likely to have the opposite result.

People who gesture appropriately often create impressions that differ from those of less-expressive people: They are rated as being more warm, casual, agreeable, and energetic. They also are viewed as more enthusiastic, considerate, approachable, and likable. On the other hand, less-expressive people are viewed as more logical, cold, and analytic. Not only are

they less persuasive; they are viewed as less likable in general.

Some kinds of gestures reveal **deception clues** (Ekman and Friesen 1974). Deceivers tend to display more hand-shrug emblems, use fewer illustrators to punctuate and emphasize their points, and engage in more face-play than do truth tellers. In other words, liars do more fiddling that is unrelated to a message, and they are likely to use more gestures that complement their verbal message.

As with almost any nonverbal behavior, the context in which gestures occur can make all the difference in the results they produce. Animated movements that will be well received in a cooperative social setting may seem like signals of aggression or attempts at domination in a more competitive setting. Fidgeting that might suggest deviousness in a bargaining session could be appropriate when you offer a nervous apology in a personal situation. In any case, trying to manufacture insincere, artificial gestures (or any other nonverbal behaviors) will probably backfire. A more useful goal is to recognize the behaviors you find yourself spontaneously delivering and to consider how they reflect the attitudes you already feel. Impression management has its uses, but it is a tricky skill.

TOUCH

Besides being the earliest means we have of making contact with others, touching is essential to our healthy development (Jones and Yarbrough 1985). During the nineteenth and early twentieth centuries a large percentage of children born every year died from a disease then called *marasmus*, which translated from Greek means "wasting away." In some orphanages the mortality rate was nearly 100 percent, but even children in the most "progressive" homes, hospitals, and other institutions

As children develop, their need for being touched continues. In his excellent book *Touching: The Human Significance of the Skin* (1971), Ashley Montagu describes research suggesting that allergies, eczema, and other health problems are in part caused by a person's lack of mother-contact as an infant. Although Montagu says that these problems develop early in life, he also cites cases where adults suffering from conditions as diverse as asthma and schizophrenia have been successfully treated by psychiatric therapy that uses extensive physical contact. Research shows that touch between therapists and clients has the potential to encourage a variety of beneficial changes: more self-disclosure, client self-acceptance, and more positive client-therapist relationships (Wilson 1982; Driscoll et al. 1988).

Touch seems to increase a child's mental functioning as well as physical health. L. J. Yarrow (1963) conducted surveys showing that babies who have been given plenty of physical stimulation by their mothers have significantly higher IQs than those receiving less contact.

Touch also plays a large part in how we respond to others and to our environment. (See Thayer 1988 for a review of research on this subject.) For example, touch increases self-disclosure, verbalization of psychiatric patients, and the preference children have for their counselors. Touch also increases compliance. In a study by Chris Kleinke (1977), subjects were approached by a female confederate who requested that they return a dime left in the phone booth from which they had just emerged. When the request was accompanied by a light touch on the subject's arm, the probability that the subject would return the dime increased significantly. In a similar experiment (Willis and Hamm 1980), subjects were asked by a male or female confederate to sign a petition or complete a rating scale. Again, subjects were more likely to cooperate when they were touched lightly on the arm. In the rating-scale variation

died regularly from the ailment (Halliday 1948). When researchers finally tracked down the causes of this disease, they found that the infants suffered from lack of physical contact with parents or nurses, rather than from lack of nutrition, medical care, or other factors. The infants hadn't been touched enough, and died as a result. From this knowledge came the practice of "mothering" children in institutions—picking the baby up, carrying it around, and handling it several times each day. At one hospital that began this practice, the death rate of infants fell from between 30 and 35 percent to below 10 percent (Bakwin 1949).

of the study, the results were especially dramatic: 70 percent of those who were touched complied, whereas only 40 percent of the untouched subjects were willing to cooperate (indicating a predisposition not to comply).

An additional power of touch is its on-the-job utility. One study showed that fleeting touches on the hand and shoulder resulted in larger tips for restaurant waiters (Crusco and Wetzel 1984).

Touch can communicate many messages. Jones and Yarbrough (1985) catalogued twelve different kinds of touches, including "positive," "playful," "control," and "ritualistic." Some types of touch indicate varying degrees of aggression. Others signify types of relationship (Heslin and Alper 1983):

> functional/professional (dental exam, haircut)
>
> social/polite (handshake)
>
> friendship/warmth (clap on back, Spanish *abrazo*)
>
> love/intimacy (holding hands, hugs)
>
> sexual arousal (some kisses, strokes)

You might object to the examples following each of these categories, saying that some nonverbal behaviors occur in several types of relationships. A kiss, for example, can mean anything from a polite but superficial greeting to the most intense arousal. What makes a given touch more or less intense? Researchers have suggested a number of factors:

> what part of the body does the touching
>
> what part of the body is touched
>
> how long the touch lasts
>
> how much pressure is used
>
> whether there is movement after contact is made
>
> whether anyone else is present
>
> the situation in which the touch occurs
>
> the relationship between the persons involved

Student Reflection

The Power of Touch

At the day-care center where I work there is a woman who is fantastic at comforting unhappy kids. She has less training than anyone there, but she has a way of calming down even the most miserable children. After watching her for a while, I realized that she is almost constantly touching the kids. She rumples hair, pats shoulders, gives hugs, and does lots of hand-holding. I'm sure there's more to her skill than that, but touching is a big part of why the kids love her so much.

From this list you can see that there is, indeed, a complex language of touch. Because nonverbal messages are inherently ambiguous, it's no surprise that they can often be misunderstood. Is a hug playful or suggestive of stronger feelings? Is a touch on the shoulder a friendly gesture or an attempt at domination? Research suggests the interpretation can depend on a variety of factors, including the sex of the people involved, ethnic background, and marital status, among others. Such ambiguity shows the importance of checking to be sure your interpretations are accurate.

In spite of the need for making physical contact with others, North American and northern European societies discourage much touching. Anyone who has traveled to other countries, particularly in Latin America, southern Europe, and parts of Africa, has noticed the differences in the amount of contact between citizens there and in the United States, Canada, and northern Europe.

The unconscious parental feelings communicated through touch or lack of touch can lead to feelings of confusion and conflict in a child. Sometimes a "modern" parent will say all the right things but not want to touch his child very much. The child's confusion comes from the inconsistency of levels: if they really approve of me so much like they say they do, why won't they touch me?

WILLIAM SCHUTZ

In the United States touching is generally more appropriate for women than for men (Jones 1986; Derlega et al. 1989). Males touch their male friends less than they touch their female friends, and also less than females touch their female friends. Fear of homosexuality seems to be a strong reason why men are reluctant to touch one another. Although females are more comfortable about touching than men, gender isn't the only factor that shapes contact. In general, the degree of touch comfort goes along with openness to expressing intimate feelings, an active interpersonal style, and satisfactory relationships (Fromme et al. 1989).

The amount of touching usually decreases with age (Knapp 1978: 244–46). Sixth graders touch each other less than do first graders. Parents touch their older children less often than their younger ones. As young children, most North Americans receive at least a modest amount of physical contact from their parents. The next time most can expect to receive this level of physical caring won't come until they have chosen a partner. Even then, the nurturing seemingly brought by physical contact will most often come only from that partner—a heavy demand for one person to carry.

Associated with (but not always the same as) love and intimacy is the sexual side of touching. It's obvious that sex can be one way of expressing caring for a partner. But especially in a touch-starved culture, sex can also serve another purpose not necessarily connected with intimate love or affection: It may simply be a socially acceptable way of touching and being touched by another human being. Although it's possible to argue that there's nothing wrong with making this kind of contact, it's sad to think that a sexual act is one of the very few ways to touch another person acceptably in a manner more personal than a handshake. Perhaps if we lived in a culture where physical contact was more acceptable, many people could achieve the touching they seem to need without resorting to sex out of desperation. Then sex would be valued and enjoyed when the time was right, not overused as the only way to bridge the gap between people.

VOICE

The voice itself is another channel of nonverbal communication. Social scientists use the term **paralanguage** to describe nonverbal, vocal messages: rate, pitch, tone, volume, and so on.

The way a message is spoken can give the same word or words many meanings. For example, note how many meanings come from a single sentence just by shifting the emphasis from one word to another:

This is a fantastic communication book.

(Not just any book, but *this* one in particular.)

This is a *fantastic* communication book.

(This book is superior, exciting.)

This is a fantastic *communication* book.

(The book is good as far as communication goes; it may not be so great as literature or drama.)

This is a fantastic communication *book*.

(It's not a play or record, it's a book.)

There are many other ways our voice communicates—through its tone, speed, pitch, volume, number and length of pauses, and **disfluencies** (such as stammering, use of "uh," "um," "er," and so on). All these factors can do a great deal to reinforce or contradict the message our words convey.

Researchers have identified the power of paralanguage through the use of content-free speech—ordinary speech that has been electronically manipulated so that the words are unintelligible, but the paralanguage remains unaffected. (Hearing a foreign language that you don't understand has the same effect.) Subjects who hear content-free speech can consistently recognize the emotion being expressed, as well as identify its strength (Scherer et al. 1972; Starkweather 1961).

The impact of paralinguistic cues is strong. In fact, listeners pay more attention to paralanguage than to the content of the words when asked to determine a speaker's attitudes (Burns and Beier 1973). Furthermore, when vocal factors contradict a verbal message (as when a speaker shouts "I am *not* angry!"), listeners judge the speaker's intention from the paralanguage, not the words themselves (Mehrabian and Weiner 1967).

Vocal changes that contradict spoken words are not easy to conceal. If the speaker is trying to hide fear or anger, the voice will probably sound higher and louder, and the rate of talk may be faster than normal. Sadness produces the opposite vocal pattern: quieter, lower-pitched speech delivered at a slower rate (Ekman 1985: 109–10).

Sarcasm is one instance in which we use both emphasis and tone of voice to change a statement's meaning to the opposite of its verbal message. Experience this reversal yourself with the following three statements. First say them literally, and then say them sarcastically.

1. "You look terrific!"
2. "I really had a wonderful time on my blind date."
3. "There's nothing I like better than calves' brains on toast."

As with other nonverbal messages, people often ignore or misinterpret the vocal nuances of sarcasm. Members of certain groups—children, people with weak intellectual skills, and poor listeners—are more likely to misunderstand sarcastic messages than are others (Andersen 1984).

Communication through paralanguage isn't always intentional. Often our voices give us away when we're trying to create an impression different than our actual feelings. For example, you've probably had experiences of trying to sound calm and serene when you were really seething with inner nervousness. Maybe your deception went along perfectly for a while—just the right smile, no telltale fidgeting of the hands, posture appearing relaxed—and then, without being able to do a thing about it, right in the middle of your relaxed comments, your voice squeaked! The charade was over.

In addition to reinforcing or contradicting messages, some vocal factors influence the way a speaker is perceived by others. People with more attractive voices are rated more highly than those whose speech sounds less attractive (Zuckerman and Driver 1989). Just what makes a voice attractive can vary. As Figure 6–1 shows, culture can make a difference. Surveys show that there are both similarities and differences between what Mexicans and Americans view as the "ideal" voice. Even in the same culture, vocal standards can differ. For example, breathiness in a man causes him to be perceived as artistic, and in a woman causes her to be perceived as

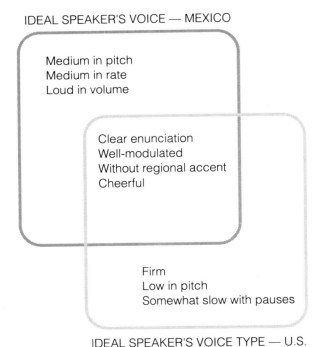

IDEAL SPEAKER'S VOICE — MEXICO

Medium in pitch
Medium in rate
Loud in volume

Clear enunciation
Well-modulated
Without regional accent
Cheerful

Firm
Low in pitch
Somewhat slow with pauses

IDEAL SPEAKER'S VOICE TYPE — U.S.

Figure 6–1   A Comparison of the Ideal Speaker's Voice
Types in Mexico and the U.S.

Reproduced from Carol A. Valentine, and Banisa Saint
Damian, "Communicative Power: Gender and Culture as
Determinants of the Ideal Voice." In *Women and
Communicative Power: Theory, Research, and Practice*,
Carol A. Valentine and Nancy Hoar, eds. Annandale, VA:
Speech Communication Association, 1988, p. 62.

The degree to which vocal factors communicate is extensive, as Lawrence Rosenfeld and Jean Civikly point out in *With Words Unspoken: The Nonverbal Experience* (1976). From vocal cues *alone* (people in these studies could not see the person speaking), we can determine age, differentiate "big" from "small" people, and judge personality characteristics, such as dominance, introversion, and sociability; we can detect certain emotions (although fear and nervousness, love and sadness, and pride and satisfaction are often confused). Interestingly, from vocal cues alone we can also determine a person's status—even on the basis of *single word cues*. We don't need more than a few seconds' worth of a speech sample.

PROXEMICS AND TERRITORIALITY

Proxemics is the study of how people and animals use the space around them. Before we discuss this fascinating area of research, try the following experiment:

Choose a partner, go to opposite sides of the room, and face each other. Very slowly begin walking toward each other while carrying on a conversation. You might simply talk about how you feel as you experience the activity. As you move closer, be aware of any change in your feelings. Continue moving slowly toward each other until you are only an inch or so apart. Remember how you feel at this point. Now, while still facing each other, back up until you're at a comfortable distance for carrying on your conversation.

During this experiment your feelings will most likely change at least three times. During the first phase, when you were across the room from your partner, you probably felt unnaturally far away. Then, as you neared a point about three feet distant, you probably felt like stopping; this is the distance at which two people in our culture normally stand while con-

petite, pretty, and shallow. Both men and women suffer being viewed as the same stereotypes when they speak with a flat voice: They are perceived as sluggish, cold, and withdrawn. Both men and women also suffer stereotyping associated with an increase in speaking rate: They are perceived as more animated and extroverted. Nasality is probably the most socially offensive vocal cue, giving rise to a host of perceived undesirable characteristics.

versing socially. If your partner wasn't someone you're emotionally close to, you probably began to feel quite uncomfortable as you moved through this normal range and came closer; it's possible that you had to force yourself not to move back. Some people find this phase so uncomfortable that they can't get closer than twenty inches or so to their partner.

The reason for your discomfort has to do with your spatial needs. Each of us carries around a sort of invisible bubble of **personal space** wherever we go. We think of the area inside this bubble as our own—almost as much a part of us as our own bodies. As you moved closer to your partner, the distance between your bubbles narrowed and at a certain point disappeared altogether: Your space had been invaded, and this is the point at which you probably felt uncomfortable. As you moved away again, your partner retreated out of your bubble, and you felt more relaxed.

Of course, if you were to try this experiment with someone close to you—your husband, wife, girlfriend, or boyfriend—you might not have felt any discomfort at all, even while touching. On the other hand, if you'd been approaching someone who made you uncomfortable—a total stranger or someone you disliked—you probably would have stopped farther away from them. The reason is that our personal bubbles vary in size according to the person we're with and the situation we're in. It's precisely the varying size of our personal space—the distance that we put between ourselves and others—that gives a nonverbal clue to our feelings.

D. Russell Crane and his associates (1987) tried just such an experiment. They tested over one hundred married couples, asking partners to walk toward one another and stop when they reached a "comfortable conversational distance." They then gave each partner a battery of tests to measure their marital intimacy, desire for change, and potential for divorce. The

Student Reflection
Distance Reflects Attitudes

Kit and I don't talk very much about our relationship, but I can always tell where we stand (no pun intended) by the distance between us. Things are good, we spend lots of time in close proximity. For example, we'll sit close together, even if we're reading or doing work. But the distance increases when something's wrong between us. One of us will come into a room and the other will leave. When we are together, we'll put the maximum amount of space between us—sitting opposite each other at the table instead of at adjacent sides, for instance. The amount of space between us is almost a barometer of our feelings.

researchers discovered that there was a strong relationship between distance and marital happiness: The average space between distressed couples was about 25 percent greater than between satisfied partners. On average, the happy couples stood 11.4 inches apart, while the distance between unhappy spouses averaged 14.8 inches.

In another study, Mark Snyder (1980) reported that the distance subjects unconsciously placed between themselves and others was a good indication of their prejudices. All the subjects were polled on their attitudes about homosexuality. Half the interviewers, who were confederates of the experimenter, wore "Gay

Drawing by Bernard Schoenbaum; © 1983
The New Yorker Magazine, Inc.

and Proud" buttons and mentioned their membership in the Association of Gay Psychologists. The other interviewers wore no buttons and simply identified themselves as graduate students. Despite their expressions of tolerance, subjects seated themselves almost a foot further away from the apparently gay interviewers of the same sex.

Anthropologist Edward T. Hall (1969) has defined four distances we use in our everyday lives. He says that we choose a particular one depending upon how we feel toward others at a given time, and that by "reading" which distance people take, we can get some insight into their feelings.

Intimate Distance The first of Hall's zones begins with skin contact and ranges out to about eighteen inches. We usually use **intimate distance** with people who are emotionally close to us, and then mostly in private situations—making love, caressing, comforting, protecting. By allowing someone to move into our intimate distance, we let them enter our personal space. When we let them in voluntarily, it's usually a sign of trust: We've willingly lowered our defenses. On the other hand, when someone invades this most personal area without our consent, we usually feel threatened. You may have had this feeling during the last exercise when your partner intruded into your space

Once I heard a hospital nurse describing doctors. She said there were beside-the-bed doctors, who were interested in the patient, and foot-of-the-bed doctors, who were interested in the patient's condition. They unconsciously expressed their emotional involvement—or lack of it—by where they stood.

EDWARD HALL

without any real invitation from you. It also explains the discomfort we sometimes feel when forced into crowded places, such as buses or elevators, with strangers. At times like these the standard behavior in our society is to draw away or tense our muscles and avoid eye contact. This is a nonverbal way of signaling, "I'm sorry for invading your territory, but the situation forced me."

In courtship situations a critical moment usually occurs when one member of a couple first moves into the other's intimate zone. If the partner being approached does not retreat, this usually signals that the relationship is moving into a new stage. On the other hand, if the reaction to the advance is withdrawal to a greater distance, the initiator should get the message that it isn't yet time to get more intimate. We remember from our dating experiences the significance of where on the car seat our companions chose to sit. If they moved close to us, it meant one thing; if they stayed jammed against the door, we got quite a different message.

Personal Distance   The second spatial zone, **personal distance,** ranges from 18 inches at its closest point to 4 feet at its farthest. Its closer phase is the distance at which most couples stand in public. If someone of the opposite sex stands this near one partner at a party, the other

partner is likely to feel uncomfortable. This "moving in" often is taken to mean that something more than casual conversation is taking place. The far range of personal distance runs from about 2 ½ to 4 feet. It's the zone just beyond the other person's reach. As Hall puts it, at this distance we can keep someone "at arm's length." His choice of words suggests the type of communication that goes on at this range: The contacts are still reasonably close, but they're much less personal than the ones that occur a foot or so closer.

Test this zone for yourself. Start a conversation with someone at a distance of about three feet, and slowly move a foot or so closer. Do you notice a difference? Does this distance affect your conversation?

Social Distance   The third zone is **social distance.** It ranges from 4 to about 12 feet out. Within it are the kinds of communication that usually occur in business situations. Its closer phase, from 4 to 7 feet, is the distance at which conversations usually occur between salespeople and customers and between people who work together. Most people feel uncomfortable when a salesclerk comes as close as 3 feet, whereas 4 or 5 feet nonverbally signals, "I'm here to help you, but I don't mean to be too personal or pushy."

We use the far range of social distance—7 to 12 feet—for more formal and impersonal situations. At this range we sit across the desk from our boss (or other authority figures). Sitting at this distance signals a far different and less relaxed type of conversation than if we were to pull a chair around to the boss's side of the desk and sit only 3 feet away.

Public Distance   **Public distance** is Hall's term for the furthest zone, running outward from 12 feet. The closer range of public distance is the one that most teachers use in the classroom. In the further reaches of public space—25 feet and beyond—two-way communication is almost impossible. In some cases it's necessary for speakers to use public distance to reach a large audience, but we can assume that anyone who chooses to use it when more closeness is possible is not interested in a dialogue.

When our spatial bubble is invaded, we respond with what are called *barrier behaviors*, behaviors designed to create a barrier (or fix a broken one) between ourselves and other people. Invade someone's personal space and notice the reaction. At first the person is most likely simply to back away, probably without realizing what is happening. Next your partner might attempt to put an object between you, such as a desk, a chair, or some books clutched to the chest, all in an effort to get some separation. Then the other person will probably decrease eye contact (the "elevator syndrome," in which we can crowd in and even touch one another so long as we avoid eye contact). Furthermore, your reluctant partner might sneeze, cough, scratch, and exhibit any variety of behaviors to discourage your antisocial behavior. In the end, if none of these behaviors achieve the desired goal of getting some space between the two of you, the other person might "counterattack," gently at first ("Move back, will you?"), then more forcefully (probably with a shove).

Writers sometimes confuse personal space with a related concept: *territoriality*. While personal space is the invisible bubble we carry around, the bubble that serves as an extension of our physical being, **territory** remains stationary. Any geographical area, such as a room, house, neighborhood, or country, to which we assume some kind of "rights" is our territory. What's interesting about territoriality is that there is no real basis for the assumption of proprietary rights, of "owning" some area, but the feeling of owning exists nonetheless. My room in my house is *my room* whether I'm there

or not (unlike my personal space that is carried around with me), and it's my room because I say it's my room. Although I could probably make a case for my room *really being* my room (as opposed to belonging to another family member or to the mortgage holder on the house), what about the desk I sit at in each class? I feel the same about the desk. It's *my desk*, even though it's certain that the desk is owned by the school and is in no way really mine.

What nonverbal messages do you send? Are you aware of all of them? Find out by asking someone who knows you well. See Activity 5 on page 200 for more details.

How can you tell if you are territorial? Ask yourself: Is there some piece of land, some area, which you would defend against others? Are you uncomfortable when someone comes into your room uninvited, or when you're not there? Does the thought of your neighborhood showing an increase in crime make you want to fight back? Does defending your country sound like a good idea? Ethographers (people who study animal behavior and attempt to make parallels with human behavior) argue that we are territorial *in nature;* that is, like other animals, we human beings are biologically programmed to defend our territory (Ardrey 1966).

Territoriality in animals serves a number of functions, such as providing a defended area for food and mating, and a place to hide from enemies. A territory also aids in the regulation of population density; only those controlling certain parts of the territory (usually the best pieces of land) tend to mate, thereby keeping the population in balance.

It is difficult to determine the advantages territoriality has for humans as a species. However, certain advantages do exist for individuals, especially for those with high status.

Generally, we grant people with higher status more personal territory and greater privacy. We knock before entering our supervisor's office, whereas the supervisor can usually walk into our work area without hesitating. In traditional schools professors have offices, dining rooms, and even toilets that are private, whereas the students, who are presumably less important, have no such sanctuaries. In the military greater space and privacy usually come with rank: Privates sleep forty to a barracks, sergeants have their own private rooms, and generals have government-provided houses.

TIME

Social scientists use the term **chronemics** to describe the study of how humans use and structure time. The way we handle time can express both intentional and unintentional messages. Social psychologist Robert Levine (1988) describes several ways that time can communicate. For instance, in a culture like ours that values time highly, waiting can be an indicator of status. "Important" people (whose time is supposedly more valuable than others) may be seen by appointment only, while it is acceptable to intrude without notice on lesser beings. To see how this rule operates, consider how natural it is for a boss to drop into a subordinate's office unannounced, while the employee would never intrude into the boss's office without an appointment. A related rule is that low-status people must never make more important people wait. It would be a serious mistake to show up late for a job interview, although the interviewer might keep you cooling your heels in the lobby. Important people are often whisked to the head of a restaurant or airport line, while presumably less-exalted masses are forced to wait their turn.

The use of time depends greatly on culture. In some cultures, punctuality is critically important, while in others it is barely considered. Punctual mainlanders often report welcoming the laid back Hawaiian approach towards time. One psychologist discovered the difference between North and South American attitudes when teaching at a university in Brazil (Levine and Wolff 1985). He found that some students arrived halfway through a two hour class, and that most of them stayed put and kept asking questions when the class was scheduled to end. A half hour after the official end of the period, the professor finally closed off discussion, since there was no indication that the students intended to leave. This flexibility of time is quite different than what is common in most North American colleges and universities!

Even within a culture, rules of time vary. Sometimes the differences are geographic. In New York City, the party invitation may say 9:00, but nobody would think of showing up before 10:30. In Salt Lake City, guests are expected to show up on time, or perhaps even a bit early. Even within the same geographic area, different groups establish their own rules about the use of time. Consider your own experience. In school, some instructors begin and end class punctually, while others are more casual. With some people you feel comfortable talking for hours in person or on the phone, while with others time seems to be precious and not "wasted."

PHYSICAL ATTRACTIVENESS

The importance of beauty has been emphasized in the arts for centuries. More recently, social scientists have begun to measure the degree to which physical attractiveness affects interaction between people. Recent findings, summarized by Knapp (1984: 141–44), Berscheid and Walster (1978), and Rosenfeld (1979), indicate that women who are perceived as attractive have more dates, receive higher grades in col-

The researchers found that children as young as three agreed as to who was attractive ("cute") and unattractive ("homely"). Furthermore, they valued their attractive counterparts—both of the same and opposite sex—more highly. Also, preschool children rated by their peers as pretty were most liked, and those identified as least pretty were least liked. Children who were interviewed rated good-looking children as having positive social characteristics ("He's friendly to other children") and unattractive children negatively ("He hits other children without reason").

Teachers, unfortunately, share this prejudice. One group rated identical school reports, some with an attractive child's photo attached and others with an unattractive child's, differently: Unattractive children were given lower grades, presumed to have lower IQs, and thought to get along less well with their peers.

Fortunately, attractiveness is something we can control without having to call the plastic surgeon. We view others as beautiful or ugly, not just on the basis of the "original equipment" they come with, but also on *how they use that equipment.* Posture, gestures, facial expressions, and other behaviors can increase the attractiveness of an otherwise unremarkable person. Exercise can improve the way each of us looks. Finally, the way we dress can make a significant difference in the way others perceive us, as you'll now see.

CLOTHING

Besides protecting us from the elements, clothing is a means of nonverbal communication. One writer has suggested that clothing conveys at least ten types of messages to others (Thourlby 1978):

1. economic level
2. educational level

lege, persuade males with greater ease, and receive lighter court sentences. Both men and women whom others view as attractive are rated as being more sensitive, kind, strong, sociable, and interesting than their less-fortunate brothers and sisters. Who is most likely to succeed in business? Place your bet with the attractive job applicant. For example, shorter men have more difficulty finding jobs in the first place, and men over 6'2" receive starting salaries that average 12.4 percent higher than comparable applicants under six feet.

The influence of attractiveness begins early in life. Preschoolers, for example, were shown photographs of children their own age and asked to choose potential friends and enemies.

We may be born naked, but we waste little time correcting the oversight. Almost from the moment we wriggle into the world, we start getting dressed. Conventional wisdom claims that clothing is simply a means of survival, but clearly there's more to it. Whether it's a couple of strategically placed shells or a suit of armor, a G-string or a caribou parka, clothing is a set of signals to all we meet. And though clothes may indeed protect us from the elements, their real job is to protect us from social opprobrium, or to make a statement—to a potential boss, a potential bride, or a very real enemy.

BANANA REPUBLIC CATALOG

3. trustworthiness
4. social position
5. level of sophistication
6. economic background
7. social background
8. educational background
9. level of success
10. moral character

Research shows that we do make assumptions about people based on their style of clothing. In one study, a male and female were stationed in a hallway so that anyone who wished to go by had to avoid them or pass between them. In one condition the conversationalists wore "formal daytime dress"; in the other, they wore "casual attire." Passersby behaved differently toward the couple, depending on the style of clothing: They responded positively with the well-dressed couple and negatively when the same people were casually dressed (Fortenberry et al. 1978). Similar re-

sults in other situations show the influence of clothing. We are more likely to obey people dressed in high-status manner. Pedestrians were more likely to return lost coins to well-dressed people than to those dressed in low-status clothing (Bickman 1974). We are also more likely to follow the lead of high-status dressers, even when it comes to violating social rules. Eighty-three percent of the pedestrians in one study followed a well-dressed jaywalker who violated a "wait" crossing signal, whereas only forty-eight followed a confederate dressed in lower-status clothing (Lefkowitz et al. 1955).

Despite their frequency, our clothing-based assumptions aren't always accurate. The stranger wearing wrinkled, ill-fitting old clothes might be a worker on vacation, a normally stylish person on the way to clean a fireplace, or even an eccentric millionaire. As we get to know others better the importance of clothing shrinks (Hoult 1954), which suggests that clothing is especially important in the early stages of a relationship, when making a positive first impression is necessary in order to encourage others to get to know us better. This advice is equally important in personal situations and in employment interviews. In both cases, your style of dress (and personal grooming) can make all the difference between the chance to progress further and outright rejection.

One setting in which dress is significant is in employment interviews. Janelle Johnson conducted a study in 1981, in which thirty-eight personnel representatives involved in recruiting and interviewing in the southwest were asked several questions about their attitudes toward applicants' appearance. One question was "What is the most predominant factor influencing your initial impression of interviewees?" Choices were physical attractiveness, resumé, appearance (dress), and manners. The majority of respondents (45 percent) indicated appearance as the most influential factor (fol-

"A general! Goodness gracious, you don't <u>look</u> like a general!"
Drawing by Richter: © 1968 The New Yorker Magazine, Inc.

lowed by resumé with 33 percent and the other two items with 11 percent each).

Another question Johnson's study asked was how the first impression created by the applicant affected the rest of the interview. Choices were not at all, not significantly, somewhat significantly, significantly, and it is the most important factor affecting the rest of the interview. The majority of respondents indicated that their first impression affected the rest of the interview either somewhat (42 percent) or significantly (37 percent).

At this point you might be thinking of the old saying "You can't judge a book by its cover." How valid is such a statement? In an attempt to answer this question, psychologist Lewis Aiken (1963) conducted a study focusing on "wearer characteristics." His goal was to see whether there is any relationship between the type of clothing a person chooses to wear and personality. Aiken focused his study on female subjects and found that clothes do offer some clues about the characteristics of the wearer. For instance, Aiken found that women who had a high concern for decoration and style in dress also scored above average on traits such as conformity and sociability. Women who dressed for comfort scored high in the areas of self-control and extroversion. A great interest in dress correlated positively with compliance, stereotypic thinking, social conscientiousness, and insecurity. Those who dressed in high conformity to style also rated above average on social conformity, restraint, and submissiveness. Finally, women who stressed economy in their dress rated high on responsibility, alertness, efficiency, and precision.

To see whether Aiken's results held for men as well as women and to bring his research up to date, Lawrence Rosenfeld and Timothy Plax (1977) conducted a follow-up investigation. They gave a battery of psychological examinations to a large number of male and female college students, and also administered a test that measured the subjects' attitudes toward clothes on four dimensions: clothing consciousness, exhibitionism, practicality, and the desire to design clothes.

Upon analyzing the results, some definite relationships between personality type and approach to clothing did emerge. For instance, both men and women who were not especially conscious of clothing style proved to be more independent than their more stylish counterparts. Highly exhibitionistic males were less sympathetic than other groups, and exhibitionistic women were more detached in their relationships. Men who dressed in a highly practical manner rated low on leadership orientation and were less motivated to form friendships, whereas those less concerned with practicality were more success-oriented and forceful.

Results such as these are fascinating, for they show that to some degree we *can* get an idea about human "books" from their covers. At the same time it's important to remember that research results are generalizations, and that not every clothes-conscious or exhibitionistic dresser fits into the pattern just described. Again, the best course is to treat your nonverbal interpretations as hunches that need to be checked out and not as absolute facts.

Patient Survey: MDs Should 'Dress for Success'

Patients surveyed at health clinics in Minnesota and Wisconsin say they are turned off by casual dress among their physicians, according to the *Minneapolis Star and Tribune.*

The survey of 292 patients found that patients had the greatest confidence in male physicians who wore shirts and ties and women MDs in skirts. A white coat and a dangling stethoscope added to the patient's perception of professionalism, the survey found.

Patients were questioned at family practice clinics in St. Paul, Minn., and in Milwaukee and Kenosha, Wis. The clinics are staffed by residents as well as staff physicians.

The patients also favored short hair—above the collar for men and women. They responded more favorably to women physicians who wore makeup, but were turned off by prominent ruffles, dangling earrings, boots, or patterned hose.

"Appearance is an important aspect of the way doctors communicate with patients, and doctors should pay attention to it," said Dwenda Gjerdingen, MD, of the Bethesda-University Family Physicians clinic in St. Paul, who directed the study.

"If doctors look good, they are taken seriously by their patients, and the patients believe they will be well taken care of," Dr. Gjerdingen added.

AMERICAN MEDICAL NEWS

ENVIRONMENT

We will conclude our look at nonverbal communication by examining how physical settings, architecture, and interior design affect communication. Begin by recalling the different homes you've visited lately. Were some of these homes more comfortable to be in than others? Certainly a lot of your feelings were shaped by the people you were with, but there are some houses where it seems impossible to relax, no matter how friendly the hosts. We've spent what seemed like endless evenings in what Mark Knapp (1978) calls "unliving rooms," where the spotless ashtrays, furniture coverings, and plastic lamp covers seemed to send nonverbal messages telling us not to touch anything, not to put our feet up, and not to be comfortable. People who live in such houses probably wonder why nobody ever seems to relax and enjoy themselves at their parties. One

---

Campuses are full of conscious and unconscious architectural symbolism. While the colleges at Santa Cruz evoke images of Italian hill towns as they might have been if the peasants had concrete, the administration building is another story. It appears to anticipate the confrontations between students and administration that marked the sixties. At Santa Cruz, administrative offices are located in a two-story building whose rough sloped concrete base with narrow slit windows gives it the look of a feudal shogun's palace. The effect is heightened by the bridge and landscaped moat that one crosses to enter the building. "Four administrators in there could hold off the entire campus," joked one student.

SYM VAN DER RYN
(CHIEF ARCHITECT, STATE OF CALIFORNIA)

---

thing is quite certain: They don't understand that the environment they have created can communicate discomfort to their guests.

The impressions that home designs communicate can be remarkably accurate. Edward Sadalla (1987) showed ninety-nine students slides of the insides or outsides of twelve upper-middle-class homes and then asked them to infer the personality of the owners from their impressions. The students were especially accurate after glancing at interior photos. The decorating schemes communicated accurate information about the homeowners' intellectualism, politeness, maturity, optimism, tenseness, willingness to take adventures, family orientations, and reservedness. The home exteriors also gave viewers accurate perceptions of the owners' artistic interests, graciousness, privacy, and quietness.

Besides communicating information about the designer, an environment can shape the kind of interaction that takes place in it. In one experiment at Brandeis University, Maslow and Mintz (1956) found that the attractiveness of a room influenced the happiness and energy of people working in it. The experimenters set up three rooms: an "ugly" one, which resembled a janitor's closet in the basement of a campus building; an "average" room, which was a professor's office; and a "beautiful" room, which was furnished with carpeting, drapes, and comfortable furniture. The subjects in the experiment were asked to rate a series of pictures as a way of measuring their energy and feelings of well-being while at work. Results of the experiment showed that while in the ugly room, the subjects became tired and bored more quickly and took longer to complete their task. Subjects who were in the beautiful room, however, rated the faces they were judging more positively, showed a greater desire to work, and expressed feelings of importance, comfort, and enjoyment. The results teach a lesson that isn't sur-

prising: Workers generally feel better and do a better job when they're in an attractive environment.

Many business people show an understanding of how environment can influence communication. Robert Sommer, a leading environmental psychologist, described several such cases. In *Personal Space: The Behavioral Basis of Design* (1969), he points out that dim lighting, subdued noise levels, and comfortable seats encourage people to spend more time in a restaurant or bar. Knowing this fact, the management can control the amount of customer turnover. If the goal is to run a high-volume business that tries to move people in and out quickly, it's necessary to keep the lights shining

brightly and not worry too much about soundproofing. On the other hand, if the goal is to keep customers in a bar or restaurant for a long time, the proper technique is to lower the lighting and use absorbent building materials that will keep down the noise level.

Furniture design also affects the amount of time a person spends in an environment. From this knowledge came the Larsen chair, which was designed for Copenhagen restaurant owners who felt their customers were occupying their seats too long without spending enough money. The chair is constructed to put an uncomfortable pressure on the sitter's back if occupied for more than a few minutes. (We suspect that many people who are careless in buying furniture for their homes get much the same result without trying. One environmental psychologist we know refuses to buy a chair or couch without sitting in it for at least half an hour to test the comfort.)

Sommer also describes how airports are designed to discourage people from spending too much time in waiting areas. The uncomfortable chairs, bolted shoulder to shoulder in rows facing outward, make conversation and relaxation next to impossible. Faced with this situation, travelers are forced to move to restaurants and bars in the terminal, where they're not only more comfortable but also more likely to spend money.

Casino owners in places such as Las Vegas also know how to use the environment to control behavior. To keep gamblers from noticing how long they've been shooting craps, playing roulette and blackjack, and feeding slot machines, they build their casinos without windows or clocks. Unless wearing a wristwatch, customers have no way of knowing how long they have been gambling or, for that matter, whether it's day or night.

In a more therapeutic and less commercial way, physicians have also shaped environments to improve communications. One study showed that simply removing a doctor's desk made patients feel almost five times more at ease during office visits. Sommer found that redesigning a convalescent ward of a hospital greatly increased the interaction between patients. In the old design seats were placed shoulder to shoulder around the edges of the ward. By grouping the chairs around small tables so that patients faced each other at a comfortable distance, the amount of conversations doubled.

Even the design of an entire building can shape communication among its users. Architects have learned that the way housing projects are designed controls to a great extent the contact neighbors have with each other. People who live in apartments near stairways and mailboxes have many more neighbor contacts than do those living in less heavily traveled parts of the building, and tenants generally have more contacts with immediate neighbors than with people even a few doors away. Architects now use this information to design buildings that either encourage communication or increase privacy, and house hunters can use the same knowledge to choose a home that gives them the neighborhood relationships they want.

So far we've talked about how designing an environment can shape communication, but there's another side to consider: Watching how people use an already existing environment can be a way of telling what kind of relationships they want. For example, Sommer watched students in a college library and found that there's a definite pattern for people who want to study alone. While the library was uncrowded, students almost always chose corner seats at one of the empty rectangular tables. After each table was occupied by one reader, new readers would choose a seat on the opposite side and at the far end, thus keeping the maximum distance between themselves and the other readers. One of Sommer's associates tried violating these "rules" by sitting next to and across from other female readers when more-distant seats were available. She found that the approached women reacted defensively, signaling their discomfort through shifts in posture, gesturing, or eventually moving away.

Research on classroom environments is extensive. Probably the most detailed study was conducted by Raymond Adams and Bruce Biddle (1970). Observing a variety of classes from grades 1, 6, and 11, they found that the main determinant of whether a student was actively and directly engaged in the process of classroom communication was that student's seating position. This finding held even when students were assigned seats, indicating that location, and not personal preferences, determined interaction.

Other studies by Robert Sommer and his colleagues (1978) found that students who sit near the teacher talk more. Also, the middle of the first row contains the students who interact most, and as we move back and to the sides of the classroom, interaction decreases markedly.

As we draw this discussion of nonverbal communication to a close, realize that we haven't tried to teach you *how* to communicate nonverbally in this chapter—you've always known how. What we do hope you've gained here is a greater *awareness* of the messages you and others send. You can use this new awareness to understand your relationships, improve them, and make them more interpersonal in the best sense of the word.

Summary

Nonverbal communication consists of messages expressed by nonlinguistic means such as distance, touch, body posture and orientation, expressions of the face and eyes, movement, time, vocal characteristics, clothing, and physical environment.

Nonverbal communication is pervasive; in fact, nonverbal messages are always available as a source of information about others. Most nonverbal behavior suggests messages about attitudes and feelings, in contrast to verbal statements which are better suited to expressing ideas. While many nonverbal behaviors are universal, their use and significance varies from one culture to another. Nonverbal communication serves many functions. It can repeat, substitute for, complement, accent, regulate, and contradict verbal messages.

Nonverbal messages differ from verbal statements in several ways. They involve multiple channels, are continuous instead of discrete, usually more ambiguous, and are more likely to be unconscious. When presented with conflicting verbal and nonverbal messages, communicators are more likely to rely on the nonverbal ones.

Activities

1. Demonstrate for yourself that it is virtually impossible to avoid communicating nonverbally by trying *not* to communicate with a friend or family member. (You be the judge of whether to tell the other person about this experiment beforehand.) See how long it takes for your partner to inquire about what is going on, and the other person to report on what he or she thinks you might be thinking and feeling.

2. Interview someone familiar with another culture or subculture and learn at least three ways in which nonverbal codes differ from the environment in which you were raised. Together, develop a list of ways you could violate unstated but important rules about nonverbal behavior in your partner's culture in three of the following areas:
   a. Eye contact

b. Posture

c. Gesture

d. Facial expression

e. Distance

f. Voice

g. Touch

h. Time

i. Clothing

j. Environmental design

k. Territory

3. Using the videotape of a television program or film, identify examples of the following nonverbal functions:

a. Repeating

b. Substituting

c. Complementing

d. Accenting

e. Regulating

f. Contradicting

If time allows, show these videotaped examples to your classmates.

4. Sharpen your ability to distinguish between observing and interpreting nonverbal behaviors by following these directions:

a. Sit or stand opposite a partner at a comfortable difference. For a one-minute period, report your observations of the other person's behavior by repeatedly completing the statement "Now I see (*nonverbal behavior*)." For example, you might report "Now I see you blinking your eyes...Now I see you looking down at the floor...Now I see you fidgeting with your hands..." Notice that no matter what your partner does, you have an unending number of nonverbal behaviors to observe.

b. For a second one-minute period, complete the sentence "Now I see (*nonverbal behavior*), and I think—," filling in the blank with your interpretation of the other person's nonverbal behavior. For instance, you might say, "Now I see you look away and I think you're nervous about looking me in the eye...Now I see you smiling and I think you're imagining that you agree with my interpretation..." Notice that by clearly labeling your interpretation you give the other person a chance to correct any mistaken hunches.

c. Repeat the first two steps, changing roles with your partner.

5. Learn more about the nonverbal messages you send by interviewing someone who knows you well: a friend, family member, or coworker, for example. Ask your interview subject to describe how he or she knows when you are feeling each of the following emotions, even though you may not announce your feelings verbally:

a. Anger or irritation

b. Boredom or indifference

c. Happiness

d. Sadness

e. Worry or anxiety

Which of these nonverbal behaviors do you display intentionally, and which are not conscious? Which functions do your nonverbal behaviors perform in the situations your partner described: repeating, substituting, complementing, accenting, regulating, and/or contradicting?

Readings

Adams, R., and B. Biddle. *Realities of Teaching: Explorations with Video Tape.* New York: Holt, Rinehart and Winston, 1970.

Aiken, L. R. "The Relationship of Dress to Selected Measures of Personality in Undergraduate Women." *Journal of Social Psychology* 80 (1963): 119–28.

Andersen, P. A. "Nonverbal Communication in the Small Group." In *Small Group Communication: A Reader,* 4th ed., R. S. Cathcart and L. A. Samovar, eds. Dubuque, IA: Wm. C. Brown, 1984.

Ardrey, R. *The Territorial Imperative.* New York: Dell, 1966.

Baker, E., and M. E. Shaw. "Reactions to Interpersonal Distance and Topic Intimacy: A Comparison of Strangers and Friends." *Journal of Nonverbal Behavior* 5 (1980): 80–91.

Bakker, C. B., and M. Bakker-Rabadau. *No Trespassing! Explorations in Human Territory.* San Francisco: Chandler and Sharp, 1973.

Bakwin, H. "Emotional Deprivation in Infants." *Journal of Pediatrics* 35 (1949): 512–21.

*Berscheid, E., and E. H. Walster. *Interpersonal Attraction,* 2d ed. Reading, MA: Addison-Wesley, 1978.

Bickman, L. "Social Roles and Uniforms: Clothes Make the Person." *Psychology Today* 7 (April 1974): 48–51.

Birdwhistell, R. L. *Kinesics and Context.* Philadelphia: University of Pennsylvania Press, 1970.

Blonston, G. "The Translator: Edward T. Hall." *Science 85* (July-August 1985): 78–85.

Booth-Butterfield, M., and F. Jordan. "'Act Like Us': Communication Adaptation Among Racially Homogeneous and Heterogeneous Groups." Paper presented at the Speech Communication Association meeting, New Orleans, 1988.

Buck, R. "Individual Differences in Nonverbal Sending Accuracy and Electrodermal Responding: The Externalizing-Internalizing Dimension." In *Skill in Nonverbal Communication: Individual Differences,* R. Rosenthal, ed. Cambridge, MA: Oelgeschlager, Gunn and Hain, 1979.

Buller, D. B., J. Comstock, R. K. Aune, and K. D. Stryzewski, "The Effect of Probing on Deceivers and Truthtellers." *Journal of Nonverbal Behavior* 13 (1989): 155–70.

Burgoon, J. K. "Nonverbal Signals." In *Handbook of Interpersonal Communication,* M. L. Knapp and G. R. Miller, eds. Beverly Hills, CA: Sage, 1985.

Burgoon, J. K., T. Birk, and M. Pfau, "Nonverbal Behaviors, Persuasion, and Credibility." *Human Communication Research* 17 (1990): 140–69.

Burgoon, J. K., D. B. Buller, and W. G. Woodall. *Nonverbal Communication: The Unspoken Dialogue.* New York: Harper & Row, 1989.

Burns, K. L., and E. G. Beier. "Significance of Vocal and Visual Channels for the Decoding of Emotional Meaning." *Journal of Communication* 23 (1973): 118–30.

Byers, P., and H. Byers. "Nonverbal Communication and the Education of Children." In *Functions of Language in the Classroom,* C. B. Cazden, V. P. John, and D. Hymes, eds. New York: Teachers College Press, 1972.

Cody, M. J., P. J. Marston, and M. Foster. "Paralinguistic and Verbal Leakage of Deception as a Function of Attempted Control and Timing of Questions." In *Communication Yearbook* 8, R. Bostrom, ed. Beverly Hills, CA: Sage, 1984.

Comadena, M. E. "Telling It Like It Isn't: A Review of Theory and Research on Deceptive Communication." *Human Communication Research* 5 (1979): 270–85.

Crane, D. R. "Diagnosing Relationships with Spatial Distance: An Empirical Test of a Clinical Principle." *Journal of Marital and Family Therapy* 13 (1987): 307–10.

Crusco, A. H., and C. G. Wetzel. "The Midas Touch: Effects of Interpersonal Touch on Restaurant Tipping." *Personality and Social Psychology Bulletin* 10 (1984): 512–17.

Darwin, C. *The Expression of Emotions in Man and Animals.* London: John Murray, 1872.

Deasy, C. M. "When Architects Consult People." *Psychology Today* 3 (March 1970): 10.

DePaulo, B. M., M. Zuckerman, and R. Rosenthal. "Detecting Deception: Modality Effects." In *Review of Personality and Social Psychology*, Vol. 1, L. Wheeler, ed., Beverly Hills, CA: Sage, 1980.

Derlega, V. J., R. J. Lewis, S. Harrison, B. A. Winstead, and R. Costanza, "Gender Differences in the Initiation and Attribution of Tactile Intimacy." *Journal of Nonverbal Behavior* 13 (1989): 83–96.

Driscoll, M. S., D. L. Newman, and J. M. Seal, "The Effect of Touch on the Perception of Counselors." *Counselor Education and Supervision* 27 (1988): 344–54.

Druckmann, D., R. M. Rozelle, and J. C. Baxter. *Nonverbal Communication: Survey, Theory, and Research.* Beverly Hills, CA: Sage, 1982.

Duncan, S. D., Jr. "Some Signals and Rules for Taking Speaking Turns in Conversation." *Journal of Personality and Social Psychology* 23 (1972): 283–92.

Duncan, S. D., Jr. "On the Structure of Speaker-Auditor Interaction During Speaking Turns." *Language in Society* 2 (1974): 161–80.

Duncan, S. D., Jr., and D. W. Fiske. "Dynamic Patterning in Conversation." *American Scientist* 67 (1979): 90–98.

Eibl-Eibesfeldt, I. "Universals and Cultural Differences in Facial Expressions of Emotions." In *Nebraska Symposium on Motivation*, J. Cole, ed. Lincoln, NB: University of Nebraska Press, 1972.

*Ekman, P. *Telling Lies: Clues to Deceit in the Marketplace, Politics, and Marriage.* New York: Norton, 1985.

Ekman, P., and W. V. Friesen. "Nonverbal Leakage and Clues to Deception." *Psychiatry* 32 (1969): 88–106.

Ekman, P., and W. V. Friesen. "Constants Across Cultures in the Face and Emotion." *Journal of Personality and Social Psychology* 17 (1971): 124–29.

Ekman, P., and W. V. Friesen. "Detecting Deception from the Body or Face." *Journal of Personality and Social Psychology* 29 (1974): 288–98.

Ekman, P., and W. V. Friesen, "Nonverbal Behavior and Psychopathology," in *The Psychology of Depression: Contemporary Theory and Research*, ed. R. J. Friedman and M. N. Katz. Washington, DC: J. Winston, 1974.

Ekman, P., and W. V. Friesen. *Unmasking the Face: A Guide to Recognizing Emotions from Facial Clues.* Englewood Cliffs, NJ: Prentice-Hall, 1975.

Ekman, P., W. V. Friesen, and J. Baer. "The International Language of Gestures." *Psychology Today* 18 (May 1984): 64–69.

Ellsworth, P. C., and L. D. Ross. "Intimacy in Response to Direct Gaze." *Journal of Experimental Social Psychology* 11 (1976): 592–613.

Ellyson, S. L., J. F. Dovidio, and R. L. Corson. "Visual Behavior Differences in Females as a Function of Self-Perceived Expertise." *Journal of Nonverbal Behavior* 5 (1981): 164–71.

Exline, R. V., S. L. Ellyson, and B. Long. "Visual Behavior as an Aspect of Power Role Relationships." In *Advances in the Study of Communication and Affect*, Vol. 2, P. Pilner, L. Krames, and T. Alloway, eds. New York: Plenum Press, 1975.

Feldman, S. D. "The Presentation of Shortness in Everyday Life. Height and Heightism in American Society: Toward a Sociology of Stature." In *Lifestyles: Diversity in American Society*, 2d ed., S. D. Feldman and G. W. Thielbar, eds. Boston: Little, Brown, 1975.

Fortenberry, J. H., J. Maclean, P. Morris, and M. O'Connell. "Mode of Dress as a Perceptual Cue to Deference." *Journal of Social Psychology* 104 (1978): 131–39.

Fromme, D. K., W. E. Jaynes, D. K. Taylor, E. G. Hanold, J. Daniell, J. R. Rountree, and M. Fromme, "Nonverbal Behavior and Attitudes Toward Touch." *Journal of Nonverbal Behavior* 13 (1989): 3–14.

Garratt, G. A., J. C. Baxter, and R. M. Rozelle. "Training University Police in Black-American Nonverbal Behaviors: An Application to Police-Community Relations." *Journal of Social Psychology* 113 (1981): 217–29.

Greene, J. O., H. D. O'Hair, M. Cody, and C. Yen. "Planning and Control of Behavior During Deception." *Human Communication Research* 11 (1985): 335–64.

Hale, J., and J. B. Stiff. "Nonverbal Primacy in Veracity Judgments." *Communication Reports* 3 (1990): 75–83.

*Hall, E. T. *The Hidden Dimension.* Garden City, NY: Anchor Books, 1969.

Hall, J. A. "Gender, Gender Roles, and Nonverbal Communication Skills." In *Skill in Nonverbal Communication: Individual Differences.* R. Rosenthal, ed. Cambridge, MA: Oelgeschlager, Gunn and Hain, 1979.

Halliday, J. L. *Psychosocial Medicine: A Study of the Sick Society.* New York: Norton, 1948.

Hegstrom, T. G. "Message Impact: What Percentage Is Nonverbal?" *Western Journal of Speech Communication* 43 (1979): 134–42.

Heslin, R., and T. Alper. "Touch: The Bonding Gesture." In *Nonverbal Interaction,* J. M. Wiemann and R. P. Harrison, eds. Beverly Hills, CA: Sage, 1983.

Hess, E. H., and J. M. Polt. "Pupil Size as Related to Interest Value of Visual Stimuli." *Science* 132 (1960): 349–50.

Hoult, T. F. "Experimental Measurement of Clothing as a Factor in Some Social Ratings of Selected American Men." *American Sociological Review* 19 (1954): 326–27.

Johnson, J. M. "The Significance of Dress in an Interview." Unpublished paper, University of New Mexico, 1981.

Jones, S. E. "Sex Differences in Touch Behavior." *Western Journal of Speech Communication* 50 (1986): 227–41.

Jones, S. E., and E. Yarbrough. "A Naturalistic Study of the Meanings of Touch." *Communication Monographs* 52 (1985): 19–56.

Jourard, S. M. "An Exploratory Study of Body Accessibility." *British Journal of Social and Clinical Psychology* 5 (1966): 221–31.

Katz, A. M., and V. T. Katz. *Foundations of Nonverbal Communication.* Carbondale, IL: Southern Illinois University Press, 1983.

Keyes, R. "The Height Report." *Esquire* (November 1979): 31–43.

Kleinke, C. R. "Compliance to Requests Made by Gazing and Touching Experimenters in Field Settings." *Journal of Experimental Social Psychology* 13 (1977): 218–23.

Kleinke, C. R., M. R. Lenga, T. B. Tully, F. B. Meeker, and R. A. Staneski. "Effect of Talking Rate on First Impressions of Opposite-Sex and Same-Sex Interactions." Paper presented at the meeting of the Western Psychological Association, Los Angeles, 1976.

Knapp, M. L. *Nonverbal Communication in Human Interaction,* 2d ed. New York: Holt, Rinehart and Winston, 1978.

Knapp, M. L. *Interpersonal Communication and Human Relationships.* Boston: Allyn and Bacon, 1984.

*La France, M., and C. Mayo. "A Review of Nonverbal Behaviors of Women and Men." *Western Journal of Speech Communication* 43 (1979): 96–107.

Lavater, J. C., *Essays in Physiognomy.* Quoted in "Lavater on Foreheads," *Psychology Today* 14 (December 1980): 95.

Leathers, D. G. *Nonverbal Communication Systems.* Boston: Allyn and Bacon, 1978.

Leathers, D. G. *Successful Nonverbal Communication: Principles and Applications.* New York: Macmillan, 1986.

Lefkowitz, M., R. R. Blake, and J. S. Mouton. "Status of Actors in Pedestrian Violation of Traffic Signals." *Journal of Abnormal and Social Psychology* 51 (1955): 704–6.

Levine, R. "The Pace of Life Across Cultures." In *The Social Psychology of Time,* J. E. McGrath, ed. Newbury Park, CA: Sage, 1988.

Levine, R., and E. Wolff. "Social Time: The Heartbeat of Culture." *Psychology Today* 19 (March 1985): 28–35.

Lieberman, D. A., T. G. Rigo, and R. F. Campain. "Age-Related Differences in Nonverbal Decoding Ability." *Communication Quarterly* 36 (1988): 290–97.

McCornack, S. A., and M. R. Parks. "What Women Know that Men Don't: Sex Differences in Determining the Truth Behind Deceptive Messages." *Journal of Social and Personal Relationships* 7 (1990): 107–18.

Manusov, V. "An Application of Attribution Principles to Nonverbal Behavior in Romantic Dyads." *Communication Monographs* 57 (1990): 104–18.

Maslow, A., and N. Mintz. "Effects of Aesthetic Surroundings: Initial Effects of Those Aesthetic Surroundings upon Perceiving 'Energy' and 'Well-Being' in Faces." *Journal of Psychology* 41 (1956): 247–54.

Mayo, C., and M. LaFrance. "Gaze Direction in Interracial Dyadic Communication." Paper presented at the meeting of the Eastern Psychological Association, Washington, D.C., 1973.

Medley, H. A. *The Neglected Art of Being Interviewed.* Belmont, CA: Wadsworth, 1978.

Mehrabian, A. "Nonverbal Betrayal of Feeling." *Journal of Experimental Research in Personality* 5 (1971): 64–73.

Mehrabian, A. *Nonverbal Communication.* Chicago: Aldine-Atherton, 1972.

Mehrabian, A., and M. Weiner. "Decoding of Inconsistent Communications." *Journal of Personality and Social Psychology* 6 (1967): 109–14.

Mehrabian, A., and M. Williams. "Nonverbal Concomitants of Perceived and Intended Persuasiveness." *Journal of Personality and Social Psychology* 13 (1969): 37–58.

Montagu, A. *Touching: The Human Significance of the Skin.* New York: Harper & Row, 1971.

Morsbach, H. "Aspects of Nonverbal Communication in Japan." *Journal of Nervous and Mental Disease* 157 (1973): 262–77.

Motley, M. T., and C. T. Camden. "Facial Expressions of Emotion: A Comparison of Posed Expressions Versus Spontaneous Expressions in an Interpersonal Communication Setting." *Western Journal of Speech Communication* 52 (1988): 1–22.

Newall, W. P. *One on One.* New York: Focus Press, 1979.

Newsweek. "Updating the Hot Line to Moscow." (April 30, 1984): 19.

Noller, P. "Gaze in Married Couples." *Journal of Nonverbal Behavior* 5 (1980): 115–29.

O'Hair, H. D., M. J. Cody, and M. L. McLaughlin. "Prepared Lies, Spontaneous Lies, Machiavellianism, and Nonverbal Communication." *Human Communication Research* 7 (1981): 325–39.

Pearson, J. C., "Communication in the Family," New York, Harper & Row, 1989.

Powell, J. L., and M. G. Lenihan. "Touch, Compliance, and Interpersonal Affect." *Journal of Nonverbal Behavior* 10 (1986): 41–50.

Richmond, V. P., J. C. McCroskey, and S. K. Payne. *Nonverbal Behavior in Interpersonal Relations.* Englewood Cliffs, NJ: Prentice-Hall, 1987.

Rosenfeld, L. B. "Beauty and Business: Looking Good Pays Off." *New Mexico Business Journal* (April 1979): 22–26.

*Rosenfeld, L. B., and J. M. Civikly. *With Words Unspoken: The Nonverbal Experience.* New York: Holt, Rinehart and Winston, 1976.

Rosenfeld, L. B., S. Kartus, and C. Ray. "Body Accessibility Revisited." *Journal of Communication* 26 (1976): 27–30.

Rosenfeld, L. B., and T. G. Plax. "Clothing as Communication." *Journal of Communication* 27 (1977): 24–31.

*Rosenthal, R., and B. M. DePaulo. "Expectancies, Discrepancies, and Courtesies in Nonverbal Communication." *Western Journal of Speech Communication* 43 (1979): 76–95.

Rubin, D. L. "Nobody Play by the Rule He Know:' Ethnic Interference in Classroom Questioning Events." In *Interethnic Communication: Recent Research,* Y. Y. Kim ed. Newbury Park, CA: Sage, 1986.

Sadalla, E. "Identity and Symbolism in Housing." *Environment and Behavior* 19 (1987): 569–87.

Scheflen, A. E. "Quasi-Courting Behavior in Psychotherapy." *Psychiatry* 228 (1965): 245–257.

Scheflen, A. E. *How Behavior Means.* Garden City, NY: Anchor Books, 1974.

Scherer, K. R., J. Kolwunaki, and R. Rosenthal. "Minimal Cues in the Vocal Communication of Affect: Judging Emotions from Content-Masked Speech." *Journal of Psycholinguistic Speech* 1 (1972): 269–85.

Smith, D. E., F. N. Willis, and J. A. Gier. "Success and Interpersonal Touch in a Competitive Setting." *Journal of Nonverbal Behavior* 5 (1980): 26–34.

Snow, P. A. "Verbal Content and Affective Response in an Interview as a Function of Experimenter Gaze Direction." Master's thesis, Lakehead University, Thunder Bay, Ontario, Canada, 1972.

Snyder, M. "The Many Me's of the Self-Monitor." *Psychology Today* 14 (March 1980): 33–40, 92.

*Sommer, R. *Personal Space: The Behavioral Basis of Design.* Englewood Cliffs, NJ: Prentice-Hall, 1969.

Sommer, R. *Tight Spaces.* Englewood Cliffs, NJ: Prentice-Hall, 1978.

Starkweather, J. A. "Vocal Communication of Personality and Human Feeling." *Journal of Communication* 11 (1961): 69.

Stiff, J. B., J. L. Hale, R. Garlick, and R. G. Rogan, "Effect of Cue Incongruence and Social Normative Influences on Individual Judgments of Honesty and Deceit," *Southern Speech Communication Journal* 55 (1990): 206–29.

Stiff, J. B., and G. R. Miller. "'Come to Think of It . . .': Interrogative Probes, Deceptive Communication, and Deception Detection." *Human Communication Research* 12 (1986): 339–58.

Streeter, L. A., R. M. Krauss, V. Geller, C. Olson, and W. Apple. "Pitch Changes During Attempted Deception." *Journal of Personality and Social Psychology* 35 (1977): 345–50.

Taylor, A. P., and G. Vlastos. *School Zone: Learning Environments for Children.* New York: Van Nostrand Reinhold, 1975.

Taylor, H. M. "American and Japanese Nonverbal Behavior." In *Papers in Japanese Linguistics* 3, J. V. Neustupny, ed. Melbourne, Australia: Monash University, 1974.

Thayer, S. "Close Encounters." *Psychology Today* 22 (March 1988): 31–36.

Thompson, J. J. *Beyond Words: Nonverbal Communication in the Classroom.* New York: Citation Press, 1973.

Thourlby, W. *You Are What You Wear.* New York: New American Library, 1978.

Valentine, C. A., and B. Saint Damian. "Communicative Power: Gender and Culture as Determinants of the Ideal Voice." In *Women and Communicative Power: Theory, Research, and Practice,* C. A. Valentine and N. Hoar, eds. Annandale, VA: Speech Communication Association, 1988.

Wachtel, P. "An Approach to the Study of Body Language in Psychotherapy." *Psychotherapy* 4 (1967): 97–100.

Watson, O. M. *Proxemic Behavior: A Cross-Cultural Study.* The Hague: Mouton, 1970.

Weitz, S., ed. *Nonverbal Communication: Readings with Commentary.* New York: Oxford University Press, 1974.

Willis, F. N., and H. K. Hamm. "The Use of Interpersonal Touch in Securing Compliance." *Journal of Nonverbal Behavior* 5 (1980): 49–55.

Wilson, G., and D. Nias. "Beauty Can't Be Beat." *Psychology Today* 10 (September 1976): 96–98, 103.

Wilson, J. M. "The Value of Touch in Psychotherapy," *American Journal of Orthopsychiatry* 52 (1982): 65–72.

Yarrow, L. J. "Research in Dimensions of Early Maternal Care." *Merrill-Palmer Quarterly* 9 (1963): 101–22.

Zuckerman, M., B. M. DePaulo, and R. Rosenthal. "Verbal and Nonverbal Communication of Deception." In *Advances in Experimental Social Psychology,* Vol. 14, L. Berkowitz, ed. New York: Academic Press, 1981.

Zuckerman, M., and R. E. Driver. "What Sounds Beautiful Is Good: The Vocal Attractiveness Stereotype." *Journal of Nonverbal Behavior* 13 (1989): 67–82.

*Items identified by an asterisk are recommended as especially useful follow-ups.

Listening

Chapter 7
Listening

After studying the material in this chapter

You should understand

1. The frequency and importance of listening.

2. The errors in some common myths about listening.

3. The components of the listening process.

4. The functions listening can serve.

5. The reasons people listen ineffectively.

6. The differences between listening for information and listening to help another person.

You should be able to

1. Identify specific instances when you listen for information reception, empathy, criticism and discrimination, and other-affirmation.

2. Identify the circumstances in which you listen ineffectively, and the poor listening habits you use in these circumstances.

3. Use the guidelines in this chapter to listen more effectively for information.

4. Identify the response style(s) you commonly use when responding to others' problems.

5. Demonstrate a combination of listening styles you could use to respond effectively to another person's problems.

Key Terms

Active listening
Advising
Ambushing
Analyzing
Assimilation to prior input
Attending
Defensive listening
Filling in the gaps

Hearing
Insensitive listening
Insulated listening
Judging
Listening
Paraphrasing
Pseudolistening
Questioning

Reflecting
Remembering
Responding
Selective listening
Stage hogging
Supporting
Understanding

The grizzled army sergeant faced a roomful of new Signal Corps cadets, about to begin their training as radio operators.

"The equipment is a snap to operate," he explained. "All you have to do to send a message is to push this button on the microphone and your voice goes out to anyone who's tuned in. Go ahead . . . give it a try."

Each recruit picked up a microphone and began speaking. The sound of thirty amplified voices all transmitting at the same time created a loud, painful squeal.

"Okay, soldiers," the sergeant announced. "You just learned the first principle of radio communication. Any fool can send a message. The only way communication works is if you're willing and able to *receive* one too."

The sergeant's lesson was a good one for every communicator. Speaking is important, but without listening, a message might as well never be sent. In this chapter you will learn just how important listening is in interpersonal communication. You will learn about the many factors that make it so difficult to listen effectively, and you will sharpen your skills in two very important kinds of listening: to gather information, and to help others.

The Importance of Listening

How important is listening? If we use frequency as a measure, it ranks at the top of the list. Over sixty years ago, Paul Rankin (1929) found that adults spent about 70 percent of their waking time communicating. Writing occupied 9 percent of that time, reading 16 percent, speaking 30 percent, and listening 45 percent. More recent studies confirm the importance of listening. Keefe (1971) found that executives spend about 63 percent of their communication time listening. The most recent survey, pictured in Figure 7–1 (Barker et al. 1981), provides the

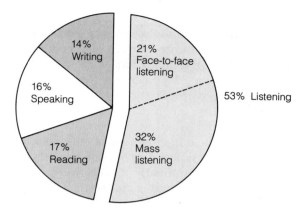

Figure 7–1 Types of communication activities

following percentages for each type of communication: writing, 14; speaking, 16; reading, 17; and listening, 53. Listening was broken down further into listening to mass communication messages, such as radio and television,

We judge a child's intelligence by how soon he or she starts talking, and we keep a record of each and every word in the baby book. I, for one, have never seen any parents go around boasting that their child is an exceptionally bright and gifted listener, much less keep a record of the first day they noticed it.

And we continue to ignore our early listeners and reward these fancy "talkers" in school, business, and industry. Oh, it's wonderful to have a command of the language, to choose just the right word from a rich vocabulary, and to beautifully articulate ideas, make friends, and influence people. But talking isn't everything. It's only one half of a communication skill—the other half is listening.

JAMES BOSWELL

and listening to face-to-face messages. The former category accounted for 21 percent of the subjects' communication time, whereas the latter accounted for 32 percent—more than any other type of communication.

Besides being the most frequent form of communication, listening is arguably just as important as speaking in terms of making relationships work. When a group of adults was asked what communication skills were most important in family and social settings, listening was ranked first (Wolvin 1984). When the same group was asked to identify the most important on-the-job communication skills, listening again ranked at the top of the list. A study examining the link between listening and career success revealed that better listeners rose to higher levels in their organizations (Sypher et al. 1989). The ability to listen well was linked to persuasive skills, showing that good listeners are also good speakers.

Despite the importance of listening, the educational system provides surprisingly little training in this communication skill. Ralph Nichols and L. A. Stevens (1957) point out that the allotment of time for communication skills is upside-down in most school systems: The greatest amount of time is spent teaching the skills used least often. Writing is taught most often and used least; reading receives the second greatest amount of attention and is the third most-used skill; speaking receives the third-greatest amount of time and is the second most-used skill; and listening—the most frequently used skill—is hardly taught at all (Steil

---

Give every man thine ear, but few thy voice.

POLONIUS IN SHAKESPEARE'S
Hamlet

1978). School, of course, isn't the only place where we learn how to communicate. Children manage to learn how to speak, for example, before setting foot in a classroom. Yet observing others outside the classroom is hardly an ideal way to learn good listening habits. Distracted parents and inattentive playmates are not always ideal models for a young child to emulate.

As you'll soon read, some poor listening is inevitable; but in other cases we can be better receivers by learning a few basic listening skills. The purpose of this chapter is to help you become a better listener by teaching you some important information about the subject. We'll talk about some common misconceptions concerning listening and show you what really happens when listening takes place. We'll discuss some poor listening habits and explain why they occur. Finally, we'll introduce you to some more-effective alternatives, to increase both your own understanding and your ability to help others.

Debunking Myths about Listening

In spite of its importance, listening is misunderstood by most people. Because these misunderstandings so greatly affect our communication, let's take a look at three common misconceptions.

LISTENING IS NOT HEARING

Hearing is the process wherein sound waves strike the eardrum and cause vibrations that are transmitted to the brain. *Listening* occurs when the brain reconstructs these electrochemical impulses into a representation of the original sound, and then gives them meaning. Barring illness, injury, or cotton plugs, hearing cannot be stopped. Your ears will pick up sound waves and transmit them to your brain whether you want them to or not.

Listening, however, is not so automatic. Many times we hear but do not listen. Sometimes we deliberately do not listen. Instead of paying attention to words or other sounds, we avoid them. Often we block irritating sounds, such as a neighbor's power lawn mower or the roar of nearby traffic. We also stop listening when we find a subject unimportant or uninteresting. Boring stories, TV commercials, and nagging complaints are common examples of messages we avoid.

There are also cases when we honestly believe we're listening although we're merely hearing. For example, recall times when you think you've "heard it all before." It's likely that in these situations you might claim you were listening when in fact you had closed your mental doors to new information.

People who confuse listening with hearing often fool themselves into thinking that they're really understanding others, when in fact they're simply receiving sounds. As you'll see by reading this chapter, true listening involves much more than the passive act of hearing.

SKILLFUL LISTENING IS NOT A NATURAL ABILITY

Another common myth is that listening is like breathing: a natural activity that people do well. "After all," this common belief goes, "I've been listening since I was a child. Why should I have to study the subject in school?"

This attitude is understandable, considering the lack of attention most schools devote to listening in comparison with other communication skills. From kindergarten to college most students receive almost constant training in reading and writing. Every year the exposure to literature continues, from Dick and Jane through Dostoyevski. Likewise, the emphasis on

---

Student Reflection

Listening Is More Than Hearing

I have one of those watches that beep every half hour, so I used it to try a little experiment. Each time the alarm went off I tried to write down what the other person was saying, just to see if I was really listening. The results were amazing. More than half the time I found that my mind was somewhere else. I couldn't write down more than a few rough ideas about what the speaker was talking about.

There were even times when I would be in the middle of a conversation with the other person, but even then I wasn't listening. Either I was busy rehearsing what I wanted to say or I was just daydreaming—nodding, smiling, and saying things like "uh huh" and "I know what you mean."

I almost always <u>hear</u> what other people say, and if I'm lucky I can repeat the words they've just spoken. But I have to confess that I'm not a very good listener.

---

writing continues without break. You could probably retire if you had a dollar for every composition, essay, research paper, and blue book you have written since the first grade. Even spoken communication gets some attention in the curriculum. It's likely that you had a chance to take a public speaking class in high school and another one in college.

Compare all this training in reading, writing, and speaking with the almost total lack of instruction in listening. Even in college, there

are few courses devoted exclusively to the subject. This state of affairs is especially ironic when you consider that over 50 percent of our communication involves listening.

The truth is that listening is a skill much like speaking: Virtually everyone listens, but few people do it well. Your own experience should prove that communication often suffers due to poor listening. How many times have others misunderstood your clearest directions or explanations? How often have you failed to understand others because you weren't receiving their thoughts accurately? The answers to these questions demonstrate the need for effective training in listening.

ALL LISTENERS DO NOT RECEIVE THE SAME MESSAGE

When two or more people are listening to a speaker, we tend to assume that they are each hearing and understanding the same message. In fact, such uniform comprehension isn't the case. Communication is *proactive:* Each person involved in a transaction of ideas or feelings responds uniquely. Recall our discussion of perception in Chapter 3, where we pointed out the many factors that cause each of us to perceive an event in a different manner. Physiological factors, social roles, cultural background, personal interests, and needs all shape and distort the raw data we hear into uniquely different messages.

Components of Listening

By now you can begin to see that there is more to listening than sitting quietly while another person speaks. In truth, **listening**—at least listening effectively—consists of five separate elements: hearing, attending, understanding, remembering, and responding.

HEARING

As we already discussed, *hearing* is the physiological aspect of listening. It is the nonselective process of sound waves impinging on the ear. Insofar as these waves range between approximately 125 and 8,000 cycles per second (frequency) and 55 to 85 decibels (loudness),

One often hears the remark, "He talks too much," but when did anyone last hear the criticism "He listens too much?"

NORMAN R. AUGUSTINE

the ear can respond. Hearing is also influenced by background noise. If a background noise is the same frequency as the speech sound, then the speech sound is said to be masked; however, if the background noise is of a different frequency than speech, it is called "white noise," and may or may not detract greatly from our ability to hear. Hearing is also affected by auditory fatigue, a temporary loss of hearing caused by continuous exposure to the same tone or loudness. People who spend an evening in a discotheque may experience auditory fatigue and, if they are exposed often enough, permanent hearing loss.

ATTENDING

While hearing is a physiological process, **attending** is a psychological one. We would go crazy if we attended to every sound we hear, and so we filter out some messages and focus on others. Needs, wants, desires, and interests determine what is attended to. Not surprisingly, research shows that we attend most carefully to messages when there's a payoff for doing so (see, for example, Smeltzer and Watson 1984). If you're thinking about attending a movie, you'll listen to a friend's description more carefully than you otherwise would have. And when you want to get better acquainted with others, you'll pay careful attention to almost anything they

say in hopes of improving the relationship. As Aubrey Fisher (1987: 389–90) suggests, our listening ability is often affected more by motivations and incentives than by any skills we have. In other words, we listen best when we attend carefully, and we attend carefully when we see the benefit of doing so.

Listening isn't as simple as it might seem. You can explore the many dimensions of listening by completing Activity 1 on page 235.

UNDERSTANDING

Paying attention—even close attention—to a message doesn't guarantee that you'll understand what's being said. **Understanding** is composed of several elements: First, of course, you must be aware of the syntactic and grammatical rules of the language. But beyond this basic ability, understanding a message depends on several other factors. One is your knowledge about the source of the message. Such background will help you decide, for example, whether a friend's insulting remark is a joke or a serious attack. The context of a message also helps you understand what's being said. A yawning response to your comments would probably have a different meaning at midnight than at noon.

© 1978 United Feature Syndicate, Inc. Reprinted by permission of UFS, Inc.

Finally, understanding often depends on the listener's mental abilities. Generally speaking, the ability to make sense of messages is closely related to the listener's intelligence (Bostrom and Waldhart 1980). As early as 1948, Ralph Nichols related successful understanding to factors including verbal ability, intelligence, and motivation. A more recent investigation completed in 1979 by Timothy Plax and Lawrence Rosenfeld showed that personality traits of listeners also affect their ability to understand messages. People who are good at interpreting disorganized messages were especially secure, sensitive to others, and willing to understand the speaker. Listeners who are successful at understanding disorganized speech proved to be more insightful and versatile in their thinking.

REMEMBERING

The ability to recall information once we've understood it, or **remembering,** is a function of several factors: the number of times the information is heard or repeated, how much information there is to store in the brain, and whether the information may be "rehearsed" or not.

Research conducted during the 1950s (Barker 1971) revealed that people remember only about half of what they hear *immediately* after hearing it. They forget half even if they work hard at listening. This situation would probably not be too bad if the half remembered right after were retained, but it isn't. Within two months, half of the half is forgotten, bringing what we remember down to about 25 percent of the original message. This loss, however, doesn't take two months: People start forgetting immediately (within eight hours the 50 percent remembered drops to about 35 percent). Given the amount of information we process every day—from teachers, friends, the radio, TV, and other sources—the *residual message* (what we remember) is a small fraction of what we hear.

This high rate of forgetfulness isn't as depressing as it might seem. While most people recall very few details of their conversations, they do retain an overall impression about the speaker, especially in important relationships (Fisher 1987: 390). The more intensity, intimacy, trust, and commitment in the relationship, the more we pay attention to what others are saying. Thus, high recall is one characteristic of healthy interpersonal relationships.

RESPONDING

All of the steps we have discussed so far—hearing, attending, understanding, and remembering—are internal activities. A final part of the listening process involves **responding** to a message—giving observable feedback to the speaker. One study of 195 critical incidents in banking and medical settings showed that a major difference between effective and ineffective listening was the kind of feedback offered (Lewis and Reinsch 1988). Good listeners showed that they were attentive by nonverbal behaviors such as keeping eye contact and reacting with appropriate facial expressions. Their verbal behavior—answering questions and exchanging ideas, for example—also demonstrated their attention. It's easy to imagine how other responses would signal less effective listening. A slumped posture, bored expression, and yawning send a clear message that you are not tuned in to the speaker.

Adding responsiveness to our listening model demonstrates the fact we discussed in Chapter 1 that communication is transactional in nature. Listening isn't just a passive activity. As listeners, we are active participants in a communication transaction. At the same time that we receive messages we also send them.

Functions of Listening

"All right," you may respond. "So I don't listen to everything I hear, I don't understand everything I listen to, and I don't remember everything I understand. I still seem to get along well enough. Why should I worry about becoming a better listener?" Author Rob Anderson (1979) suggests four benefits that can come from improving your listening skills.

INFORMATION RECEPTION

People who can understand and retain more information have a greater chance of becoming successful, however you define that term (Floyd 1985). In school the advantages of listening effectively are obvious. Along with the skills of effective writing and reading, the ability to receive and understand the spoken word is a major key to academic success. The same holds true in the business and professional worlds. Understanding the instructions and advice of superiors and colleagues, learning about the needs and reactions of subordinates, and discovering the concerns of clients and other members of the public are important in virtually every job.

How much time do you spend listening? What kinds of listening do you do? How important a role does listening play in your life? You can answer these questions by completing Activity 2 on page 235.

Even in personal life, the ability to receive and understand information is a key to success. Being a good listener can help you learn everything from car repair to first aid for houseplants to the existence of cheap restaurants. Socially, everyone knows the benefits of being able to

Student Reflection

Listening Builds Relationships

I've just discovered that a great way to make people feel good about themselves is to let them talk about what they think is important, not what I think is important.

Instead of stage hogging, I decided to ask questions. (That way I still get to talk!) The results have been fantastic. People open up when you ask questions. Conversations are more enjoyable and stimulating. And I learned patience! By taking an active interest in my friends' lives, I got closer to them.

I learned that stage hogging is really a way to keep your distance from others. If other people never get a chance to say anything, you don't have to deal with them. Being a good listener is a sincere way to tell others you care, and to get closer to them.

hear and remember information about others whom we'd like to know better.

EMPATHY

A listener who was *only* able to receive and recall large amounts of information efficiently would be no more likable or valuable as a friend than a computer. Although the ability to receive data is admirable, personally helpful listeners also are able to empathize: to understand and "feel with" the emotions and thoughts of a speaker. An impressive body of research supports the idea that the ability to empathize is an important element in effective communication for many social roles: business supervisors, teachers, therapists and counselors, and of course, friends.

It's obvious that listening empathically can be a valuable way to help someone else with a problem, but developing the ability to empathize can also have personal payoffs for you as a listener. The most obvious one is the reward of having helped solve another person's problems. In addition, as an empathic listener, you can broaden your own understanding and often learn how to deal with issues in your own life. Just as it's helpful to hear all about a new place before traveling there yourself, listening to another person's personal experiences can teach you what to think and do when you encounter similar circumstances.

CRITICISM AND DISCRIMINATION

In their interesting book *Teaching as a Subversive Activity,* Neil Postman and Charles Weingartner (1969) discuss this function of listening in their chapter "Crap Detecting." They define a crap detector as someone who not only functions in a society, but *observes* it, noting its obsessions, fears, strengths, and weaknesses. Critical listeners are able to hear a speaker's words and understand the ideas without accepting them totally. The ability to listen analytically and critically differs radically from the kind of empathic reception just discussed, but it is equally important. Critical listeners can help individuals and societies understand themselves and evaluate their ideas.

The greatest compliment that was ever paid to me was when one asked me what I thought, and attended to my answer.

HENRY DAVID THOREAU

OTHER-AFFIRMATION

As Chapters 1 and 10 explain, a basic human need is to be recognized and acknowledged by others. Listening is one of the most fundamental means of giving such acknowledgment. The act of listening, of *choosing* to listen, is itself an affirmation of the speaker. Whenever you listen, you are sending a nonverbal message suggesting that the person speaking is important. Of course, there are varying degrees of importance, and there are also various degrees of listening intensity reflecting this range of valuing. A brief affirmation can come from a few minutes of chitchat with an acquaintance, whereas a much stronger message of acknowledgment is reflected in your willingness to spend hours hearing a friend talk over a personal problem.

Barriers to Listening

Given the importance of receiving information, building empathy, critically discriminating, and affirming others, it's obvious that listening well can be valuable for both the receiver and the speaker. In spite of this fact, we often do not listen with much energy or concern. Why? Sad as it may be, it's impossible to listen *all* the time. Research has identified a variety of reasons why people listen ineffectively (see, for example, Hulbert 1989). There are plenty of barriers to good listening: One study identified twenty-five of them (Golan 1990). A look at some of the reasons why we listen poorly shows the challenges every communicator faces.

HEARING PROBLEMS

If a person suffers from a physical impairment that prevents either hearing sounds at an adequate volume or receiving certain auditory frequencies, then listening will obviously suffer. Once a hearing problem has been diagnosed, it's often possible to treat it. The real tragedy occurs when a hearing loss goes undiagnosed. Both the person with the defect and those surrounding can become frustrated and annoyed at the ineffective communication that takes place. If you suspect that you or someone you know might have a hearing loss, it's wise to have a physician or audiologist perform an examination.

INFORMATION OVERLOAD

The sheer amount of speech most of us encounter every day makes it impossible to listen carefully to everything we hear. Many of us spend almost half the time we're awake listening to verbal messages from teachers, coworkers, friends, family, salespeople, and total strangers (Barker et al. 1981). We often spend five or more hours a day listening to people talk. If you add these hours to the amount of time we listen to radio and TV, you can see that it's virtually impossible for us to keep our attention totally focused for so long. Therefore, we periodically let our attention wander.

PERSONAL CONCERNS

A third reason we don't always listen carefully is that we're often wrapped up in personal concerns of more immediate importance to us than the messages others are sending. It's hard to pay attention to someone else when we're anticipating an upcoming test or thinking about the wonderful time we had last night with good friends. When we still feel we have to "listen" politely to others, listening becomes a charade.

RAPID THOUGHT

Listening carefully is also difficult for a physiological reason. Although we're capable of understanding speech at rates up to 600 words per minute (Goldhaber 1970), the average person

Student Reflection

Drowning in a Sea of Talk

I'm an accounting major, so I decided to keep track of my listening in a typical day. Here's what I found:

Listening to lectures	2 hours, 25 minutes
Face-to-face conversation with professor	21 minutes
Conversations with other students	43 minutes
Talking with salespeople, waiters, etc.	32 minutes
Phone conversations	54 minutes
Conversation over meals	1 hour, 5 minutes
Conversations around the house	25 minutes
Conversations at party	3 hours, 45 minutes

All this added up to over ten hours of communicating. Even if you subtract the time that I was talking in conversations, I'm sure I listened for over six hours.

Before this exercise I felt badly because I knew I didn't listen carefully or well all the time. Now I understand why. There isn't enough time or energy in the day to pay careful attention to everyone.

I'm not sure what the answer is. Perhaps I should try to spend more time away from people so I can really listen when I am around them. Or maybe I need to accept the fact that I won't listen well much of the time and just concentrate on the really important messages.

speaks between 100 and 140 words per minute. Therefore we have a lot of "spare time" to spend with our minds while someone is talking. The temptation is to use this time in ways that don't relate to the speaker's ideas, such as thinking about personal interests, daydreaming, planning a rebuttal, and so on. The trick is to use this spare time to understand the speaker's ideas better, rather than letting your attention wander.

"NOISE"

Finally, our physical and mental worlds often present distractions that make it hard to pay attention to others. The sounds of other conversations, traffic, and music, as well as the kinds of psychological noise discussed in Chapter 1, all interfere with our ability to hear well. Also, fatigue or other forms of discomfort can distract us from paying attention to a speaker's remarks. Consider, for example, how the efficiency of your listening decreases when you are seated in a crowded, hot, stuffy room full of moving people and other noises. In such circumstances even the best intentions aren't enough to ensure cogent understanding.

Before going any further, we want to make it clear that intensive listening isn't always desirable, even when the circumstances permit. Given the number of messages to which we're exposed, it's impractical to expect yourself to listen well 100 percent of the time. Many of the messages sent to us aren't even worthwhile: boring stories, deceitful commercials, and remarks

---

One advantage of talking to yourself is that you know at least somebody is listening.

FRANKLIN P. JONES

---

we've heard many times before. Nonlistening behaviors are therefore often reasonable. Our only concern is that you have the ability to be an accurate receiver when it really does matter.

Poor Listening Habits

Although effective listening may not be necessary or desirable all the time, it's sad to realize that most people possess one or more bad habits that keep them from understanding truly important messages. As you read about the following poor listening behaviors, see which ones describe you.

No one is a perfect listener. You can discover your poor listening habits by completing Activity 3 on page 235.

PSEUDOLISTENING

The habit of **pseudolistening** is an imitation of the real thing. "Good" pseudolisteners give the appearance of being attentive: They look you in the eye, nod and smile at the right times, and even answer you occasionally. Behind that appearance of interest, however, something entirely different is going on, for pseudolisteners use a polite facade to mask thoughts that have nothing to do with what the speaker is saying. Often pseudolisteners ignore you because of something on their mind that's more important to them than your remarks. Other times they may simply be bored, or think that they've heard what you have to say before, and so tune out your remarks. Whatever the reasons, the significant fact is that pseudolistening is really counterfeit communication.

STAGE HOGGING

Those engaged in **stage hogging** are interested only in expressing their ideas and don't care

Drawing by Leo Cullum, © 1990 The New Yorker Magazine, Inc.

about what anyone else has to say. These people allow you to speak from time to time, but only so they can catch their breath and use your remarks as a basis for their own babbling or keep you from running away. Stage hogs really aren't conversing when they dominate others with their talk—they're making a speech and at the same time probably making an enemy.

Interruptions are usually a hallmark of stage hogging. Besides preventing the listener from learning potentially valuable information, they can damage the relationship between the interrupter and the speaker. For example, applicants who interrupt the questions of employment interviewers are likely to be rated less favorably than job seekers who wait until the interviewer has finished speaking before they respond (McComb and Jablin 1984).

Not all interruptions are attempts at stage hogging. Anthony Mulac and his associates (1988) discovered a difference between male and female interrupters. Men typically interrupted conversations far more often than women. Their goals were usually to control the discussion. Women interrupted for very different reasons: to communicate agreement, to elaborate on the speaker's idea, or to participate in the topic of conversation. These sorts of responses are more likely to be welcomed as a contribution to the discussion, and not as attempts to grab the stage.

SELECTIVE LISTENING

Selective listeners respond only to the parts of a speaker's remarks that interest them, rejecting

---

Student Reflection

Poor Listening

After reading this chapter I decided to ask my best friend what kinds of poor listening behaviors I used with her. Her first reply was "do you really want to know?" When I convinced her that I was sincerely interested, she began to rattle off a whole list of faults.

I managed to keep quiet for the first few minutes, but inside I was making up all sorts of justifications for her criticism. After a while I just had to speak up and defend myself. "You see," she said. "You asked me to tell you what I thought, and now you don't want to hear it."

What could I say? She was right. I don't even listen well when the subject is listening!

---

everything else. All of us engage in **selective listening** from time to time; for instance, we screen out media commercials and music as we keep an ear cocked for a weather report or an announcement of time. In other cases selective listening occurs in conversations with people who expect a thorough hearing, but get attention only when the subject turns to their partner's favorite topic—money, sex, a hobby, or some particular person. Unless and until they bring up one of these pet subjects, they might as well talk to a tree.

FILLING IN GAPS

People who are **filling in gaps** like to think that what they remember makes a whole story. We remember half or less of what we hear, but these people manufacture information so that when they retell what they listened to, they can give the impression they "got it all." Of course, filling in the gaps is as dangerous as selective listening: The message that's left is a distorted (not merely incomplete) version of the real message.

ASSIMILATION TO PRIOR MESSAGES

We all have a tendency to interpret current messages in terms of similar messages remembered from the past. This phenomenon is called **assimilation to prior input.** A problem arises for those who go overboard with this tendency. They push, pull, chop, squeeze, and in other ways mutilate messages they receive to *make sure* the new messages are consistent with what they heard in the past. This unfortunate situation occurs when the current message in some way conflicts with past beliefs.

INSULATED LISTENING

The habit of **insulated listening** is almost the opposite of selective listening. Instead of looking for something, these listeners avoid it. Whenever a topic arises they'd rather not deal with, insulated listeners simply fail to hear or acknowledge it. You remind them about a problem—an unfinished job, poor grades, or the like—and they'll nod or answer you and then promptly forget what you've just said.

DEFENSIVE LISTENING

People who engage in **defensive listening** take innocent comments as personal attacks. Teenagers who perceive parental questions about friends and activities as distrustful snooping are defensive listeners, as are insecure breadwinners who explode any time their mates mention money, or touchy parents who view any questioning by their children as a threat to their authority and parental wisdom. It's fair to assume that many defensive listeners are suffering from shaky presenting images, and avoid admitting it by projecting their own insecurities onto others.

AMBUSHING

Someone who is **ambushing** will listen carefully to you, but only because he or she is collecting information that will be used to attack what you have to say. The cross-examining prosecuting attorney is a good example of an ambusher. Needless to say, using this kind of strategy will justifiably initiate defensiveness on the other's side.

INSENSITIVE LISTENING

People who engage in **insensitive listening** offer the final example of people who don't receive another person's messages clearly. As we've said before, people often don't express their thoughts or feelings openly but instead communicate them through subtle and unconscious choice of words and/or nonverbal clues. Insensitive listeners aren't able to look beyond the words and behavior to understand hidden meanings. Instead, they take a speaker's remarks at face value.

When we speak we do not listen, my son and I.
I complain of slights, hurts inflicted on me.
He sings a counterpoint, but not in harmony.
Asking a question, he doesn't wait to hear.
Trying to answer, I interrupt his refrain.
This comic opera excels in disharmony only.

LENNI SHENDER GOLDSTEIN

It's important not to go overboard in labeling listeners as insensitive. Often a seemingly mechanical comment is perfectly appropriate. Most often it is proper in situations involving *phatic* communication, in which a remark derives its meaning totally from context. For instance, the question "How are you?" doesn't call for an answer when you pass an acquaintance on the street. In this context the statement means no more than "I acknowledge your existence and I want to let you know that I feel friendly toward you." It is not an inquiry about the state of your health. Although insensitive listening is depressing, you would be equally discouraged to hear a litany of aches and pains every time you asked, "How's it going?"

Informational listening doesn't just occur in lectures. Understanding others is an important part of interpersonal relationships. You can practice your skill as an informational listener by following the steps in Activity 4 on page 235.

Informational Listening

After reading the last few pages, you might decide that listening well is impossible. Fortunately, with the right combination of attitude and skill, you can do a reasonably good job. The first step is to realize that different types of listening are suited for different purposes. With informational listening the goal is to make sure you are accurately receiving the same thoughts the other person is trying to convey—not always an easy feat when you consider the forces that interfere with understanding.

The situations that call for informational listening are endless and varied: following the directions of an instructor or boss, listening to a friend's account of a vacation, learning about

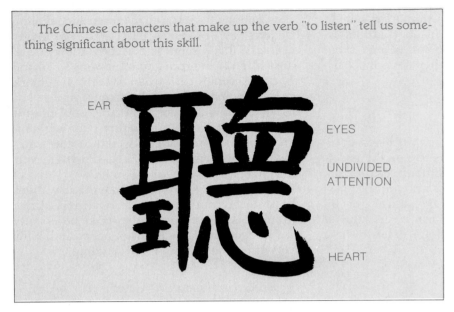

The Chinese characters that make up the verb "to listen" tell us something significant about this skill.

EAR

EYES

UNDIVIDED ATTENTION

HEART

Calligraphy by Angie Au.

your family history from a relative's tales, swapping ideas in a discussion about religion or politics...the list goes on and on. You can become a more effective informational listener by following several guidelines.

TALK LESS

Zeno of Citium put it most succinctly: "We have been given two ears and but a single mouth, in order that we may hear more and talk less." If your true goal is to understand the speaker, avoid the tendency to hog the stage and shift the conversation to your ideas. Talking less doesn't mean you should remain completely silent. As you'll soon read, feedback that clarifies your understanding and seeks new information is an important way to understand a speaker. Nonetheless, most of us talk too much when we're claiming to understand others.

GET RID OF DISTRACTIONS

Some distractions are external: ringing telephones, radio or television programs, friends dropping in, and so on. Other diversions are internal: preoccupation with your own problems, an empty stomach, and so on. If the information you're seeking is really important, do everything possible to eliminate the internal and external noise that interferes with careful listening.

As friends, we don't see eye to eye. But then, we don't hear ear to ear either.

BUSTER KEATON

DON'T JUDGE PREMATURELY

Most people would agree with the principle that it's essential to understand a speaker's ideas before **judging** them. Despite this common-sense fact, all of us are guilty of forming snap judgments, evaluating others before hearing them out. This tendency is greatest when the speaker's ideas conflict with our own. Conversations that ought to be exchanges of ideas turn into verbal battles, with the "opponents" trying to ambush one another in order to win a victory. Disagreements aren't the only kind of conversation in which the tendency to judge others is strong: It's also tempting to counterattack when others criticize you, even when those criticisms may contain valuable truths and when understanding them may lead to a change for the better. Even if there is no criticism or disagreement, we tend to evaluate others based on sketchy first impressions, forming snap judgments that aren't at all valid. Not all premature judgments are negative. It's also possible to jump to overly favorable conclusions about the quality of a speaker's remarks when we like that person or agree with the ideas being expressed. The lesson contained in these negative examples is clear: Listen first. Make sure you understand. *Then* evaluate.

LOOK FOR KEY IDEAS

It's easy to lose patience with long-winded speakers who never seem to get to the point—or *have* a point, for that matter. Nonetheless, most people do have a central idea. By using your ability to think more quickly than the speaker can talk, you may be able to extract the central idea from the surrounding mass of words you're hearing. If you can't figure out what the speaker is driving at, you can always ask in a tactful way by using the skills of questioning and paraphrasing, which we'll examine now.

ASK QUESTIONS

So far we have been discussing listening methods basically passive in nature; that is, those that can be carried out silently. It's also possible to verify or increase your understanding in a more active way by **questioning** the speaker to be sure you are receiving the speaker's thoughts and feelings accurately.

Although the suggestion to ask questions may seem so obvious as to be trivial, honestly ask yourself whether you take full advantage of this simple but effective method. It's often tempting to remain silent instead of being a questioner for two reasons. Sometimes you may be reluctant to show your ignorance by asking for further explanation of what seems as if it should be an obvious point. This reluctance is especially strong when the speaker's respect or liking is important to you. At such times it's a good idea to remember a quote attributed to Confucius: "He who asks a question is a fool for five minutes. He who does not ask is a fool for life."

A second reason people are often disinclined to ask questions is that they think they already understand a speaker, but do we in fact understand others as often or as well as we think? You can best answer by thinking about how often people misunderstand *you* while feeling certain that they know what you've meant. If you are aware that others should ask questions of you more often, then it's logical to assume that the same principle holds true in reverse.

Questioning is often a valuable tool for increasing understanding. Sometimes, however, it won't help you receive a speaker's ideas any more clearly, and it can even lead to further communication breakdown. To see how, consider the common example of asking directions to a friend's home. Suppose you've received these instructions: "Drive about a mile and then turn left at the traffic signal." Now imagine that a few common problems exist in this simple

Student Reflection

Paraphrasing for Information

My brother and I are complete political opposites. I'm a red-white-and-blue conservative and he's a flaming radical. We've almost given up talking about politics, since our "conversations" almost always turned into arguments.

But yesterday when we were watching news about the elections I decided to give paraphrasing a chance. Instead of arguing with him, I tried to say what I thought he was getting at in my own words.

At first he thought I was trying to trick him. But once I convinced Derrick that I was really trying to understand him, something interesting happened. I certainly didn't change my mind, but I began to see that he had some arguments that were hard to dispute. We talked for almost an hour, and when we were finished I felt like I had actually learned something. It also felt good to have a decision that wasn't a fight.

go?" to which your friend replied that the house is the third from the corner. Clearly, if you parted after this exchange, you would encounter a lot of frustration before finding the elusive residence.

What was the problem here? It's easy to see that questioning might not have helped you, for your original idea of how far to drive and where to turn were mistaken. Such mistakes exemplify the biggest problem with questioning: Your inquiries don't tell you whether you have accurately received information that has *already* been sent.

PARAPHRASE

Now consider another kind of feedback—one that would tell you whether you understood what had already been said before you asked additional questions. Such feedback as **paraphrasing** involves restating in your own words the message you thought the speaker just sent, without adding anything new: "So you're telling me to drive down to the traffic light by the high school and turn toward the mountains, is that it?" Immediately sensing the problem, your friend could then reply, "Oh no, that's way too far. I meant that you should drive to the four-way stop by the park and turn there. Did I say stop light? I always do that when I mean stop sign!"

Paraphrasing is the best way to make sure you understand another speaker, but it isn't as easy as it seems. Sharpen your skill at paraphrasing by trying Activity 5 on page 235.

This simple step of restating what you thought the speaker said before proceeding with the conversation is commonly termed *paraphrasing*, and it is an important tool for effec-

message. First, suppose that your friend's idea of a mile differs from yours: Your mental picture of the distance is actually closer to two miles, whereas your friend's is closer to 300 yards. Next, consider that "traffic signal" really means "stop sign"; after all, it's common for us to think one thing and say another. Keeping these problems in mind, suppose you tried to verify your understanding of the directions by asking, "After I turn at the light, how far should I tive listening. Remember that what is significant in paraphrasing is to *reword* the sender's words, not to parrot them. In other words, restate what you think the speaker has said in your own terms as a way of cross-checking the information. If you simply repeat the speaker's comments verbatim, you'll sound foolish or hard-of-hearing, and just as important, you still might be misunderstanding what's been said.

Because it's an unfamiliar way of responding, paraphrasing may feel awkward at first; but if you start by paraphrasing occasionally and then gradually increase the frequency of such responses, you can begin to learn the benefits of this method.

Listening to Help

We may be **listening** for information out of self-interest. Another reason for listening, however, is to help the speaker solve a problem, perhaps a personal dilemma such as "I don't know whether we should stay together or split up," "I keep getting turned down for jobs I want," "I can't get along with my family." The problem needn't be so profound, however. A friend might be trying to decide what birthday gift to buy or how to spend the weekend.

There's no question about the value of receiving help with personal problems. "Comforting ability" has been shown to be one of the most important communication skills a friend can have (Burleson 1991). The value of personal support is clear when big problems arise, but research shows that smaller, everyday distresses and upsets can actually take a bigger toll on mental health and physical well-being (Ekenrode 1984).

What kinds of responses are comforting? Gary Kreps (1990) has identified five characteristics of therapeutic communication. The first is *empathy*. It is reassuring to know that

Student Reflection
Listening as Comforting Communication

Last Tuesday Jenny, one of the tutors where I work, came in crying. It turned out that her family had just had their cat (which she had owned since the first grade) put to sleep. I felt completely helpless. I'm not a pet lover myself, and I didn't know how to offer her comfort. We talked for ten or fifteen minutes, and she told me how difficult it was to make the decision of whether or not to let the cat die naturally. I didn't know what I would have done, and so all I did was listen to her without offering advice or even telling her I thought she had done the right thing.

On Thursday Jenny came to work and thanked me for helping her so much. I was surprised, since I hadn't felt very helpful at all. "You were there," she said. "You listened to me. That's what I needed."

someone understands you, even if there is no solution to your problem. A second feature of helpful communication is *trust:* the knowledge that you can share your concerns without risk of being ridiculed or criticized, and with the assurance that your secrets are safe. A third characteristic of therapeutic responses is *honesty.* Knowing that the other person's responses are sincere is comforting in itself, while the thought that a response might be phony can create even more stress. *Validation* is a fourth feature of helpful responses. We don't need others to agree with everything about our position,

If you think communication is all talk, you haven't been listening

ASHLEIGH BRILLIANT

but the acknowledgement that our concerns are legitimate can help us begin to feel better. All of these features together represent *caring*, the final characteristic of therapeutic communication. Knowing that our welfare is important to others is in itself reassuring, and can result in less feelings of distress. There are a number of specific responses to problems. By examining each of them we can see how well they meet these characteristics of comforting communication.

ADVISING

When approached with another's problem, the most common reaction is **advising** (Notarius and Herrick 1988). Although suggestions are sometimes valuable, often they aren't as helpful as they might seem. In interviews with bereaved people who had recently lost a loved one to death, almost half of the mourners received sympathy gestures consisting of advice, yet the suggestions were rated helpful only 3 percent of the time (Davidowitz and Myrick 1984).

What listening styles do you use when responding to others' problems? How helpful are your responses, and what can you do to be even more helpful? You can discover the answers to these questions by completing Activity 6 on page 236.

There are several reasons why advice isn't helpful. First, it may not offer the best suggestion about how to act. In fact, it might even be harmful. There's often a temptation to tell others how we would behave in their place, but it's important to realize that what's right for one person may not be right for another. A related consequence of advising is that it often allows others to avoid responsibility for their decisions. A partner who follows a suggestion of yours that doesn't work out can always pin the blame on you. Finally, people often don't want advice: They may not be ready to accept it, instead needing simply to talk out their thoughts and feelings.

Before offering advice, then, be sure three conditions are present:

■ Be confident that the advice is correct. Resist the temptation to act like an authority on matters you know little about or to make suggestions when you aren't positive that they are the best choice. Realize that just because a course of action worked for you doesn't guarantee that it will be correct for everybody.

- Be sure that the person seeking your advice is truly ready to accept it. In this way you can avoid the frustration of making good suggestions, only to find that the person with the problem had another solution in mind all the time.
- Be certain that the receiver won't blame you if the advice doesn't work out. You may be offering the suggestions, but the choice and responsibility for accepting them is up to the recipient of your advice.

JUDGING

A **judging** response evaluates the sender's thoughts or behaviors in some way. The judgment may be favorable ("That's a good idea" or "You're on the right track now") or unfavorable ("An attitude like that won't get you anywhere"). In either case it implies that the person judging is in some way qualified to pass judgment on the speaker's thoughts or actions.

Sometimes negative judgments are purely critical. How many times have you heard such responses as "Well, you asked for it!" or "I *told* you so!" or "You're just feeling sorry for yourself"? Although such comments can sometimes serve as a verbal slap that "knocks sense" into the problem holder, they usually make matters worse by arousing defensiveness in that person. After all, suggesting that someone is foolish or mistaken is an attack on the presenting image which most people would have a hard time ignoring or accepting.

Other times, negative judgments are less critical. These involve what we usually call con-

---

Many receive advice, few profit by it.

PUBLILIUS SYRUS

THE FAR SIDE   By GARY LARSON

4-27   © 1987 Universal Press Syndicate

Man, Bernie, you're a mess!... You ain't itchin' anywhere, are you? Man, I had a cast on my leg years ago and <u>boy</u> did it itch!...Drove me crazy! Y'know what I'm sayin'?... 'Cause you can't scratch it, y'know... Don't think about itching anywhere, Bernie, 'cause it'll drive you <u>nuts</u>!

© 1988 Universal Press Syndicate.
Reprinted with permission.

structive criticism, which is intended to help the problem holder improve in the future. Friends give this sort of response about everything from the choice of clothing, to jobs, to friends. Another common setting for constructive criticism is school, where instructors evaluate students' work in order to help them master concepts and skills. Even constructive criticism can arouse defensiveness because it may threaten the self-concept of the person at whom it is directed.

Judgments have the best chance of being received when two conditions exist:

- The person with the problem should have requested an evaluation of you. Occasionally an unsolicited judgment may bring someone to

It is hard to know what to say to a person who has been struck by tragedy, but it is easier to know what not to say. Anything critical of the mourner ("don't take it so hard," "try to hold back your tears, you're upsetting people") is wrong. Anything which tries to minimize the mourner's pain ("it's probably for the best," "it could be a lot worse," "she's better off now") is likely to be misguided and unappreciated. Anything which asks the mourner to disguise or reject his feelings ("we have no right to question God," "God must love you to have selected you for this burden") is wrong as well.

HAROLD S. KUSHNER
When Bad Things Happen to Good People

their senses, but more often this sort of uninvited evaluation will trigger a defensive response.

■ Your judgment should be genuinely constructive and not designed as a putdown. If you are tempted to use judgments as a weapon, don't fool yourself into thinking that you are being helpful. Often the statement "I'm telling you this for your own good..." simply isn't true.

If you can remember to follow these two guidelines, your judgments will probably be less frequent and better received.

ANALYZING

In **analyzing** a situation, the listener offers an interpretation to a speaker's message ("I think what's really bothering you is..."; "She's doing it because..."; or "Maybe the problem started when he..."). Interpretations are often effective in helping people with problems to con-

sider alternative meanings of a situation—meanings they would have never thought of without your help. Sometimes a clear analysis will clarify a confusing problem, either suggesting a solution or at least providing an understanding of what is going on.

In other cases, an analysis can create more problems than it solves. There are two reasons why: First, your interpretation may not be correct, in which case the problem holder may become even more confused by accepting it. Second, even if your analysis is accurate, sharing it with the problem holder might not be useful. There's a chance that it will arouse defensiveness (analysis implies being superior and in a position to evaluate). Besides, the problem holder may not be able to understand your view of the problem without working it out personally.

How can you know when it's helpful to offer an analysis? There are several guidelines to follow:

■ Offer your interpretation in a tentative way rather than as absolute fact. There's a big difference between saying "Maybe the reason is..." and insisting, "This is the truth."
■ Your analysis ought to have a reasonable chance of being correct. An inaccurate interpretation—especially one that sounds plausible—can leave a person more confused than before.

■ You ought to be sure that the other person will be receptive to your analysis. Even if you're completely accurate, your thoughts won't help if the problem holder isn't ready to consider them.
■ Be sure that your motive for offering an analysis is truly to help the other person. It can be tempting to offer an analysis to show how brilliant you are or even to make the other person feel bad for not having thought of the right answer in the first place. Needless to say, an analysis offered under such conditions isn't helpful.

QUESTIONING

A few pages ago we talked about questioning as one way for you to understand others better. A questioning response can also be a way of helping others think about their problem and understand it more clearly. For example, questioning can help a problem holder define vague ideas more precisely. You might respond to a friend with a line of questioning: "You said Greg has been acting 'differently' toward you lately. What has he been doing?" "You told your roommates that you wanted them to be more helpful in keeping the place clean. What would you like them to do?"

Questions can also encourage a problem holder to examine a situation in more detail by talking about either what happened or personal feelings. For example: "How did you feel when they turned you down? What did you do then?" Such questioning is particularly helpful when you are dealing with someone who is quiet or is unwilling under the circumstances to talk about the problem very much.

Although questions have the potential to be helpful, they also run the risk of confusing or distracting the person with the problem. The best questioning follows these principles:

- Don't ask questions just to satisfy your own curiosity. You might become so interested in the other person's story that you will want to hear more. "What did he say then?" you might be tempted to ask. "What happened next?" Responding to questions like these might confuse the person with the problem, or even leave him or her more agitated than before.
- Be sure your questions won't confuse or distract the person you're trying to help. For instance, asking someone "When did the problem begin?" might provide some clue about how to solve it— but it could also lead to a long digression that would only confuse matters. As with advice, it's

important to be sure you're on the right track before asking questions.
- Don't use questions to disguise your suggestions or criticism. We've all been questioned by parents, teachers, or other figures who seemed to be trying to trap us or indirectly to guide us. In this way, questioning becomes a strategy that can imply that the questioner already has some idea of what direction the discussion should take, but isn't willing to tell you directly.

SUPPORTING

Supporting can take several forms. Sometimes it involves reassuring: "You've got nothing to worry about—I know you'll do a good job." In other cases, support comes through comforting: "Don't worry. We all love you." We can also support people in need by distracting them with humor, kidding, and joking.

Sometimes a person needs encouragement, and in these cases a supporting response can be the best thing. In many other instances, this kind of comment isn't helpful at all; in fact, it can even make things worse. Telling a person who is obviously upset that everything is all right, or joking about what seems like a serious problem can trivialize the problem. People might see your comments as a putdown, leaving them feeling worse than before. As with the other styles we've discussed, supporting can be helpful, but only in certain circumstances:

- Make sure your expression of support is sincere. Phony agreement or encouragement is probably worse than no support at all, since it adds the insult of your dishonesty to whatever pain the other person is already feeling.
- Be sure the other person can accept your support. Sometimes we become so upset that we aren't ready or able to hear anything positive.

REFLECTING

A **reflecting** response (sometimes also called **active listening**) goes beyond simply paraphrasing the speaker's message. It mirrors both the *thoughts* and the *feelings* you hear being expressed. This conversation between two friends shows how reflecting can offer support and help a person find the answer to her own problem:

Jill: I've had the strangest feeling about my boss lately.

Mark: What's that? (A simple question invites Jill to go on.)

Jill: I'm starting to think maybe he has this thing about women—or maybe it's just about me.

Mark: You mean he's coming on to you? (Mark paraphrases what he thinks Jill has said).

Jill: Oh no, not at all! But it seems like he doesn't take women—or at least me—seriously. (Jill corrects Mark's misunderstanding and explains herself.)

Mark: What do you mean? (Mark asks another simple question to get more information.)

Jill: Well, whenever we're in a meeting or just talking around the office and he asks for ideas, he always seems to pick men. He gives orders to women—men too—but he never asks the women to say what *they* think.

Mark: So you think maybe he doesn't take women seriously, is that it? (Mark paraphrases Jill's last statement.)

Jill: Yeah. Well, he sure doesn't seem interested in their ideas. But that doesn't mean he's a total woman-hater or a male chauvinist pig. I know he counts on some women in the office. Our accountant Teresa has been there forever, and he's always saying he couldn't live without her. And when Brenda got the new computer system up and running last month, I know he appreciated that. He gave her a day off and told everybody how she saved our lives.

Mark: Now you sound confused. (He reflects her apparent feeling.)

Jill: I *am* confused. I don't think it's just my imagination. I mean I'm a good producer, but he has never—not once—asked me for my ideas about how to improve sales or anything. And I can't remember a time when he's asked any other women. But maybe I'm overreacting.

Mark: You're not positive whether you're right, but I can tell that this has you concerned. (Mark paraphrases both Jill's central theme and her feeling.)

Jill: Yes. But I don't know what to do about it.

Mark: Maybe you should...(starts to offer advice, but catches himself and decides to ask a sincere, nonleading question instead). So what are your choices?

Jill: Well, I could just ask him if he's aware that he never asks women's opinions. But that might sound too aggressive and angry.

Mark: And you're *not* angry? (He tries to clarify how Jill is feeling.)

Jill: Not really. I don't know whether I *should* be angry because he's not taking ideas seriously, or whether he just doesn't take *my* ideas seriously, or whether it's nothing at all.

Mark: So you're mostly confused. (He reflects Jill's apparent feeling again.)

Jill: Yes! I don't know where I stand with my boss, and not being sure is starting to get to me. I wish I knew what he thinks of me. Maybe I could just tell him I'm confused about what is going on here and ask him to clear it up. But what if it's nothing? Then I'll look insecure.

Mark: (He thinks Jill should confront her boss, but isn't positive that this is the best approach, so he paraphrases what Jill seems to be saying.) And

that would make you look bad.

Jill: I'm afraid maybe it would. I wonder if I could talk it over with anybody else in the office and get their ideas....

Mark: See what they think....

Jill: Yeah. Maybe I could ask Brenda. She's easy to talk to, and I do respect her judgment. Maybe she could give me some ideas about how to handle this.

Mark: Sounds like you're comfortable with talking to Brenda first.

Jill: (warming to the idea) Yes! Then if it's nothing, I can calm down. But if I do need to talk to the boss, I'll know I'm doing the right thing.

Mark: Great. Let me know how it goes.

Reflecting a speaker's ideas and feelings in this way can be surprisingly helpful. First, it helps clarify the other person's concerns. In the dialog you just read, Mark's paraphrasing helped Jill pin down the real source of her concern: what her boss thinks of her, and not whether he doesn't take women seriously. If a restatement is accurate, the speaker has a clear picture of the problem; and if the guess is wrong, the speaker can correct it and in doing so clarify the situation.

Reflecting emotions can open up an important, unexplored area of concern. The emotional responses we have to problems are often more important than the problems themselves. In the dialog you just read, Jill's feelings of insecurity were far more important than the specifics of one project or another. By encouraging Jill to express those feelings, Mark helped her tackle the biggest problem that was bothering her.

Along with skill, attitude is an important requirement for successful reflecting when you want to help another person. The goal is to strive for a state of *empathy* with the speaker: As one unknown writer put it, "To see with the eyes of another, to hear with the ears of another, to feel with the heart of another." The purpose of expressing empathy is, according to Byrnes and Yamamoto (1981: 343), "to create an atmosphere of reassurance and understanding so that the feelings of the client [or any other person with whom you are interacting] may be expressed without mistrust or fear."

Since empathy is the ingredient that makes paraphrasing thoughts and feelings helpful, it's a mistake to think of reflective listening as a technique that you can use mechanically (Bruneau 1989, Cissna and Anderson 1990). It's essential to realize that empathy is a relational matter and not a something that can be created just by paraphrasing, or by any other kind of behavior. As psychologist Carl Rogers (1986: 376) put it, "I am *not* trying to 'reflect feelings.'" I am trying to determine whether my understanding of the client's inner world is correct— whether I am seeing it as he or she is experiencing it at this moment." In other words, reflecting is not an end in itself; rather, it is one way to help others by understanding them better.

While empathy is an important goal, it's important to realize that even the best listening won't result in complete rapport with another person (see Arnett, Nakagawa 1983; and Stewart 1983). Most importantly, empathy requires setting aside one's prejudices, values, and beliefs, which is partially, but not completely possible. Also, complete empathy means experiencing another's world, but all we can do is imagine how *we* would feel in the other's position. These restrictions don't make the pursuit of empathy any less worthwhile. They simply show that empathy is an ideal toward which to strive, not a state we can ever reach.

There are several reasons why reflecting works so well. First, it takes the burden off you as a friend. Simply being there to understand what's on someone's mind often makes it possible to clarify the problems. You don't have to know all the answers to help. Also, helping by reflecting means you don't need to guess at reasons or solutions that might not be correct. Thus, both you and your friend are saved from going on a wild goose chase after incorrect solutions.

Another advantage of reflecting is that it's an efficient way to get through layers of hidden meanings. Often people express their ideas, problems, or feelings in strangely coded ways. Reflecting can sometimes help cut through to the real meaning. Not too long ago a student came to an instructor and asked, "How many people get Ds and Fs in this class?" The instructor could have taken the question at face value and answered it, but instead he tried reflecting. He replied, "Sounds like you've got some fears of doing poorly in here." After a few minutes of listening, the instructor learned that the student was afraid that getting a low grade in a communication class would be equal to failing as a person.

A third advantage of reflecting is that it's usually the best way to encourage people to share more of themselves with you. Knowing that you're interested will make them feel less threatened, and many will be willing to let down some of their defenses. In this sense reflecting is simply a good way to learn more about someone, and a good foundation on which to build a relationship.

Although the immediate goal of reflective listening is to help the other person, an additional payoff is that the relationship between speaker and listener improves. Judy Pearson (1989: 272–75) summarizes research showing that couples who communicate in ways that show they understand one another's feelings and ideas are more satisfied with their marriages than couples who express less understanding. The opposite is also true: In marriages where husbands do not give emotional responses to their wives, the stress level grows.

Regardless of the advantages, reflecting isn't

appropriate in all situations when someone wants help. Sometimes people are simply looking for information and not trying to work out their feelings. At such times reflecting would be out of place. If someone asks you for the time of day, you'd do better simply to give the information than to respond by saying, "You want to know what time it is." If you're fixing dinner and someone wants to know when it will be ready, it would be exasperating to reply, "You're interested in knowing when we'll be eating."

However, people do often hide an important feeling behind an innocent-sounding statement or question, and in such cases reflecting can usually bring their real concern into the open. But don't go overboard with the technique. Usually, if there's a feeling hidden behind a question you'll recognize some accompanying nonverbal clue—a change in your friend's facial expression, tone of voice, posture, and so on. It takes attention, concentration, and caring on your part.

You should realize that the success of reflecting depends on the attitude you bring to a situation. Too often people think of reflecting as a kind of gimmick they can use when some unpleasant situation arises. If you think about the technique this way, it is almost sure to fail. In fact, unless you truly mean what you say, you'll come across as manipulative, phony, and uncaring. As you practice reflecting, try to keep these points in mind:

- *Don't reflect unless you truly want to help the person.* There's nothing wrong with being too busy or preoccupied to help. You'll be doing both yourself and the other person a disservice if you pretend to care when you really don't.

- *Don't reflect if you're not willing to take the necessary time.* Listening with feedback isn't easy. If you're willing to make the effort, you'll probably be rewarded, but you'll only lose the speaker's trust if you commit yourself and then don't follow through.

- *Don't try to impose your ideas on the other person.* Reflecting means accepting other people's feelings and trusting that they can find their own solutions. Your efforts to moralize, to suggest, or to change the speaker might be helpful, but if you decide to use these approaches, do so honestly— don't mask them in the guise of reflecting.

- *Keep your attention focused on the problem holder.* Sometimes, as you listen to others share feelings, it's easy to become defensive, to relate their thoughts to your own life, or to seek further information just to satisfy your own curiosity. Remember that reflecting is a form of helping someone else. The general obligation to reciprocate the other person's self-disclosure with information of your own isn't necessary when the goal is to solve a problem. Research shows that speakers who reveal highly intimate personal information don't expect, or even appreciate, the same kind of disclosure from a conversational partner (Hosman 1987). Rather, the most competent and socially attractive response is one that sticks to the same topic but is lower in intimacy. In other words, when we are opening up to others, we don't appreciate their pulling a conversational takeaway such as "You're worried? So am I! Let me tell you about how I feel. . . . "

- *Mix reflecting with other response styles.* To sound natural, reflecting needs to be mixed with other types of helping responses. If you do nothing but paraphrase, you are likely to sound phony and annoying. This risk is especially great if you suddenly begin to use reflecting a great deal. The switch in your behavior will be so out of character that others will find it distracting. A far better way to use reflecting is to gradually introduce it into your repertoire of helping responses, so that your skill and comfort with it develop over time. Another way to develop your skill at reflecting is to start using that approach on real but relatively minor problems, so that you will be more adept at knowing how and when to use it when a crisis occurs.

WHICH STYLE TO USE?

By now it's clear that there are many ways to help others—probably more than you use. You can also see that each helping style has its advantages and drawbacks. This leads us to the important question of which style or styles are most helpful. There isn't a simple answer to this question. Research shows that *all* styles can help others accept their situation, feel better, and have a sense of control over their problems (Silver and Wortman 1981; Young et al. 1982). Furthermore, communicators who are able to use a wide variety of helping styles are usually more effective than those who rely on just one or two approaches (Burleson 1988, 1991; Samter et al. 1988).

You can boost the odds of choosing the best helping style in each situation by considering three factors. First, think about the *situation* and match your response to the nature of the problem. Sometimes people need your advice. In other cases your encouragement and support will be most helpful, and in still other instances your analysis or judgment may be truly useful. And, as you have seen, there are times when your probes and paraphrasing can help others find their own answer.

Besides considering the situation, you also should think about the *other person* when deciding which approach to use. Some people are able to consider advice thoughtfully, while others use suggestions to avoid making their own decisions. Many communicators are extremely defensive, and aren't capable of receiving analysis or judgments without lashing out. Still others aren't equipped to think through problems clearly enough to profit from paraphrasing and probing. Sophisticated helpers choose a style that fits the person.

Finally, think about *yourself* when deciding how to respond. Most of us reflexively use one or two helping styles. You may be best at listening quietly, offering a prompt or reflecting from time to time. Or perhaps you are especially insightful, and can offer a truly useful analysis of the problem. Of course, it's also possible to rely on a response style that is *unhelpful.* You may be overly judgmental or too eager to advise, even when your suggestions aren't invited or productive. As you think about how to respond to another's problems, consider both your strengths and weaknesses.

Summary

Listening is both more frequent and less emphasized than speaking. Despite its relative invisibility, listening is arguably at least as important as speaking. Along with its lack of attention, understanding of listening suffers from several misconceptions, which communicators need to correct. Listening—at least listening effectively—is quite different from merely hearing a message. Skillful listening is not a natural skill; rather, it requires much effort and talent. Even careful listening does not guarantee that all listeners will receive the same message. A wide variety of factors discussed in this chapter can result in widely varying interpretations of even simple statements.

Listening consists of several components: attending to a message, understanding the statement, recalling the message after the passage of time, and responding to the speaker.

Listening can serve several functions. It can allow us to empathize with others, critically analyze their messages, and affirm their value. Whatever the goal, several barriers can hamper effective listening: hearing problems, information overload, rapid thought, and both internal and external noise.

A number of poor habits can interfere with effective listening. The chapter described pseudolistening, stage hogging, selective listening, filling in gaps, assimilation to prior messages, insulated listening, defensive listening, ambushing, and insensitive listening.

When the goal is to listen for information, several simple steps can increase comprehension. Focusing on the speaker and talking less is a good start. Removing distractions can help listeners pay better attention. Withholding judgment, looking for key ideas, asking questions, and paraphrasing were all recommended.

When the goal is to help the other person, listeners have a variety of response styles at their disposal: Advising, judging, analyzing, questioning, supporting, and reflecting all have their advantages and drawbacks. The most effective helpers use several styles, depending on the situation, the other person, and their own personal styles.

Activities

1. You can overcome believing in some common myths about listening by recalling specific instances when
   a. You heard another person's message, but did not attend to it.
   b. You attended to a message, but forgot it prematurely.
   c. You attended and remembered a message, but did not understand it accurately.
   d. You understood a message, but did not respond sufficiently to convey your understanding to the sender.

2. Keep a one day's journal of your listening behavior. Note the amount of waking time you spend in each of the following types of listening:
   a. Informational
   b. Empathic
   c. Critical and discriminating
   d. Other-affirming
   After completing your survey, calculate the percentage of your waking day spent listening.

3. Explain the list of poor listening habits on pages 218–221 to a companion who knows you well. Work together to identify which of these habits you fall prey to. Discuss with your partner the consequences of these behaviors. Finally, consider how you might listen more effectively in the situations you identified here.

4. Informational listening doesn't just occur in lectures. Describe a specific situation in one of your important interpersonal relationships when you will need to listen for information. Arrange a conversation with your relational partner and apply each of the informational listening principles described on pages 222–225. After the conversation, answer the following questions:
   a. How did this conversation differ from others in which you weren't consciously following the guidelines listed in this chapter?
   b. What informational listening skills learned here can you apply in your everyday life?

5. Practice your ability to paraphrase to understand others by following these steps.
   a. Choose a partner, and designate one of yourselves as A and the other as B. Find a subject

on which you and your partner seem to disagree—a personal dispute, a philosophical or moral issue, or perhaps a matter of personal taste.

c. A begins by making a statement on the subject. B's job is to paraphrase the idea. In this step B should feed back only what he or she heard A say without adding any judgment or interpretation. B's job here is simply to *understand* A—not to agree or disagree with A.

d. A responds by telling B whether or not the response was accurate, and by making any necessary additions or corrections to clarify the message.

e. A then paraphrases the revised statement. This process should continue until A is sure that B understands him or her.

f. Now B and A reverse roles and repeat the procedure in steps a–e. Continue the conversation until both partners are satisfied that they have explained themselves fully and have been understood by the other person.

After the discussion has ended, consider how this process differed from typical conversations on controversial topics. Was there greater understanding here? Do the partners feel better about one another? Finally, ask yourself how your life might change if you used paraphrasing more in everyday conversations.

6. Explore the various types of helping responses by completing the following steps.

a. Join with two partners to form a trio. Label members as A, B, and C.

b. A begins by sharing a current, real problem with B. The problem needn't be a major life crisis, but it should be a real one. B should respond in whatever way seems most helpful. C's job is to categorize each response by B as advising, judging, analyzing, questioning, supporting, or reflecting.

c. After a four- to five-minute discussion, C should summarize B's response styles. A then describes which of the styles were most helpful, and which were not helpful.

d. Repeat the same process two more times, switching roles so that each person has filled all of the positions.

e. Based on their findings, the threesome should develop conclusions about what combination of response styles can be most helpful.

Readings

Anderson, R. *Students as Real People: Interpersonal Communication and Education.* Rochelle Park, NJ: Hayden, 1979.

Arnett, R. C., and G. Nakagawa. "The Assumptive Roots of Empathic Listening: A Critique." *Communication Education* 32 (October 1983): 368–78.

Baddeley, A. D. *The Psychology of Memory.* New York: Basic Books, 1976.

Banville, T. G. *How to Listen—How to Be Heard.* Chicago: Nelson-Hall, 1978.

*Barker, L. L. *Listening Behavior.* Englewood Cliffs, NJ: Prentice-Hall, 1971.

Barker, L., R. Edwards, C. Gaines, K. Gladney, and F. Holley. "An Investigation of Proportional Time Spent in Various Communication Activities by College Students." *Journal of Applied Communication Research* 8 (1981): 101–9.

Beier, E. G., and E. G. Valens. *People-Reading: How We Control Others, How They Control Us.* New York: Stein and Day, 1975.

*Bostrom, R. N. *Listening Behavior.* New York: Guilford, 1990.

Bostrom, R. N., and C. L. Bryant. "Factors in the Retention of Information Presented Orally: The Role of Short-Term Listening." *Western Journal of Speech Communication* 44 (1980): 137–45.

*Bostrom, R. N., and E. S. Waldhart. "Components in Listening Behavior: The Role of Short-Term Memory." *Human Communication Research* 6 (1980): 221–27.

Bruneau, J. "Empathy and Listening: A Conceptual Review and Theoretical Directions." *Journal of the International Listening Association* 3 (1989): 1–20.

Burgoon, J. K., D. B. Buller, J. L. Hale, and M. A. de Turck. "Relational Messages Associated with Nonverbal Behaviors." *Human Communication Research* 10 (1984): 351–78.

Burleson, B. "Comforting Communication: Does It Really Matter?" Paper presented at the annual convention of the Western Speech Communication Association, San Diego, 1988.

Burleson, B. R. "Comforting Messages: Their Significance and Effects." In *Communicating Strategically: Strategies in Interpersonal Communication*, J. A. Daly and J. M. Wiemann, eds. Hillsdale, NJ: Erlbaum, 1991.

Byrnes, D. A., and K. Yamamoto. "Some Reflections of Empathy." *School Counselor* 28 (1981): 343–45.

Cissna, K. N., and R. Anderson. "The Contributions of Carl R. Rogers to a Philosophical Praxis of Dialogue." *Western Journal of Speech Communication* 54 (1990): 137–47.

Davidowitz, M., and R. Myrick. "Responding to the Bereaved: An Analysis of 'Helping' Styles." *Death Education* 8 (1984): 1–10.

Dittmann, A. T. "Developmental Factors in Conversational Behavior." *Journal of Communication* 22 (1972): 404–23.

Ekenrode, J. "Impact of Chronic and Acute Stressors on Daily Reports of Mood." *Journal of Personality and Social Psychology* 46 (1984): 907–18.

Fisher, B. A. *Interpersonal Communication: Pragmatics of Human Relationships*. New York: Random House, 1987.

*Floyd, J. J. *Listening: A Practical Approach*. Glenview, IL: Scott, Foresman, 1985.

Foulke, E., and T. Stricht. "Review of Research in Time-Compressed Speech." In *Time-Compressed Speech*, S. Duker, ed. Metuchen, NJ: Scarecrow Press, 1974.

Golan, S. "A Factor Analysis of Barriers to Effective Listening." *Journal of Business Communication* 27 (1990): 25–36.

Goldhaber, G. M. "Listener Comprehension of Compressed Speech as a Function of the Academic Grade Level of Subjects." *Journal of Communication* 20 (1970): 167–73.

Goss, B. *Processing Communication: Information Processing in Interpersonal Communication*. Belmont, CA: Wadsworth, 1982.

Haase, R. F., and D. T. Tepper. "Non-Verbal Components of Empathic Communication." *Journal of Counseling Psychology* 19 (1972): 417–24.

Hosman, L. A. "The Evaluational Consequences of Topic Reciprocity and Self-Disclosure Reciprocity." *Communication Monographs* 54 (1987): 420–35.

Hulbert, J. E. "Barriers to Effective Listening." *Bulletin for the Association for Business Communication* 52 (1989): 3–5.

Katz, J. J., and J. A. Foder. "The Structure of a Semantic Theory." In *Readings in the Philosophy of Language*, J. F. Rosenberg and C. Travis, eds. Englewood Cliffs, NJ: Prentice-Hall, 1971.

Keefe, W. F. *Listen Management*. New York: McGraw-Hill, 1971.

Kelley, C. M. "Empathic Listening." In *Small Group Communication: A Reader*, 4th ed., R. Cathcart and L. Samovar, eds. Dubuque, IA: Wm. C. Brown, 1984.

Kreps, G. "The Nature of Therapeutic Communication." In *Talking to Strangers: Mediated Therapeutic Communication*. G. Gumpert and S. L. Fish, eds. Norwood, NJ: Ablex, 1990.

Lewis, M. H., and N. L. Reinsch, Jr. "Listening in Organizational Environments." *Journal of Business Communication* 25 (1988): 49–67.

McComb, K. B., and F. M. Jablin. "Verbal Correlates of Interviewer Empathic Listening and Employment Interview Outcomes." *Communication Monographs* 51 (1984): 367.

Mulac, A., J. M. Wyeman, S. J. Widenmann, and T. W. Gibson, "Male/Female Language Differences and

Effects in Same Sex and Mixed-Sex Dyads: The Gender-Linked Language Effect," *Communication Monographs,* 55 (1988): 315–335.

Nichols, R. G. "Factors in Listening Comprehension." *Speech Monographs* 15 (1948): 154–63.

*Nichols, R. G., and L. A. Stevens. *Are You Listening?* New York: McGraw-Hill, 1957.

Notarius, C. I., and L. R. Herrick, "Listener Response Strategies to a Distressed Other." *Journal of Social and Personal Relationships* 5 (1988): 97–108.

Pearson, J. *Communication in the Family* New York: Harper & Row, 1989.

Plax, T. G., and L. B. Rosenfeld. "Receiver Differences and the Comprehension of Spoken Messages." *Journal of Experimental Education* 48 (1979): 23–28.

Postman, N., and C. Weingartner. *Teaching as a Subversive Activity.* New York: Delacorte Press, 1969.

Rankin, P. "Listening Ability." In *Proceedings of the Ohio State Educational Conference's Ninth Annual Session,* 1929.

Rogers, C. R. *On Becoming a Person.* Boston: Houghton-Mifflin, 1961.

Rogers, C. R. "Reflection of Feelings." *Person-Centered Review* 1 (1986): 375–77.

Samter, W., B. R. Burleson, and L. B. Murphy. "Comforting Conversations: The Effects of Strategy Type of Evaluations of Messages and Message Producers." *Southern Speech Communication Journal* 52 (1987): 263–84.

Silver, R., and C. Wortman. "Coping with Undesirable Life Events." In J. Garber and M. Seligman, eds. *Human Helplessness: Theory and Applications* New York: Academic Press, 1981.

Smeltzer, L. R., and K. W. Watson. "Listening: An Empirical Comparison of Discussion Length and Level of Incentive." *Central States Speech Journal* 35 (1984): 166–70.

Steil, L. K. "Listen My Students...and You Shall Learn." *Towards Better Teaching* 11 (Fall 1978).

Steil, L. K., L. L. Barker, and K. W. Watson. *Effective Listening: Key to Your Success.* Reading, MA: Addison-Wesley, 1983.

Stewart, J. "Interpretive Listening: An Alternative to Empathy." *Communication Education* 32 (October 1983): 379–91.

Sypher, B. D., R. N. Bostrom, and J. H. Seibert. "Listening Communication Abilities and Success at Work." *Journal of Business Communication* 26 (1989): 293–303.

Weaver, C. *Human Listening: Processes and Behavior.* Indianapolis: Bobbs-Merrill, 1972.

*Wolff, F., N. C. Marsnik, W. S. Tacey, and R. G. Nichols. *Perceptive Listening* New York: Holt, Rinehart and Winston, 1983.

Wolvin, A. D. "Meeting the Communication Needs of the Adult Learner." *Communication Education* 33 (1984): 267–71.

*Wolvin, A. D., and C. Coakley. *Listening,* 3d ed. Dubuque, IA: Wm. C. Brown, 1988.

Young, C. E., D. E. Giles, and M. C. Plantz. "Natural Networks: Help-Giving and Help-Seeking in Two Rural Communities." *American Journal of Community Psychology* 10 (1982): 457–69.

*Items identified by an asterisk are recommended as especially useful follow-ups.

Part Four

Relational Dimensions of
Interpersonal Communications

Relationships

Chapter 8
Relationships

After studying the material in this chapter

You should understand

1. The goals participants seek to satisfy in interpersonal relationships.

2. The ways content and relational messages are communicated in interpersonal relationships.

3. The strategies that can be used to gain compliance in a relationship.

4. The reasons why people choose others as potential relational partners.

5. The stages of relational development and deterioration, and the characteristics of movement between these stages.

6. The communication-related characteristics that distinguish high-quality relationships.

7. The pressures that operate against friendships.

8. Gender-related variables that influence friendships.

9. Various types of love.

You should be able to

1. Identify the social needs that you and the other person are trying to satisfy at a given point in one of your interpersonal relationships.

2. Describe the distribution of control in an important relationship.

3. Choose the most promising compliance-gaining strategy you could use in a given situation.

4. Identify the bases of interpersonal attraction in one of your relationships.

5. Describe the current stage of an important personal relationship and describe whether and how that relationship might move to a more satisfying stage.

6. Describe how you can apply the guidelines on page 280 to maintain or improve an important relationship.

Key Terms

Affinity
Agape
Avoiding
Bonding
Circumscribing
Complementary relational
    structure

Compliance gaining
    strategy
Content message
Control
Differentiating
Direct request
Eros

Exchange theory
Experimenting
Face maintenance strategy
Indirect appeal
Initiating
Integrating
Intensifying

There's no question that personal relationships matter. To understand just how important they are, imagine how your life would suffer without them: no friends, family, fellow workers, or romantic partners. Almost as bad would be poor relationships with these key people. It's no surprise that respondents to one survey identified interpersonal relationships as more important than anything else in making their lives meaningful (Campbell et al. 1976).

Despite such importance, most people have a difficult time defining the word "relationship." The dictionary definition reads, "the mode in which two or more things stand to one another." This is true as far as it goes. You are tall in relation to some people and short in relation to others, and we are more or less wealthy only by comparison to others; but physical and economic relationships don't tell us much that is useful about interpersonal communication.

Interpersonal relationships involve the way people deal with one another *socially.* In other words, we judge the quality of an interpersonal relationship by how well it satisfies our social needs. In a moment we will describe just what those needs are. For now, though, we can define the term **interpersonal relationship** as an association in which the people meet each other's social needs to some degree.

Goals of Interpersonal Relationships

What do we seek in interpersonal relationships? Certainly some of our goals involve meeting the day-to-day challenges of life: helping us feed ourselves, succeed on the job, get from place to place, and so on. As important as these tasks may be, we don't need *interpersonal* relationships to accomplish them. We seek out interpersonal relationships to satisfy four less tangible but equally important needs: intimacy, control, affiliation, and respect.

INTIMACY

Three kinds of **intimacy** help determine the importance of a relationship: intellectual, emo-

> What is peculiarly characteristic of the human world is above all that something takes place between one being and another the like of which can be found nowhere in nature . . . It is rooted in one being turning to another as another, as this particular other being, in order to communicate with it in a sphere . . . *the sphere of "between."*
>
> MARTIN BUBER
> *Between Man and Man*

243

tional, and physical. It is possible to be intimate with someone in one of these ways and not in others. You may, for example, share a relationship in which you're not physically close, but highly intimate on an emotional level.

There's more to intimacy than sex. You can analyze the kinds and level of intimacy in one of your relationships by following the directions in Activity 1 on page 281.

A high level of intimacy isn't a goal in every relationship (Delia 1980). We aren't interested in getting closer to most of the people we encounter every day: salesclerks, telephone operators, and so on. Great intimacy isn't even important in every interpersonal relationship. It's possible to have a very satisfying association with some friends, neighbors, fellow workers, or even family members without a high amount of personal sharing. You can probably think of several personal relationships that have moderate or even low amounts of intimacy. In fact, you might feel uncomfortable if the other people in these relationships sought more intimacy. Nonetheless, it's fair to assume that most of us need some relationships that are emotionally, physically, and intellectually close.

The **social penetration model** (see Figure 8–1) is a useful way to visualize the development of intimacy (Altman and Taylor 1973; Taylor and Altman 1987). This model suggests that relationships develop in increments, moving from superficial to more personal levels. As two people learn more about each other, primarily through the process of self-disclosure, the relationship gains importance. Depending on the *breadth* of the information shared (for example, the number of topics you discuss) and the *depth* of that information, a relationship can be defined as casual or intimate. In the case of a casual relationship, the breadth may be high, but not the depth. A more intimate relationship is likely to have high breadth and high depth. Altman and Taylor visualize these two factors as an image of concentric circles. Depth increases as you disclose information that is central to the relationship, information not available unless you provide it; for example, your personal goals, fears, and self-images. Altman and Taylor see relationship development as a progression from the periphery to the center of the circle, a process that typically takes time.

Using this theory of social penetration, you can visualize a diagram in which a husband's relationship with his wife has high breadth and high depth, his relationship with his friend has low breadth and high depth, and his relationship with his boss is one of low breadth and low depth. Imagine what your own relationship with various people would look like. Figure 8–2 provides a typical example.

Figure 8–1   Sample model of social penetration illustrating a college student's relationship with a friend

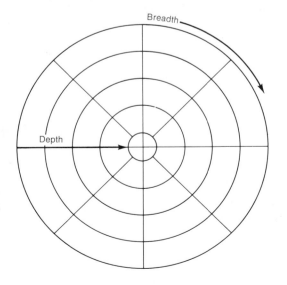

The Altman-Taylor model of social penetration

Figure 8–2   Mean intimacy ratings of relationship terms in two cultures
Items are rated on a nine-point scale.   **1 = most intimate**   **9 = least intimate**

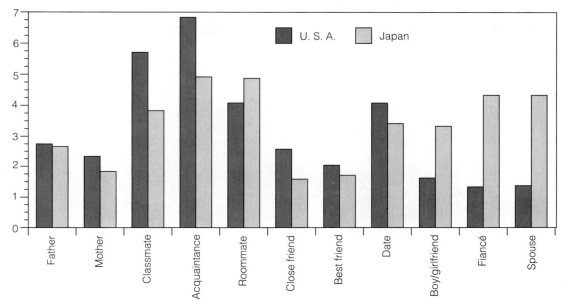

Adapted from W. B. Gudykunst and T. Nishida, "The Influence of Cultural Variability on Perceptions of Communication Behavior Associated with Relationship Terms." *Human Communication Research* 13: (1986) 147–66

The Altman-Taylor model can be used to predict a variety of relationships. According to the theory, relationships proceeding rapidly to the central areas can be fragile. For example, an experience such as a "one-night stand" of sexual intimacy often lacks the accompanying transactions that build trust and understanding. When interpersonal conflict erupts, the relationship crumbles.

The degree of intimacy we seek in relationships can vary from one culture to another. For example, Gudykunst and Nishida (1986) examined the way American and Japanese viewed the level of intimacy in various relationships. As Figure 8–2 shows, the expectation of closeness is very similar in some cases, such as father and mother. In other cases, however,

the level of intimacy varied. Japanese seem to expect more intimacy in friendships, while Americans look for more intimacy in romantic relationships: boy or girlfriend, fiancé, and spouse. Differences like these illustrate the challenges that people from different cultures can face when they try to build relationships.

AFFINITY

Another dimension of relationships is **affinity**—the degree to which the partners like or appreciate one another. Not all interpersonal relationships are friendly. Colleagues who have worked together for years and who have struggled for most of the time may not like each other much, but they are still intensely involved with

That Certain Someone, Inc.
INTRODUCTION SERVICE
● MEMBERSHIP
● STRICT CONFIDENTIALITY
● COMPUTERIZED
● INQUIRIES
● GUARANTEED

"My preference is for someone who's afraid of closeness, like me."

Drawing by Weber; © 1989, *The New Yorker Magazine, Inc.*

each other. Likewise, friends who disagree or lovers who constantly argue are partners in relationships. In this sense, liking and disliking (both signs that we *care* about the other person) are much more closely related to each other than either is to indifference.

RESPECT

At first glance, **respect** might seem identical to affinity, but the two attitudes are different. It's possible to like others without respecting them. For instance, you might like—or even probably love—your two-year-old cousin without respecting her. In the same way, you might have a great deal of affection for some friends, yet not respect the way they behave. The reverse is also true: It's possible to respect people we don't like. You might hold an acquaintance in high esteem

for being a hard worker, honest, talented, or clever—yet not particularly enjoy that person's company.

Sometimes being respected is more important than being liked. Think about occasions in school when you were offended because an instructor or fellow students didn't seem to take your comments or questions seriously. The same principle holds on the job, where having your opinions count often means more than being popular. Even in more personal relationships, conflicts often focus on the issue of respect. Being taken seriously is a vital ingredient of self-esteem.

CONTROL

Influencing others, or **control,** is one of the most fundamental goals in most relationships

(Berger 1985; Wiemann and Kelly 1981). We try to influence other people over a wide range of topics (Dillard 1989): Persuading them to change their life-style, take better care of their health, modify their opinions, give us assistance, spend time with us, and behave differently in relationships. Sometimes the subject of discussion is less important than the sheer act of influencing others. You've probably experienced this fact for yourself: You find yourself arguing about a trivial topic—whether one film is or isn't better than another or whether an article of clothing is blue or green. The dispute here isn't really about the apparent subject. Rather, it focuses on who will influence whom—who's in control.

What is the balance of control in your relationships? Do you share power willingly or struggle to gain the upper hand? Find out by completing Activity 2 on page 281.

Communication scholars frequently use the scheme introduced by Bateson (1937), developed by Watzlawick et al. (1967) and later modified by Phillips and Wood (1983) and Wilmot (1987) to describe the distribution of control in a relationship. This scheme identifies three distinct relational structures: *complementary, symmetrical,* and *parallel.* A **complementary relational structure** is based on differences between the partners that complete each other. By their different behaviors, each fulfills the other's needs. For example, a traditional marriage with a dominant husband and submissive wife is a complementary relationship. The male is expected to earn the money on which to live, while the female is expected to stay home and take care of the house and children. The relationship is stable; they work as a team, and both perceive they can do more together than either could do individu-

ally. According to Phillips and Wood (1983: 151), two individuals in a complementary relationship "go together so that each works better in combination than alone."

Several attributes define a complementary relationship (Phillips and Wood 1983; Wilmot 1987): The relationship is based on differences between the partners; one partner occupies the superior or "one-up" position and the other occupies the submissive or "one-down" position; both individuals need each other to confirm their identities (for example, the submissive spouse is submissive only in the presence of the dominant spouse); each partner has distinct roles, rights, and obligations; the relationship reduces the partners' ability to function independently; and if the relationship is terminated, both partners are debilitated. Stability characterizes the relationship and is its avowed virtue.

Unlike the complementary structure, the **symmetrical structure** implies equality. A symmetrical structure is a balanced one: Each of the individuals contributes equally to all facets of the relationship with the goal of balance or reciprocity. Balance and reciprocity are often a result of similarity between the partners; in fact, this similarity may be a source of attraction (Hinde 1979).

These attributes define a symmetrical relationship (Phillips and Wood 1983; Wilmot 1987): Power is distributed equally between the partners; partners behave as if they are of equal status; each partner may initiate action; partners are highly independent (for example, each claims the right to make personal decisions, keep a private domain both inside and outside the relationship, and pursue a career); and both partners attempt to be either "one-up" or "one-down," that is, dominant or submissive. Partners in a symmetrical relationship believe that the structure of their relationship helps preserve their individuality.

A **parallel relational structure** combines the features of both the complementary and symmetrical structures. In this structure, participants are willing to employ both the complementary and symmetrical communication patterns in their relationship (Phillips and Wood 1983).

Here are the attributes of a parallel structure (Phillips and Wood 1983; Wilmot 1987): Part-

ners are committed to a common direction; partners realize that contributions to the relationship will vary from time to time and situation to situation; partners believe a certain amount of independence is necessary in some areas of the relationship; and both partners pursue common activities while retaining some separate interests. Flexibility is the hallmark of this relationship structure, with partners using either complementary or symmetrical interchanges depending upon the apparent needs of the relationship at a given moment.

In a 1984 investigation of perceptions of partners in each of the three types of relational structures, M. R. Harrington found that the parallel relationship structure was favored by the vast majority of subjects. Apparently the open nature of the relationship allowed each of the subjects to maintain the relationship without

---

Most conversations seem to be carried out on two levels, the verbal level and the emotional level. The verbal level contains those things which are socially acceptable to say, but it is used as a means of satisfying emotional needs. Yesterday a friend related something that someone had done to her. I told her why I thought the person had acted the way he had and she became very upset and started arguing with me. Now, the reason is clear. I had been listening to her words and had paid no attention to her feelings. Her words had described how terribly this other person had treated her, but her emotions had been saying, "Please understand how I felt. Please accept my feeling the way I did." The last thing she wanted to hear from me was an explanation of the other person's behavior.

HUGH PRATHER

compromising individual identity. The parallel structure also reflects the current popular view of a progressive relationship. The flexibility of the structure allows for greater social adaptability, an important and attractive asset in a rapidly changing social and professional world. The most rejected relationship was the complementary one with the female dominant and the male submissive, results that confirm Kaplan and Sedney's (1980) conclusion that in the United States people currently perceive such a family structure as pathological and a negative influence on children.

Another study revealed that changes in popular romance novels over the years reflect the evolving social image of the ideal male-female relationship (Hubbard 1985). In the 1950s romantic relationships were basically complementary, with a Cinderella-type heroine and a male hero who strongly resembled Prince Charming. Themes in the 1960s and 1970s reflected the emerging womens' movement: a struggle for symmetrical power between a rebellious female and a male still seeking dominance. By the early 1980s, symmetry earned equal billing with parallel relationships in which liberated heroines and equally powerful male partners shared the stage.

Communication in Interpersonal Relationships

By now it is clear that interpersonal relationships can be described in terms of their intimacy, locus of control, affinity, and respect. How are these dimensions communicated?

CONTENT AND RELATIONAL MESSAGES

As you learned in Chapter 1, every message has a **content** and a **relational** dimension. The most obvious component of most messages is their

---

Student Reflection

Negotiating the Relational Balance of Power

Our daughter turned thirteen this year, and nothing I read about adolescence has prepared me for the struggles we've gone through. We've fought over everything you can imagine: curfew deadlines, clothes, homework, music, diet—you name it. Now I realize that the struggle for control is the theme running through all our battles. When she was younger, our daughter was willing to be the one-down person in our relationship. Now, though, she wants to take charge of her life. As parents we have to realize that she does deserve to have more control, but our daughter has to accept the fact that we still need to make the final decision in some important areas. Until we can agree on a fair "balance of power" I'm afraid we're in for more battles.

---

content—the subject being discussed. The content of statements like "It's your turn to do the dishes" or "I'm busy Saturday night" is obvious.

Content messages aren't the only information being exchanged when two people communicate. In addition, every message—both verbal and nonverbal—also has a second, *relational* dimension, which makes statements about how the parties feel toward one another (Watzlawick et al. 1967: 80–83). These relational messages deal with one or more of the social needs we have been discussing. Consider the two examples we just mentioned:

Student Reflection

Indirect and Overt Relational Messages

I call it "the sigh." My friend Bess hates to fight and she tries to hide it when she's mad at me, but she gives herself away by letting off a huge sigh and rolling her eyes. When I ask her what's wrong she says "Nothing" and sighs again.

Sometimes I can guess what's bothering her, but I wish she would talk about it. I'm getting tired of guessing and begging her to talk. Bess isn't fooling anybody (except maybe herself) when she says everything is fine. Sometimes I think about how much easier it would be if she was willing to try a little metacommunication.

■ Imagine two ways of saying, "It's your turn to do the dishes," one that is demanding and another that is matter-of-fact. Notice how the different nonverbal messages make statements about how the sender views control in this part of the relationship. The demanding tone says, in effect, "I have a right to tell you what to do around the house," whereas the matter-of-fact one suggests, "I'm just reminding you of something you might have overlooked."

■ You can easily imagine two ways to deliver the statement "I'm busy Saturday night," one with little affection and the other with much liking.

Like these messages, every statement we make goes beyond discussing the subject at hand and says something about the way the speaker feels about the recipient. You can prove this fact by listening for the relational messages implicit in your own statements to others and theirs to you.

Most of the time we are unaware of the relational messages that bombard us every day. Sometimes these messages don't capture our awareness because they match our belief about the amount of control, liking, or intimacy that is appropriate in a relationship. For example, you probably won't be offended if your boss tells you to drop everything and tackle a certain job, because you agree that supervisors have the right to direct employees. However, if your boss delivered the order in a condescending, sarcastic, or abusive tone of voice, you would probably be offended. Your complaint wouldn't be with the order itself, but with the way it was delivered. "I may work for this company," you might think, "but I'm not a slave or an idiot. I deserve to be treated like a human being."

EXPRESSION OF RELATIONAL MESSAGES

Exactly how are relational messages communicated? As the boss-employee example suggests, they are usually expressed nonverbally. To test this fact for yourself, imagine how you could act while saying, "Can you help me for a minute?" in a way that communicates each of the following relationships:

superiority

helplessness

friendliness

aloofness

sexual desire

irritation

Although nonverbal behaviors are a good source of relational messages, remember that they are ambiguous. The sharp tone you take as a personal insult might be due to fatigue, and the interruption you take as an attempt to ignore your ideas might be a sign of pressure that has nothing to do with you. Before you jump to conclusions about relational clues, it is a good idea to verify the accuracy of your interpretation with the other person: "When you cut me off, I got the idea you're angry at me. Is that right?"

Not all relational messages are nonverbal. Social scientists use the term **metacommunication** to describe messages that refer to other messages. In other words, metacommunication is communication about communication. Whenever we discuss a relationship with others, we are metacommunicating: "I wish we could stop arguing so much," or "I appreciate how honest you've been with me." Verbal metacommunication is an essential ingredient in successful relationships. Sooner or later there are times when it becomes necessary to talk about what is going on between you and the other person. The ability to focus on the kinds of issues described in this chapter can be the tool for keeping your relationship on track.

But despite its importance, overt metacommunication isn't a common feature of most relationships (Wilmot 1987: 127). In fact, there seems to be an aversion to it, even among many intimates. When ninety people were asked to identify the taboo subjects in their personal relationships, the most frequent topics involved metacommunication (Baxter and Wilmot 1985). For example, people were reluctant to discuss the state of their current relationships and the norms ("rules") that governed their lives together. Other studies suggest that when metacommunication does occur, it sometimes threatens the recipient and provokes conflict (Hocker and Wilmot 1991).

By now it's clear that metacommunication can be both important and risky. The key to its success is the skill with which you deliver metacommunicative messages. Because this skill is so important, Chapters 9, 10 and 11 of this book offer guidelines that can help you become more effective at delivering relational messages.

Strategies in Interpersonal Relationships

Whether the goal is gaining control, affection, or respect, we use communication to get what we seek. Sometimes the choice of approaches is conscious: If you are trying to impress a potential boss or romantic partner, you will probably think carefully about what to say or do. Once relationships develop, we still do our share of strategizing. A teenager who wants to borrow the family car, a spouse who wants to propose a vacation that his or her mate might not like, or a friend who needs to explain why he or she forgot to show up for a date all are likely to weigh their words before speaking. In other cases we don't consciously strategize, but even then it's likely that as competent communicators we consider a number of ways to get what we seek before choosing what we hope will be the best approach.

TYPES OF COMPLIANCE
GAINING STRATEGIES

Social scientists use the term **compliance gaining strategies** to define the tactics we use to persuade others to think or act in a desired way. Over the last quarter century researchers have devised a variety of ways to describe compliance-gaining strategies (see, for example, Table 8–1 and Trenholm 1989: 311–12; and Goss and O'Hair 1988: 241–43). The particular strategies we use to get what we seek from others can vary from one type of relationship to another. For example, dating couples who want to intensify their relationship use the strategies listed in Table 8–1. When the goal is to increase the level of physical intimacy, a wide range of approaches can be used, including logic, pleading,

Table 8–1   Compliance Strategies Used to Intensify Dating Relationships (Listed in Order of Frequency)

39.2% *Increased contact:* Interact with partner more often and for longer periods of time.

29.1% *Relationship negotiation:* Initiates or engages in direct give-and-take discussion of relationship.

26.1% *Social support and assistance:* Asking for advice, assistance, or support.

17.6% *Increase rewards:* Compliment, do favors, perform tasks to increase rewards.

16.6% *Direct relational bid:* Direct request or bid, without discussion, for a more serious exclusive relationship.

16.1% *Token of affection:* Gives gifts, cards, flowers, sentimental items to partner.

15.1% *Personalized communication:* Self-disclosure or use of language that reflects uniqueness of relationship (e.g., pet names).

14.1% *Verbal expressions of affection:* Directly expresses feelings of affection to partner.

13.1% *Suggestive actions:* Hints, flirts, playing hard to get and other deceptive or non-open methods to communicate feelings.

12.1% *Nonverbal expressions of affection:* Touching, sustained eye contact, etc.

11.6% *Social enmeshment:* Getting to know friends and family of the partner or getting the partner to know one's own friends and family.

 9.5% *Accept definitional bid:* Agree to a direct request for a more serious/exclusive relationship.

 9.5% *Personal appearance:* Attempt to look physically attractive for one's partner.

From James H. Tolhuizen, "Communication Strategies for Intensifying Dating Relationships: Identification, Use and Structure." *Journal of Social and Personal Relationships* 6 (1989): 413–434.

bargaining, flattery, and physical impositions (Christopher and Fransden 1990).

You may not think of yourself as a conniving person, but you probably do use compliance gaining strategies in your relationships. To explore how, see Activity 3 on page 281.

The following list of approaches combines most of the elements in previous taxonomies. As you read each category, think of times when you have used it, or when it has been used by others to gain your compliance.

Direct Requests   The most straightforward way to gain compliance is to ask for it, or make a **direct request.** We usually preface a request with a reason: "I have to work late tonight ..." and then make a polite request, "so could you pick up a few things downtown for me?" (Tracy 1984). Along with its simplicity and honesty, this approach is a surprisingly effective way to get what you want. College students have reported that the best way to get social support is to ask for it (Conn and Peterson 1989). This approach even works well with strangers. One famous study illustrates its power (Langer 1978). Experimenters waiting in line to use a copying machine asked to move ahead of others by asking "May I use the Xerox machine because I'm

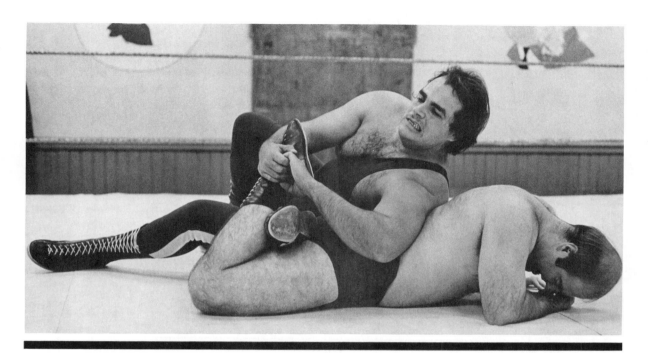

in a rush?" Over 90 percent of the customers let the requester go ahead. People were almost as willing to comply when the reason was a lame one: ("May I use the Xerox machine because I have to make some copies?"). Even without a reason for letting the requester cut in, over 60 percent of the people complied.

Indirect Appeals   When it is awkward or ineffective to make a direct request, we often use **indirect appeals,** hoping that the other person will infer or assume the our real intent (Goss and O'Hair 1988: 242). Indirect appeals usually take the form of hints: "You're driving downtown? What a coincidence—I was just going to catch a bus myself!" "You're tired of that sweater? I think it's great!"

While hints are strategic by definition, they are often a sensible and ethical way to seek compliance. Asking others directly may make them uncomfortable or put them on the spot. For example, it's usually inappropriate to invite

yourself to a party, but hinting that you're free gives the host a chance to include you—or pretend not to have noticed the unspoken request. The risk of hints is that the other person might not recognize them. Nonetheless, they are a useful part of a repertoire for getting what you want from others.

Exchange and Reciprocity   Even if others aren't inclined to do what we want just because we ask them, they will often comply because of the powerful social **norm of reciprocity**—the convention that obligates us to return the favors others have extended to us—even when we dislike the other person (Cialdini, 1988: 25; Garko 1990). If I have given you a ride or helped you study, you are likely to do me a favor when I ask, even though you might prefer not to.

When used in a manipulative manner, the norm of reciprocity provides a good way to trick people into doing things they otherwise wouldn't do. A devious person might, for

Charm is a way of getting the answer yes without asking a clear question.

ALBERT CAMUS

instance, offer to lend you cash, knowing you don't need it so that you'll feel obliged to extend a loan the next time he asks. But in many cases reciprocity is a kind of social lubricant that keeps relationships running. By supporting others, we wind up feeling altruistic and helping ourselves. In this sense, reciprocity can be a win-win approach, in which both parties profit.

Reward and Punishment   Sometimes we comply because there's a clear payoff for doing so: "If you fix dinner tonight, I'll wash the dishes and pay for a movie later." The flip side of rewards, of course are punishments: "If you try anything like that again, we're through!"

Not all threats and promises have immediate outcome. Sometimes they lay out more general consequences. A dentist might counsel a patient to floss daily in order to avoid oral surgery or tooth loss later in life. Likewise, an English teacher might tell students that people who can't read or write are headed for dead-end jobs.

Rewards or punishments may be blatant: "I'll give you $5.00 for washing my dirty clothes" or "If you don't pay the rent on time I'm moving out." Sometimes the positive or negative consequences we project are more subtle: acting more friendly when another person cooperates or becoming less talkative when things don't go your way.

Some relationships are better suited than others to the use of power-based appeals of reward and punishments. A boss might reason-

It's only a suggestion, but let's not forget who's making it.

ably persuade an employee to work harder by suggesting that promotions go to workers who make an extra effort on the job, for example. But even in relationships where power is distributed unevenly, rewards and punishments aren't used as often as we might think. One study compared the compliance-gaining methods of parents on prime-time family television shows with the approaches used by real-life parents. Television parents used commands 39 percent of the time—much more often than real families (Haefner and Comstock 1990).

Face Maintenance   Rewards aren't always obvious. Sometimes we appeal to others by stroking their ego, inducing them to comply because it makes them feel better about themselves. **Face maintenance strategies** lead others to act in ways that reinforce their presenting self . . . and at the same time provide what we want (Goss and O'Hair 1988). You might, for example, get a friend to help you work on a tough assignment by saying "You're so smart and so good at explaining things. I know I could do better if you gave me a hand." Since the desire to maintain a presenting self is strong, others may provide what you are seeking for their sake, because it enhances their image. Your friend might not feel like helping you study, but lending a hand lets her think "I really *am* pretty smart, and I'm helpful too. I'm a pretty good person!"

Face maintenance strategies aren't always cynical attempts to manipulate others. They are often a way to shape others in a socially desirable manner. A parent might urge a child to perform a task by using this approach: "Now that you're six years old, I know you can clean up your room without me having to nag you." Likewise, a boss might give an employee an important assignment, saying "I know I can count on you to do a good job." In cases like this face maintenance can create a self-fulfilling prophecy. By creating idealized images of other people, we can induce them to become the person they (and we) want to be.

Relational Appeals   Sometimes we comply with others out of respect or affection. **Relational appeals** fall into this category. They consist of strategies that rely on the target's relationship with the person making the request. Some referent appeals are straightforward requests for help: "I know you think those jokes are funny, but I'm embarrassed when you tell them. Would you stop telling them for me?"

Other referent appeals may be just as sincere, but more calculating. "If you really care about me you won't drink and drive." In every case, a relational appeal offers no other reason for complying beyond honoring the wishes of someone whose feelings are important to you. These appeals are most effective in intimate relationships, where the partners already feel a strong obligation to support one another (Roloff et al. 1988). This explains why the requests of intimate partners are less elaborate than those of mere acquaintances. They contain fewer apologies, explanations, and inducements. Simply making the request seems to include the implied reasoning: "You owe it to me to do what I ask."

WHICH STRATEGY TO CHOOSE?

There is no single best compliance-gaining strategy. As you learned in Chapter 1, competent communicators have a wide repertoire of strategies and are skillful at choosing the best one for the circumstances. Some skill at compliance gaining comes with age. Research shows that, as children become older, they become more skillful and flexible in their compliance-gaining approaches. Between the ages of two and five, preschoolers become more skilled at adjusting to one another and managing conflicts (Haslett 1983). The flexibility in choosing the best approach continues to develop with age. A study of five-, nine-, and thirteen-year-old girls showed that the number and variety of appeals grew as the children grew older (Finley and Humphreys 1974).

Once we have developed the skill to consider alternate ways to gain compliance, we weigh a number of factors in choosing the most promising approach. Some factors to weigh include the level of intimacy (spouse vs. neighbor), dominance (employee vs. boss), resistance (agreeable vs. reluctant target), rights (reasonable vs. unreasonable request), personal benefits of the persuader (high or low reward), and consequence of rejection (Cody et al. 1983; Cody and McLaughlin 1980).

Although there is no single "best" strategy for gaining compliance, three principles can help you choose the best approach for a given situation (Cody et al. 1981).

Which Strategy Has the Best Chance for Immediate Success?   Since your goal is to gain the other's cooperation, you need to choose the approach that promises to have the best chance of success. This means you must tailor your approach to the personal characteristics of the person involved. The approach that might work with a friend might fail with a professor, or even another friend. Unlike public speakers who often have to persuade a diverse audience, you can tailor your approach to the characteristics of the single person you want to reach.

As you analyze the other party, consider all the appeals listed on pages 251–255, and then select the one that seems most promising. Is the other person likely to prefer a straightforward request, or would an indirect approach work better? Are you better off using logic to support your bid, or should you ask for compliance as a personal favor? Do your respective social roles make the promise of reward or punishment appropriate, or should you try a different tack?

How Will the Strategy Affect the Long-term Well-being of the Relationship?   As you consider which approach to use, don't focus exclusively on short-term gains. Be sure to communicate in a way that keeps the long-term quality of the relationship comfortable. For example, you might be able to persuade a reluctant partner to give up studying to join you for an evening on the town by using a combination of relational and face-maintaining appeals ("I really was looking forward to spending the evening with you") and threats ("If you don't go tonight, don't expect me to party next time you ask"). Even if you succeed in this short-term goal, pestering the other person to do something that really isn't appealing is probably not worth the cost.

Does the Strategy Conform to Your Values and Personal Style?   Some approaches are clearly unethical. For example, Scott Christopher and Michael Fransden (1990) point out the unfortunate fact that some dating partners rely on ridicule, guilt, alcohol, and persistence to gain sexual favors. Most people would agree that telling outright lies isn't justified, although you may feel justified using the kinds of equivocation and "white lies" described in Chapter 9. In any case, you should feel comfortable with whatever approaches you take. One test is whether you would be embarrassed to confess your strategy to the other person involved if he or she confronted you.

In addition to ethical considerations, the strategies you use should fit your personal style of communicating. You probably feel more comfortable with some of the strategies listed above than with others. Your preferred style might be to make straightforward requests, perhaps backing them up with evidence. Or you might be more inclined to demonstrate the desirability of cooperating by emphasizing the face-maintaining benefits and other rewards.

Don't rule out a particular strategy just because you aren't used to using it. You may feel a bit awkward trying a seldom-used approach, but it still may be the best for a particular situation. Compliance gaining, like any skill, takes time to develop. Whatever strategy you use, the short- and long-term success probably depend on your sincerity. If you are going to compliment the other person, be sure your praise is sincere. If you ask the other person to comply because the request is personally important, be sure you mean what you say. If you seem to be deceiving or manipulating the other person, your chances for success will shrink, as will your ability to be persuasive in the future.

Why We Form Relationships

Why do we form relationships with some people and not with others? Sometimes we have no choice: Children can't select their parents, and most workers aren't able to choose their colleagues. In many other cases, however, we seek out some people and actively avoid others. Social scientists have collected an impressive body of research on interpersonal attraction (see Berscheid and Walster 1978; Hamachek 1982; Poole et al. 1987).

APPEARANCE

Most people claim that we should judge others on the basis of how they act, not how they look. The reality, however, is quite the opposite, especially in the early stages of a relationship. In one study, a group of over 700 men and women were matched as blind dates, allegedly for a "computer dance." After the party was over, they were asked whether or not they would like to date their partners again. The result? The more physically attractive the person (as judged in advance by independent raters), the more likely

he or she was to be seen as desirable. Other factors—social skills and intelligence, for example—didn't seem to affect the decision (Walster et al. 1966).

What attracts you to others? What makes you an attractive person? Explore these questions by following the directions in Activity 4 on page 282.

The influence of physical attractiveness begins early in life. From age five on, overweight boys are viewed by peers as socially offensive; tall, thin ones are judged as introverted and nervous; and muscular and athletic youngsters are seen as outgoing, active, and popular (Lemer and Gillert 1969; Staffieri 1967). The same principle continues into adult life. Handsome men and beautiful women are seen as more sensitive, kind, interesting, strong, poised, modest, sociable, outgoing, and exciting than their less attractive counterparts (Dion et al. 1972). Attractiveness continues to be important well into middle age. Gerald Adams and Ted Huston (1975) found that adults in this group viewed attractive peers as more socially outgoing, more pleasant, and of higher social status than their less-attractive counterparts.

What makes us view someone as attractive? Recent studies reveal that some long-held assumptions are incorrect (Langlois and Roggman 1990). First, beauty is not culture-specific: Many of the attributes of attractiveness are shared around the world. When raters from a variety of cultural and ethnic backgrounds were presented with images of culturally and racially diverse people, there was strong agreement about who was attractive.

Another mistaken assumption is that standards of attractiveness are learned slowly by exposure to media and culture. In fact, when infants as young as three months old are shown pictures of faces that have been rated attractive and unattractive by adult judges, they prefer attractive ones.

Although we might assume that attractive people are radically different from their more unfortunate cousins, the truth is that we view the familiar as beautiful. Raters were presented with two types of photos: Some were images of people from North European, Asian, and Hispanic backgrounds, while others were computer-generated images that combined the characteristics of several individuals. Surprisingly, the judges consistently preferred the composite photos of both men and women. When the features of eight or more individuals were combined into one image, viewers rated the picture as more attractive than one of a single person or a smaller combination of people. Thus, we seem to be drawn to people who represent the best qualities of ourselves and those people we know. In other words, beautiful people aren't different from the rest of us. Rather, they're "radically similar."

Even if your appearance isn't beautiful by any standards, consider these encouraging facts: First, ordinary-looking people with pleasing personalities are likely to be judged as being attractive (Berscheid and Walster 1978). Second, physical factors become less important as a relationship progresses. As Hamachek (1982: 59) puts it, "Attractive features may open doors, but apparently, it takes more than physical beauty to keep them open."

SIMILARITY

It's comforting to know someone who likes the things we like, who has similar values, and who may even be of the same race, economic class, or educational standing. This basis for the relationship, commonly and most appropriately known as the *similarity thesis,* is the most well substantiated of the several bases of relationship formation. The most common sim-

ilarities between partners include age, education, race, religious and ethnic background, and socioeconomic status (Buss 1985).

There are at least two possible hypotheses to study in the dynamics of similarity and interpersonal attraction: (1) People with similar attitudes are attracted to each other; and (2) people who are attracted to each other perceive themselves as similar, whether or not that's actually the case. Experiments support both of these ideas.

We like people who like what we like, and who dislike what we dislike. Several logical reasons exist for feeling this way. First of all, the other person serves as an external indication—a social validation—that we are not alone in our thinking, that we're not too "weird." Someone else *did* like the same controversial book as you. Therefore, this other person offers good support for you, reinforcing your own sense of what is right.

Second, when someone is similar to you, you can make fairly accurate predictions—whether the person will want to eat at the Mexican restaurant or hear the concert you're so excited about. This ability to make confident predictions reduces uncertainty and anxiety.

There's a third explanation for the similarity thesis. It may be that when we learn that other people are similar to us, we assume they'll probably like us, so we in turn like them. The self-fulfilling prophecy creeps into the picture again.

Donn Byrne (Byrne 1969; Byrne and Blaylock 1963) verified that people are attracted to others they think similar. These researchers told subjects they would be participating in a group discussion, and that some of the other participants (strangers) would have similar opinions to theirs, whereas others would not. As expected, students expressed more liking for people who supposedly had views similar to their own, and judged these strangers to be more intelligent, better informed, more moral,

and better adjusted than those assumed to have dissimilar attitudes. Recent evidence indicates, however, that rejection of an attitudinally dissimilar other decreases after conversation (Sunnafrank 1985).

Research studies also support the second attraction-similarity relationship: When we like a person, we perceive that similarities exist with that individual. Studies by Byrne and Blaylock (1963) as well as by Levinger and Breedlove (1966) have found that the actual amount of similarity between husbands and wives is significantly less than the amount the partners *assume* to exist. In discussion of these findings, Ellen Berscheid and Elaine Walster (1978) speculate that couples deemphasize their disagreements in the interest of maintaining a harmonious relationship.

For either direction observed in this attraction-similarity relationship, the research indicates that specific aspects of similarity must be considered. For example, does it matter that the person is similar to you in attitudes, but not in personality (or the converse)? The answer is yes. *Attitude similarity* carries more weight than *personality similarity*. Does it matter that you and the other person are similar on a small number of issues of greater importance to you both, than on a large number of other issues of lesser significance? Again, yes. Finally, are there any limitations to the degree of similarity and attraction between two people? Yes: A relationship can become *too* predictable, *too* patterned. This situation is the "I'm bored!" test of the relationship. It has also been found that people who are less anxious about whether or not others like them will associate with people who have different appearances, experiences, and attitudes.

The most important kind of similarity changes as a relationship develops (Neimeyer and Mitchell 1988). In the earliest stages of

Student Reflection

Similarity, Complementarity, and Friendships

I used to think the ideal partner was somebody who was just like me: talkative, ambitious, and a dreamer. But now that I've met Chris, I realize that our differences complement one another. She's a great listener, and even though she supports my goal to become a lawyer, she's happy to paint and sculpt for her own enjoyment. But most important, her common sense balances my wild schemes. We are similar in ways, too: We both love small towns, the outdoors, dancing, and traveling to new places. This combination of being similar and different is a nice mix.

interaction, attitude similarity is most powerful. If your opinion about politics, music, or school match a potential friend's, the relationship is likely to develop. When we get to know others better, similar evaluations of acquaintances take on more importance. Do you both get along with the same friends? If so, your times together will be more pleasant than if your social preferences don't match. Similarity of ability and intelligence is important when we are seeking social partners; but when we are looking for someone to help us get a job done, we understandably prefer to pair up with someone who seems more gifted than we are (Yinon et al. 1989).

Similarity turns from attraction to dislike when we encounter people who are like us in many ways but who behave in a strange or socially offensive manner (Cooper and Jones 1969; Taylor and Mette 1971). For instance, you have probably disliked people others have said were "just like you" but who talked too much, were complainers, or had some other unappealing characteristic. In fact, there is a tendency to have stronger dislike for similar but offensive people than for those who are offensive but different. One likely reason is that such people threaten our self-esteem, causing us to fear that we may be as unappealing as they are. In such circumstances, the reaction is often to put as much distance as possible between ourselves and this threat to our ideal self-image.

COMPLEMENTARITY

The old saying "opposites attract" seems to contradict the principle of similarity we just described. In truth, though, both are valid. Differences strengthen a relationship when they are *complementary*—when each partner's characteristics satisfy the other's needs. Couples, for instance, are more likely to be attracted to each other when one partner is dominant and the other passive (Winch 1958). Relationships also work well when the partners agree that one will exercise control in certain areas ("You make the final decisions about money") and the other will take the lead in different ones ("I'll decide how we ought to decorate the place"). Strains occur when control issues are disputed.

In Chapter 1 we talked about how communication can satisfy human needs. We discussed Maslow's hierarchy of needs: physiological, safety, social, self-esteem, and self-actualization. We also looked at Schutz's theory that humans seek inclusion, control, and affection. These theories reflect the need-fulfillment thesis: the idea that people seek each other out and establish certain types of relationships because of the needs they want fulfilled at that time in their lives.

Studies that have examined successful and unsuccessful couples over a twenty-year period show the interaction between similarities and differences (Kelley 1977: 625–26). The research demonstrates that partners in successful marriages were similar enough to satisfy each other physically and mentally, but were different enough to meet each other's needs and keep the relationship interesting. The successful couples found ways to keep a balance between their similarities and differences, adjusting to the changes that occurred over the years.

RECIPROCITY

Knowing that others like us is a strong source of attraction, especially in the early stages of a relationship (Aron 1989; Backman and Secord 1959). Conversely, we will probably not feel good about people who either attack or seem indifferent to us. After we get to know others, their liking becomes less of a factor. By then we form our preferences more from the other reasons listed in this section.

It's no mystery why reciprocal liking builds attractiveness. People who approve of us bolster our feelings of self-esteem. This approval is rewarding in its own right, and it can also confirm a self-concept that says, "I'm a likable person."

You can probably think of times when you haven't liked people who seemed to like you. These experiences usually fall into two categories. Sometimes we think the other person's supposed liking is counterfeit—an insincere device to get something from us. The acquaintance who becomes friendly when asking to borrow your car or the employee whose flattery of the boss seems to be a device to get a raise are examples. This sort of behavior really isn't "liking" at all.

The second category of unappealing liking occurs when the other person's approval doesn't fit with our own self-concept. We cling to an

Student Reflection

Balancing Relational Accounts

Toni and I are comanagers of a restaurant. She is a terrible bookkeeper, so I wind up doing a lot of paperwork that's really her job. She can be very moody at times, and when she gets in a bad mood I have to be careful what I say. Also, Toni hates to confront people, so I have to handle all the personnel problems, like firing employees who don't work out.

Why do I put up with her? Because Toni does a lot for me. She's always there when I need to talk about a problem. If I want to take an extra day off to go skiing, she'll cover for me. I don't have any relatives nearby, and she goes out of her way to include me in her family on holidays. We're sort of an odd couple, but I think it works because each of gets at least as much out of the relationship as we put in.

existing self-concept even when it is unrealistically unfavorable. When someone says you're good-looking, intelligent, and kind, but you believe you are ugly, stupid, and mean, you may choose to disregard the flattering information and remain in your familiar state of unhappiness. Groucho Marx summarized this attitude when he said he would never join any club that would have him as a member.

EXCHANGE

Some relationships are based on an economic model called **exchange theory** (Homans 1961; Thibaut and Kelley 1959). This theory sug-

A proposal of marriage in our society tends to be a way in which a man sums up his social attributes and suggests to a woman that hers are not so much better as to preclude a merger or partnership in these matters.

ERVING GOFFMAN

gests that we often seek out people who can give us rewards—either physical or emotional—that are grater than or equal to the costs we encounter in dealing with them. When we operate on the basis of exchange, we decide (often unconsciously) whether dealing with another person is "a good deal" or "not worth the effort."

At its most blatant level, an exchange approach seems cold and calculating, but in some situations it can be reasonable. A healthy business relationship is based on how well the parties help each other out, and some friendships are based on an informal kind of barter: "I don't mind listening to the ups and downs of your love life because you rescue me when the house needs repairs." Even close relationships have an element of exchange. Husbands and wives tolerate each other's quirks because the comfort and enjoyment they get make the unhappy times worth accepting. Most deeply satisfying relationships, however, are built on more than just the benefits that make them "a good deal."

COMPETENCY

We like to be around talented people, probably because we hope their skills and abilities will rub off on us. On the other hand, we are uncomfortable around those who are *too* competent—probably because we look bad by comparison (Bales 1958).

Elliot Aronson and his associates (1966) demonstrated how competence and imperfection combine to affect attraction by having subjects evaluate tape recordings of candidates for a quiz program. One was a "perfect" candidate who answered almost all the questions correctly, and modestly admitted that he was an honor student, athlete, and college yearbook editor. The "average" candidate answered fewer questions correctly, had average grades, was a less successful athlete, and was a low-level member of the yearbook staff. Toward the end of half the tapes, the candidates committed a blunder, spilling coffee all over themselves. The remaining half of the tapes contained no such blunder.

These, then, were the four experimental conditions: (1) a person with superior ability who blundered; (2) a superior person who did not blunder; (3) an average person who blundered; and (4) an average person who did not.

The students who rated the attractiveness of these four types of people revealed an interesting and important principle of interpersonal attraction. The most attractive person was the superior candidate who blundered. Next was the superior person who did not blunder. Third was the average person who did not blunder. The least attractive person was the average person who committed the blunder.

Aronson's conclusion was that we like people who are somewhat flawed because they remind us of ourselves. There are some qualifications to this principle, however. People with especially positive or negative self-esteem find "perfect" people more attractive than those who are competent but flawed (Helmreich et al. 1970). Furthermore, women tend to be more impressed by uniformly superior people, whereas men find desirable but "human" subjects especially attractive (Deaux 1972). On the whole, though, the principle stands: The best way to gain the liking of others is to be good at what you do, but to admit your mistakes.

PROXIMITY

As common sense suggests, we are likely to develop relationships with people we interact with frequently. In many cases, proximity leads to liking. We're more likely to develop friendships with close neighbors than with distant ones, for instance; and several studies show that the chances are good that we'll choose a mate with whom we cross paths often. Facts like these are understandable when we consider that proximity allows us to get more information about other people and benefit from a relationship with them.

Familiarity, on the other hand, can also breed contempt. Evidence to support this fact comes from police blotters as well as university laboratories. Thieves frequently prey on nearby victims, even though the risk of being recognized is greater. Most aggravated assaults occur within the family or among close neighbors. Within the law, the same principle holds: You are likely to develop strong personal feelings of either like or dislike toward others you encounter frequently.

DISCLOSURE

Telling others important information about yourself can help build liking. Sometimes the basis of this attraction comes from learning about ways we are similar, either in experiences ("I broke off an engagement myself") or in attitudes ("I feel nervous with strangers, too"). Self-disclosure also increases liking because it indicates regard. Sharing private information is a form of respect and trust—a kind of liking that we've already seen increases attractiveness.

Self-disclosure is a good measure of the depth of a relationship. A study of first-year college students living in dormitories demonstrated this fact (Rubin and Shenker 1978). Students who were close friends revealed personal information, while those who were physically close but didn't consider themselves close

---

Student Reflection

Proximity and Friendship

Last year my neighbor Pat moved across town. We used to talk almost every day, and we told each other everything. I don't think I've ever had a better friend.

We're still friends, but since Pat moved our relationship has changed. It used to be easy to spend time with one another—we'd bump into one another picking up the mail or in the parking lot and end up talking for an hour. But now that we have to make an effort to get together, it doesn't happen so often. Work, school, and family keep us both busy and there just doesn't seem to be time. It's spooky to realize how important proximity is in keeping a friendship going.

---

friends shared less personal information. In other words, proximity alone isn't enough to guarantee that a relationship will develop.

Not all disclosure leads to liking. Research shows that the key to satisfying self-disclosure is *reciprocity:* getting back an amount and kind of information equivalent to that which you reveal (Altman 1973; Derlega et al. 1976). A second important ingredient in successful self-disclosure is *timing.* It's probably unwise to talk about your sexual insecurities with a new acquaintance or express your pet peeves to a friend at your birthday party. The information you reveal ought to be appropriate for the setting and stage of the relationship (Archer and Berg 1978; Wortman et al. 1976). Chapter 9 contains a great deal of information on the subject of self-disclosure.

Relational Trajectories

Relationships go through stages. Your own experience will prove this fact: The novelty and curiosity you and a new acquaintance feel about one another can develop into a comfortable and familiar friendship. Likewise, the infatuation you feel in the early stages of a love affair can never last: Soon it changes, perhaps into a less intense but more comfortable kind of love, perhaps into a friendship, or even into the recognition that the association was not meant to last at all.

STAGES OF A RELATIONSHIP

Communication theorists have attempted to explain the patterns that relationships follow. One of the best known models was developed by Mark Knapp (1984), who has broken the rise

and fall of relationships into ten steps (see Table 8–2).

There's truth to the saying "Life imitates art." Learn more about how relational stages operate by analyzing films and literature. For details, see Activity 5 on page 282.

Initiating   The goals in the **initiating** stage are to show that you are interested in making contact and to show that you are the kind of person worth talking to. Communication during this stage is usually brief, and it generally follows conventional formulas: handshakes, remarks about innocuous subjects like the weather, and friendly expressions. Such behavior may seem superficial and meaningless, but it is a way of signaling that you're interested in building

Table 8–2   An Overview of Relational Stages

Process	Stage	Representative Dialogue
Coming Together	Initiating	"Hi, how ya doin'?" "Fine. You?"
	Experimenting	"Oh, so you like to ski…so do I." "You do?! Great. Where do you go?"
	Intensifying	"I…I think I love you." "I love you too."
	Integrating	"I feel so much a part of you." "Yeah, we are like one person. What happens to you happens to me."
	Bonding	"I want to be with you always." "Let's get married."
Coming Apart	Differentiating	"I just don't like big social gatherings." "Sometimes I don't understand you. This is one area where I'm certainly not like you at all."
	Circumscribing	"Did you have a good time on your trip?" "What time will dinner be ready?"
	Stagnating	"What's there to talk about?" "Right. I know what you're going to say and you know what I'm going to say."
	Avoiding	"I'm so busy. I just don't know when I'll be able to see you." "If I'm not around when you try, you'll understand."
	Terminating	"I'm leaving you…and don't bother trying to contact me." "Don't worry."

Reprinted with permission from Mark L. Knapp, *Interpersonal Communication and Human Relationships* Boston: Allyn and Bacon, 1984.

some kind of relationship with the other person. It allows us to say without saying, "I'm a friendly person, and I'd like to get to know you."

Making contact and talking long enough to get beyond the initiating stage does require skill. One study revealed that several strategies are both efficient and socially acceptable ways to learn about others (Douglas 1987). The first is *networking*—getting information about the other person from a third party that helps the first moments of contact go well. Another strategy is *offering*—putting yourself in a favorable position to be approached by the desired partner. Offering strategies might include picking a

Student Reflection

Early Stages in Relational Development

I used to hate parties where I didn't know anyone but the host. The small talk seemed so stupid and predictable, and I felt like a hypocrite standing around saying the same things as if I were speaking a script. Now I see that the small talk is OK as a way to find out what people have in common. I've also started listening to what people say and asking sincere questions, and it isn't bad at all!

seat in class near the person you'd like to meet or hanging around the hors d'oeuvres at a party until the attractive person drops by for a snack. A third technique is *approaching*—signaling your desire for contact, either verbally or nonverbally. Typical approaches include smiles and self-introductions. (Incredibly, there are people who never even try such seemingly obvious strategies, instead waiting for interesting people to approach them.) A final initiating strategy is *sustaining*—behaving in ways to keep the conversation going. Asking questions is a typical sustaining technique.

Other styles proved less effective, either because they didn't work or because they were socially inappropriate. Expressing feelings ("Do you like me?") was too forward for most initial contacts. Remaining silent (either to be coy or from an inability to know what to say) didn't work. Seeking favors that were inconvenient to the other person was rarely successful. Finally, diminishing one's self ("I'm such a dope!") rarely met with success.

Experimenting   After making contact with a new person, we generally begin the search for common ground. This search usually begins with the basics: "Where are you from? What's your major?" From there we look for other similarities: "You're a runner too? How many miles do you do a week?"

The hallmark of **experimenting** is small talk. As Knapp (p. 36) says, this small talk is like Listerine: We hate it, but we take large quantities every day. We tolerate the ordeal of small talk because it serves several functions. First, it is a useful way to find out what interests we share with the other person. It also provides a way to "audition" the other person—to help us decide whether a relationship is worth pursuing. In addition, small talk is a safe way to ease into a relationship. You haven't risked much as you decide whether to proceed further. Finally, small talk *does* provide some kind of link to others. It's often better than being alone.

The quality of communication changes after even a small amount of experimenting. In one study, strangers met with each other for two, four, or six minutes (Douglas 1990). In every case, researchers found that, as the parties learned more about one another, they asked fewer questions and disclosed more personal information. In addition, as the amount of information the partners knew about one another increased, so did their attraction for one another.

Intensifying   At the next stage the kind of truly interpersonal relationship defined in Chapter 1 begins to develop. Dating couples use a wide range of communication strategies to express their feelings of attraction (Tolhuizen 1990). In this **intensifying** stage, about a quarter of the time they express their feelings directly, using metacommunication to discuss the state of the relationship. More often they use less direct methods of communication: spending an in-

A lot of people didn't expect our relationship to last, but we just celebrated our two months' anniversary.

BRITT EKLAND

creasing amount of time together, asking for support from one another, doing favors for the partner, giving tokens of affection, hinting and flirting, expressing feelings nonverbally, getting to know the partner's friends and family, and trying to look more physically attractive.

Although commitment grows as a relationship intensifies, communication between partners shows that doubts can still remain. Romantic couples use a variety of strategies to test the commitment of one another (Baxter and Wilmot 1984; Bell and Buerkel-Rothfuss 1990). These approaches include asking direct questions, "testing" the partner by presenting challenges that require proof of commitment, hinting in order to gain expressions of commitment, asking third parties for information, and attempts at making the partner jealous. While these behaviors are frequent in the early stages of a relationship, they decline as the partners spend more time together.

Integrating As the relationship strengthens, the individuals begin to take on an identity as a social unit. Invitations begin to come addressed to the couple. Social circles merge. The partners begin to take on each other's commitments: "Sure we'll spend Thanksgiving with your family." Common property may begin to be designated—our apartment, our car, our song (Baxter 1987). In this sense, the stage of **integrating** is a time when we give up some characteristics of our old selves and become different people.

Some Western cultures have rituals to mark the progress of a friendship and to give it public legitimacy and form. In Germany, for example, there's a small ceremony called *Duzen*, the name itself signifying the transformation in the relationship. The ritual calls for the two friends, each holding a glass of wine or beer, to entwine arms, thus bringing each other physically close, and to drink up after making a promise of eternal brotherhood with the word *Bruderschaft*. When it's over, the friends will have passed from a relationship that requires the formal *Sie* mode of address to the familiar *du*.

LILLIAN B. RUBIN
Just Friends: The Role of Friendship in Our Lives

As we become more integrated with others, our sense of obligation to them grows (Roloff et al. 1988). We feel obliged to provide a variety of resources such as class notes and money, whether or not the other person asks for them. When intimates do make requests of one another, they are relatively straightforward. Gone are the elaborate explanations, inducements, and apologies. In short, partners in an integrated relationship expect more from one another than they do in less intimate associations.

Bonding   During the **bonding** stage, the parties make symbolic public gestures to show the world that their relationship exists. These gestures can take the form of a contract to be business partners or a license to be married. Bonding generates social support for the relationship. Custom and law both impose certain obligations on partners who have officially bonded.

Bonding marks one turning point in relationships. Up to now the relationship may have developed at a steady pace: Experimenting gradually moved into intensifying and then into integrating. Now, however, there is a spurt of commitment. The public display and declaration of exclusivity make this a critical period in the relationship. Although most people would agree that turning points do occur, research shows that couples don't always agree about what specific events marked those points in their relationships. About 45 percent of the time, the partners do not identify the same events (Baxter and Bullis 1986) as turning points.

Differentiating   Now that the two people have formed this commonality, they need to reestablish individual identities. How are we different? How am I unique? Former identifications as "we" now emphasize "I." **Differentiating** often first occurs when a relationship begins to experience the first, inevitable stress. Whereas happy employees might refer to "our company," the description might change to "their company" when a raise or some other request isn't forthcoming. We see this kind of differentiation when parents argue over the misbehavior of a child: "Did you see what *your* son just did?"

Differentiation can be positive, too, for people need to be individuals as well as parts of a relationship. The key to successful differentiation is maintaining commitment to a relationship while creating the space for being individuals as well. Partners use a variety of strategies to gain privacy from one another (Burgoon et al. 1989). Sometimes they confront the other party directly, explaining that they don't want to continue a discussion. In other cases they are less direct, offering nonverbal cues, changing the topic, or leaving the room.

Circumscribing   So far we have been looking at the growth of relationships. Although some reach a plateau of development, going on successfully for as long as a lifetime, others pass through several stages of decline and dissolution. In the **circumscribing** stage, communication between members decreases in quantity and quality (see Duck 1987). Subtle hints of dissatisfaction grow more evident. Working late at the office, less and less romance, more and more arguments begin to form a pattern that is hard to ignore. Ironically, both partners in a circumscribed relationship still cooperate in one way: suppressing the true status of the relationship. They hide its decline from others, and even from themselves (Vaughn 1987). Restrictions and restraints characterize this stage, and dynamic communication becomes static. Rather than discuss a disagreement (which requires some degree of energy on both parts), members opt for withdrawal: either mental (silence or daydreaming and fantasizing) or physical (where people spend less time together). Circumscribing doesn't involve total avoidance, which comes later. Rather, it entails a certain shrinking of interest and commitment.

Stagnation   If circumscribing continues, the relationship begins to stagnate. Members behave toward each other in old, familiar ways without much feeling. No growth occurs. The **stagnating** relationship is a hollow shell of its former self. We see stagnation in many workers who have lost enthusiasm for their job, yet continue to go through the motions for years. The same sad event occurs for some couples who unenthusiastically have the same conversations, see the same people, and follow the same routines without any sense of joy or novelty.

Avoiding   When stagnation becomes too unpleasant, people in a relationship begin to create distance between each other by **avoiding.** Sometimes they do it under the guise of excuses ("I've been sick lately and can't see you") and sometimes directly ("Please don't call me; I

When he pictured their introduction . . . it seemed nothing more than the beginning of their parting. When she had looked up at him that first night and rattled the ice cubes in her paper cup, they were already moving toward their last edgy, miserable year together, towards those months when anything either of them said was wrong, toward that sense of narrowly missed connections. They were like people who run to meet, holding out their arms, but their aim is wrong; they pass each other and keep running. It had all amounted to nothing, in the end.

ANNE TYLER
The Accidental Tourist

don't want to see you now"). In either case, by this point the handwriting is on the wall about the relationship's future.

Terminating   Characteristics of this final stage include summary dialogues of where the relationship has gone and the desire to dissociate. The relationship may end with a cordial dinner, a note left on the kitchen table, a phone call, or a legal document stating the dissolution. Depending on each person's feelings, this **terminating** stage can be quite short, or it may be drawn out over time, with bitter jabs at each other. In either case, termination doesn't have to be totally negative. Understanding each other's investments in the relationship and needs for personal growth may dilute the hard feelings.

Communication theorists used to believe that the ending of a relationship was little more than a reversal of the stages of coming together. Recent studies show that the matter isn't so simple. When both parties agree to end their relationship, the amount and kind of sharing does resemble a mirror image of that during the growth stages (Bordagaray-Sciolino 1984).

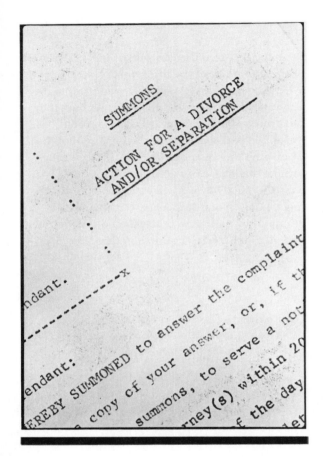

When one partner wants out and the other wants to keep the relationship together, however, the communication changes significantly.

The way a relationship ends depends on several factors, which Leslie Baxter (1984) identified after examining the breakups of ninety-seven heterosexual romantic relationships. In addition to whether both or only one partner want to end the relationship, these factors matter: whether the onset of relational problems is sudden or gradual, whether the partners use direct or indirect actions to dissolve the relationship, whether negotiations about the disen-

gagement are brief or lengthy, whether there are attempts to save the relationship, and whether the final outcome is termination of the relationship or its continuation in some other form.

Besides these factors, Baxter (1982) and Cody (1982) found that the strategy partners use to disengage depends on the degree of intimacy their relationship had reached. In the least intimate relationships, one partner simply withdraws (physically or emotionally) from the other. In slightly more intimate relationships, one partner is likely to request they see less of each other. When intimacy has been greater, the disengaging partner makes an effort to explain the reason for leaving in a way that takes the other's feelings into account. In the most intimate relationships, the initiator expresses grief over the disengagement. In fact, Cody (1982) found that the more intimate the relationship, the greater the feeling of obligation to justify terminating it.

How do the individuals deal with one another after a romantic relationship has ended? The best predictor of whether the individuals will become friends is whether they were friends before their romantic involvement (Metts et al. 1989). The way the couple split up also makes a difference. It's no surprise to find that friendships are most possible when communication during the breakup was positive: expressions that there were no regrets for time spent together and other attempts to minimize hard feelings. When communication during termination was negative (manipulative, complaining to third parties), friendships were less likely.

What happens to the degree of self-disclosure when a relationship ends? Danielle Bordagaray-Sciolino (1984) found that the *breadth* (number of topics chosen for disclosure) remains the same, but the *depth* of disclosure varies from one partner to the other. The person who wants to maintain the relationship decreases the *level* of intimacy (probably to avoid "rocking the boat," scaring the other away), whereas the partner who wants to end it decreases the *amount* of information disclosed, while keeping the depth of disclosure about the same. Why would someone looking for a way out of a relationship keep disclosing personal information? One explanation is that this strategy allows for a graceful, relatively painless withdrawal that is less traumatic for the person left behind.

Survivors of terminated relationships offer a number of reasons why their relationships didn't last (Cupah and Metts 1986). These reasons are summarized in Table 8–3. The tendency is to blame the breakup on the other person more than on oneself, although divorced women are more likely to blame themselves, while men are more likely to pin the responsibility on their ex-wives or on outside forces.

Table 8–3   Reasons Offered for Relationship Termination

I. Characteristics of the individuals themselves

"My former husband decided he was unhappy."
"I began to feel lonely."
"She said she felt trapped."
"He was too conservative."

II. Lack of fulfillment of relational roles

"He found no joy in being a father."
"There were no sexual relations."
"He tried to tell me what I had to do to be his wife."
"She went back to school."

III. Unsatisfactory relational cohesiveness and intimacy

"We no longer wanted the same things in life."
"We did nothing together as a couple."
"We had different needs."

IV. Poor regulation of interaction

"He wouldn't listen."
"All our discussions ended in arguments."
"He threatened me."

V. Third-party involvements

"I had an affair with an exciting older man."
"When I found out she'd been seeing other guys, I was very hurt."
"The unexpected pregnancy was more than we could handle."
"I lost my job."

Adapted from W. R. Cupah and S. Metts, "Accounts of Relational Dissolution: A Comparison of Marital and Non-Marital Relationships," *Communication Monographs* 53 (1986): 311–54.

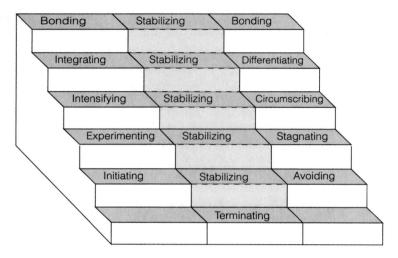

Figure 8–3   Staircase Model of Relational Stages

Reprinted with permission from Mark L. Knapp, *Interpersonal Communication and Human Relationships* Boston: Allyn and Bacon, 1984, p. 50.

MOVEMENT WITHIN AND BETWEEN STAGES

After outlining the ten steps of relational growth and decay, Knapp discusses the characteristics of movement between stages by presenting a **staircase model of relational stages** (see Figure 8–3). This model suggests several characteristics of relational development.

Movement Occurs Within Stages   According to Knapp's model, a relationship can exist in only one stage at a time. At any moment it will exhibit the most predominant traits of just one of the ten levels pictured in Figure 8–3. Despite this fact, there are usually elements of other levels present. For example, two lovers deep in the throes of integrating may still do their share of experimenting and have differentiating disagreements. Likewise, a couple who spend most of their energy avoiding one another may have an occasional good spell in which their former attraction briefly intensifies. Even though there may be overtones of several stages, one will predominate.

No relationship is stable, so it's reasonable to expect that from day to day the interaction between two people will change. Nonetheless, if you take a step back from any relationship, you will probably be able to find a common theme that characterizes one of the ten stages.

Movement Between Steps Is Generally Sequential   Typically relationships move from one stage to another in a step-by-step manner as they develop and deteriorate. This doesn't mean that every relationship will move through all ten stages. Some reach a certain point and then go no further. When this occurs, movement is usually across the staircase to the corresponding point of deterioration. For example, two people who have just met at a party may move from initiating to avoiding, whereas a couple that has progressed to intensifying is likely to begin circumscribing their relationship before it decays into stagnation and avoidance.

There are exceptions to the rule of sequential development. Occasionally partners may skip a stage: Sudden elopements and desertions are an example. Nonetheless, most of the time sequential, one-step-at-a-time progression allows the relationship to unfold at a pace that is manageable for the partners.

Relationships Are Constantly Changing   Relationships are certainly not doomed to deteriorate. But even the strongest ones are rarely stable for long periods of time. In fairy tales a couple may live "happily ever after," but in real life this sort of equilibrium is less common. Consider a husband and wife who have been married for some time. Although they have formally bonded, their relationship will probably shift forward and backward along the spectrum of stages. Sometimes the partners will feel the need to differentiate from one another. The relationship may become more circumscribed, or even stagnant. From this point the marriage may fail, but this fate isn't certain. With effort, the partners may move across the staircase, from stagnating to experimenting or from circumscribing to intensifying.

This back-and-forth movement reflects three contradictions that tug at the parties in every relationship (Baxter 1990). The first contradiction centers on alternating desires for *connection and autonomy*. Each of us wants—even needs to have associations with others, yet we also begin to feel suffocated if we lose complete freedom to operate independently. Another pull is between the needs for both *openness and privacy*. Self-disclosure and mutual understanding are characteristics of interpersonal relationships, but too much openness leaves us feeling invaded. The third tug is between the desires for *predictability and novelty*. Too much predictability leaves us feeling bored, but too much novelty leaves us feeling uncertain about the relationship. Given these tensions, it's not surprising that relationships are constantly in flux.

Movement Is Always to a New Place   Even though a relationship may move back to a stage

it has experienced before, it will never be the same as before. For example, most healthy long-term relationships will go through several phases of experimenting, when the partners try out new ways of behaving with one another. Though each phase is characterized by the same general features, the specifics will feel different each time. As you learned in Chapter 1, communication is irreversible. Partners can never go back to "the way things were." Sometimes this fact may lead to regrets: It's impossible to take back a cruel comment or forget a crisis. On the other hand, the irreversibility of communication can make relationships exciting, since it lessens the chance for boredom.

How healthy are your friendships? What can you do to make them stronger? Find out by trying Activity 6 on page 282.

Friendship: A Special Relationship

Romantic and career relationships may come and go, but friendships are the interpersonal bond that can exist throughout a lifetime. Because friendship is so important, it deserves a special look in this chapter.

WHAT MAKES A FRIEND?

You probably have a variety of friends. If you are lucky, you have a few people whom you can count as special friends. Exactly what is it about these relationships that distinguish them from less personal ones? Michael Argyle and Monika Henderson (1984) found six rules that distinguish high-quality friendships from lower-quality ones—rules that seem to be mandatory if a friendship is to thrive:

1. Standing up for the other person when you are apart.
2. Sharing news of success with the other person.

3. Showing emotional support.
4. Trusting and confiding in each other.
5. Volunteering to help in time of need.
6. Striving to make the other happy when you are together.

These rules are similar to the eight characteristics that Muriel James and Louis Savary (1976) defined as important to friendships. Notice that the following traits take on different levels of importance as a friendship matures.

Availability and *shared activities* are particularly important in the initial stages of a relationship (Griffin and Sparks 1990). You expect to spend time with the other person, getting together to work on the term project, having lunch or dinner, or maybe talking during TV commercials. If these expectations are not met, the relationship may never develop beyond an acquaintanceship. In most cases, being available presumes face-to-face interactions, but there are also times when we maintain availability through written letters or telephone calls. When you're feeling down and depressed, you may surprise yourself by what you do. Sometimes you call someone you haven't spoken to in months, someone who may not even be a "close" friend, and at other times you write to someone who presumes you died or ran off for a tour of the world. No matter, the person is still available, and that's what is important.

Expectations common to the intermediate phases of relationships include *caring, honesty, confidentiality,* and *loyalty.* You expect them from the other person, and you expect to provide them yourself if the relationship is to be reciprocal. Sometimes we forget that others expect the same treatment from us!

Although the degree of caring will vary with the type of relationship, James and Savary offer the following definition:

> Caring is not the same as using the other person to satisfy one's own needs. Neither is it to be confused with such things as well-wishing, or simply having an interest in what happens to another. Caring is a process of helping others grow and actualize themselves. It is a transforming experience.

In like manner, honesty, confidentiality, and loyalty are expected in all types of relationships. Honesty in a relationship does not mean that you need to tell everything to the other person, but that you are honest about matters relevant to that relationship, while maintaining a respect for the other person's sense of privacy. Confidentiality and loyalty are two agreements made in relationships, at times in unstated and assumed ways, and sometimes in a formal (written) legal manner.

Understanding and *empathy* are the "bonuses" of a relationship. Many relationships can maintain themselves based on the other characteristics, but those that are particularly strong have a mutually high degree of understanding and empathy. Sue and Mary each understand how the other works and thinks, and they can empathize with each other's feelings. It's not that they are so predictable as to be boring, but they do know each other's ways of thinking and feeling almost as well as they know their own. Usually, these features of a relationship take time to develop, and they require clear communication between the two people involved. Each must be willing to express needs, feelings, and wishes as accurately as possible, and each must practice the skills of active listening for the other person.

PRESSURES ON FRIENDSHIPS

Many times strong friendships wither away. Sad as this change may be, it's not surprising, for there are both external and internal pressures on friendships. The *external* pressures include physical circumstances, such as moving away from friends or changing jobs, and the existence of other competing people and relationships. Two people who have been friends throughout their school years, for example, may experience new tensions when one marries. For example, married men disclose less of their personal thoughts and feelings to friends than do single men (Tschann 1988). There's no mystery about this shift: with a spouse to confide in, these men had less need (and probably less time) to open up to their buddies. Interestingly, women do not share less with their friends after marriage. This fact probably grows from the general tendency of females to focus more on relational issues than men: If males disclose only rarely, then the "intrusion" of a wife is likely to have a strong effect on his communication with friends.

Friends usually come in pairs, and there's a good reason why that's so. In three-person interactions it is almost impossible for one participant to extend attention to both of the other two simultaneously. Unless each person is quite secure both in the relationship and apart from it, most triadic arrangements cannot survive the tensions.

Internal factors can also pressure a friendship. Caldwell and Peplau (1977) found that women see friendships as a means for sharing feelings, whereas men determine friends according to similar interests in physical activities. Another common internal pressure occurs when partners grow at different rates. For instance, a relationship that was born out of one person's dependency on the other loses its main reason for existing if the weaker partner becomes more self-reliant. Similarly, a friendship once based on agreement to avoid discussing any conflicts will be threatened if one of the friends suddenly becomes willing to tackle disputes directly. When such changes occur, maintaining the friendship depends on the ability of both persons to adapt to the new conditions. Therefore, friendships lasting for long periods are often quite different now than they were when they began. The partners were wise enough to adapt to their personal changes rather than clinging to the old ways of relating that may have been comfortable and enjoyable, but are now gone.

Not all friendships can survive these pressures. But the end of a friendship does not always mean that the people have failed. Rather, it may simply reflect the fact that one or both partners have changed and now seek a different (not necessarily better) type of interaction. Of course, such an ending is easier to accept if both people have other relationships that can support their needs.

One way to avoid the brutal self-attacks that can follow a separation is to see the friendship not as a *fraction* of you, but as what James and Savary call an additional, "third self." There's you, me, and *us*. If the friendship changes or dissolves, the separate entities of you and me still exist intact and completely, and a new friendship will bring with it another third self.

In one study, respondents reported having only about 60 percent as many close friends of the opposite sex as compared with same-sex friendships (Shellen and Cole 1982). Neither men nor women find same-sex friendships as comfortable or easy to establish as relationships with members of the opposite sex. Roughly 40 percent did not even express a desire to have friends of the opposite sex (Block 1980: 100). One problem with these relationships is the issue of sex. A majority of respondents confess that sexual dynamics intrude into the friendship, often creating problems for one or both people: "Too tempting," they say. "Looking for trouble," "bound to evolve into something sexual," "won't work" are similar reactions. The

potential for sexual complications is especially great when at least one of the friends is married.

Given these pressures, it's not surprising that roughly 70 percent of the people surveyed report that the nature of mixed-sex friendships is different than same-sex friendships. The most frequent differences cited were the ability to communicate openly about personal topics with same-sex friends, different interests and activities, and the issue of sex which we have already discussed (Shellen and Cole 1982: 15).

Despite the pressures working against mixed-sex friendships, the figures show that these relationships *are* possible. Because they are less common, male-female friendships are especially precious. Rather than writing them off as hopeless, a smarter approach is to treasure them when they do occur. Most people who do have close friends of the opposite sex are conscious of not allowing sexual or romantic interest to jeopardize the relationship, and they proceed slowly or back away from it if it happens.

GENDER AND FRIENDSHIP

Social scientists have discovered that friendship has different properties for men and women. Think about it yourself: Do you have the same number of male and female friends? Do you appreciate them in the same way? Do you talk about the same subjects with men and women? If you are like most people, the answers to these questions will most often be "no."

Even in early childhood, differences between same-sex friendships are different for boys and girls (Block 1980). Boys are most likely to form competitive play groups, while girls' play is more often cooperative. Thus, patterns for traditional sex roles are set. In friendship surveys focusing on preteen play, men recall being highly responsive to the sex-role opinions of other boys, while girls are less susceptible to pressures of conforming to stereotyped sex roles. The worst label for most boys is "sissy," while being called a "tomboy" is less common and less hurtful in an era of coeducational soccer and unisex clothing.

As adults, same-sex friendships of men and women differ in some important ways (Sherrod 1989). Men report having more of these relationships, while women describe their same-sex friendships as being more intimate. Women are more than three times as likely to have an intimate confidante (Aires and Johnson 1983). In general, the topics men and women discuss in same-sex friendships differ. As some writers have put it, women are more likely to talk about who they are, while men traditionally talk about what they do (Steward et al. 1986). Women's conversations focus more on relational, personal, and family matters and involve a greater sharing of emotions, while men are more likely to talk about less personal topics such as current events, sports, money, and music (Haas and Sherman 1982).

When problems arise, the response in same-sex friendships also varies by gender. Women friends are more likely to listen noncritically and offer mutual support. If a man finds that his friend is unhappy, a more common response is to change the subject. This is not necessarily a sign of being unconcerned. Rather, it reflects both a form of respect for the other's privacy and a strategy of diverting the attention of the troubled friend (Howell 1982).

LIKING AND LOVING

The word "friend" is rather vague. Although we clearly see a relationship with a friend as more intimate than one with a "co-worker" or "pal" and less intimate than one with a "spouse," "lover," or "steady" (Knapp et al. 1980), it is hard to define exactly how intimate a friendship relationship really is. This difficulty may stem from our inability to draw the line between "liking" and "loving."

The unabridged edition of the *Random House Dictionary of the English Language* (1969) defines "like" as "to take pleasure in; find agreeable or congenial to one's taste...to regard with favor...find attractive...." The definition of "love" takes up twice the space of "like" and, unfortunately, does not provide twice the clarity. "Love" is defined as "the profoundly tender or passionate affection for a person of the opposite sex...a feeling of warm personal attachment or deep affection... beloved person; sweetheart..." and so on for twenty different definitions and usages, including number nineteen: "like."

Some of the confusion about love comes from its equivocal nature. In truth, people use the word "love" in a variety of ways, even to describe their romantic relationships. After surveying Canadian and English subjects, John Alan Lee (1973) identified several very different uses of the term. To make these distinctions more clear, he gave each type its own label.

Eros Sexual love is **eros** and the erotic lover regards love as life's most important activity. Attraction to the partner is strong, and the relationship is intense, both emotionally and physically. The erotic lover prefers that feelings be mutual but does not demand it: There is little possessiveness or fear of rivals.

Ludus The Latin word for play is **ludus,** and the ludic lover considers love a game, a pleasant pastime, which requires neither much feeling nor commitment. The game is played for mutual enjoyment; it requires self-control and detachment, with just the right level of intensity. Lies and insincerity are often part of the rules of this game, although there is no desire to hurt the other person.

Storge Storgic love, or **storge,** is love without intensity or excitement: It is an extension of friendship and affection. Storgic lovers have a relaxed relationship that is part of their ongoing lives. Characteristic of this type of love is the tendency to share interests and activities, but not feelings about the relationship itself.

Mania Often called "romantic love," **mania** or manic love is intense, obsessive, and painful. Manic lovers are out of control, continuously creating problems to intensify how they feel. Life without the partner's love is not worth living, so manic lovers abuse themselves to win the other's love, to force the other into greater and greater expressions of love. A rather dramatic relationship, manic love rarely ends happily.

Pragma The Greek word for heed or life work is **pragma,** and the pragmatic lover looks for contentment, a mate with whom a long-term compatible relationship can be formed. Emotional extremes are avoided because they can get in the way of reciprocated affection and mutual problem solving.

Agape Agapic love, derived from a Greek word, **agape,** is completely altruistic and deeply compassionate, given without ulterior motives or expectations of something in return. The agapic lover cares for the other, whether the other wants it or not, whether the love is deserved or not.

Beliefs about love vary according to a number of factors, including gender and age (Frazier and Esterly 1990). College-age men scored higher than their female counterparts on romanticism (the belief in love at first sight, that love comes only once, that there is only one ideal partner, and that love is mysterious and uncontrollable). Men also scored higher on the quality of agape—all giving, selfless love—than females. Both men and women become less romantic with age, and women become more pragmatic, believing that love develops slowly and that relationships take effort. For both men and women, satisfaction in a relationship is correlated most highly with higher levels of eros and agape, as well as the length of a relationship. There is a negative relationship between ludic game playing and relational satisfaction.

METAPHORS FOR LOVE

One way to recognize which type of love people are seeking or describing is through the metaphors they use. Philosopher Robert Solomon (1981) suggests that the metaphor we use when thinking about love both shapes and reflects the way we behave with a partner. Solomon outlines a number of metaphors for love and describes the consequences of using each.

Love as a Game We often hear people talking about love as if it were a contest in which one person emerges as the winner. The term itself is a common one: the "game" of love. People "play the field," often trying to "score." Strategies—including lying and flattery—that lead to domination are common: after all, "All's fair. . . ." "Playing hard to get" is another common tactic. For most game players, relationships are short-lived.

Love as a Fair Exchange This view of love is based on the economic model of receiving fair value for one's goods and services. People who adopt this metaphor talk about their relationship being "a good arrangement" and say they are getting "a good (or lousy) deal" from their partners. When things go wrong, the complaint is "It isn't worth it anymore." As these metaphors suggest, the overriding question for these love traders is "What am *I* getting out of this?" The value of the relationship is measured by whether the return on one's investment (of time, energy, money, good will, and so on) is worth the effort. Social exchange theory, introduced earlier in this chapter, explores this economic metaphor.

Love as Communication   Some people (including a few students in communication courses, we fear) measure love in terms of how well the lovers send and receive messages. For them, Solomon suggests, the essential moment is the "heavy conversation." "We really get through to each other," they say proudly. Their "feedback" is good, and "openness" is the ultimate goal—regardless of whether the messages are supportive or hostile. In other words, in the communication model, *expression* of feelings is more important than the content of those emotions. The result of this attitude is interaction that is all form and little substance: *making* love as opposed to *loving.*

Communication is important in a loving relationship, of course, but as a *means*, and not an end in itself. When expression of feelings becomes more important than the content of those feelings, something is wrong.

Love as Work   Some people view love as an important job, and their language reflects this attitude. They "work on," "work out," or "work at" the relationship. They see nothing wrong with having fun, but their primary objective is to build a successful relationship in the face of life's inevitable obstacles. Solomon points out that some devotees of the work model pick the most inept or inappropriate partners "rather like buying a rundown shack—for the challenge" (p. 87). They feel somehow superior to couples who are merely happy together, and admire those who have survived years of fights and other pain for "making it work."

Love as a Flame   Solomon states that "red-hot" lovers act as if they were Mr. Coffee machines, "bubbling over, occasionally overflowing, getting too hot to handle, and occasionally bursting from too much pressure" (p. 94). Partners who expect this sort of emotional fire can become disappointed when things "cool down" and may look for ways to "spice up their relationship." Unfortunately, the likelihood of those flames of love burning brightly for a long period is slim; and rather than settling for mere warmth, these romantic pyromaniacs frequently find themselves looking for a new flame.

Love as Banal   Banal lovers stand in almost direct opposition to their red-hot counterparts. Although few lovers intentionally seek a relationship based on blandness, this approach is a common one. Bland, unexcited lovers use bland, unexciting metaphors. The word "thing" is overused. It can describe a sex organ, profession or hobby ("doing one's thing"), or a problem. The bland, high-level abstraction that banal lovers often use is "relationship": clinically accurate, but hardly suggestive of any emotion.

Solomon presents other metaphors, including the dramatic model, in which lovers strive for catharsis (often playing before onlookers); the contract model, which emphasizes "commitment" and "obligation"; and the biological metaphor, which stresses that people are "made for each other."

People rarely select a metaphor consciously. In the case of love, the linguistic model we use is likely to come from the models to which we're exposed, both in the media and in our personal experience. Once a metaphorical view of love exists, we tend to behave in ways that support it. We can speculate that one source of difficulty for many couples is the partners' fundamentally different views of how their relationship "ought" to be. What metaphor do you use? Is it appropriate?

MAKING FRIENDSHIPS WORK

In a study called "Happily Ever After and Other Relationship Styles: Advice on Interpersonal Relations in Popular Magazines, 1951–1973," Virginia Kidd (1975) described two media views of relationships. First, there is a static vision: "Relationships don't change, and people live happily ever after." Second, there is a more realistic vision that emphasizes the dynamic nature of communication. Individuals are constantly changing, and so too are the relationships they share. This second vision implies that we can improve our relationship effectiveness if we understand the transactional nature of the communication process and practice such communication skills as active listening, conflict management, and self-disclosure.

In accordance with Kidd's categories of relationships, William Wilmot (1987) discusses four important principles about relationships:

Relationships Do Change   Change is inevitable, and relationships are no exception to the rule. Unfortunately, sometimes we do get stuck in our relationships. We stifle ourselves and others with expectations that each of us remain the same. We impose restrictions and often fight to keep relationships from being redefined. An extreme case can be observed in a parent who continues to treat a forty-six-year-old son as the baby, not as an adult and friend. Consider your own relationships. Do you accept the fact that your relationships will change?

Relationships Require Attention   As Wilmot notes, "Participants have to *keep working on their relationships until the day they die.*" He makes another comment: "If we all worked on our relationships as much as we did our jobs, we would have a richer emotional life." Work takes at least forty hours a week of your time. How much time do you devote to developing your close relationships?

Good Relationships Meet the Expectations of the Participants   Your satisfaction with a relationship is a function of how well that relationship meets *your* goals. For example, people get married for a variety of reasons: companionship, status, love, a good sex life, a name, money. So long as the two people sharing that relationship fulfill their expectations, the relationship is satisfying for them. Conflicts arise when the expectations differ and cannot be met with that relationship. What expectations do you have? What do you want from your relationships?

Relationships Can Be Improved by Dealing Directly with Relational Issues   The nature of the relationship and its functions are defined by the people, not by some mystical outside force. Knowing how a relationship forms and how it can change should increase the quality of that relationship. Rather than hoping problems won't occur and avoiding them when they do arise, do you use your best communication skills to prevent and confront your interpersonal problems?

Summary

The quality of an interpersonal relationship can be measured by how well the parties meet one another's social needs. There are four such needs: intimacy (intellectual, emotional, and physical), affinity, respect, and control. These relational messages are communicated almost constantly in addition to content messages. Sometimes relational messages are expressed overtly via metacommunication; more frequently they are conveyed nonverbally.

Communicators use a variety of compliance-gaining strategies to achieve their relational goals. These strategies include direct requests, indirect appeals, exchanging resources, promising or delivering rewards and punishments, acting in ways that maintain the other's face, and making relational appeals. The choice of a particular compliance-gaining strategy depends on several short- and long-term considerations.

We choose certain people as relational partners for a variety of factors including physical appearance, similarity, complementarity, reciprocal obligations, an exchange of resources, competency, physical proximity, and the amount of self-disclosure. Once we have identified a potential partner, the relationship can pass through several stages. Knapp's "staircase" model of relational development outlines ten stages and describes how movement within and between these stages can occur.

A variety of rules characterize most friendships. Despite their benefits, friendships can suffer from a variety of pressures, both external ones and from personal changes experienced by one or both partners. The confusing distinction between friendship and love grows in part from the many meanings of that term. Whether the partners define their relationship as liking or loving, a friendship can profit by following several principles which are outlined in this chapter.

Activities

1. Identify an important interpersonal relationship. If you aren't involved in such a relationship now, choose one from the past.
   a. Define the types and degree of intimacy (intellectual, emotional, physical) that help make this relationship interpersonal.
   b. Use the social penetration model to how the level of intimacy varies from one part of the relationship to another.

   Based on your observations, answer the following questions:
   a. How satisfied are you with the level of intimacy in your relationship?
   b. What can you do to make the level of intimacy more satisfactory?

2. Identify examples of complementary, symmetrical, and parallel distributions of control in relationships you have observed or ones in which you have been involved. You may choose different relationships to describe each type of control, or you may describe how a single relationship exhibited each distribution of power at a different time.

3. What compliance gaining strategies do you use? Interview someone with whom you have an important relationship such as a family member, friend, roommate, or fellow worker. Follow these instructions:
   a. Explain the types of compliance gaining behaviors listed on pages 252–255.

b. Ask which of these strategies you use. Do you rely on the same strategies most of the time, or does your approach vary from one situation to another?

c. Invite your partner to explain his or her reaction to these strategies. Are they acceptable, or do they cause friction in the relationship? Would your partner prefer that you use different strategies?

4. What attracts you to others? Choose five *voluntary* relationships you are currently involved in. (Attraction usually isn't an issue in involuntary relationships such as families and job partners.) Describe which factors listed on pages 257–263 of this chapter first attracted you to the other person, and which factors encourage you to maintain the relationship.

5. Use films, television programs, books, and newspaper articles to illustrate each stage in Knapp's staircase model of relational trajectories.

6. Identify an important personal friendship. How would you describe the current strength of that relationship? Do any of the definitions of loving on pages 277–280 describe it? How can you use the guidelines on page 280 to strengthen this friendship?

Readings

Adams, G. R., and T. L. Huston. "Social Perception of Middle-Aged Persons Varying in Physical Attractiveness." *Developmental Psychology* 11 (1975): 657–58.

Altman, I. "Reciprocity of Interpersonal Exchange." *Journal for the Theory of Social Behavior* 3 (1973): 249–61.

*Altman, I., and D. Taylor. *Social Penetration: The Development of Interpersonal Relationships.* New York: Holt, Rinehart and Winston, 1973.

Archer, R., and J. Berg. "To Encourage Intimacy, Don't Force It." *Psychology Today* (November 1978): 39–40.

Argyle, M., and M. Henderson. "The Rules of Friendship." *Journal of Social and Personal Relationships* 1 (1984): 211–37.

Aries, E. J., and F. L. Johnson. "Close Friendship in Adulthood: Conversational Content Between Same-Sex Friends," *Sex Roles* 9 (1983): 1183–1196.

Aron, A., D. G. Dutton, E. N. Aron, and A. Iverson. "Experiences of Falling in Love." *Journal of Social and Personal Relationships* 6 (1989): 243–57.

Aronson, E., B. Willerman, and J. Floyd. "The Effect of a Pratfall on Increasing Interpersonal Attractiveness." *Psychonomic Science* 4 (1966): 227–28.

Backman, C. W., and P. F. Secord. "The Effect of Perceived Liking on Interpersonal Attraction." *Human Relations* 12 (1959): 379–84.

Bales, R. "Task Roles and Social Roles in Problem Solving Groups." In *Readings in Social Psychology,* 3d ed., E. E. Maccoby, T. M. Newcomb, and E. L. Hartley, eds. New York: Holt, Rinehart and Winston, 1958.

Bateson, G. *Naven.* Cambridge: Cambridge University Press, 1937.

Baxter, L. A. "Dialectical Contradictions in Relationship Development." *Journal of Social and Personal Relationships* 7 (1990): 69–88.

Baxter, L. A. "Strategies for Ending Relationships: Two Studies." *Western Journal of Speech Communication* 46 (1982): 223–41.

Baxter, L. A. "Symbols of Relationship Identity in Relationship Culture." *Journal of Social and Personal Relationships* 4 (1987): 261–80.

Baxter, L. A. "Trajectories of Relationship Disengagement." *Journal of Social and Personal Relationships* 1 (1984): 29–48.

Baxter, L. A., and C. Bullis. "Turning Points in Developing Romantic Relationships." *Human Communication Research* 12 (1986): 469–94.

Baxter, L. A., and W. W. Wilmot. "Taboo Topics in Close Relationships." *Journal of Social and Personal Relationships* 2 (1985): 253–69.

Bell, R. A., and N. L. Buerkel-Rothfuss. "(S)he Loves Me, S(he) Loves Me Not: Predictors of Relational Information-Seeking in Courtship and Beyond." *Communication Quarterly* 38 (1990): 64–82.

Berger, C. R. "Social Power and Interpersonal Communication." In *Handbook of Interpersonal Communication*, M. L. Knapp and G. R. Miller, eds. Beverly Hills, CA: Sage, 1985: 439–99.

*Berscheid, E., and E. H. Walster. *Interpersonal Attraction*, 2d ed. Reading, MA: Addison-Wesley, 1978.

Block, J. D. *Friendship* New York: Macmillan, 1980.

Bordagaray-Sciolino, D. *The Role of Self-Disclosure as a Communication Strategy During Relationship Termination.* Thesis, University of North Carolina at Chapel Hill, 1984.

Burgoon, J. K., and J. L. Hale. "Validation and Measurement of the Fundamental Themes of Relational Communication." *Communication Monographs* 54 (1987): 19–41.

Burgoon, J. K., R. Parrott, B. A. LePoire, D. L. Kelley, J. B. Walther, and D. Perry. "Maintaining and Restoring Privacy Through Different Types of Relationships." *Journal of Social and Personal Relationships* 6 (1989): 131–58.

Buss, D. M. "Human Mate Selection." *American Scientist* 73 (January-February 1985): 47–51.

Byrne, D. "Attitudes and Attraction." In *Advances in Experimental Social Psychology* 4, L. Berkowitz, ed. New York: Academic Press, 1969.

Byrne, D., and B. Blaylock. "Similarity and Assumed Similarity of Attitudes Between Husbands and Wives." *Journal of Abnormal and Social Psychology* 67 (1963): 636–40.

Caldwell, M. A., and L. A. Peplau. "Sex Differences in Friendship." Paper presented to the Western Psychological Association Convention, Seattle, Washington, April 1977.

Campbell, A., P. E. Converse, and W. L. Rogers. *The Quality of Married Life.* New York: Russell Sage Foundation, 1976.

Carson, R. C. *Interaction Concepts of Personality.* Chicago: Aldine, 1969.

Christopher, F. S., and M. M. Frandsen. "Strategies of Influence in Sex and Dating." *Journal of Social and Personal Relationships* 7 (1990): 89–105.

*Cialdini, R. B. *Influence: Science and Practice.* Glenview, IL: Scott-Foresman, 1988.

Cody, M. J. "A Typology of Disengagement Strategies and Examination of the Role of Intimacy, Reactions to Inequity, and Relational Problems in Strategy Selection." *Communication Monographs* 49 (1982): 148–70.

Cody, M. J., and M. L. McLaughlin. "Perceptions of Compliance Gaining Situations: A Dimensional Analysis." *Communication Monographs* 47 (1980): 132–48.

Cody, M. J., M. L. McLaughlin, and M. J. Schneider. "The Impact of Relational Consequences and Intimacy on the Selection of Interpersonal Persuasion Tactics: A Reanalysis." *Communication Quarterly* 28 (1981): 91–106.

Cody, M. J., M. L. Woelfel, and W. J. Jordan. "Dimensions of Compliance-Gaining Situations." *Human Communication Research* 9 (1983): 99–113.

Conn, M. K., and C. Peterson. "Social Support: Seek and Ye Shall Find." *Journal of Social and Personal Relationships* 6 (1989): 345–58.

Cooper, J., and E. E. Jones. "Opinion Divergence as a Strategy to Avoid Being Miscast." *Journal of Personality and Social Psychology* 13 (1969): 23–30.

Cupah, W. R., and S. Metts. "Accounts of Relational Dissolution: A Comparison of Marital and Non-Marital Relationships." *Communication Monographs* 53 (1986): 311–34.

*Davis, K. "Near and Dear: Friendship and Love Compared." *Psychology Today* 19 (February 1985): 22–30.

Deaux, K. "To Err Is Humanizing: But Sex Makes a Difference." *Representative Research in Social Psychology* 3 (1972): 20–28.

Delia, J. G. "Some Tentative Thoughts Concerning the Study of Interpersonal Relationships and Their Development." *Western Journal of Speech Communication* 44 (1980): 97–103.

Derlega, V. J., M. Wilson, and A. L. Chaikin. "Friendship and Disclosure Reciprocity." *Journal of Personality and Social Psychology* 34 (1976): 578–82.

*Dillard, J. P. *Seeking Compliance: The Production of Interpersonal Influence Messages.* Scottsdale, AZ: Gorsuch Scarisbrick, 1990.

Dion, K., E. Berscheid, and E. Walster. "What Is Beautiful Is Good." *Journal of Personality and Social Psychology* 24 (1972): 285–90.

Douglas, W. "Affinity-Testing in Initial Interactions." *Journal of Social and Personal Relationships* 4 (1987): 3–16.

Douglas, W. "Uncertainty, Information-Seeking, and Liking During Initial Interaction." *Western Journal of Speech Communication* 54 (1990): 66–81.

*Duck, S. "How to Lose Friends Without Influencing People." In *Interpersonal Processes: New Directions in Communication Research,* M. E. Roloff and G. R. Miller, eds. Beverly Hills, CA: Sage, 1987.

*Duck, S. *Human Relationships: An Introduction to Social Psychology.* London: Sage, 1986.

Duck, S. " A Topography of Relationship Disengagement and Dissolution." In *Personal Relationships 4: Dissolving Personal Relationships,* S. Duck, ed. London: Academic Press, 1982.

Duck, S., and D. Perlman, eds. *Understanding Personal Relationships: An Interdisciplinary Approach.* London: Sage, 1984.

Feezel, J. D., and P. E. Shepherd. "Cross-Generational Coping with Interpersonal Relationship Loss." *Western Journal of Speech Communication* 51 (1987): 317–27.

Feinberg, M. R., G. Feinberg, and J. J. Tarrant. *Leavetaking.* New York: Simon and Schuster, 1978.

Finley, G. E., and C. A. Humphreys. "Naive Psychology and the Development of Persuasive Appeals in Girls." *Canadian Journal of Behavioral Science* 6 (1974): 75–80.

Fitzpatrick, M. A., and J. Winke. "You Always Hurt the One You Love: Strategies and Tactics in Interpersonal Conflict." *Communication Quarterly* 27 (1979): 3–11.

Frazier, P. A., and E. Esterly. "Correlates of Relationship Beliefs: Gender, Relationship Experience and Relationship Satisfaction." *Journal of Social and Personal Relationships* 7 (1990): 331–52.

Garko, M. G. "Perspectives on and Conceptualizations of Compliance and Compliance-Gaining." *Communication Quarterly* 38 (1990): 138–57.

Goss, B., and D. O'Hair. *Communicating in Interpersonal Relationships.* New York: Macmillan, 1988.

Griffin, E., and G. G. Sparks. "Friends Forever: A Longitudinal Exploration of Intimacy in Same-Sex and Platonic Friends." *Journal of Social and Personal Relationships* 7 (1990): 29–46.

Gudykunst, W. B., and T. Nishida. "The Influence of Cultural Variability on Perceptions of Communication Behavior Associated with Relationship Terms." *Human Communication Research* 13 (1986): 147–66.

Haas, A., and M. A. Sherman. "Reported Topics of Conversation Among Same-Sex Adults." *Communication Quarterly* 30 (1982): 332–42.

Haefner, M. J., and J. Comstock. "Compliance Gaining on Prime Time Family Programs." *Southern Communication Journal* 55 (1990): 402–20.

Hamachek, D. E. *Encounters with Others: Interpersonal Relationships and You.* New York: Holt, Rinehart and Winston, 1982.

Harrington, M. R. *The Relationship Between Psychological Sex-Type and Perceptions of Individuals in Complementary, Symmetrical, and Parallel Relationships.* Thesis, University of North Carolina at Chapel Hill, 1984.

Haslett, B. "Communicative Functions and Strategies in Children's Conversations." *Human Communication Research* 9 (1983): 114–29.

Helmreich, R., E. Aronson, and J. Lefan. "To Err Is Humanizing—Sometimes: Effects of Self-Esteem, Competence, and a Pratfall on Interpersonal Attraction." *Journal of Personality and Social Psychology* 16 (1970): 259–64.

*Hendrick, C., and S. Hendrick. *Liking, Loving, and Relating.* Monterey, CA: Brooks/Cole, 1983.

Hinde, R. A. *Towards Understanding Relationships.* London: Academic Press, 1979.

Hocker, J., and W. W. Wilmot. *Interpersonal Conflict,* 3d ed. Dubuque, IA: William C. Brown, 1991.

Homans, G. C. *Social Behavior: Its Elementary Form.* New York: Harcourt, Brace, 1961.

Howell, W. S. *The Empathic Communicator.* Belmont, CA: Wadsworth, 1982.

Hubbard, R. C. "Relationship Styles in Popular Romance Novels, 1950–1983." *Communication Quarterly* 33 (1985): 113–25.

James, M., and L. M. Savary. *The Heart of Friendship.* New York: Harper & Row, 1976.

Kaplan, A. G., and M. A. Sedney. *Psychology and Sex Roles: An Androgynous Perspective.* Boston: Little, Brown, 1980.

Kelley, E. L., cited in J. V. McConnell. *Understanding Human Behavior,* 2d ed. New York: Holt, Rinehart and Winston, 1977.

Kelley, H. H. *Personal Relationships: Their Structure and Processes.* Hillsdale, NJ: Lawrence Erlbaum Associates, 1979.

Kidd, V. "Happily Ever After and Other Relationship Styles: Advice on Interpersonal Relations in Popular Magazines, 1951–1973." *Quarterly Journal of Speech* 61 (1975): 31–39.

*Knapp, M. L. *Interpersonal Communication and Human Relationships.* Boston: Allyn and Bacon, 1984.

Knapp, M. L., D. G. Ellis, and B. A. Williams. "Perceptions of Communication Behavior Associated with Relationship Terms." *Communication Monographs* 47 (1980): 262–78.

Langer, E. "Rethinking the Role of Thought in Social Interaction." in *New Directions in Attribution Research,* vol. 2, J. H. Harvey, W. J. Ickes, and R. F. Kidd, eds. New York: John Wiley & Sons, Inc., 1978.

Langlois, J. H., and L. A. Roggman. "Attractive Faces Are Only Average." *Psychological Science* 1 (1990): 115–21.

Leary, T. *Interpersonal Diagnosis of Personality.* New York: Ronald, 1957.

Leary, T. "The Theory and Measurement Methodology of Interpersonal Communication." *Psychiatry* 18 (1955): 147–61.

Lee, J. A. *The Colors of Love: An Exploration of the Ways of Loving.* Don Mills, Ontario, Canada: New Press, 1973.

Lemer, R. M., and E. Gillert. "Body Build Identification, Preference, and Aversion in Children." *Developmental Psychology* 1 (1969): 456–63.

Levinger, G., and J. Breedlove. "Interpersonal Attraction and Agreement." *Journal of Personality and Social Psychology* 3 (1966): 367–72.

Metts, S., W. R. Cupach, and R. A. Bejllovec. "'I Love You too Much to Ever Start Liking You': Redefining Romantic Relationships." *Journal of Social and Personal Relationships* 6 (1989): 259–74.

Millar, F., and L. E. Rogers. "Relational Dimensions of Interpersonal Dynamics." In *Interpersonal Processes: New Directions in Communication Research,* M. E. Roloff and G. R. Miller, eds. Beverly Hills, CA: Sage, 1987.

Neimeyer, R. A., and K. A. Mitchell. "Similarity and Attraction: A Longitudinal Study." *Journal of Social and Personal Relationships* 5 (1988): 141–48.

*O'Keefe, D. J. *Persuasion: Theory and Research.* Newbury Park, CA: Sage, 1990.

Parlee, M. B., and the editors of *Psychology Today.* "The Friendship Bond: PT's Survey Report on Friendship in America." *Psychology Today* 13 (October, 1979): 43–45, 49–50, 53–54, 113.

Phillips, G. M., and J. T. Wood. *Communication and Human Relationships: The Study of Interpersonal Relationships.* New York: Macmillan, 1983.

Poole, M. S., J. P. Folger, and D. E. Hewes. "Analyzing Interpersonal Attraction." In *Interpersonal Processes: New Directions in Communication Research,* M. E. Roloff and G. R. Miller, eds. Beverly Hills, CA: Sage, 1987.

Rogers, C. "The Characteristics of a Helping Relationship." In C. Rogers, *On Becoming a Person.* Boston: Houghton Mifflin, 1961.

Roloff, M. E. "Communication and Reciprocity Within Intimate Relationships." In *Interpersonal Processes: New Directions in Communication Research,* M. E. Roloff and G. R. Miller, eds. Beverly Hills, CA: Sage, 1987.

Roloff, M., C. A. Janiszewski, M. A. McGrath, C. S. Burns, and L. A. Manrai. "Acquiring Resources from Intimates: When Obligation Substitutes for Persuasion," *Human Communication Research* 14 (1988): 364–96.

*Rubin, L. B. *Just Friends: The Role of Friendships in Our Lives.* New York: Harper & Row, 1985.

*Rubin, Z. *Liking and Loving.* New York: Holt, Rinehart and Winston, 1973.

Rubin, Z., and S. Shenker. "Friendship, Proximity and Self-Disclosure." *Journal of Personality* 46 (1978): 1–22.

Schnall, M. "Commitmentphobia." *Savvy* 2 (1981): 37–41.

Selman, R. L., and A. P. Selman. "Children's Ideas About Friendship: A New Theory." *Psychology Today* 13 (October 1979): 71–72, 74, 79–80, 114.

Shellen, W. N., and C. M. Cole. "Friendly Relations: Same and Opposite Sex Friendships Among the Married and Unmarried." Paper presented at the Western Speech Communication Association meeting, Denver, 1982.

Sherrod, D. "The Influence of Gender on Same-Sex Friendship." In *Close Relationships,* C. Hendrick, ed. Newbury Park, CA: Sage, 1989.

Solomon, R. C. "The Love Lost in Clichés." *Psychology Today* 15 (October 1981): 83–94.

Staffieri, J. "A Study of Social Stereotype of Body Image in Children." *Journal of Personality and Social Psychology* 7 (1967): 101–4.

Steward, L. P., P. J. Cooper, and S. A. Friedley. *Communication Between the Sexes: Sex Differences and Sex-Role Stereotypes.* Scottsdale, AZ: Gorsuch Scarisbrick, 1986.

Sunnafrank, M. "Attitude Similarity and Interpersonal Attraction During Early Communicative Stages: A Research Note on the Generalizability of Findings to Opposite-Sex Relationships." *Western Journal of Speech Communication* 49 (1985): 73–80.

Taylor, D. A., and I. Altman. "Communication in Interpersonal Relationships: Social Penetration Processes." In *Interpersonal Processes: New Directions in Communication Research,* M. E. Roloff and G. R. Miller, eds. Beverly Hills, CA: Sage, 1987: 257–77.

Taylor, S., and D. Mette. "When Similarity Breeds Contempt." *Journal of Personality and Social Psychology* 20 (1971): 75–81.

Thibaut, J. W., and H. H. Kelley. *The Social Psychology of Groups.* New York: Wiley, 1959.

Tolhuizen, J. H. "Communication Strategies for Intensifying Dating Relationships: Identification, Use and Structure." *Journal of Social and Personal Relationships* 6 (1989): 413–34.

Tracy, K. "The Discourse of Requests: Assessment of a Compliance-Gaining Approach." *Human Communication Research* 10 (1984): 513–38.

Trenholm, S. *Interpersonal Communication.* Belmont, CA: Wadsworth, 1988.

Trenholm, S. *Persuasion and Social Influence.* Englewood Cliffs, NJ: Prentice-Hall, 1989.

Tschann, J. M. "Self-Disclosure in Adult Friendship: Gender and Marital Status Differences." *Journal of Social and Personal Relationships* 5 (1988): 65–81.

Vaughn, D. "The Long Goodbye." *Psychology Today* 21 (July 1987): 37–42.

Walster, E., E. Aronson, D. Abrahams, and L. Rottman. "Importance of Physical Attractiveness in Dating Behavior." *Journal of Personality and Social Psychology* 4 (1966): 508–16.

*Walster, E., and M. Walster. *A New Look at Love.* Reading, MA: Addison-Wesley, 1978.

Watzlawick, P., J. Beavin, and D. D. Jackson. *Pragmatics of Human Communication.* New York: W. W. Norton, 1967.

Werner, C. M., and L. M. Haggard. "Temporal Qualities of Interpersonal Relationships." In *Handbook of Interpersonal Communication,* M. L. Knapp and G. R. Miller, eds. Beverly Hills, CA: Sage, 1985.

Wiemann, J. M., and C. W. Kelly. "Pragmatics of Interpersonal Competence." In *Rigor and Imagination: Essays from the Legacy of Gregory Bateson,* C. Wilder-Mott and J. H. Weakland, eds. New York: Praeger, 1981.

*Wilmot, W. W. *Dyadic Communication,* 3d ed. New York: Random House, 1987.

Winch, R. *Mate-Selection: A Study of Complementary Needs.* New York: Harper & Row, 1958.

Witteman, H., and M. A. Fitzpatrick. "Compliance-Gaining in Marital Interaction: Power Bases, Processes, and Outcomes." *Communication Monographs* 53 (1986): 130–43.

Wortman, C. B., P. Adosman, E. Herman, and R. Greenberg. "Self-Disclosure: An Attributional Perspective." *Journal of Personality and Social Psychology* 33 (1976): 184–91.

Wright, P. H. "Toward a Theory of Friendship Based on a Conception of Self." *Human Communication Research* 4 (1978): 196–207.

Yinon, Y., A. Bizman, and D. Yagil, "Self-Evaluation Maintenance and the Motivation to Interact." *Journal of Social and Personal Relationships* 6 (1989): 475–86.

*Items identified by an asterisk are recommended as especially useful follow-ups.

Self-Disclosure

Chapter 9
Self-Disclosure

After studying the material in this chapter

You should understand

1. How self-disclosure is defined.

2. How the Johari Window represents the degrees of self-disclosure in a dyadic relationship.

3. How receivers judge whether another's message is self-disclosing.

4. Eight reasons people self-disclose, and which are most common in various contexts.

5. The types, functions, and extent of equivocation and white lies.

6. How gender affects self-disclosure.

7. The risks and benefits of self-disclosure.

You should be able to

1. Identify the degree to which you engage in self-disclosure with individuals in your life and the circumstances in which you do so.

2. Use the Johari Window model to represent the level of self-disclosure in one of your relationships.

3. Express the reasons you self-disclose in a selected relationship.

4. Compose responses to a situation that reflects varying degrees of candor and equivocation.

5. Name the potential risks and benefits of disclosing in a selected situation.

6. Use the guidelines in this chapter to decide whether or not to disclose important information in one of your relationships.

Key Terms

Equivocal language
Johari Window
Lie
Self-disclosure
White lie

The dream is a common one. You suddenly find yourself without clothes—on the street, at work, at school, or maybe in a crowd of strangers. Everyone else is fully dressed, while you stand alone, naked, and vulnerable. Maybe others see you and respond with curiosity or hostility or laughter. Possibly you seem to be invisible, searching for shelter before you are recognized. Whatever the details, dreams of this sort are usually disturbing.

You needn't be a psychoanalyst to figure out that the nakedness here is symbolic, representing the fear of disclosing oneself in other ways, dropping the masks and facades that we often show to the world. Laughter hides pain; a relaxed pose covers tension; a veneer of certainty masks confusion, and we fear being found out.

Why are we often afraid of opening up to others? Why not let others know who we really are? In his thoughtful book *What Are You Afraid Of?: A Guide to Dealing with Your Fears*, John T. Wood (1976) suggests an answer:

> I am afraid to be who I am with you...I am afraid to be judged by you. I am afraid you will reject me. I am afraid you will say bad things about me. I am afraid you will hurt me. I am afraid, if I really am myself, you won't love me—and I need your love so badly that I will play the roles you expect me to play and be the person that pleases you, even though I lose myself in the process.

There probably isn't a person over the age of six who wouldn't understand these words. At one time or another all of us are afraid to disclose personal information to others. As Wood suggests, the biggest reason for hiding this information is usually fear of rejection. As we'll soon see, there are other reasons as well.

Because the issue of **self-disclosure** is such a crucial one in interpersonal communication, we want to spend this chapter looking at it in detail. We'll talk about what self-disclosure is and how it differs from other types of communication. We'll see how one's gender influences disclosure. We will look at the benefits and apparent drawbacks of disclosing. Finally, we'll offer some suggestions for when self-disclosure is appropriate...and when it is not. Let's begin by defining our terms.

What Is Self-Disclosure?

What do we mean when we use the term "self-disclosure"? How does the process operate in interpersonal relationships? We need to begin our discussion by answering these questions.

What is the level of self-disclosure in one of your important relationships? How would your relational partner answer this question? Find out by completing Activity 1 on page 319.

A DEFINITION OF SELF-DISCLOSURE

You might argue that aside from secrets, it's impossible *not* to make yourself known to others. After all, every time you open your mouth to speak, you're revealing your tastes, interests, desires, opinions, beliefs, or some other bit of information about yourself. Even when the subject isn't a personal one, your choice of what to speak about tells the listener something about who you are. If you recall Chapter 6, each of us

Which of us has known his brother?
Which of us has looked into his father's heart:
Which of us has not remained forever prison-bent?
Which of us is not forever a stranger and alone?

THOMAS WOLFE

Student Reflection

Self-Disclosure: Quality and Quantity

At first I thought Beth and I had a special friendship. From the first time we met she told me things about herself that seemed very personal: about her family, her growing up, and her plans for the future. I was flattered that she trusted me enough to share so much.

Now I've found out that she's this open with almost <u>everybody</u>. At a party last weekend I heard her talking about the history of cancer in her family, and yesterday on the bus she started talking to a complete stranger about her broken engagement.

I suppose Beth is just a very open person, and there's nothing wrong with that. But knowing that she discloses personal information to almost anybody makes our relationship feel less special.

communicates nonverbally even when we're not speaking. For instance, a yawn may mean that you're tired or bored, a shrug of your shoulders may indicate uncertainty or indifference, and how close or how far you choose to stand from your listener may be taken as a measure of your friendliness or comfort.

If every verbal and nonverbal behavior in which you engage is self-revealing, how can self-disclosure be distinguished from any other act of communication? Psychologist Paul Cozby (1973) begins to answer this question. He suggests that in order for a communication act to be considered self-disclosing it must meet the following criteria: (1) It must contain personal information about the sender; (2) the sender must communicate this information verbally; and (3) another person must be the target. Put differently, the content of self-disclosing communication is the *self,* and information about the self is *purposefully communicated to another person.*

Although this definition is a start, it ignores the fact that some messages intentionally directed toward others are not especially revealing. For example, telling an acquaintance "I don't like clams" is quite different from announcing that "I don't like you." Let's take a look at several factors that further distinguish self-disclosure from other types of communication.

Honesty   It almost goes without saying that true self-disclosure has to be honest. It's not revealing to say, "I've never felt this way about anyone before" to every Saturday night date, or to preface every lie with the statement "Let me be honest…."

What about times when individuals do not know themselves well enough to present accurate information? Are these unintentionally false statements self-disclosing? For our purposes, the answer is yes. As long as you are honest and accurate to the best of your knowledge, the communication can qualify as an act of self-disclosure. On the other hand, both painting an incomplete picture of yourself (telling only part of what's true), or avoiding saying anything at all about yourself, are not self-disclosive acts.

Depth   A self-disclosing statement is generally regarded as being personal—containing relatively "deep" rather than "surface" information. Of course, what is personal and intimate for one person may not be for another. You might feel comfortable admitting your spotty academic record, short temper, or fear of spiders to anyone who asks, whereas others would be embarrassed to do so. Even basic information such as "How old are you?" can be extremely revealing for some people.

Availability of Information   Self-disclosing messages must contain information the other person is not likely to know at the time or be able to obtain from another source without a great deal of effort. For example, describing your conviction for a drunk-driving accident might feel like an act of serious disclosure, for the information concerns you, is offered intentionally, is honest and accurate, and considered personal. However, if the other person could obtain that information elsewhere without much trouble—from a glance at the morning newspaper or from various gossips, for example—your communication would not be an act of self-disclosure.

Context of Sharing   Sometimes the self-disclosing nature of a statement comes from the setting in which it is uttered (Officer and Rosenfeld 1985). For instance, relatively innocuous information about family life seems more personal when a teacher shares it with the class. This sort of sharing creates a more personal atmosphere because it changes the relationship from a purely "business" level to a more personal one.

Culture   Research shows that natives of the United States are more disclosing than members of any other culture studied (Gudykunst and Kim 1984: 181; Gudykunst and Ting-Toomey 1987: 197–98; Ting-Toomey 1987). For example, people in the United States are likely to disclose more about themselves to acquaintances, and even strangers. By contrast, Germans tend to disclose little about themselves except in intimate relationships with a select few, and Japanese reveal very little about themselves in even their closest relationships.

Cultural differences like this mean that what counts as disclosing communication varies from one culture to another. If you were raised in the United States you might view people from other cultures as undisclosing, or even standoffish. But the amount of personal information that the nonnatives reveal might actually be quite personal and revealing according to the standards of their culture. The converse is also true: To members of other cultures, North Americans probably appear like exhibitionists who spew personal information to anyone within earshot.

When communicating with people from different cultures it's important to consider their norms for appropriate disclosure. On the one hand, don't mistakenly judge them according to your own standards. Likewise, be sensitive about honoring their standards when talking about yourself. In this sense, choosing the proper level of self-disclosure isn't too different from choosing the appropriate way of dressing or eating when encountering members of a different culture: What seems familiar and correct at home may not be suitable with strangers.

We can summarize our definitional tour by saying that **self-disclosure** (1) has the self as content; (2) is intentional; (3) is directed at another person; (4) is honest; (5) is revealing; (6) contains information generally unavailable from other sources; and (7) gains much of its intimate nature from the context and culture in which it is expressed.

Although many acts of communication may be self-revealing, this definition makes it clear that few of our statements may be classified as self-disclosure. Pearce and Sharp (1973) estimate that as little as 2 percent of our communication qualifies as self-disclosure. Other writers agree with the point, if not the exact percentage (Berne 1964; Powell 1968; Steele 1975). Consider your own communication. How often do you disclose?

A MODEL OF SELF-DISCLOSURE

One way to illustrate how self-disclosure operates in communication is to look at a model called the **Johari Window,** developed by Joseph Luft and Harry Ingham (Luft 1969).

Imagine a frame that contains everything there is to know about you: your likes and dislikes, your goals, your secrets, your needs—everything (Figure 9–1).

Figure 9–1

Of course, you aren't aware of everything about yourself. Like most people, you're probably discovering new things about yourself all the time. To represent this, we can divide the frame containing everything about you into two parts: the part you know about, and the part of which you are not aware (Figure 9–2).

Figure 9–2

We also can divide the frame containing everything about you in another way. In this division one part represents the things about you that others know, and the second part contains the things about you that you keep to yourself. Figure 9–3 represents this view.

When we place these two divided frames one atop the other, we have a Johari Window. By

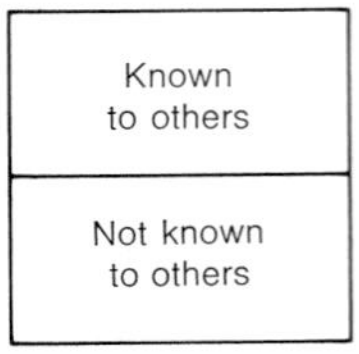

Figure 9–3

looking at Figure 9–4, you can see that it divides everything about you into four parts.

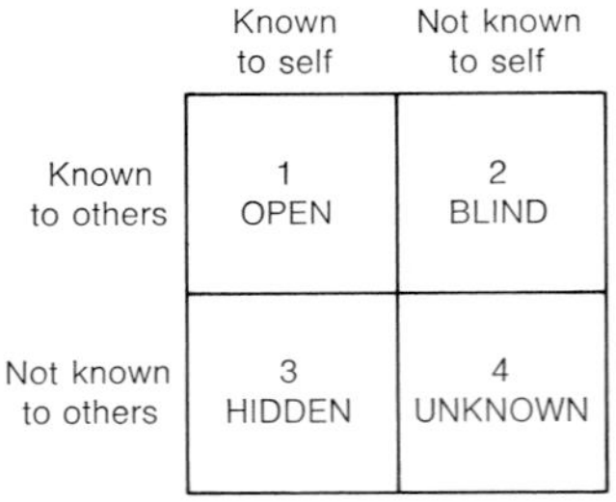

	Known to self	Not known to self
Known to others	1 OPEN	2 BLIND
Not known to others	3 HIDDEN	4 UNKNOWN

Figure 9–4

Part 1 represents the information of which both you and the other person are aware. This part is your *open area.* Part 2 represents the *blind* area: information of which you are unaware, but the other person knows. You learn about information in the blind area primarily through feedback. Part 3 of the Johari Window represents your *hidden area:* information that you know but aren't willing to reveal to others. Items in this hidden area become public primarily through self-disclosure, which is the focus of this chapter. Part 4 of the Johari Window represents information that is *unknown* to both you and others. At first the unknown area seems impossible to verify. After all, if neither you nor others know what it contains, how can you be sure it exists at all? We can deduce its existence because we are constantly discovering new things about ourselves. It is not unusual to discover, for example, that you have an unrecognized talent, strength, or weakness. Items move from the unknown area either directly into the open area when you share your insight, or through one of the other areas first.

What would a Johari Window representing one of your relationships look like? What could it tell you about the relationship? You can answer these questions by following the directions in Activity 2 on page 320.

The relative size of each area in our personal Johari Windows changes from time to time, according to our moods, the subject we are discussing, and our relationship with the other person. Despite these changes, most people's overall style of disclosure could be represented by a single Johari Window. Figure 9–5 pictures windows representing four extreme interaction styles.

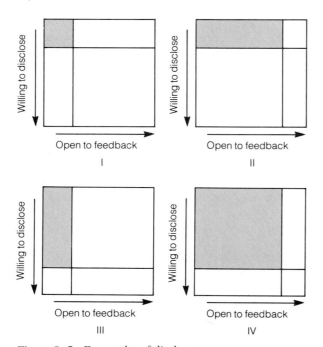

Figure 9–5   Four styles of disclosure

Style 1 depicts a person who is neither receptive to feedback nor willing to self-disclose. This person takes few risks, and may appear aloof and uncommunicative. The largest quadrant is the unknown area: Such people have a lot to learn about themselves, as do others.

Style 2 depicts a person who is open to feedback from others but does not voluntarily self-disclose. This person may fear exposure, possibly because of a distrust of others. People who fit this pattern may appear highly supportive at first. After all, they want to hear _your_ story, and appear willing to deny themselves by remaining quiet. Then this first impression fades, and eventually you see them as distrustful and detached. A Johari Window describing such people has a large hidden area.

Style 3 in Figure 9–5 describes people who discourage feedback from others, but disclose freely. Like the people pictured in Style 1, they may distrust others' opinions. They certainly seem self-centered. Their largest quadrant is the blind area: They do not encourage feedback and so fail to learn much about how others view them.

Style 4 depicts people who are both willing to disclose information about themselves and open to others' ideas. They are trusting enough to seek the opinions of others and share their own. In extreme, this communication style can be intimidating and overwhelming because it violates the usual expectations of how nonintimates ought to behave. In moderation, however, this open style provides the best chance for developing highly interpersonal relationships.

Interpersonal communication of any significance is virtually impossible if the individuals involved have little open area. Going a step further, you can see that a relationship is limited by the individual who is less willing to disclose. Figure 9–6 illustrates this situation with Johari Windows. _A's_ window is set up in reverse so that _A's_ and _B's_ open areas are adjacent. Notice that the amount of communication (represented by the arrows connecting the two open areas) is dictated by the size of the smaller open area of A. The arrows originating from B's open area and being turned aside by A's hidden and blind areas represent unsuccessful attempts to communicate.

You have probably found yourself in situations that resemble Figure 9–6. Perhaps you have experienced the frustration of not being able to get to know someone who was too reserved. Perhaps you have blocked another person's attempts to build a relationship with you in the same way. Whether you picture yourself more like Person A or Person B, the fact is that self-disclosure on both sides is necessary for the development of any interpersonal relationship. This chapter will describe just how much self-disclosure is optimal and of what type it is.

THE RECEIVER'S PERCEPTION

So far we have been looking at self-disclosure from the sender's (discloser's) viewpoint. After all, a receiver can't always be certain whether a given act of communication is truly intentional,

honest, and revealing, and contains information unavailable elsewhere. Suppose, for example, that at a party you met someone who remarked, "I've never felt comfortable in places like this." Is your companion disclosing? The content of the communication concerns the self and is directed at another person (you); but is the statement intentional, honest, revealing, and unavailable elsewhere? You might guess at the answers to these questions, but you could not know for sure.

Although the sender may be best suited to judge whether a message is self-disclosive, the receiver of the message also makes judgments about the communication. Whether or not these judgments are accurate, they are certainly powerful—in some ways more powerful than the sender's real intentions. In one study of fifty dating couples, the degree to which the partners *perceived* their mate to be disclosing was a better predictor of affection than the actual amount of self-disclosure (Sprecher 1987).

What characteristics of a message or sender impress receivers as being most disclosive? Recent investigations have begun to answer this question. In a series of studies conducted by Gordon Chelune (1981; Chelune et al. 1981), sub-

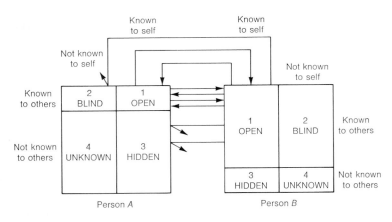

Figure 9–6   How limited disclosure blocks communication

> Sometimes a neighbor whom we have disliked for a lifetime for his arrogance and conceit lets fall a single commonplace remark that shows us another side, another man, really; a man uncertain, puzzled, and in the dark like ourselves.
>
> WILLA CATHER

jects were asked to rate the degree to which they believed a speaker was self-disclosing from 0 (indicating the speaker totally withheld personal information) to 100 (indicating total disclosure). These ratings were then compared to a number of objective behaviors exhibited by the speakers:

Self-references: statements descriptive of the speaker

Self-reference percent: number of self-references divided by the total number of statements made

Positive self-reference percent: percentage of statements describing favorable attributes of the speaker

Negative self-reference percent: percentage of statements describing unfavorable attributes of the speaker

Intimacy: depth of verbal content, measured on a five-point scale

Affective manner of presentation: degree of congruence between the intimacy level and the manner in which it was presented

Rate of disclosure: number of self-references per minute

Results indicate that all of these factors shape a receiver's evaluation of how much self-disclosure a sender is exhibiting. The single best predictor of subjects' ratings was intimacy, with rate of disclosure and congruent affective manner the next most influential factors.

Chelune also found, interestingly, that men were consistently seen as being more disclosing than women (for both male and female raters), possibly reflecting the stereotyped notion that men do not self-disclose very much; hence, any disclosure is "a lot."

Other elements of a communication situation also affect the receiver's perception of another's self-disclosure. Chris Kleinke (1979) discusses variables such as social context (location, subject, people), the appropriateness of the information disclosed (highly intimate disclosure early in a relationship is usually viewed as inappropriate), attributions made about the discloser's motives ("Why is she telling me this?"), and individual characteristics of both the sender and receiver (self-image, dogmatism, neuroticism, anxiety, and need for approval). All of these factors need to be considered in determining how much and what kind of self-disclosure is appropriate.

Why do you self-disclose? Discover some reasons by completing Activity 3 on page 320.

Reasons for Self-Disclosure

Although the amount of self-disclosure varies from one person to another, all of us share important information about ourselves at one time or another. For what reasons? Derlega and Grzelak (1979) present a variety of reasons a person might have for disclosing in any particular situation. We can build upon their work and divide these reasons into several categories.

CATHARSIS

Sometimes you might disclose information in an effort to "get it off your chest." In a moment of candor you might, for instance, share your regrets about having behaved badly in the past.

The personality of man is not an apple that has to be polished, but a banana that has to be peeled. And the reason we remain so far from one another, the reason we neither communicate nor interact in any real way, is that most of us spend our lives in polishing rather than peeling.

Man's lifelong task is simply one, but it is not simple: to remove the discrepancy between his outer self and his inner self, to get rid of the "persona" that divides his authentic self from the world.

This persona is like the peeling on a banana: It is something built up to protect from bruises and injury. It is not the real person, but sometimes (if the fear of injury remains too great) it becomes a lifelong substitute for the person.

The "authentic personality" knows that he is like a banana, and knows that only as he peels himself down to his individuated self can he reach out and make contact with his fellows by what Father Goldbrunner calls "the sheer maturity of his humanity." Only when he himself is detached from his defensive armorings can he then awaken a true response in his dialogue with others.

Most of us, however, think in terms of the apple, not the banana. We spend our lives in shining the surface, in making it rosy and gleaming, in perfecting the "image." But the image is not the apple, which may be wormy and rotten to the taste.

Almost everything in modern life is devoted to the polishing process, and little to the peeling process. It is the surface personality that we work on—the appearance, the clothes, the manners, the geniality. In short, the salesmanship: We are selling the package, not the product.

SYDNEY J. HARRIS

SELF-CLARIFICATION

Sometimes you can clarify your beliefs, opinions, thoughts, attitudes, and feelings by talking about them with another person. This sort of "talking the problem out" occurs in many psychotherapies, but it also goes on in other relationships, ranging all the way from good friends to bartenders or hairdressers.

SELF-VALIDATION

If you disclose information ("I think I did the right thing . . . ") with the hope of seeking the listener's agreement, you are seeking validation of your behavior—confirmation of a belief you hold about yourself. On a deeper level, this sort of self-validating disclosure seeks confirmation of important parts of your self-concept.

RECIPROCITY

A well-documented conclusion from research is that one act of self-disclosure begets another (Derlega and Chaikin 1975). Thus, in some situations you may choose to disclose information about yourself to encourage another person to begin sharing.

IMPRESSION FORMATION

Sometimes we reveal personal information to make ourselves more attractive. Helen Wintrob (1987) makes this point bluntly, when she asserts that self-disclosure has become another way of "marketing" ourselves. Consider a couple on their first date. It's not hard to imagine how one or both partners might share personal information to appear more sincere, interesting, sensitive, or interested in the other person. The same principle applies in other situations. A salesperson might say "I'll be honest with you . . . " primarily to show that he is on your side, and a new acquaintance might talk about the details of her past to seem more friendly and likeable.

RELATIONSHIP MAINTENANCE AND ENHANCEMENT

A large body of research supports the obvious fact that, in order to stay healthy, relationships need to be nourished by self-disclosure (Aronson 1984: 316). For example, there is a strong relationship between the amount and quality of self-disclosure and marital satisfaction (Fincham and Bradbury 1989). Not surprisingly, partners who reveal personal information to one another avoid the sorts of misunderstandings that lead to unhappiness. The same princi-

ple applies in other relationships. The bond between grandparents and grandchildren, for example, grows stronger when the honesty and depth of sharing between them is high (Downs 1988) Even relative strangers who work together in groups are more productive, cohesive, and committed to their job when they are encouraged to share their feelings about the task at hand (Elias et al. 1989).

SOCIAL CONTROL

As you learned in Chapter 8, self-disclosure can be an effective compliance-gaining strategy. Revealing personal information may increase your control over the other person, and some-

"Bob, as a token of my appreciation for this wonderful lunch I would like to disclose to you my income-tax returns for the past four years."

Drawing by Ziegler; © 1984 The New Yorker Magazine, Inc.

times over the situation in which you and the other person find yourselves. For example, an employee who tells the boss that another firm has made overtures probably will have an increased chance of getting raises and improvements in working conditions.

MANIPULATION

Although most of the preceding reasons might strike you as being manipulative, they often aren't premeditated strategies. There are cases, however, when an act of self-disclosure is calculated in advance to achieve a desired result. Of course, if a disclosure's hidden motive ever becomes clear to the receiver, the results will most likely be quite unlike the intended ones.

To determine which of these reasons for self-disclosing are most important, Lawrence Rosenfeld and Leslie Kendrick (1984) asked college students to describe which ones would be their reasons for disclosing in a variety of situations. The situations varied in three respects:

the target of the self-disclosure (friend or stranger)

the setting (alone or in a group)

intimacy (intimate or nonintimate)

For example, the *friend alone/intimate* situation was "It's evening and you are alone with your boyfriend or girlfriend in his or her home." The *friend alone/nonintimate* situation was "You are in the library with a friend." The *group of strang-*

ers/nonintimate situation was "You are introduced to a group of strangers."

The study showed that whether the target was a stranger or a friend had the strongest influence on the reason for disclosing. When the target was a friend, the top three reasons for disclosing were (from most to least important) relationship maintenance and enhancement, self-clarification, and reciprocity. The primary objective of disclosing to friends appears to be to help the relationship grow and solidify, with reciprocity functioning as the process that allows this growth to happen. The importance of self-clarification shows that friendships also have a personal (as opposed to relational) function. It appears that friendships provide a secure environment in which we can share our private thoughts in an attempt to sort things out.

When the target was a stranger, the top reason for disclosing was reciprocity. People offer information to elicit information from others. The information provides a basis for deciding whether to continue the relationship and how personal it is likely to be. The second reason for disclosing to strangers was impression formation. In other words, we often reveal information to strangers that will make us look good. This information, of course, is usually positive—at least in the early stages of a friendship.

Alternatives to Self-Disclosure

While self-disclosure plays an important role in interpersonal relationships, it isn't the only type of communication available. To understand why complete honesty isn't always an easy or ideal choice, consider some familiar dilemmas:

> A new acquaintance is much more interested in becoming friends than you are. She invites you to a party this weekend. You aren't busy, but you don't want to go. What would you say?

Student Reflection
Honesty May Not Always Be the Best Policy

I've become a sort of unofficial "big brother" to two eight-year-old boys who were on the softball team I used to coach. We spend one or two afternoons a week together, and I know it's good for them—neither one of them has a dad at home.

One of the kids (I'll call him Sam) is a great little guy. But the other one (I'll call him Joe) isn't a very nice kid. He always whines, he's selfish, and he's afraid to try anything new. I know a lot of his problems come from a lousy family background, but that doesn't make taking care of him any more fun.

Here's my problem: Last week Joe said "you don't like me as much as Sam, do you?" I've always told the kids that it's important to tell the truth, but I just couldn't bring myself to tell Joe he was right—that I didn't like him very much. Instead I said something vague like "You guys are different. There's something special about each of you."

I suppose this answer was a cop-out, but I still think it was better than telling him the plain truth. I guess some things are more important than honesty.

Your boss, whose divorce from a ten-year marriage just became final, asks you what you think of his new wardrobe. You think it's cheap and flashy. Would you tell him?

Hateful to me as are the gates of hell
Is he, who hiding one thing in his heart,
Utters another.

HOMER
Iliad

You're attracted to your best friend's spouse, who has confessed feeling the same way about you. You both agreed that you won't act on your feelings, and that even bringing up the subject would make your friend feel terribly insecure. Now your friend has asked whether you're attracted at all to the spouse. Would you tell the truth?

You've just been given a large, extremely ugly painting as a gift by a relative who visits your home often. How would you respond to the question "Where will you hang it?"

These situations show that while honesty is desirable in principle, it often has risky, potentially unpleasant consequences. It's tempting to avoid situations where self-disclosure would be awkward, but evasion isn't always possible, and even silence sends a message. There are two common alternatives to self-disclosure: lies and equivocation.

According to research, almost no one communicates with complete honesty. When might you tell white lies or equivocate? You can find out by trying Activity 4 on page 320.

LYING

A **lie** is a deliberate attempt to hide or misrepresent the truth. To most of us, lying seems to be a breach of ethics. At first glance it appears that the very possibility of a society depends on the acceptance of truthfulness as a social norm (Jaska and Pritchard, 1988; Winch 1959–60). While lying to gain unfair advantage over an unknowing victim seems clearly wrong, another kind of mistruth—the "white lie"—isn't so easy to dismiss as completely unethical. **White lies** are defined (at least by the people who tell them) as being unmalicious, or even helpful to the person to whom they are told.

Whether or not they are innocent, white lies are certainly common. In one study, 130 subjects were asked to keep track of the truthfulness of their everyday conversational statements (Turner et al. 1975). Only 38.5 percent of these statements—slightly more than a third—proved to be totally honest.

Reasons for Lying   What reasons do people give for being so deceitful? When subjects in the study were asked to give a lie-by-lie account of their motives for concealing or distorting the truth, five major reasons emerged.

To save face   Over half of the lies were justified as a way to prevent embarrassment. Such lying is often given the approving label "tact," and is used "when it would be unkind to be honest but dishonest to be kind" (Bavelas 1983). Sometimes a lie saves face for the recipient, as when you pretend to remember someone at a party in order to save the person from the embarrassment of being forgotten. Married couples are especially likely to lie in order to protect the feelings of their spouse (Metts 1989). In other cases a lie protects the teller from humiliation. You might, for instance, cover up your mistakes by blaming them on outside forces: "You didn't receive the check? It must have been delayed in the mail."

To avoid tension or conflict   Sometimes it seems worthwhile to tell a small lie to prevent a large conflict. You might, for example, say you're not upset at a friend's teasing to prevent the hassle that would result if you showed your annoyance. It's often easier to explain your behavior in dishonest terms than to make matters worse. You might explain your apparent irritation by saying "I'm not mad at you; it's just been a tough day."

To guide social interaction   Sometimes we lie to make everyday relationships run smoothly. You might, for instance, pretend to be glad to see someone you actually dislike or fake interest in a dinner companion's boring stories to make a social event pass quickly. Children who aren't skilled or interested in these social lies are often a source of embarrassment for their parents.

To expand or reduce relationships   Some lies are designed to make the relationship grow: "You're going downtown? I'm headed that way. Can I give you a ride?" "I like science fiction too. What have you read lately?" Lies that make the teller look good also fit into this category. You might try to impress a potential employer by calling yourself a management student when you've only taken a course or two in business. Sometimes we tell untruths to reduce interaction with others. Lies in this category often allow the teller to escape unpleasant situations: "I really have to go. I should be studying for a test tomorrow." In other cases people lie to end a relationship entirely: "You're really great, but I'm just not ready to settle down yet."

To gain power   Sometimes we tell lies to show we're in control of a situation. Turning down a last-minute request for a date by claiming you're busy can be one way to put yourself in a one-up position, saying in effect, "Don't expect me to sit around waiting for you to call." Lying to get confidential information—even for a good cause—also falls into the category of achieving power.

This five-part scheme isn't the only ways to categorize lies (see, for example, Lippard 1988). The taxonomy outlined in Table 9–1 is more complicated than the five-part one above, and covers some types of lies that don't fit into the simpler scheme. Exaggerations, for example, are lies told to boost the effect of a story. In exaggerated tales the fish grow larger, hikes grow longer and more strenuous, and so on. The stories may be less truthful, but they become more interesting—at least to the teller.

Most people think white lies are told for the benefit of the recipient. In the study cited above, the majority of subjects claimed such lying was "the right thing to do." Other research paints a less flattering picture of who benefits most from lying. One study found that two out of every three lies are told for "selfish reasons" (Hample 1980). A look at Table 9–1 seems to make this figure too conservative. Of the 322 lies recorded, 75.8 percent were for the benefit of the liar. Less than 22 percent were for the benefit of the person hearing the lie, while a mere 2.5 percent were intended to aid a third person.

Before we become totally cynical, however, the researchers urge a charitable interpretation. After all, most intentional communication behavior—truthful or not—is designed to help the speaker achieve a goal. Therefore, it's unfair to judge white lies more harshly than other types of messages. If we define selfishness as the extent to which some desired resource or interaction is denied to the person hearing the lie or to a third party, then only 111 lies (34.5 percent) can be considered truly selfish. This figure may be no worse than the degree of selfishness in honest messages.

Effects of Lies on the Recipient   What are the consequences of learning that you've been lied to? In an interpersonal relationship, the discovery can be traumatic. As we grow closer to oth-

Table 9–1   Types of White Lies and Their Frequency

	Benefit Self	Benefit Other	Benefit Third Party
Basic Needs	68	1	1
A. Acquire resources	29	0	0
B. Protect resources	39	1	1
Affiliation	128	1	6
A. Positive	65	0	0
1. Initiate interaction	8	0	0
2. Continue interaction	6	0	0
3. Avoid conflict	48	0	0
4. Obligatory acceptance	3	0	0
B. Negative	43	1	3
1. Avoid interaction	34	1	3
2. Leave-taking	9	0	0
C. Conversational control	20	0	3
1. Redirect conversation	3	0	0
2. Avoid self-disclosure	17	0	3
Self-Esteem	35	63	1
A. Competence	8	26	0
B. Taste	0	18	1
C. Social desirability	27	19	0
Other	13	5	0
A. Dissonance reduction	3	5	0
B. Practical joke	2	0	0
C. Exaggeration	8	0	0

From Camden, C., M. T. Motley, and A. Wilson. "White Lies in Interpersonal Communication: A Taxonomy and Preliminary Investigation of Social Motivations." *Western Journal of Speech Communication* 48 (1984): 315.

ers, our expectations about their honesty grow stronger (Buller 1988; Stiff et al. 1989). After all, discovering that you've been deceived requires you to redefine not only the lie you just uncovered, but also many of the messages you previously took for granted. Was last week's compliment really sincere? Was your joke really funny, or was the other person's laughter a put-on? Does the other person care about you as much as he or she claimed?

Recent research has shown that deception does, in fact, threaten relationships (McCornack and Levine 1990). Not all lies are equally devastating, however. Feelings like dismay and betrayal are greatest when the relationship is most intense, the importance of the subject is high, and when there was previous suspicion that the other person wasn't being completely honest. Of these three factors, the importance of the information lied about proved to be the key factor in provoking a relational crisis. We may be able to cope with "misdemeanor" lying, but "felonies" are a grave threat.

An occasional white lie in an otherwise honest relationship doesn't pose much threat. Major deception, though—especially when it is part of a pattern of deceit—is likely to provoke a relational crisis. In fact, the discovery of major deception can lead to the end of the relationship. More than two-thirds of the subjects in McCornack and Levine's study reported that their relationship had ended since they discovered a lie. Furthermore, they attributed the breakup directly to the deception.

The lesson here is clear: Lying about major parts of your relationship can have the most grave consequences. If preserving a relationship is important, honesty—at least about important matters—really does appear to be the best policy.

EQUIVOCATION

Lying isn't the only alternative to self-disclosure. When faced with the choice between lying and telling an unpleasant truth, communicators can—and often do—equivocate. As Chapter 5 explained, **equivocal language** has two or more equally plausible meanings.

Sometimes we send equivocal messages without meaning to, resulting in confusion. "I'll meet you at the apartment" could refer to more than one place. But other times we are deliberately vague. For instance, when a friend asks what you think of an awful outfit, you could say "It's really unusual—one of a kind!" Likewise, if you are too angry to accept a friend's apology but don't want to appear petty, you might say "Don't mention it."

The value of equivocation becomes clear when you consider the alternatives. Consider the dilemma of what to say when you've been given an unwanted present—an ugly painting, for example—and the giver asks what you think of it. How can you respond? On the one hand, you need to choose between telling the truth and lying. At the same time, you have a choice of whether to make your response clear or vague. Figure 9–7 displays these choices.

After considering the alternatives, it's clear that the first option—an equivocal, true response—is far preferable to the other choices in several respects. First, it spares the receiver from embarrassment. For example, rather than flatly saying "No" to an unappealing invitation, it may be kinder to say "I have other plans"—even if those plans are to stay home and watch TV.

Besides saving face for the recipient, honest equivocation can be less stressful for the sender than either telling the truth bluntly or lying. Because equivocation is often easier to take than the cold, hard truth, it spares the teller from feeling guilty. It's less taxing on the conscience to say "I've never tasted anything like this" than to say "this meal tastes terrible," even though the latter comment is more precise. Few people *want* to lie, and equivocation provides an alternative to deceit.

Equivocal language also saves the speaker from being caught lying. If a potential employer asks about your grades during a job interview, you would be safe saying "I had a B average last semester," even though your overall grade average is closer to C. The statement isn't a complete answer, but it is honest as far as it goes. As Bavelas et al. (1990: 171) put it, "equivocation is neither a false message nor a clear truth, but rather an alternative used precisely when both of these are to be avoided."

Given these advantages, it's not surprising that most people will usually choose to equivocate rather than tell a lie. In a series of experiments, subjects chose between telling a face-saving lie, the truth, and equivocating. Only 6 percent chose the lie and between 3 and 4 percent chose the hurtful truth. By contrast, over 90 percent chose the equivocal response (Bavelas et al. 1990).

THE ETHICS OF EVASION

It's easy to see why people choose white lies and equivocations over complete honesty so much of the time. These evasions provide a way to manage difficult situations that is easier than the alternatives for both the speaker and the receiver of the message. In this sense, successful liars and equivocators can be said to possess a

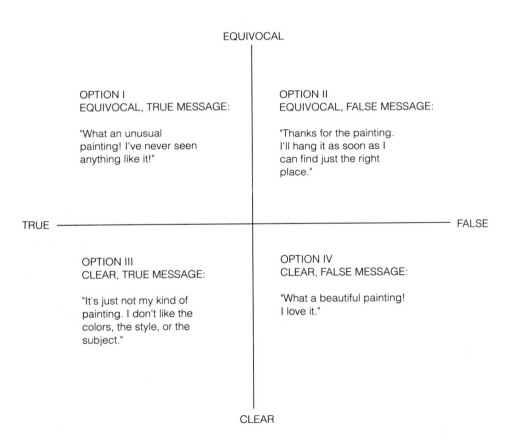

EQUIVOCAL

OPTION I
EQUIVOCAL, TRUE MESSAGE:

"What an unusual painting! I've never seen anything like it!"

OPTION II
EQUIVOCAL, FALSE MESSAGE:

"Thanks for the painting. I'll hang it as soon as I can find just the right place."

TRUE ——————————————— FALSE

OPTION III
CLEAR, TRUE MESSAGE:

"It's just not my kind of painting. I don't like the colors, the style, or the subject."

OPTION IV
CLEAR, FALSE MESSAGE:

"What a beautiful painting! I love it."

CLEAR

Adapted from J. B. Bavelas, A. Black, N. Chovil, and J. Mullett. *Equivocal Communication*. Newbury Park, CA: Sage, 1990, p. 178.

Figure 9–7   Dimensions of Truthfulness and Equivocation

certain kind of communicative competence or skill. On the other hand, there are certainly times when honesty is the right thing to do, even if it's painful. At times like these, evaders could be viewed as lacking the competence or the integrity to handle a situation most effectively.

Are white lies and equivocations an ethical alternative to self-disclosure? Although we hesitate to answer the question with an unqualified "yes," the research cited in these pages makes it clear that few people are totally honest. Perhaps the right questions to ask are whether a small lie or an equivocation is truly in the interests of the receiver, and whether this sort of evasion is the only effective way to behave. Another test is to imagine how others would respond if they knew what you were really thinking or feeling. Would they accept your reasons for not disclosing?

Even if you are satisfied that an evasive response is ethically defensible, it's important to realize that anything less than completely honest communication does have a cost. Every time you lie or hedge an answer, you distance yourself from the other person. By definition, non-disclosing messages reduce intimacy. Even if the other person *thinks* you are telling everything, you know the truth—and you know that a gap has opened between yourself and your partner. Some white lies and equivocation may be justified, but even so they create distance between the two of you. If intimacy is the most important goal, then self-disclosure has a high probability of being the best policy.

Gender Differences in Self-Disclosure

Are men and women equally willing to communicate in a disclosing way? Sidney Jourard (1971) was one of the first researchers to explore this question. Using his Self-Disclosure Questionnaire, he found that females disclose more than males. He explained his results by discuss-

Student Reflection

Gender and Self-Disclosure

I don't like to think of myself as the John Wayne type, but I guess it's true in some ways. It's very hard for me to open up to my male friends, especially about problems or worries. I've always found it easier to talk about my feelings to a girl friend or close female friend. With men, I hold back because I imagine I'll sound like a wimp if I start talking about myself. I know this attitude isn't logical, and that I'd be better off disclosing more to my closest men friends. That's going to take some courage.

ing what he called the "lethal male role"—that is, males are socialized not to disclose and so build up more tension in their daily lives, which results in early death—and the notion that females are socialized to be open and self-disclosing.

Some research supports the notion that women disclose more than men (Cline 1986). But other studies aren't so clear. For example one study (Derlega and Chaikin 1975) found that men reveal more strengths than women, following the stereotypical image of the powerful male. On the other hand, a second experiment (Hatch and Leighton 1986) found that women scored higher on disclosure of their strengths than men.

Inconsistencies like this begin to clear up when we realize that gender isn't the only variable that influences self-disclosure. Another factor is the *target* of the disclosure. While both men and women prefer to open up to members of the opposite sex (Rosenfeld 1981), males usually disclose more to strangers than females do, while females are more willing to open up to people they know well (Rosenfeld et al. 1979). Another variable is the *subject* of the disclosure. Men are more willing to share superficial information about themselves: work, attitudes, and opinions. Conversely, females are more willing to reveal personal feelings. A third variable is *self-image*. Cash and Soloway (1975) found that men who perceive themselves as attractive disclose more than other males, whereas females who view themselves as attractive disclose less than other women. A final factor that interacts with gender is what Rebecca Cline (1989) called *self-perceived interpersonal power:* the degree to which communicators are willing to act in accordance with their own standards instead of deferring to the expectations of others. She discovered that women with high interpersonal power are most willing to reveal personal information to others. Men—especially those with low interpersonal power—disclose less than women.

Self-disclosure in families differs according to gender. A study by Victor Daluiso (1972) reported that daughters received the lion's share of disclosure from the parents and, probably as a consequence, had a more accurate perception of their parents. Sons received less disclosure than they gave, and they gave less than their sisters did. This information suggests that the pattern for later life may be established in the family: Males have a tendency to disclose less intimate information about themselves than females do.

Adrienne Abelman (1976) uncovered some fascinating connections between self-disclosure and family relationships. Among her many conclusions were the following: (1) Mutual self-disclosure exists, but primarily between parents and children of the same sex; (2) a daughter's satisfaction with her family is related to her father's degree of self-disclosing to his wife; (3) men seem to rely on self-disclosing with their wives to obtain family satisfaction, whereas women seem to rely on self-disclosing with their children in order to obtain the same thing (which may account for why a father's disclosure to his wife is a determinant of their daughter's satisfaction); (4) information family members have about each other is related to how much each family member self-discloses.

Men and women differ in their self-disclosing behaviors, but do they *avoid* opening up for the same or different reasons? Rosenfeld (1979) investigated this question in a study in which men and women in beginning speech courses were asked to evaluate reasons why people might avoid self-disclosure. (See Table 9–2.) Before reading the results of the survey, you might want to complete the questionnaire for yourself.

Use the following scale to indicate the extent to which you use each reason to avoid self-disclosing.

1. Almost always
2. Often
3. Sometimes
4. Rarely
5. Almost never

An analysis of responses to the questionnaire indicated a great deal of similarity between why males and females avoid self-disclosure. The reason most commonly identified by both men and women was "If I disclosed, I might project an image I do not want to project."

Important differences exist, too. For males, subsequent reasons (in order of importance) included: "If I disclosed, I might give information that makes me appear inconsistent"; "If I disclosed, I might lose control over the other person"; and "Self-disclosure might threaten

Table 9–2   Reasons for Nondisclosure

_____ 1. I can't find the opportunity to self-disclose with this person.

_____ 2. If I disclosed, I might hurt the other person.

_____ 3. If I disclosed, I might be evaluating or judging the other person.

_____ 4. I cannot think of topics that I would disclose.

_____ 5. Self-disclosure would give the other person information to use against me at some time.

_____ 6. If I disclosed, it might cause me to make personal changes.

_____ 7. Self-disclosure might threaten relationships I have with people other than the close acquaintance to whom I disclose.

_____ 8. Disclosure is a sign of weakness.

_____ 9. If I disclosed, I might lose control over the other person.

_____ 10. If I disclosed, I might discover I am less than I wish to be.

_____ 11. If I disclosed, I might project an image I do not want to project.

_____ 12. If I disclosed, the other person might not understand what I was saying.

_____ 13. If I disclosed, the other person might evaluate me negatively.

_____ 14. Self-disclosure is a sign of some emotional disturbance.

_____ 15. Self-disclosure might hurt our relationship.

_____ 16. I am afraid that self-disclosure might lead to an intimate relationship with the other person.

_____ 17. Self-disclosure might threaten my physical safety.

_____ 18. If I disclosed, I might give information that makes me appear inconsistent.

_____ 19. Any other reason:_____

From L. B. Rosenfeld, "Self-Disclosure Avoidance: Why I Am Afraid to Tell You Who I Am" _Communication Monographs_ 46 (1979): 63–74.

relationships I have with people other than the close acquaintance to whom I disclose." Taken as a group, these reasons provide insight into the predominant reason why men avoid self-disclosure: "If I disclose to you, I might project an image I do not want to, which could make me look bad and cause me to lose control over you. This trouble might go so far as to affect relationships I have with people other than you." _The object is to maintain control,_ which may be hampered by self-disclosure.

For females, reasons in addition to "If I disclosed, I might project an image I do not want to project" included (in order of importance): "Self-disclosure would give the other person information to use against me at some time"; "Self-disclosure is a sign of some emotional disturbance"; and "Self-disclosure might hurt our relationship." Taken as a group, these reasons add up to the following: "If I disclose to you, I might project an image I do not want to, such as my being emotionally ill, which you might use

---

Student Reflection

Self-Disclosure Requires Discretion

George is one of my best friends. He works in the Communication department office, and he knows things that most students don't ever find out. I've learned a lot from listening to George: personal gossip about the professors and some students, and also tips that have helped me do better in my classes.

Even though I like George a lot and I do listen to his stories, I don't tell him anything personal about myself. Knowing that he's not willing or able to keep a secret leaves me not trusting him.

---

against me and which might hurt our relationship." *The object is to avoid personal hurt and problems with the relationship,* both of which may result from self-disclosure.

Other analyses have supplemented these results. Males are expected not to disclose (Lewis 1978). Men are socialized to compete, and sharing private information can seem incompatible with winning. Also, some men may be reluctant to share positive feelings toward others of the same sex because of *homophobia,* the fear of homosexuals or of appearing to be a homosexual. Expressions of vulnerability are perceived as feminine, as are expressions of affection.

Women, on the other hand, are expected to be more disclosing than men (Hacker 1981). Women have been taught to value relationships and develop intimacy. Also, females are more likely to have had positive experiences when

self-disclosing as children, and they expect that future disclosure will lead to continued positive results.

Risks and Benefits of Self-Disclosure

Is self-disclosure "good" or "bad"? There are two answers to this question: "Both" and "It depends." On the one hand, disclosure is both a means and an end of interpersonal relationships. Revealing important information about ourselves is a way to grow closer and build trust. The information we learn about others through disclosure is often what transforms our relationships from superficial, stereotyped role-playing arrangements into unique, deeply fulfilling ones. On the other hand, too much disclosure or disclosure that is poorly timed can lead to consequences ranging from mild annoyance and disappointment to downright rage and grief. We need to look, then, at both the benefits and risks of disclosing to gain a clearer idea of when it is—and isn't—an effective type of communication.

Should you open up to others? Help answer this question by completing a cost-benefit analysis of self-disclosure in your life. See Activity 5 on page 320 for details.

RISKS OF SELF-DISCLOSURE

The reasons for avoiding self-disclosure are summed up best by John Powell, who answers the questions posed in the title of his book, *Why Am I Afraid to Tell You Who I Am?* (1968):

> I am afraid to tell you who I am, because, if I tell you who I am, you may not like who I am, and that's all I have.

Revealing private information can be risky, both for the person who does the disclosing and those who hear it. These risks fall into several categories:

Self-disclosure Might Lead to Rejection   The risk of disapproval is a powerful one. Sometimes our fear of rejection is exaggerated and illogical, but there are real dangers in revealing personal information:

A: I'm starting to think of you as more than a friend. To tell the truth, I think I love you.
B: I think we should stop seeing one another.

i think of my poems and songs
as hands
and if i don't hold them out to you
i find i won't be touched
if i keep them
in my pocket
i would never get to see you
seeing me
seeing you
and though i know from experience
many of you
for a myriad of reasons
will laugh
and spit
and walk away unmoved
still
to meet those of you
who do reach out
is well worth the risk
the pain
so
here are my hands
do what you will

RIC MASTEN

Before I built a wall I'd ask to know
What I was walling in or walling out,
And to whom I was like to give offense.
Something there is that doesn't love a wall,
That wants it down.

ROBERT FROST,
"Mending Wall"

Self-disclosure Might Lead to the Projection of a Negative Image   Even if disclosure of unappealing information doesn't lead to total rejection, it can create a negative impression that diminishes both the other person's respect and your self-esteem.

A: I earned a C average last semester.
B: Really? You must be a real dummy!

Self-disclosure Might Lead to a Decrease in the Satisfaction Obtained from a Relationship   Relationships can be weakened when the wants and needs of the individuals are different.

A: Let's get together with Wes and Joanne Saturday night.
B: To tell you the truth, I'm tired of seeing Wes and Joanne. I don't have much fun with them.
A: But they're my best friends . . .

Self-disclosure Might Lead to a Loss of Control in the Relationship   Once you confess a secret weakness, your control over how the other person views you has diminished.

A: I'm sorry I was sarcastic. That's my way of hiding how inferior I feel sometimes.
B: Is that it? I'll never let you put me down again!

"Hah! This is the Old King Cole nobody ever sees."

Drawing by Dana Fradon; © 1983 The New Yorker Magazine, Inc.

Self-disclosure Might Hurt the Other Person
Revealing hidden information may leave you feeling temporarily better, but it leaves others, especially insecure people, with lowered self-esteem.

A: Well, since you asked, I have been bored lately when we've been together.
B: I know. It's my fault. I don't see how you can stand me at all!

Lying Often Appears to Have Greater Benefit for the Listener   Honesty doesn't always seem to be the best policy.

A: I worked three months on this painting, and I want you to have it. What do you think of it?
B: The thought is really sweet, but I don't like the painting.

The above risks make it clear that self-disclosure doesn't always lead to happily-ever-after outcomes. In addition to these situational hazards, there are cultural dangers associated with disclosing. Like it or not, many people view revealing personal information—even in close relationships—as a kind of weakness, exhibitionism, or mental illness. Although these beliefs seem to be growing less pervasive, it is still important to consider whether the other person will welcome the information you share.

Paradoxical as it sounds, a final risk of self-disclosure is that it often leads to increased awareness. As you reveal yourself to others, you often learn more about yourself. This awareness can expose a need for you to change, which might be difficult or painful. If ignorance is bliss, self-awareness can sometimes be quite the opposite—at least temporarily.

BENEFITS OF SELF-DISCLOSURE

Although revealing personal information has its risks, the potential benefits are at least as great. Self-disclosure—of the right type, communicated at the right time, in the right way—has three benefits.

Better Relationships The effect of self-disclosure on personal relationships works in two directions: We like people with whom we reciprocally disclose, and we disclose with people whom we like. Cozby (1973) describes a study in which subjects who had just spent a short time getting acquainted chose to disclose the greatest amount of information to partners whom they liked the most, and the smallest amount of information to those they liked the least. After a period of interaction, the subjects were asked again to rate their liking for their partners. An analysis showed that the partners who had disclosed the greatest amount of information were liked the best.

Self-disclosure plays a very important role in our close relationships. According to Derlega

(1984: 4), "It enables the relationship partners to coordinate necessary actions and to reduce ambiguity about each other's intentions and the meaning of their behavior." Perhaps because of this, the importance of self-disclosure in marriage is well documented. Self-disclosure has been found to be positively related to marital satisfaction (Miller and Lefcourt 1982; Waring and Chelune 1983). One recent study revealed that distressed couples who sought counseling disclosed less information to each other and communicated more ambiguously than non-distressed couples did (Chelune et al. 1985). Couples recognize the value of disclosure: Disclosing couples give their present relationships higher evaluations and have more positive expectations than do partners who disclose less (Troost 1977). In one sample of fifty couples, the amount of overall disclosure in their relationships was a good predictor of whether the partners remained together over the four years in which they were studied (Sprecher 1987).

Whether lack of self-disclosure is a cause or a symptom of troubled marriages isn't clear. However, couples who learn to change their communication styles are likely to find their relationships grow stronger. A number of studies have demonstrated that increased self-disclosure can improve troubled marriages (Jacobson 1984; Waring 1981). With the guidance of a skilled counselor or therapist, partners can learn constructive ways to open up. Many of the guidelines for constructive disclosure are contained in this chapter. Often, however, a couple with a backlog of hidden hurts and resentments needs the help of a third party to unload their emotional baggage without causing more damage.

Whether or not the relationship is an intimate one, it's a mistake to believe that if some self-disclosure is good, then more disclosure is better. In fact, as Figure 9–8 shows, there is a curvilinear relationship between liking and self-disclosure (Cozby 1972; Lange and Grove 1981). People who disclose too little are not well liked for an obvious reason: It's impossible to get to know them. On the other hand, those who disclose too much aren't popular either. They are viewed as lacking judgment and trustworthiness. One key to better relationships, then, is to engage in a moderate amount of self-disclosure.

Mental Health   Besides being necessary for the success of interpersonal relationships, appropriate self-disclosure promotes mental health. Cozby summarizes the research in this area:

> Persons with positive mental health (given that they can be identified) are characterized by high disclosure to a few significant others and medium disclosure to others in the social environment. Individuals who are poorly adjusted (again assuming a suitable identification can be made) are characterized by either high or low disclosure to virtually everyone in the social environment. (Cozby 1973: 78)

The relationship between self-disclosure and mental health is obvious, if somewhat circular. Most experts consider the ability to form and maintain satisfying interpersonal relationships as one element of mental health. Because it is impossible to carry on these relationships with-

out a degree of self-disclosure, it follows that self-disclosure and mental health go hand in hand.

There is an additional way in which self-disclosure and personal adjustment are related. It takes a great deal of energy to keep feelings hidden from significant others. Withholding important information can create stress that leads to less-effective behavior and even physical discomfort (Jourard 1971; Mowrer 1968). The feelings we experience when we have finally opened up—freedom, relief, "as if a weight were taken off your shoulders"—come from freeing up the energy used to keep the information private. Mentally healthy people are not burdened by an excessive load of unexpressed feelings and ideas.

Self-Understanding   Sharing your thoughts and feelings appropriately can lead to learning more about yourself. Disclosure leads to self-understanding in two steps. First, the act of sharing information often leads to new insights. Simply talking about a subject aloud often reduces the confusion that comes from turning a feeling over and over in your mind. Second, your disclosure boosts the odds that the other person will also reveal information—about you, the subject you are discussing, and the relationship you share. Research shows that disclosure is reciprocal: The more information you reveal, the more you are likely to receive (Chelune 1979). In this way, feedback from others can lead to increased self-awareness.

When to Self-Disclose

Self-disclosure is a special kind of sharing, not appropriate for every situation. Let's take a look at some guidelines that can help you recognize how to express yourself in a way that's rewarding for you and the others involved.

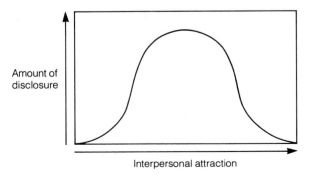

Figure 9–8   Relationship between self-disclosure and interpersonal attraction

IS THE OTHER PERSON IMPORTANT TO YOU?

There are several ways in which someone might be important. Perhaps you have an ongoing relationship deep enough so that sharing significant parts of yourself justifies keeping your present level of togetherness intact. Perhaps the person to whom you're considering disclosing is someone with whom you've previously related on a less personal level. Now you see a chance to grow closer, and disclosure may be the path toward developing that personal relationship.

There's still another category of "important person" to whom self-disclosure is sometimes appropriate: strangers who are players in what has been called the "bus rider phenomenon." Sometimes when we meet a total stranger whom we'll probably never see again (on a bus, plane, or elsewhere), we reveal the most intimate parts of our lives. It's sometimes possible to call such strangers "important people" because they provide a safe outlet for expressing important feelings that otherwise would go unshared.

IS THE RISK OF DISCLOSING REASONABLE?

Most people intuitively calculate the potential benefits of disclosing against the risks of doing so (Fisher 1986). The approach makes sense. Even if the probable benefits are great, opening yourself up to almost certain rejection may be asking for trouble. For instance, it might be foolhardy to share your important feelings with someone you know is likely to betray your confidences or ridicule them. On the other hand, knowing your partner will respect the information makes the prospect of speaking out more reasonable.

Revealing personal thoughts and feelings can be especially risky on the job (Eisenberg 1990; Eisenberg and Witten, 1987). The politics of the workplace sometimes require communicators to keep feelings to themselves in order to

accomplish both personal and organizational goals. You might, for example, find the opinions of a boss or customer personally offensive but decide to bite your tongue rather than risk your job or lose goodwill for the company.

There are several criteria to look for when choosing an audience for your disclosures. These include trustworthiness, sincerity, likability, good listening, warmth, and openness (Petronio et al. 1984). All other factors being equal, both men and women prefer to share personal information with partners whom they view as having similar personalities to themselves (Skoe and Ksionzky 1985).

Holding back with people with whom you don't feel comfortable may not be a bad idea. A study of almost one hundred people, some suffering from depression and others with no symptoms, revealed that the subjects who were high in defensiveness had lower lifetime histories of psychiatric disorders such as depression, anxiety, and substance abuse (Bower 1990). By contrast, less defensive subjects were more likely to suffer from these problems. Defensiveness, it seems, is a protective trait. Self-disclosure is not necessarily the only way to achieve mental health. There may, however, be a physiological trade-off: High defensiveness is linked to greater rates of hypertension, elevated heart rate, and some forms of cancer.

In anticipating the risks of disclosing, be sure that you are realistic. It's sometimes easy to imagine all sorts of disastrous consequences of opening up, when in fact such horrors are quite unlikely to occur.

IS THE SELF-DISCLOSURE APPROPRIATE?

Self-disclosure isn't an all-or-nothing proposition. It's possible to reveal information in some situations and keep it to yourself in others. One important variable is the relational stage (Vanlear 1987; Won-Doornick 1979). Research shows

"I'm a very sensual person. How about you, Mr. Gellerman?"

Drawing by Stan Hunt; © 1982 The New Yorker Magazine, Inc.

that sharing personal information is appropriate during the integrating stage of a relationship, where partners grow closer by disclosing. But once the same relationship has reached a maintenance stage, the frequency of personal disclosures drops (Fisher 1987: 376). This makes sense, for by this time the partners have already shared much of their private selves. Even the closest long-term relationships are a mixture of much everyday, nonintimate information and less frequent but more personal messages. Finally, realize that even intimate partners need to be sensitive to the timing of a message. If the other person is tired, preoccupied, or grumpy, it may be best to postpone an important conversation.

IS THE DISCLOSURE RELEVANT TO THE SITUATION AT HAND?

The kind of disclosure that is often a characteristic of highly personal relationships usually isn't appropriate in less personal settings. For instance, a study of classroom communication revealed that sharing all feelings—both positive and negative—and being completely honest resulted in less cohesiveness than a "relatively" honest climate in which pleasant but superficial relationships were the norm (Rosenfeld and Gilbert 1989).

Even in personal relationships—with close friends, family members, and so on—constant disclosure isn't a useful goal. The level of sharing in successful relationships rises and falls in cycles. You may go through a period of great disclosure and then spend another interval of relative nondisclosure (Vanlear 1987).

Even during a phase of high disclosure sharing *everything* about yourself isn't necessarily constructive. Usually the subject of appropriate self-disclosure involves the relationship rather than personal information (Sillars et al. 1987). Furthermore, it is usually most constructive to focus your disclosure about the relationship on the "here and now" as opposed to "there and then." "How am I feeling now?" "How are we doing now?" These are appropriate topics for sharing personal thoughts and feelings. There are certainly times when it's relevant to bring up the past, but only as it relates to what's going on in the present.

IS THE DISCLOSURE RECIPROCATED?

There's nothing quite as disconcerting as talking your heart out to someone, only to discover that the other person has yet to say anything to you that is half as revealing. You think to yourself, "What am I doing?" Unequal self-disclosure creates an unbalanced relationship, one doomed to fall apart.

With married couples, the balance of disclosure can be even more important than the amount. One study revealed that the greater the discrepancy between the partners' disclosure of feelings, the lower was their marital adjustment (Davidson et al. 1988). In other words, a couple who build a nondisclosing relationship are more likely to be satisfied than one in which one partner wants more disclosing communication than the other. Even neurotics recognize that nonreciprocal disclosure is not as appropriate as two-way revelations (Strassberg et al. 1988).

The reciprocal nature of effective disclosure doesn't mean that you are obliged to match another person's personal revelations on a tit-

Student Reflection

Self-Disclosure as a Weapon

Last week my wife hinted about my putting on too much weight. I know she's right, but I got defensive and said back to her "Well, I don't like the sound of your voice, but I've never complained about it." (It's sort of high-pitched and squeaky.)

As soon as I said the words I realized what a mistake I'd made. I was trying to hurt her because she hurt me, which was a stupid reaction. Besides, I may be able to lose weight by dieting, but there's nothing she can do about her voice. I can see clearly now that honesty can be a dangerous weapon. I wish I hadn't used it this way.

for-tat basis. You might reveal personal information at one time, while the other person could open up at a later date. There are even times when reciprocal self-disclosure can be taken as stage hogging. For instance, if a close friend is talking about his opinion of your relationship, it's probably better to hear him out and bring up your perspective later, after he's made his point.

There are few times when one-way disclosure is acceptable. Most of them involve formal, therapeutic relationships in which a client approaches a trained professional with the goal of resolving a problem. For instance, you wouldn't necessarily expect your physician to begin sharing his or her personal ailments with you during an office visit.

WILL THE EFFECT BE CONSTRUCTIVE?

Self-disclosure can be a vicious tool if it's not used carefully. Every person has a psychological "beltline," and below that beltline are areas about which the person is extremely sensitive. Jabbing at a "below the belt" area is a surefire way to disable another person, usually at great cost to the relationship. It's important to consider the effects of your candor before opening up to others. Comments such as "I've always thought you were pretty unintelligent" or "Last year I made love to your best friend" *may* sometimes resolve old business and thus be constructive, but they also can be devastating—to the listener, to the relationship, and to your self-esteem.

IS THE SELF-DISCLOSURE CLEAR AND UNDERSTANDABLE?

When expressing yourself to others, it's important that you share yourself in a way that's intel-ligible. This means describing the *sources* of your message clearly. For instance, it's far better to describe another's behavior by saying, "When you don't answer my phone calls or drop by to visit anymore..." than to complain vaguely, "When you avoid me..."

It's also vital to express your *thoughts* and *feelings* explicitly. "I feel worried because I'm afraid you don't care about me" is more understandable than "I don't like it..."

Summary

Self-disclosure consists of honest, revealing messages about the self that are intentionally directed towards others. Disclosing communication contains information that is generally unavailable via other sources. It gains much of its intimate nature from cultural rules and the context in which it is delivered. Revealing personal information does not guarantee that this communication will be perceived as disclosing by others. A number of factors govern whether a communicator will be judged as being a high- or low-level discloser.

The Johari Window model is a useful way to illustrate self-disclosure. A window representing a single person can illustrate the amount of information that individual reveals to others, hides, is blind to, and unaware of. Windows representing two communicators reveal how differing levels of disclosure can affect the level of intimacy in a relationship.

Communicators disclose personal information for a variety of reasons: catharsis, self-clarification, self-validation, reciprocal obligations, impression formation, relationship maintenance and enhancement, social control, and manipulation.

The percentage of messages that are self-disclosing is relatively low. Two alternatives to revealing personal facts, feelings, and opinions are lies and equivocations. Unmalicious "white lies" serve a variety of functions: saving face for the sender or receiver, avoiding tension or con-

flict, guiding social interaction, managing relationships, and gaining power. When discovered by the recipient, lies have the potential to provoke a relational crisis, especially if the content of the information lied about is significant. Equivocal messages are an attractive alternative to lying and direct honesty. They allow a communicator to be honest without being blunt and causing undesirable reaction.

Gender is an important factor in influencing both who self-discloses and the preferred target of that disclosure. Early findings that women disclose more than men have been qualified by later studies revealing that a variety of other variables interact with gender to influence who discloses: the target of the disclosure, the nature of the topic, the self-image, and the self-perceived power of the communicator.

Self-disclosure poses a variety of risks, both to the sender and recipient of the message. These potential risks are offset by the promise of many benefits. When deciding whether or not to disclose, communicators should consider a number of questions.

Activities

1. Use the definition on page 293 to calculate the amount and quality of self-disclosing communication that you express in one of your interpersonal relationships. Answer the following questions, and invite your relational partner to answer them independently:
   a. What percentage of your communication is truly disclosing? Is this amount optimal? Too high? Too low?

   b. What topics form the bulk of your disclosing messages? Are there any important topics that do not receive a sufficient amount of disclosure?

   Compare your answers with those of your partner. If the results are significantly different, use the information on pages 292–293 to consider why your partner does not perceive your level of disclosure in a way that matches yours. Consider what steps you might take to reconcile your perception of your disclosing behavior with your partner's.

2. Create a figure similar to the two Johari Windows pictured in Figure 9–6 to represent the balance of self-disclosure on a key topic in one of your relationships. How does the equality or imbalance of disclosure between you and the other person affect your relationship?

3. List examples from your personal experience that illustrate each of the reasons for self-disclosure described on pages 297–301. Which of these reasons are the most common motives for your disclosure? Are you satisfied with these motives?

4. Based on your personal experience, list five situations where complete honesty would be damaging to you or the other persons involved. For each situation, develop a white lie and an equivocal response. Then use the criteria in this chapter to decide which response would be best from an ethical and strategic point of view.

5. Compose a disclosing message you could share with each of the following people: an instructor, a friend, a family member, and someone with whom you work. For each person, describe the risks and benefits of sharing your message, and explain your choice about whether or not to deliver it.

Readings

Abelman, A. K. "The Relationship Between Family Self-Disclosure, Adolescent Adjustment, Family Satisfaction, and Family Congruence." *Dissertation Abstracts International* 36 (1976): 4248A.

Aronson, E. *The Social Animal*, 4th ed. New York: W. H. Freeman, 1984.

Bavelas, I. "Situations That Lead to Disqualifications." *Human Communication Research* 9 (1983): 130–45.

Bavelas, J. B., A. Black, N. Chovil, and J. Mullett. *Equivocal Communication*. Newbury Park, CA: Sage, 1990.

Berne, E. *Games People Play*. New York: Grove Press, 1964.

Bower, B. "Defensiveness Reaps Psychiatric Benefits." *Science News* 137 (1990): 309.

Buller, D. B. "Deception by Strangers, Friends, and Intimates: Attributional Biases Due to Relationship Development." Paper presented at the annual meeting of the Speech Communication Association, Boston, MA, 1988.

Burke, R. J., T. Weir, and D. Harrison. "Disclosure of Problems and Tensions Experienced by Marital Partners." *Psychological Reports* 38 (1976): 531–42.

Camden, C., M. T. Motley, and A. Wilson. "White Lies in Interpersonal Communication: A Taxonomy and Preliminary Investigation of Social Motivations." *Western Journal of Speech Communication* 48 (1984): 309–25.

Cash, T. F., and D. Soloway. "Self-Disclosure Correlates of Physical Attractiveness: An Exploratory Study." *Psychological Reports* 36 (1975): 579–86.

*Chelune, G. J., ed. *Self-Disclosure*. San Francisco: Jossey-Bass, 1979.

Chelune, G. J. "Toward an Empirical Definition of Self-Disclosure: Validation in a Single Case Design." *Western Journal of Speech Communication* 45 (1981): 269–76.

Chelune, G. J., L. B. Rosenfeld, and E. M. Waring. "Spouse Disclosure Patterns in Distressed and Nondistressed Couples." *American Journal of Family Therapy* 13 (1985): 24–32.

Chelune, G. J., S. T. Skiffington, and C. Williams. "A Multidimensional Analysis of Observers' Perceptions of Self-Disclosing Behavior." *Journal of Personality and Social Psychology* 41 (1981): 599–606.

Cline, R. J. "The Effects of Biological Sex and Psychological Gender on Reported and Behavioral Intimacy and Control of Self-Disclosure." *Communication Quarterly* 34 (1986): 41–54.

Cline, R. W. "The Politics of Intimacy: Costs and Benefits Determining Disclosure Intimacy in Male-Female Dyads." *Journal of Social and Personal Relationships* 6 (1989): 5–20.

*Cozby, P. C. "Self-Disclosure: A Literature Review." *Psychological Bulletin* 79 (1973): 73–91.

Cozby, P. C. "Self-Disclosure, Reciprocity, and Liking." *Sociometry* 35 (1972): 151–60.

Daluiso, V. E. "Self-Disclosure and Perception of that Self-Disclosure Between Parents and Their Teen-Age Children." *Dissertation Abstracts International* 33 (1972): 420B.

Davidson, B., J. Balswich, and C. Halverson. "Affective Self-Disclosure and Marital Adjustment: A Test of Equity Theory." *Journal of Marriage and the Family* 45 (1983): 93–102.

Derlega, V. J. "Self-Disclosure and Intimate Relationships." In *Communication, Intimacy, and Close Relationships*, V. J. Derlega, ed. Orlando: Academic Press, 1984.

*Derlega, V. J., and A. L. Chaikin. *Sharing Intimacy: What We Reveal to Others and Why.* Englewood Cliffs, NJ: Prentice-Hall, 1975.

Derlega, V. J., B. Durham, B. Gockel, and D. Sholis. "Sex Differences in Self-Disclosure: Effects of Topic Content, Friendships, and Partner's Sex." *Sex Roles* 7 (1981): 433–48.

Derlega, V. J., and J. Grzelak. "Appropriateness of Self-Disclosure." In *Self-Disclosure*, G. J. Chelune, ed. San Francisco: Jossey-Bass, 1979.

Derlega, V., B. Winstead, P. Wong, and M. Greenspan. "Self-Disclosure and Relationship Development: An Attributional Analysis." In *Interpersonal Processes: New Directions in Communication Research*, M. E. Roloff and G. R. Miller, eds. Beverly Hills, CA: Sage, 1987.

Dillard, J. P. "Types of Influence Goals in Personal Relationships." *Journal of Social and Personal Relationships* 6 (1989): 293–308.

Downs, V. G. "Grandparents and Grandchildren: The Relationship Between Self-Disclosure and Solidarity in an Intergenerational Relationship." *Communication Research Reports* 5 (1988): 173–79.

Eisenberg, E. M. "Jamming: Transcendence Through Organizing." *Communication Research* 17 (1990): 139–64.

Eisenberg, E. M., and M. G. Witten. "Reconsidering Openness in Organizational Communication." *Academy of Management Review* 12 (1987): 418–28.

Elias, F. G., M. E. Johnson, and J. B. Fortman. "Task-Focused Self-Disclosure: Effects on Group Cohesiveness, Commitment to Task, and Productivity." *Small Group Behavior* 20 (1989): 87–96.

Fincham, F. D., and T. N. Bradbury. "The Impact of Attributions in Marriage: An Individual Difference Analysis." *Journal of Social and Personal Relationships* 6 (1989): 69–85.

Fisher, B. A. *Interpersonal Communication: Pragmatics of Human Relationships.* New York: Random House, 1987.

Fisher, D. V. "Decision-Making and Self-Disclosure." *Journal of Social and Personal Relationships* 3 (1986): 323–36.

Garcia, P. A., and J. S. Geisler. "Sex and Age/Grade Differences in Adolescents' Self-Disclosure." *Perceptual and Motor Skills* 67 (1988): 427–32.

Gilbert, S. J., and G. G. Whiteneck. "Toward a Multidimensional Approach to the Study of Self-Disclosure." *Human Communication Research* 2 (1976): 347–55.

*Goodstein, L. D., and V. M. Reinecker. "Factors Affecting Self-Disclosure: A Review of the Literature." In *Progress in Experimental Personality Research* VII, B. A. Maher, ed. New York: Academic Press, 1974.

Gudykunst, W. B., and Y. Y. Kim. *Communicating with Strangers: An Approach to Intercultural Communication.* Reading, MA: Addison-Wesley, 1984.

*Gudykunst, W. B., and S. Ting-Toomey. *Culture and Interpersonal Communication.* Newbury Park, CA: Sage, 1987.

Hacker, H. M. "Blabbermouths and Clams: Sex Differences in Self-Disclosure in Same-Sex and Cross-Sex Friendship Dyads." *Psychology of Women Quarterly* (Spring 1981): 385–401.

Hatch, D. and L. Leighton "Comparison of Men and Women on Self-Disclosure." Psychological Report, 58 (1986): 175–178.

Hample, D. "Purposes and Effects of Lying." *Southern Speech Communication Journal* 46 (1980): 33–47

Hendrick, S. S. "Self-Disclosure and Marital Satisfaction." *Journal of Personality and Social Psychology* 40 (1981): 1150–59.

Jacobson, N. S. "A Component Analysis of Behavioral Marital Therapy: The Relative Effectiveness of Behavior Exchange and Communication/Problem-Solving Training." *Journal of Consulting and Clinical Psychology* 52 (1984): 295–305.

*Jaska, J. A., and M. S. Pritchard. *Communication Ethics: Methods of Analysis.* Belmont, CA: Wadsworth, 1988.

Jourard, S. M. "Healthy Personality and Self-Disclosure." *Mental Hygiene* 43 (1959): 499–507.

*Jourard, S. M. *The Transparent Self,* 2d ed. Princeton, NJ: Van Nostrand, 1971.

Kleinke, C. L. "Effects of Personal Evaluations." In *Self-Disclosure,* G. J. Chelune, ed. San Francisco: Jossey-Bass, 1979.

Lange, J. I., and T. G. Grove. "Sociometric and Autonomic Responses to Three Levels of Self-Disclosure in Dyads." *Western Journal of Speech Communication* 45 (1981): 335–62.

Lewis, R. A. "Emotional Intimacy Among Men." *Journal of Social Issues* 34 (1978): 108–21.

Lippard, P. V. "Ask Me No Questions, I'll Tell You No Lies: Situational Exigencies for Interpersonal Deception." *Western Journal of Speech Communication* 52 (1988): 91–103.

Luft, J. *Of Human Interaction.* Palo Alto, CA: National Press Books, 1969.

Lyons, A. "Personality of High and Low Self-Disclosers." *Journal of Humanistic Psychology* 18 (1978): 83–86.

McCornack, S. A., and T. R. Levine. "When Lies Are Uncovered: Emotional and Relational Outcomes of Discovered Deception." *Communication Monographs* 57 (1990): 119–38.

Metts, S. "An Exploratory Investigation of Deception in Close Relationships" *Journal of Social and Personal Relationships* 6 (1989): 159–179.

Miller, R. S., and H. M. Lefcourt. "The Assessment of Social Intimacy." *Journal of Personality Assessment* 46 (1982): 514–18.

Moriwaki, S. Y. "Self-Disclosure, Significant Others and Psychological Well-Being in Old Age." *Journal of Health and Social Behavior* 14 (1973): 226–32.

Mowrer, O. H. "Loss and Recovery of Community: A Guide to the Theory and Practice of Integrity Therapy." In *Innovations to Group Psychotherapy,* G. M. Gazda, ed. Springfield, IL: Charles C. Thomas, 1968.

Officer, S. A., and L. B. Rosenfeld. "Self-Disclosure to Male and Female Coaches by High School Female Athletes." *Journal of Sport Psychology* 7 (1985): 360–70.

Pearce, W. B., and S. M. Sharp. "Self-Disclosing Communication." *Journal of Communication* 23 (1973): 409–25.

Petronio, S., J. Martin, and R. Littlefield. "Prerequisite Conditions for Self-Disclosing: A Gender Issue." *Communication Monographs* 51 (1984): 268–73.

Powell, J. *Why Am I Afraid to Tell You Who I Am?* Niles, IL: Argus Communications, 1968.

Rosenfeld, L. B. "Self-Disclosure and Small Group Interaction." In *Small Group Communication,* 5th ed., R. S. Cathcart and L. A. Samovar, eds. Dubuque, IA: Wm. C. Brown, 1988.

Rosenfeld, L. B. "Self-Disclosure and Target Characteristics." Unpublished manuscript, University of New Mexico, 1981.

*Rosenfeld, L. B. "Self-Disclosure Avoidance: Why I Am Afraid to Tell You Who I Am" *Communication Monographs* 46 (1979): 63–74.

Rosenfeld, L. B., J. M. Civikly, and J. R. Herron. "Anatomical Sex, Psychological Sex, and Self-Disclosure." In *Self-Disclosure*, G. J. Chelune, ed. San Francisco: Jossey-Bass, 1979.

Rosenfeld, L. B., and J. R. Gilbert. "The Measurement of Cohesion and Its Relationship to Dimensions of Self-Disclosure in Classroom Settings." *Small Group Behavior* 20 (1989): 291–301.

Rosenfeld, L. B., and W. L. Kendrick. "Choosing to Be Open: Subjective Reasons for Self-Disclosing." *Western Journal of Speech Communication* 48 (1984): 326–43.

Rosenfeld, L. B., and S. M. Welsh. "Differences in Self-Disclosure in Dual-Career and Single-Career Marriages." *Communication Monographs* 52 (1985): 253–63.

Rubin, Z. "Lovers and Other Strangers: The Development of Intimacy in Encounters and Relationships." *American Scientist* 62 (1974): 182–90.

Sillars, A. L., J. Weisberg, C. S. Burggraf, and E. A. Wilson. "Content Themes in Marital Conversations." *Human Communication Research* 13 (1987): 495–528.

Skoe, E. E., and S. Ksionzky. "Target Personality Characteristics and Self-Disclosure: An Exploratory Study." *Journal of Clinical Psychology* 41 (1985): 14–21.

Sprecher, S. "The Effects of Self-Disclosure Given and Received on Affection for an Intimate Partner and Stability of the Relationship." *Journal of Social and Personal Relationships* 4 (1987): 115–28.

Steele, F. *The Open Organization: The Impact of Secrecy and Disclosure on People and Organizations.* Reading, MA: Addison-Wesley, 1975.

Stiff, J. B., H. J. Kim, and C. N. Ramesh. "Truth-Biases and Aroused Suspicion in Relational Deception." Paper presented at the annual meeting of the International Communication Association, San Francisco, 1989.

Strassberg, D. S., T. B. Adelstein, and M. M. Chemers. "Adjustment and Disclosure Reciprocity." *Journal of Social and Clinical Psychology* 7 (1988): 234–45.

Ting-Toomey, S. "A Comparative Analysis of the Communicative Dimensions of Love, Self-Disclosure, Maintenance, Ambivalence, and Conflict in Three Cultures: France, Japan, and the United States." Paper presented at the International Communication Association convention, Montreal, 1987.

Troost, K. M. "Communication in Marriage." *Dissertation Abstracts* 37 (1977): 8003A.

Turner, R. E., C. Edgely, and G. Olmstead. "Information Control in Conversation: Honesty Is Not Always the Best Policy." *Kansas Journal of Sociology* 11 (1975): 69–89.

Vanlear, C. A. "The Formation of Social Relationships: A Longitudinal Study of Social Penetration." *Human Communication Research* 13 (1987): 299–322.

Waring, E. M. "Facilitating Marital Intimacy Through Self-Disclosure." *American Journal of Family Therapy* 9 (1981): 33–42.

Waring, E. M., and G. J. Chelune. "Marital Intimacy and Self-Disclosure." *Journal of Clinical Psychology* 39 (1983): 183–90.

Wheeless, L. R., and J. Grotz. "The Measurement of Trust and Its Relationship to Self-Disclosure." *Human Communication Research* 3 (1977): 250–57.

Winch, P. "Nature and Convention." *Proceedings of the Aristotelian Society* 60 (1959–60): 242.

Wintrob, H. L. "Self-Disclosure as a Marketable Commodity." *Journal of Social Behavior and Personality* 2 (1987): 77–88.

Won-Doornick, M. J. "On Getting to Know You: The Association Between the Stage of Relationship and Reciprocity of Self-Disclosure." *Journal of Experimental Social Psychology* 15 (1979): 229–41.

Wood, J. T. *What Are You Afraid of?: A Guide to Dealing with Your Fears.* New York: Spectrum Books, 1976.

---

*Items identified by an asterisk are recommended as especially useful follow-ups.

Communication Climate

Chapter 10
Communication Climate

After studying the material in this chapter

You should understand

1. The definition of communication climate.

2. The basic characteristics of confirming and disconfirming responses.

3. The nature of positive and negative communication spirals.

4. Types of disconfirming responses.

5. The relationship between the presenting self and defensive responses.

6. Types of defensive responses.

7. The types of messages that are likely to build confirming communication climates.

8. The ways of responding nondefensively to critical messages.

You should be able to

1. Identify some confirming and disconfirming messages in your own relationships.

2. Identify your defensive responses in a relationship, the parts of your presenting self you are defending, and the consequences.

3. Supply more confirming alternatives to a given set of disconfirming messages.

4. Supply appropriate nondefensive responses to real or hypothetical criticism.

Key Terms

Ambiguous response
Apathy
Communication climate
Compensation
Confirming response
Controlling communication
Descriptive communication
Disconfirming response
Dissonance

Evaluative language
Face
Face-threatening act
"I" language
Impersonal response
Impervious response
Incongruous response
Interrupting response
Irrelevant response

Problem orientation
Rationalization
Regression
Repression
Spiral
Tangential response
Verbal aggression
"You" language

How would you describe your most important relationships? Fair and warm? Stormy? Hot? Cold? Just as physical locations have characteristic weather patterns, interpersonal relationships have unique climates, too. You can't measure the interpersonal climate by looking at a thermometer or glancing at the sky, but it's there nonetheless. Every relationship has a feeling, a pervasive mood that colors the goings-on of the participants.

What Is Communication Climate?

The term **communication climate** refers to the social tone of a relationship. A climate doesn't involve specific activities as much as the way people feel about each other as they carry out those activities. Consider two interpersonal communication classes, for example. Both meet for the same length of time and follow the same syllabus. It's easy to imagine how one of these classes might be a friendly, comfortable place to learn, whereas the other could be cold and tense—even hostile. The same principle holds for families, coworkers, and other relationships: Communication climates are a function of the way people feel about one another, not so much the tasks they perform.

Like their meteorological counterparts, communication climates are shared by everyone involved. It's rare to find one person describing a relationship as open and positive, while the other characterizes it as cold and hostile. Also, just like the weather, communication climates can change over time. A relationship can be overcast at one time and sunny at another.

CONFIRMING AND DISCONFIRMING CLIMATES

What makes some climates positive and others negative? A short but accurate answer is that communication climate is determined by the degree to which people see themselves as valued. Communicators who perceive others in a relationship as being concerned about their welfare feel positive, whereas those who feel unimportant or abused bring negative attitudes to the relationship.

The kinds of messages that deny the value of others have been called **disconfirming responses.** A disconfirming response expresses a lack of regard for the other person, either by disputing or ignoring some important part of that person's message. This disregard, of course, is a severe blow to the receiver's self-esteem. It's disturbing enough to be told your idea is "wrong," but at least this sort of attack leaves some room for argument. More extreme types of disconfirming responses go beyond criticizing the content of a particular message to assault the worth of the person who is speaking—either overtly or simply by disregarding the person entirely.

A **confirming response,** on the other hand, is one in which the speaker acknowledges the other person as important. Unlike disconfirming responses, which are likely to make us feel unappreciated or ignored, confirming responses lead us to feel valued: Our existence is acknowledged and our importance is confirmed.

Studies by Sieburg (1969), Mix (1972), and others suggest that the most important single factor affecting outcomes in family settings is

The finer qualities of our nature, like the bloom on fruits, can only be preserved by the most delicate handling, yet we do not treat ourselves nor one another thus tenderly.

HENRY DAVID THOREAU

Student Reflection

Confirming Communication and Valuing

Dave and John both kid me about a lot of things: being a Celtics fan, my looks, my grades—almost anything you can think about. It drives me crazy when Dave does that kind of teasing, because it feels like a put-down. I don't mind John's teasing at all, though. I think that's because I know John likes me and would do anything I asked. So in a way, his teasing is a kind of affection. I guess it's not so much the <u>words</u> (or even the nonverbal communication) that make the difference. It's the attitude behind the message.

communication that implies acceptance or rejection, confirmation or disconfirmation (Pearson 1989: 270–276). For example, Clarke (1973) found that perceived confirmation was a better predictor of marital satisfaction and attraction than self-disclosure, and Cissna and Keating (1979), who also studied married couples, found that husbands and wives whose spouses communicated with them in a direct and empathic way were likely to feel confirmed by their partners.

Confirmation and disconfirmation also has been studied in educational settings. Sundell (1972) studied the behavior of teachers and students in junior high schools and found that confirming teachers were confirmed by their students, and disconfirming teachers were disconfirmed by their students. Jacobs (1973) found that reactions to interviews between professors and students were determined to a large extent by the professors' confirming behavior. Students who were deliberately disconfirmed by their professors during the interview were more dissatisfied with the interview experience and their own performance than those who were deliberately confirmed. Lawrence Rosenfeld (1983) found that supportiveness is of major importance for distinguishing liked from disliked classes, with liked classes described as more supportive. (The level of defensiveness was about the same in both classes.) Teacher behavior in liked classes was described primarily as *empathic*, whereas teacher behavior in disliked classes was described primarily as *superior*. Investigations by Rosenfeld and Jarrard (1985, 1986) found that the climate of classes with male professors perceived as sexist was less supportive, more defensive, and less involving than that of professors perceived as nonsexist. Perceived sexism in female professors was found to be unrelated to descriptions of climate.

Finally, a study by Heineken (1980) focused on the therapeutic setting in an attempt to determine whether psychiatric patients disconfirm more than "normal" individuals. She found that the frequency of disconfirming responses was significantly higher for groups of psychiatric patients.

HOW COMMUNICATION CLIMATES DEVELOP

As soon as two people start to communicate, a climate begins to develop. Verbal messages certainly contribute to the tone of a relationship, but many climate-shaping messages are nonverbal. The very act of approaching others is confirming, whereas avoiding them can be disconfirming. Smiles or frowns, the presence or absence of eye contact, tone of voice, use of personal space . . . all these cues and others send messages about how people feel about one another.

Once a communication climate is formed, it can take on a life of its own. The pattern can be either positive or negative. In one study of married couples, each spouse's response in conflict situations was similar to the other's statement (Burggraf and Sillars 1987). Conciliatory statements (for example, support, accepting responsibilities, agreeing) were likely to be followed by conciliatory responses. Confrontive acts (for example, criticism, hostile questions, faultfinding) were likely to trigger an aggressive response. The same pattern held for other kinds of messages: Avoidance begat avoidance, analysis evoked analysis, and so on. This was also found in a recent study on disagreements of married couples (Newton and Burgoon 1990): Videotaped interactions revealed that accusations from one partner triggered accusations in response, and that communication satisfaction was highest when both partners used supportive, rather than accusatory tactics.

This reciprocal pattern can be represented as a **spiral** (Wilmot 1987: 150–56). Some spirals are negative. In poorly adjusted married couples, for example, one spouse's complaint is likely to produce a countercomplaint or denial by the other (Alberts 1990). You can probably recall this sort of negative spiral from your own experience: One attack leads to another, until a skirmish escalates into a full-fledged battle:

A: *(mildly irritated)* Where were you? I thought we agreed to meet here a half hour ago.
B: *(defensively)* I'm sorry. I got hung up at the library. I don't have as much free time as you do, you know.

Friendship is like a fishhook: The further it goes in, the harder it is to pull out.

GERALD SUTTLES

A: I wasn't *blaming* you, so don't get so touchy. I do resent what you just said, though. I'm plenty busy. And I've got lots of better things to do than wait around for you!

B: Who's getting touchy? I just made a simple comment. You've sure been defensive lately. What's the matter with you?

Fortunately, spirals can work in a positive direction too (Wilmot 1987). One confirming behavior leads to a similar response from the other person, which in turn leads to further confirmation by the first party.

Spirals—whether positive or negative—rarely go on indefinitely. When a negative spiral gets out of hand, the partners might agree to back off from their disconfirming behavior. "Hold on," one might say, "this is getting us nowhere." At this point there may be a cooling-off period, or the partners might work together more constructively to solve their problem. If the partners pass the "point of no return," the relationship may end (Leary 1955). As you read in Chapter 1, it's impossible to take back a message once it has been sent, and some exchanges are so lethal that the relationship can't survive them. Positive spirals also have their limit: Even the best relationships go through rocky periods,

in which the climate suffers. The accumulated goodwill and communication skill of the partners, however, can make these times less frequent and intense. Therefore, most relationships pass through cycles of progression and regression, as pictured in Figure 10–1.

Levels of Confirming Messages

It's obvious that confirming messages are more desirable than disconfirming ones. But what characteristics distinguish such messages? Actually, it's an oversimplification to talk about one type of confirming message: Confirming communication occurs on three increasingly positive levels (Cissna and Seiberg 1981).

RECOGNITION

The most fundamental act of confirmation is to recognize the other person. Recognition seems easy and obvious, and yet there are many times when we do not respond to others on this basic level. Failure to write to or visit a friend is a common example. So is failure to return a phone message. Likewise, avoiding eye contact and not approaching someone you know sends

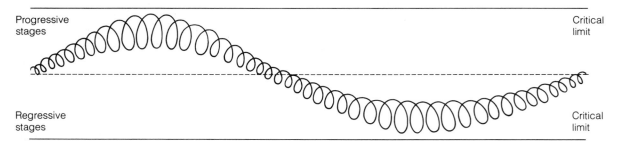

Figure 10–1　Progressive and regressive spiral phases of a marital dyad (William W. Wilmot, *Dyadic Communication*, 3d ed. New York: Random House, 1987: 154).

a negative message. Of course, this lack of recognition may simply be an oversight. You may not notice your friend, or the pressures of work and school may prevent you from staying in touch. Nonetheless, if the other person *perceives* you as avoiding contact, the message has the effect of being disconfirming.

ACKNOWLEDGMENT

Acknowledging the ideas and feelings of others is a stronger form of confirmation. Listening is probably the most common form of acknowledgment. Silently and attentively paying attention to another person's words is one measure of your interest. Of course, counterfeit listening —ambushing, stage hogging, pseudolistening, and so on—has the opposite effect of acknowledgment. More active acknowledgment includes asking questions, paraphrasing, and reflecting. As you read in Chapter 7, reflecting the speaker's thoughts and feelings can be a powerful way to offer support when others have problems.

ENDORSEMENT

Whereas acknowledgment means you are interested in another's ideas, endorsement means that you agree with them. It's easy to see why endorsement is the strongest type of confirming message, since it communicates the highest form of valuing. The most obvious form of endorsement is agreeing. Fortunately, it isn't necessary to agree completely with other people in order to endorse their message. You can probably find something in the message that you endorse. "I can see why you were so angry," you might reply to a friend, even if you don't approve of his outburst. Of course, outright praise is a strong form of endorsement, and one you can use surprisingly often once you look for opportunities to compliment others.

Student Reflection

Levels of Confirmation

I like it best when Tina agrees with me, but I'd rather have her disagree than say, "You're entitled to your opinion" and walk away as she sometimes does. Arguing shows that Tina cares. Ignoring me means I'm not even important enough to fight with.

Characteristics of Disconfirming Communication

Disconfirming communication is common enough and damaging enough that it deserves special attention.

How would you describe the communication climate in your most important interpersonal relationship? What do you do to create that climate? To find out the answers, see Activity 1 on page 353.

DISCONFIRMING MESSAGES

Disconfirming messages communicate a lack of appreciation for the recipient. These disconfirming messages can take several forms.

Verbal Aggression   The most obvious type of disconfirming response is **verbal aggression:** communication that appears to be meant to cause psychological pain to another person. In a survey of over 6,000 nationally representative families, about three quarters of the husbands and wives reported being the target of abusive verbal messages over the most recent year

Drawing by Menkoff; © 1990 The New Yorker Magazine, Inc.

MANKOFF

(Straus et al. 1989). Where verbal aggression exists in a relationship, it is seldom an isolated event. Most of the respondents reported several cases of aggression, with an average of thirteen incidents.

Complaining   Aggression isn't the only kind of disconfirming behavior. Simple complaining is a less intense but still discouraging sort of message. A survey of couples, both married and cohabitating, revealed five types of complaints (Alberts 1989). The most frequent was about *behavior* (not doing the laundry, talking too much on the phone, and so on). In declining order, the other types of complaints were about *personal characteristics* (being selfish, unfriendly, and the like), *performance* (driving too fast, drinking too much), *complaints* (e.g., being too critical, complaining too much, and so on), and *personal appearance* (such as being overweight or sloppy).

Both verbal aggression and complaining are obviously disconfirming. But other types of messages are more subtle. Sieburg and Larson (1971) describe seven such types of disconfirming responses.

Impervious Response   An **impervious response** fails to acknowledge the other person's communicative attempt, either verbally or nonverbally. Failing to return a phone call is an impervious response, as is not responding to

No more fiendish punishment could be desired, were such a thing physically possible, than that one should be turned loose in society and remain absolutely unnoticed by all the members thereof.

WILLIAM JAMES
The Principles of Psychology

another's letter. Impervious responses also happen in face-to-face settings. They are especially common when adults and children communicate. Parents often become enraged when they are ignored by their children; likewise, children feel diminished when adults pay no attention to their questions, comments, or requests.

Interrupting Response   As its name implies, an **interrupting response** occurs when one person begins to speak before the other is through making a point.

Customer: I'm looking for an outfit I can wear on a trip I'm...
Salesperson: I've got just the thing. It's part wool and part polyester, so it won't wrinkle at all.
C: Actually wrinkling isn't that important. I want something that will work as a business outfit and...
S: We have a terrific blazer that you can dress up or down, depending on the accessories you choose.
C: That's not what I was going to say. I want something that I can wear as a business outfit, but it ought to be on the informal side. I'm going to...
S: Say no more. I know just what you want.
C: Never mind. I think I'll look in some other stores.

Irrelevant Response   It is disconfirming to respond with an **irrelevant response,** making comments totally unrelated to what the other person was just saying.

A: What a day! I thought it would never end. First the car overheated and I had to call a tow truck, and then the computer broke down at work.
B: Listen, we have to talk about a present for Ann's birthday. The party is on Saturday, and I only have tomorrow to shop for it.
A: I'm really beat. You won't believe what the boss did. Like I said, the computer was down, and in the middle of that mess he decided he absolutely had to have the sales figures for the last six months.

Student Reflection

Ignoring as Disconfirming Behavior

My brother Paul's behavior with our father stands as my best example of an impervious response. When he was very young he would watch TV, and when Dad would call, completely ignore him. He never moved his eyes from the tube! He wouldn't budge a muscle! He sat there—at least until Dad would come in, see the situation, and scream. Now, when I sit in class and raise my hand to ask something and the teacher fails to see me (or sees me and ignores me), I get a clue about how my father felt.

B: I just can't figure what would suit Ann. She's been so generous to us, and I can't think of anything she needs.
A: Why don't you listen to me? I beat my brains out all day and you don't give a damn.
B: And you don't care about me!

Tangential Response   Unlike the three behaviors just discussed, a **tangential response** does acknowledge the other person's communication. However, the acknowledgment is used to steer the conversation in another direction. Tangents can come in two forms: (1) the tangential "shift," which is an abrupt change in conversation; and (2) the tangential "drift," which makes a token connection with what the other person is saying and slowly moves the conversation in another direction entirely.

Consider the following situation: A student rushes up to the teacher at the end of class to discuss the grade on a recent exam.

Student: Dr. Jones, I'd like to talk about my grade on the exam.
Dr. Jones: Fine. But you'd better hurry along so you're not late for your next class.

This response is a tangential shift, executed rather adroitly. Jones acknowledges the student's remark ("Fine"), then abruptly changes direction ("hurry along..."). Following is an example of a tangential drift:

Dr. Jones: Fine. We'll have to discuss the test. I also used to be concerned with understanding things I got wrong on tests. Of course, I was also concerned with punctuality! You'd better hurry along now so you're not late for the next class.

In this case, Jones indicates readiness to discuss the examination, but goes on to talk about something unrelated. A tangential response, if done well, can keep the other person guessing about how the change in the conversation's direction was accomplished.

Impersonal Response In an **impersonal response,** the speaker conducts a monologue filled with impersonal, intellectualized, and generalized statements. The speaker never really interacts with the other on a personal level.

Employee: I've been having some personal problems lately and I'd like to take off early a couple of afternoons to clear them up.
Boss: Ah, yes. We all have personal problems. It seems to be a sign of the times.

Ambiguous Response An **ambiguous response** contains a message with more than one meaning. The words are highly abstract or have meanings private to the speaker alone.

A: I'd like to get together with you soon. How about Tuesday?

B: Uh, maybe so. Anyhow, see you later.

C: How can I be sure you mean it?

D: Who knows what anybody means?

Incongruous Response An **incongruous response** contains two messages that seem to deny or contradict each other, one at the verbal level and the other at the nonverbal level.

He: Darling, I love you!

She: I love you too. *(giggles)*

Teacher: Did you enjoy the class?

Student: Yes. *(yawns)*

It's important to note that disconfirming messages, like virtually every other type of communication, are a matter of perception. A message that might not be intended to devalue the other person can be interpreted as disconfirming. For example, your failure to return a phone call or respond to the letter of an out-of-town friend might simply be the result of a busy schedule; but if the other person views the lack of contact as a sign that you don't value the relationship, the effect will be just as strong as if you had deliberately intended to convey a slight to them.

DEFENSIVE RESPONSES

Probably no type of communication clouds an interpersonal climate more quickly or severely than a defensive spiral. One verbal attack leads to another, and soon the dispute gets out of control, leaving an aftermath of hurt and bitterness that is difficult—sometimes even impossible—to repair. The results of one study demonstrate why defensiveness is so damaging. Subjects were asked to choose terms that answered the question "What does it mean to feel defensive?" The responses fell into seven categories including tense, discomforted, estranged, and mentally confused (Gordon 1988). It's easy to see how communication can suffer when one or both people are feeling such emotions.

What are you protecting when you are defensive? What effects does your defensiveness have on your relationships? Find out by completing Activity 2 on page 353.

The word "defensiveness" suggests protecting yourself from attack, but what kind of attack? Few of the times you become defensive involve a physical threat. If you're not threatened by bodily injury, what *are* you guarding against? To answer this question, we need to talk more about notions of presenting self and face, both of which were introduced in Chapter 2. Recall that the presenting self consists of the physical traits, personality characteristics, attitudes, aptitudes, and all the other parts of the image you want to present to the world. Actually, it is a mistake to talk about a single face: We try to project different selves to different people. You might, for instance, try to impress a potential employer with your seriousness but want your friends to see you as a joker. Of course, not all parts of your presenting self are equally significant. Letting others know that you are right-handed or a Gemini is probably less important to you than convincing them you are good-looking or loyal.

The qualities that make a person socially desirable vary from one time and place to another, so the **face** that is most desirable in

They defend their errors as if they were defending their inheritance.

EDMUND BURKE

Student Reflection

The Cost of Saving Face

Lately I've realized that a major part of my presenting self-image is to be "cool"—not to be shaken up by anybody or anything. I think that my apathetic front has cost me both my girlfriend and my job. When my girlfriend said she was thinking of leaving me, instead of telling her that I didn't want her to go, I acted apathetic and said, "If that's how you feel, I can't stop you." After she left I couldn't concentrate on school or work. When my boss asked why I had been so flaky lately, I said I didn't know what he meant instead of explaining my problem. A couple of weeks later he fired me.

I suppose people do think I'm a cool character, but the cost of putting up this front has been more than I can afford.

one setting may not be at all like that in a different one (Lim 1990). For example, most Americans value candor: Being called straightforward and honest is usually considered a compliment. On the other hand, in Japanese culture diplomacy is valued much more highly. A straight-from-the-hip style would be considered blunt and rude.

Whatever the particulars, the universal tendency is to save face by defending our presenting self when we perceive it has been attacked by what social scientists call **face-threatening acts.** To understand the process, imagine what might happen if someone attacked an important part of your presenting self. Suppose that

- An instructor labeled you an idiot, when you regard yourself as reasonably bright.

- An acquaintance accused you of being snobbish, when you believe you are friendly.

- An employer called you lazy, when you see yourself as a hard worker.

You have four choices in such situations: accept, attack, distort, or avoid.

Accepting the Critic's Judgment   When faced with an attack on your presenting self, you can agree with the critic. In the situations above, you could agree that you are stupid, snobbish, or lazy. If you sincerely accepted these evaluations, you would not feel or act defensively. Instead, you would adjust your presenting self—at least to this critic—to include the new judgment.

Sometimes, however, you aren't willing to accept attacks on your presenting self. The accusations of your critic may be false. You might, for instance, be working extremely hard on a job when you're accused of laziness. In a more extreme example, you might be telling the truth when someone accuses you of lying. Even in such cases, when defensive *feelings* are justified, defensive *behavior* is usually counterproductive. Complaining, justifying, and other defensive reactions rarely change a critic's mind. In fact, they usually intensify the attack. Also, defensive responses reduce the chance of gaining your partner's cooperation or enhancing your relationship. The final section of this chapter will suggest more productive ways to communicate when you have been criticized unfairly.

You might also be unwilling to accept criticism even when it *is* valid because it doesn't support the image you want to project. It's difficult to admit you were cheap, unfair, or foolish—especially since these traits aren't

It is a curious psychological fact that the man who seems to be "egotistic" is not suffering from too much ego, but from too little.

SYDNEY J. HARRIS

likely to gain the companionship and approval you are seeking.

If you aren't willing to accept the judgments of others, you are faced with what Leon Festinger (1957) called **dissonance:** a clash between the presenting face you want to show the world and the impression you seem to be making. Dissonance is an uncomfortable condition, and communicators try to resolve it in three ways.

Attacking the Critic   Counterattacking follows the old maxim that the best defense is a good offense. Attacks can take several forms.

■ *Verbal aggression* Sometimes the recipient directly assaults the critic. "Where do you get off calling me sloppy?" you might storm to a roommate. "You're the one who leaves globs of toothpaste in the sink and dirty clothes all over the bedroom!" This sort of response shifts the blame onto the critic without acknowledging that the original judgment might be true. Other attacks on the critic are completely off the subject: "You're in no position to complain about my sloppiness. At least I pay my share of the bills on time." Again, this response resolves the dissonance without ever addressing the validity of the criticism.

■ *Sarcasm* Disguising the attack in a barbed, humorous message is a less direct form of aggression. "You think I ought to study more? Thanks for taking a break from watching soap operas and eating junk food to run my life." Sarcastic responses might score high on wit and quick thinking, but their hostile, disconfirming nature usually leads to a counterattack and a mutually destructive defensive spiral.

"What do you mean 'Your guess is as good as mine'? My guess is a hell of a lot <u>better</u> than your guess!"
Drawing by Ross; © 1983 The New Yorker Magazine, Inc.

Student Reflection

Sarcasm as a Weapon

My goal is to stop making sarcastic comments about my boyfriend's social life. We have an agreement to see others while we date. If we argue about his current "other," he claims my dislike for her is a reflex action. I tell him, sarcastically, "Oh, no, I'm not jealous—I disliked her <u>before</u> you met her!" Yesterday we had a huge fight and I responded as defensively as ever. I know this will drive him away—I wouldn't want to be with me either. Why can't I just admit that I <u>do</u> feel threatened when he dates other people?

Distorting the Critical Information   A second way of defending a perceived self that is under attack is somehow to distort the information in a way that leaves the presenting self intact—at least in the eyes of the defender. There are a number of ways to distort dissonant information:

■ *Compensation* When we emphasize a strength in one area to cover up a weakness in another, we engage in **compensation.** A guilty parent might keep up the facade of being conscientious by protesting: "I may not be around much, but I give those kids the best things money can buy!" Likewise, you might try to convince yourself and others that you are a good friend by compensating: "Sorry I forgot your birthday. Let me give you a hand with that job." There's nothing wrong with most acts of compensation in themselves. The harm comes when they are used insincerely to maintain a fictitious presenting image.

■ *Rationalization* A communicator who uses **rationalization** invents logical but untrue explanations of undesirable behavior. "I would help you out, but I really have to study," you might say as a convenient way to avoid an unpleasant chore. "I'm not overeating," you might protest to another critic who you secretly admit is on target. "I have a busy day ahead, and I need to keep my strength up."

■ *Regression* Another way to avoid facing attack is to use **regression,** playing helpless, claiming you *can't* do something when in truth you *don't want* to do it. "I'd like to have a relationship with you, but I just can't: I'm not ready." "I wish I could do the job better, but I just can't: I just don't understand it." The test for regression is to substitute the word "won't" for "can't." In many cases it becomes clear that "It's not my fault" is a fiction.

Avoiding Dissonant Information   A third way to protect a threatened presenting image is to avoid information altogether. Avoidance can take several forms:

■ *Physical avoidance* Steering clear of people who attack a presenting self is an obvious way to avoid dissonance. Sometimes physical avoidance may be wise. There's little profit in being battered by hostile or abusive criticism. In other cases, however, the relationship may be important enough and the criticism valid enough that avoiding the situation only makes matters worse.

■ *Repression* Sometimes we use **repression** to mentally block out dissonant information. You might, for instance, know that you ought to discuss a problem with a friend, boss, or instructor, yet put the idea out of your mind whenever it arises. It's even possible to repress a problem in the face of a critic. Changing the subject, acting as if you don't understand, and even pretending you don't hear the criticism all fall into this category.

- *Apathy* Another avoidance response is to use **apathy,** acknowledging unpleasant information but pretending you don't care about it. You might, for instance, sit calmly through a friend's criticism and act as if it didn't bother you. Similarly, you might respond to the loss of a job by acting indifferently: "Who cares? It was a dumb job anyhow."

It's important to recognize that, in their purest sense, all these defensive reactions involve two kinds of deception: The first involves convincing the critic (and possibly others) that your presenting image is valid. Just as central is the need to convince *yourself* that the presenting image is accurate.

Creating Positive Communication Climates

Despite their undesirability, poor communication climates do occur. They are rarely deliberate creations: More often they grow from either lack of communication skill or carelessness.

It's reassuring to know that even potentially defense-arousing messages such as criticism and complaints can be expressed in confirming ways. This positive approach is possible because of the two-dimensional nature of communication: On a content level you might be expressing dissatisfaction with the other person, but on the relational level you can be saying—explicitly or nonverbally—that you value him or her. The possibility of handling potentially delicate issues in a way that improves your relationships may seem like too much to expect, but the following pages will offer suggestions for preventing stormy climates from developing and for changing unhealthy climates that now exist.

INITIATING POSITIVE CLIMATES

The best time to create a positive climate is at the beginning of a relationship, when there's no negative history to overcome. It's at this time that you can most easily create messages that allow people to believe you value them.

You can build a more positive communication climate in your important relationships. The process isn't complicated or mysterious, but it does take time and effort. To find out more, see Activity 3 on page 353.

Notice the word *believe* in the preceding sentence. It isn't enough to care about others: They have to *know* that you care. Sometimes communicating this concern can be difficult. You may have to overcome the other person's insecurities ("Why would anyone care about me?"). You might need to overcome a suspicious attitude ("What's he after, being so nice?"). Finally, you might have to overcome a bad reputation ("I've heard about *her*"), whether or not it's deserved.

Researchers have defined the elements of a positive climate (for example, Barbour and Goldberg 1974; Eadie 1982; Gibb 1961). Many of their descriptions are too vague to be of much use: "Be accepting," "Be empathic," and so on. The following guidelines translate abstract advice into behaviors you can use to create confirming climates in your own relationships.

Acknowledge the Other Person   Acknowledging isn't as obvious as it might seem. Pseudolistening (described in Chapter 7) is as disconfirming as it is common. A wandering glance, vacant expression, and inattentive posture all suggest you aren't really paying attention to a conversational partner. In addition, the disconfirming behaviors listed on pages 331–335 also show a lack of acknowledgment: Besides ig-

noring the person outright, you can interrupt, give irrelevant, tangential, ambiguous, or incongruous responses, and act impersonally—all behaviors that imply a disconfirming "I don't care about you" attitude.

By contrast, an acknowledging response shows that you understand the speaker. A complete acknowledgment combines two elements. The first is understanding of the speaker's *ideas*. One way to confirm another's position is to ask intelligent questions. An even clearer way to show you understand is to paraphrase the message, using the skill outlined in Chapter 7:

"So you think I'm making a big mistake by dropping the class, both because I'll be quitting and because I might need the information someday—is that it?"

"It sounds like you think we're going overboard on holiday presents again this year, and that we have to find a way of cutting back."

Notice that messages like these don't agree or disagree with the sender. Rather, they show that you understand what the other person is saying. Conveying this sort of understanding might seem trivial until you realize how often others fail to acknowledge your ideas, and how frustrated this lack of acknowledgment leaves you.

A second, more thorough kind of acknowledgment conveys your understanding of the speaker's *feelings*, as well as thoughts. Again, the best way to show your understanding is by reflecting:

"You really feel confident that changing the work schedule will work, huh? It sounds like you're excited about giving it a try."

"I never realized it before, but it sounds like you resent the way I kid you about your accent. You think I'm putting you down, and that's what makes you angry. Is that right?"

This sort of reflecting response accomplishes two things: First, it guarantees that you have indeed understood the other person accurately. If your reflection is incorrect, your partner can correct you: "It's not so much that I get mad when you tease me about my accent. It's that I feel hurt." In addition, paraphrasing shows that you respect others enough to hear them out—a genuine confirmation of their value.

Realize that acknowledging a message isn't the same thing as *agreeing* with it. You can still respond with your own ideas; but taking time first to understand the other person can make the difference between a positive, constructive climate and a negative, defensive spiral.

Demonstrate an Open-Minded Attitude Communicators with closed minds state or imply, "I don't care what you have to say—my mind is made up." Gibb (1961) terms this disconfirming attitude "certainty," and he points out how it is likely to generate a defensive reaction. The communication climate will be far more positive if you listen to others' ideas without immediately disputing them. Ask questions, by all means, but make sure they are sincere requests for information and not ambushes. Notice the difference between a genuine question ("Can you explain how that would work?") and a hostile one ("Are you crazy? How can you even imagine that would work?"). Sometimes the difference between a sincere question and a veiled attack lies in the way you ask it. Imagine confirming and disconfirming ways of saying, "Why do you want to do that?"

Edward deBono (1973) suggests a method for thinking and communicating open-mindedly. Rather than taking sides on an issue, he suggests, you and the other person should cooperatively explore all the positive aspects of an issue, then consider all the negative aspects, and finally think about all the aspects that are nei-

ther positive nor negative, but still interesting. Working *with* the other person to develop these lists sends the confirming relational message "I care about what you have to say," whereas staking out an opposing position communicates the opposite.

Agree Whenever Possible Public speakers have always realized the importance of emphasizing "common ground" they share with an audience. The same principle is just as valuable in other settings: Emphasizing shared beliefs makes it easier to discuss disagreements. A moment's thought will show that you probably share many important beliefs with others—even those whose positions you dislike. Both pro- and anti-abortionists, for example, can agree that an unwanted pregnancy poses a terrible dilemma for many women. Most supporters *and* opponents of the Equal Rights Amendment believe that women should be treated equally under the law. Recognizing such shared beliefs won't resolve disagreements but can create a climate that makes discussion more productive.

Describe, Don't Evaluate Statements that judge another person are likely to provoke a defensive reaction (Gibb 1961). **Evaluative language** has often been described as **"you" language,** since most such statements contain an accusatory use of that word. For example:

> "You made a fool of yourself last night."
> "You smoke too much."
> "You're not doing your share of the work."

In contrast to this sort of evaluative language is **descriptive communication** often characterized as **"I" language.** Rather than judging another's behavior, a descriptive statement explains the personal effect of the other's action. For example, instead of saying, "You talk too much," a descriptive communicator might say,

And I tell you that on the day of judgment, you must give account for every careless word you speak; for by your words will you be justified, and by your words you will be condemned.

MATTHEW 12:36–37

"When you don't give me a chance to say what's on my mind, I get frustrated." This sort of descriptive statement contains three elements: (1) an account of the other person's behavior, (2) an explanation of the consequences of that behavior, and (3) a description of the speaker's feelings. Notice how the three statements listed above become more confirming when rephrased as descriptions:

> "When you told those jokes last night, everyone seemed uncomfortable. I was really embarrassed."

> "When you smoke so much, I worry about your health. I wonder what might happen to you—and me—if you keep it up."

> "When you take a break every 10 or 15 minutes, I wind up doing most of the work. I don't mind that once in a while, but I'm getting fed up."

Show Concern for the Other Person's Interests Defensiveness is likely when one person tries to impose an idea on others with little regard for their needs or interests. This sort of **controlling communication** isn't only disconfirming—it's often unnecessary. A more productive attitude is what Gibb terms **problem-orientation:** asking "How can we solve this problem?" instead of "How can I overcome the other person?"

Using descriptive "I" language can improve the climate of most relationships. To get practice mastering this important skill, see Activity 4 on page 353.

A problem-oriented approach works on large issues (How can we live together with such different personalities?) and small ones (How can we watch different TV shows at the same hour?). In every case, the key to success is to strive for an answer that satisfies everyone's needs. Chapter 11 offers detailed information on this sort of "win-win" problem solving. For now it's important to recognize that simply *striving* for such an outcome builds a positive communication climate.

Communicate Honestly One of the surest ways to cloud a communication climate is to get caught lying. Dishonesty and manipulation are

Reprinted with special permission of King Features Syndicate, Inc.

disconfirming for two reasons: First, they imply that you don't have the other person's best interests in mind. Second, they suggest that you thought you could deceive the other person, and almost no one likes to be regarded as gullible.

Paradoxical as it seems, candor too can be a kind of manipulation. Some people use honesty in a calculating way, revealing just enough information to get what they want. When discovered, such candor can backfire, for it leaves the victim feeling like a sucker—hardly the kind of outcome that leads to a positive climate.

Honest messages are confirming only when they meet two conditions: First, they must grow out of a sincere concern for the other person's welfare. Honesty used as a weapon can destroy a relationship more quickly than almost any other type of communication: "You want honesty? To tell the truth, I think you're stupid!" Second, the honest message needs to be delivered at the right time and in a way that is easy for the other person to understand. This means using the kinds of communication described earlier in this section, such as common ground and descriptive language. Saying, "You look terrible in that outfit" isn't confirming. Notice how much better it is to say, "I think it's great that you're trying to change your look, but I'd like you better in another color." For more advice about how to combine honesty and effectiveness, refer to the guidelines for self-disclosure in Chapter 9.

There is no guarantee that these constructive, confirming behaviors will build a positive communication climate. The other person may simply not be receptive. But the chances for a constructive relationship will be greatest when communication consists of the kind of supportive behaviors described here. Besides boosting the odds of getting a positive response from others, supportive communication can leave you feeling better in a variety of ways: more in control of your relationships,

more comfortable, and more positive toward others (Gordon 1988).

TRANSFORMING NEGATIVE CLIMATES

The preceding pages have described how to build a positive communication climate at the beginning of a relationship and how to maintain a positive climate once it's started. What about times when negative feelings already exist? Changing such climates is like slowing down a runaway horse: You have to stop the animal before you can begin to move toward your destination.

One of the biggest barriers to overcoming poor climates is the torrent of negative criticism characterizing so many of them. Because the problem of handling criticism is so difficult and important, we'll devote the rest of this chapter to it. When you're finished reading, you should have acquired some workable skills to help you in these difficult cases.

It takes practice and self-control to respond nondefensively when you are being criticized. To improve your skill in this important area, try Activity 5 on page 354.

In order to handle criticism constructively, you need honest, nonmanipulative ways of dealing with criticism which don't require self-justification or a counterattack. There are two such methods, each of which at first appears to be almost childishly simple, yet in practice has proved over and over to be among the most valuable assertive skills (see also Smith 1975).

When Criticized, Seek More Information Seeking more information makes good sense when you realize that it's foolish to respond to a critical attack until you understand it. Even comments that upon first consideration appear to

be totally unjustified or foolish often prove to contain at least a grain of truth, and sometimes much more.

Many readers object to the idea of asking for details when they are criticized. Their resistance grows from confusing the act of *listening open-mindedly* to a speaker's comments with *accepting* them. Once you realize that you can listen to, understand, and even acknowledge the most hostile comments without necessarily

Placing the blame is a bad habit, but taking the blame is a sure builder of character.

O. A. BATTISTA

accepting them, it becomes much easier to hear another person out. If you disagree with a speaker's objections, you will be in a much better position to explain yourself once you understand them. On the other hand, after carefully listening to the other's remarks, you just might see that they are valid, in which case you have learned some valuable information about yourself. In either case, if you can agree without compromising your principles, you have everything to gain and nothing to lose by hearing the critic out.

Of course, after years of instinctively resisting criticism, the habit of hearing the other person out will take some practice. To make matters clearer, here are several ways to seek additional information from your critics.

Ask for specifics Often the vague attack of a critic is practically useless, even if you sincerely want to change. Abstract accusations such as "You're being unfair" or "You never help out" can be difficult to understand. In such cases it is a good idea to request more specific information from the sender. "What do I *do* that's unfair?" is an important question to ask before you can judge whether the accusation is correct. "When haven't I helped out?" you might ask prior to agreeing with or disputing the accusation.

If you solicit specifics by using questions and are accused of reacting defensively, the problem may be in the *way* you ask. Your tone of voice and facial expression, posture, or other nonverbal clues can give the same words radically different connotations. For example, think of how you could use the words "Exactly what are you talking about?" to communicate either a genuine desire to know or your belief that the speaker is crazy. It's important to request specific information only when you genuinely want to learn more from the speaker, for asking under any other circumstances will only make matters worse.

Guess about specifics   On some occasions even your sincere and well-phrased requests for specific details of another's criticism won't meet with success. Sometimes your critics won't be able to define precisely the behavior they find offensive. In these instances you'll hear such comments as "I can't tell you exactly what's wrong with your sense of humor—all I can say is that I don't like it." In other cases your critics may know the exact behavior they don't like but seem to get a perverse satisfaction out of making you struggle to figure it out. Then you hear such comments as "Well, if you don't know what you did to hurt my feelings, I'm certainly not going to tell you!"

Needless to say, failing to learn the details of another's criticism when you genuinely want to know them can be a frustrating experience. In such instances you can often learn more clearly what is bothering your critic by *guessing* at the specifics of a complaint. In a sense you become both detective and suspect, with the goal being to figure out exactly what "crime" you have committed. Like the technique of asking for specifics, guessing must be done with good will if it's to produce satisfying results. You need to convey to the critic that for both of your sakes you're truly interested in finding out what is the matter. Once you have communicated this intention, the emotional climate generally becomes more comfortable, because in effect both you and the critic are seeking the same goal.

Here are some typical questions you might hear from someone guessing about the details of another's criticism:

Love your enemies, for they tell you your faults.

BENJAMIN FRANKLIN

"So you object to the language I used in writing the paper. Was my language too formal?"

"OK, I understand that you think the outfit looks funny. What is it that's so bad? Is it the color? Does it have something to do with the fit? The fabric?"

"When you say that I'm not doing my share around the house, do you mean that I haven't been helping enough with the cleaning?"

Reflect the speaker's ideas   Another strategy for learning more about criticism is to draw out confused or reluctant speakers by reflecting their thoughts and feelings, using the listening skills described in Chapter 7. Reflecting is especially good in helping others solve their problems. Given that people generally criticize you because your behavior creates some problem for them, the method is especially appropriate.

One advantage of reflecting is that you don't have to guess specifically why your behavior might be offensive. By clarifying or amplifying what you understand critics to be saying, you'll learn more about their objections. A brief dialogue between a disgruntled customer and a store manager especially talented at paraphrasing might sound like this one:

Customer: The way you people run this store is disgusting! I just want to tell you that I'll never shop here again.
Manager: *(reflecting the customer's feeling)* It seems that you're quite upset. Can you tell me your problem?
C: It isn't *my* problem, it's the problem your salespeople have. They seem to think it's a great inconvenience to help a customer find anything around here.
M: So you didn't get enough help locating the items you were looking for, is that it?
C: Help? I spent twenty minutes looking around in here before I even talked to a clerk. All I can say is that it's a hell of a way to run a store.

M: So what you're saying is that the clerks seemed to be ignoring the customers?

C: No. They were all busy with other people. It just seems to me that you ought to have enough help around to handle the crowds that come in at this hour.

M: I understand now. What frustrated you the most was that we didn't have enough staff to serve you promptly.

C: That's right. I have no complaint with the service I get once I'm waited on, and I've always thought you had a good selection here. It's just that I'm too busy to wait so long for help.

M: Well, I'm glad you brought this to my attention. We certainly don't want loyal customers going away mad. I'll try to see that it doesn't happen again.

This conversation illustrates two advantages of paraphrasing. First, often the intensity of the attack abates once the critic realizes that the complaint is being heard. Criticism can grow from the frustration of unmet needs—in this case, a lack of attention. As soon as the manager genuinely demonstrated interest in the customer's plight, the customer began to feel better and was able to leave the store relatively calm. Of course, such paraphrasing won't always mollify your critic, but even when it doesn't, there's still another benefit that makes the technique worthwhile. In the sample conversation, for instance, the manager learned some valuable information by taking time to understand the customer. The manager discovered that there were certain times when the number of employees was insufficient to help the crowd of shoppers, and that the delays at these times seriously annoyed at least some shoppers, threatening a loss in business. Such knowledge is certainly important, and by reacting defensively to the customer's complaint, the manager would not have learned from it. As you read earlier, even apparently outlandish criticism often contains at least a grain of truth, so a person who is genuinely interested in improving would be wise to hear it out.

Ask about the consequences of your behavior As a rule people complain about your actions only when some need of theirs is not being met. One way to respond to such criticism is to find out exactly what troublesome consequences your behavior has for them. You'll often find that actions that seem perfectly legitimate to you cause some difficulty for your critic; once you have understood this consequence, comments that previously sounded foolish take on a new meaning:

A: You say that I ought to have my cat neutered. Why is that important to you?

B: Because at night he picks fights with my cat, and I'm tired of paying the vet's bills.

C: Why do you care whether I'm late to work?

D: Because when the boss asks where you are, I feel obligated to make up some story so you won't get in trouble, and I don't like to lie.

E: Why does it bother you when I lose money at poker? You know I never gamble more than I can afford.

F: It's not the cash itself. It's that when you lose you're in a grumpy mood for two or three days, and that's no fun for me.

Solicit additional complaints Although the idea might at first sound outlandish, once you've understood one complaint, it's often beneficial to see if anything else about your behavior bothers your critic. Soliciting additional complaints can be a good idea for the simple reason that if you can learn one valuable lesson from a single criticism, you ought to double your knowledge by hearing two.

Of course, it isn't always wise to seek additional gripes, at least not immediately. You should be sure that you understand the first complaint before tackling another one at the same time. Resolving the complaint sometimes means agreeing to the other's demands for change, but in other circumstances it can mean hearing out the other's request and promising to think about it. In still other instances, the critic really doesn't expect you to change; resolution can simply mean that you've taken the time and spent the effort to understand the criticism.

You can see how solicitation of additional criticism works by returning to the conversation between the store manager and a disgruntled customer:

M: I can promise you that I'll see what I can do about having more employees on hand during busy periods. While you're here, I'd like to know if you can think of any other ways we could improve our operation.
C: What? You really want to know what else I think you're doing wrong?
M: Sure. If we're not aware of ways we could do better, we'll never change.
C: Well, the only other thing I can think of is the parking situation. A lot of times I'll come by and have to wait several minutes for a delivery truck to unload before I can get into the lot from the south side. I wish you could have the trucks park somewhere else or unload at a quieter hour.
M: That's a good point. We can't always control when the drivers from other companies will show up, but I can sure give their dispatchers a call and see what can be done. I want to say that I appreciate your thoughts. Even when we have our bad days around here, it's important to us that we do everything we can to make this a good place to shop.

Sometimes soliciting and understanding more information from a critic isn't enough. What do you do, for instance, when you fully

---

Student Reflection

Agreeing and Saving Face

My father told me to write up a resumé since I'm graduating this semester—that I needed to "get on the ball." I told him I didn't need to yet, that there was plenty of time. Of course he was right and I knew he had my best interests at heart. I should simply have agreed with him: "You're right, I am behind on writing a resumé. I will do it today." But I still disagreed with him! I have this need to make other people wrong so that I can be right. Being right, and having to be right all the time, also means spending a lot of time alone. People don't like to lose, and if that's all I allow them, they would just as soon keep away from me.

---

understand the other person's objections and still feel a defensive response on the tip of your tongue? You know that if you try to protect yourself you'll wind up in an argument; on the other hand, you simply can't accept what the other person is saying about you. The solution to such a dilemma is outrageously simple, and is discussed in the following section.

When Criticized, Agree with the Speaker   But, you protest, how can you honestly agree with comments that you don't believe are true? The following pages will show that in virtually every situation you can honestly accept the other person's point of view and still maintain your position. To see how, you need to realize that there are four different types of agreement, each of which you can express in different circumstances.

Agree with the truth   Agreeing with the truth is easy to understand, though not always easy to practice. You agree with the truth when another person's criticism is factually correct:

"You're right, I am angry."

"I suppose I was being defensive."

"Now that you mention it, I did get pretty sarcastic."

Agreeing with the facts seems quite sensible when you realize that certain matters are indisputable. If you agree to be somewhere at 4:00 and don't show up until 5:00, you *are* late, no matter how good your explanation for tardiness is. If you've broken a borrowed object, run out of gas, or failed to finish a job you started, there's no point in denying the fact. In the same way, if you're honest you will have to agree with many interpretations of your behavior, even when they're not flattering. You do get angry, act foolishly, fail to listen, and behave inconsiderately. Once you rid yourself of the myth of perfection, it's much easier to acknowledge these truths.

If it's so obvious that the descriptions others give of your behaviors are often accurate, why is it so difficult to accept them without being defensive? The answer to this question lies in a confusion between agreeing with the *facts* and accepting the *judgment* that so often accompanies them. Most critics don't merely describe the action that offends them, they also evaluate it, and it's the evaluation that we resist:

"It's silly to be angry."
"You have no reason for being defensive."
"You were wrong to be so sarcastic."

It's such judgments that we resent. By realizing that you can agree with—even learn from—the descriptive part of many criticisms and still not accept the accompanying evaluations, you'll often have a response that is both honest and nondefensive. A conversation between a teacher and a student illustrates this point:

Teacher: Look at this paper! It's only two pages long and it contains twelve misspelled words. I'm afraid you have a real problem with your writing.
Student: You're right. I know I don't spell well at all.
T: I don't know what's happening in the lower grades. They just don't seem to be turning out people who can write a simple, declarative sentence.
S: You're not the first person I've heard say that.
T: I should think you'd be upset by the fact that after so much time in English composition classes you haven't mastered the basics of spelling.
S: You're right. It does bother me.

Notice that in agreeing with the teacher's comments the student did not in any way demean herself. Even though there might have been extenuating circumstances to account for her lack of skill, the student didn't find it necessary to justify her errors because she wasn't saddled with the burden of pretending to be perfect. By simply agreeing with the facts, she was able to maintain her dignity and avoid an unproductive argument.

Of course, in order to reduce defensiveness it's important that your agreements with the facts be honest and admitted without malice. It's humiliating to accept inaccurate descriptions, and maliciously pretending to agree with these only leads to trouble. You can imagine how unproductive the above conversation would have been if the student had spoken the same words in a sarcastic tone. Only agree with the facts when you can do so sincerely. Although it won't always be possible, you'll be surprised at how often you can use this simple response.

Agreeing with criticism is fine, but by itself it isn't an adequate response to your critic. For instance, once you've admitted to another that you are defensive, habitually late, or sarcastic, you can expect the other to ask what you intend to do about this behavior. Such questions are fair. In most cases it would be a mistake simply to understand another's criticism, to agree with the accusations, and then to go on behaving as before. Such behavior makes it clear that you have no concern for the speaker. The message that comes through is "Sure, now I understand what I've done to bother you. You're right, I have been doing it and I'll probably keep on doing it. If you don't like the way I've been behaving, that's tough!" Such a response might be appropriate for dealing with people you genuinely don't care about—manipulative solicitors, abusive strangers, and so on—but it is clearly not suitable for people who matter to you.

Before reading on, then, understand that responding nondefensively to criticism is only the *first step* in resolving the conflicts that usually prompt another's attack. In order to resolve your conflicts fully, you'll need to learn the skills described in Chapter 11.

Agree with the odds Sometimes a critic will point out possible unpleasant consequences of your behavior:

"If you don't talk to more people, they'll think you're a snob."

"If you don't exercise more, you'll wind up having a heart attack one of these days."

"If you run around with that crowd, you'll probably be sorry."

Often such comments are genuinely helpful suggestions that others offer for your own good. In other cases, however, they are really devices for manipulating you into behaving the way your critic wants you to. For instance, "If we go to the football game, you might catch cold" could mean "I don't want to go to the football game." "You'll probably be exhausted tomorrow if you stay up late" could be translated as "I want you to go to bed early." Chapter 11 will have more to say about such methods of indirect aggression, but for now it is sufficient to state that such warnings often generate defensiveness. A mother-son argument shows this outcome:

Mother: I don't see why you want to ride that motorcycle. You could wind up in an accident so easily. *(states the odds for an accident)*
Son: Oh, don't be silly. I'm a careful driver, and besides you know that I never take my bike on the freeway. *(denies the odds)*
M: Yes, but every time I pick up the paper I read about someone being hurt or killed. There's always a danger that some crazy driver will miss seeing you and run you off the road. *(states the odds of an injury)*
S: Oh, you worry too much. I always look out for the other driver. And besides, you have a lot better maneuverability on a motorcycle than in a car. *(denies the odds for an injury)*
M: I know you're careful, but all it takes is one mistake and you could be killed. *(states the odds for being killed)*
S: Somebody is killed shaving or taking a shower every day, but you don't want me to stop doing those things, do you? You're just exaggerating the whole thing. *(denies the odds for being killed)*

From this example you can see that it's usually counterproductive to deny another's predictions. You don't convince the critic, and your opinions stay unchanged as well. Notice the difference when you agree with the odds (though not the demands) of the critic.

M: I don't see why you want to drive that motorcycle. You could wind up in an accident so easily. *(states the odds for an accident)*

S: I suppose there is a chance of that. *(agrees with the odds)*

M: You're darned right. Every time I pick up the newspaper, I read about someone being hurt or killed. There's always a danger that some crazy driver will miss seeing you and run you off the road. *(states the odds for an injury)*

S: You're right, that could happen *(agrees with the odds),* but I don't think the risk is great enough to keep me off the bike.

M: That's easy for you to say now. Some day you could be sorry you didn't listen to me. *(states the odds for regret)*

S: That's true. I really might regret driving the bike some day. *(agrees with the odds)*

Notice how the son simply considers his mother's predictions and realistically acknowledges the chance that they might come true. While such responses might at first seem indifferent and callous, they can help the son to avoid the pitfall of indirect manipulation. Suppose the conversation were a straightforward one in which the mother was simply pointing out the danger of motorcycle riding to her son. He acknowledged that he understood her concern and even agreed with the possibility that her prediction could come true. If, however, her prediction was really an indirect way of saying, "I don't want you to ride anymore," then the son's response would force her to clarify her demand so that he could deal with it openly. At this point they might be able to figure out a solution that lets the son satisfy his need for transportation and excitement and at the same time allows the mother to alleviate her concern.

In addition to bringing hidden agendas into the open for resolution, agreeing with the odds also helps you become aware of some possible previously unconsidered consequences of your actions. Instead of blindly denying the chance that your behavior is inappropriate, agreeing with the odds will help you look objectively at whether your course of action is in fact the best one. You might agree with your critic that you really should change your behavior.

Agree in principle Often criticism comes in the form of abstract ideals against which you're unfavorably compared:

> "I wish you wouldn't spend so much time on your work. Relaxation is important too, you know."

> "You shouldn't expect so much from your kids. Nobody's perfect."

> "What do you mean, you're not voting? The government is only going to get better when people like you take more of an interest in it."

> You mean you're still upset by that remark? You ought to learn how to take a joke better."

In such instances it's entirely possible for you to accept the principle upon which the criticism is based and still behave as you have been doing. This apparent inconsistency is sensible for two reasons. First, no abstract statement applies to every instance of human behavior. For example, although relaxation is important, there are occasions when it is appropriate to throw yourself totally into your work for a period of time. While it is unfair to put excessive demands on one's children, in some cases it becomes necessary for them to behave in an exceptional manner. As the Bible says, there is a time for every purpose, and what may usually be right isn't always so.

A second reason why you might agree in principle with a criticism but not change your behavior is that people *are* inconsistent. Not being totally rational, we often do things that aren't in our best interests or those of another person. Again the myth of perfection needs debunking: You're not a saint, so it's unrealistic to expect that you'll always behave like one. As authors and teachers of assertive communication, we can relate to this principle. There are occasions when we find ourselves behaving in a very unassertive manner: failing to define our problems and goals behaviorally, expecting ourselves to improve in some way all at once instead of changing in gradual steps, and (ironically enough) becoming defensive in the face of criticism. In the face of such situations, our inner dialogues often go something like this:

Top dog: Boy, are you a hypocrite. Here you are, the expert on assertiveness, and you can't even take a little criticism yourself. Do as I say, not as I do, eh?

Underdog: *(whining)* Well, it's not just my fault, you know. I do the best I can, but sometimes other people are so obnoxious that...Wait a second. You're right *(agreeing with principle)*. I probably ought to be able to accept criticism better, but I guess I still haven't managed totally to master everything I teach. Maybe after a little longer I'll get better. I sure hope so for everybody's sake!

Agree with the critic's perception What about times when there seems to be no basis whatsoever for agreeing with your critics? You've listened carefully and asked questions to make sure you understand the objections, but the more you listen, the more positive you are that they are totally out of line: There is no truth to the criticisms, you can't agree with the odds, and you can't even accept the principle the critics put forward. Even here there's a way of agreeing—this time not with the critics' conclusions, but with their right to perceive things their way:

A: I don't believe you've been all the places you were just describing. You're probably just making all this up so we'll think you're hot stuff.

B: Well, I can see how you might think that. I've known people who lie to get approval.

C: I want to let you know right from the start that I was against hiring you for the job. I think the reason you got it was because you're a woman.

Student Reflection

Coping with Criticism as a Martial Art

I've been taking self-defense lessons for a year and I think there are a lot of similarities between judo and agreeing with your critic. In both techniques you don't resist your attacker. Instead you use the other person's energy to your advantage. You let your opponent defeat himself.

Last week I used "verbal judo" on a very judgmental friend who called me a hypocrite because I'm a vegetarian but still wear leather shoes. I knew that nothing I could say would change his mind, so I just agreed with his perception by saying "I can see why you think I'm not consistent." No matter what he said I replied "I understand why it looks that way to you." It drove him crazy, but it left me feeling very powerful.

I won't always agree with my critics this way, any more than I'll always use judo. But it sure is a useful approach to have at my disposal.

D: I can understand why you'd believe that with all the antidiscrimination laws on the books. I hope that after I've been here for a while you'll change your mind.

E: I don't think you're being totally honest about your reasons for wanting to stay home. You say that it's because you have a headache, but I think you're avoiding Mary and Walt.

F: I can see why that would make sense to you since Mary and I got into an argument the last time we were together. All I can say is that I do have a headache.

Such responses tell critics that you're acknowledging the reasonableness of their perceptions, even though you don't agree or wish to change your behavior. This coping style is valuable, for it lets you avoid the debates over who is right and who is wrong, which can turn an exchange of ideas into an argument. Notice the difference in the following scenes between Amy and Bob.

Disputing the perception:

Amy: I don't see how you can stand to be around Josh. The guy is so crude that he gives me the creeps.
Bob: What do you mean, crude? He's a really nice guy. I think you're just touchy.
A: Touchy! If it's touchy to be offended by disgusting behavior, then I'm guilty.
B: You're not guilty about anything. It's just that you're too sensitive when people kid around.
A: Too sensitive, huh? I don't know what's happened to you. You used to have such good judgment about people....

Agreeing with the perception:

A: I don't see how you can stand to be around Josh. The guy is so crude that he gives me the creeps.
B: Well, I enjoy being around him, but I guess I can see how his jokes would be offensive to some people.
A: You're damn right. I don't see how you can put up with him.
B: Yeah. I guess if you didn't appreciate his humor, you wouldn't want to have much to do with him.

Notice how in the second exchange Bob was able to maintain his own position without attacking Amy's in the least. Such acceptance is the key ingredient for successfully agreeing with your critics' perceptions: Using acceptance, you clarify that you are in no way disputing their views. Because you have no intention of attacking your critics' views, they are less likely to be defensive.

All of these responses to criticism may appear to buy peace at the cost of denying your feelings. However, as you can see by now, counterattacking usually makes matters worse. The nondefensive responses you have just learned won't solve problems or settle disputes by themselves. They *will* make a constructive dialogue possible, setting the stage for a productive solution. How to achieve productive solutions is the topic of Chapter 11.

Summary

Communication climate refers to the social tone of a relationship. The most influential factor in shaping a communication climate is the degree to which the people involved see themselves as being valued. Messages that deny the value of others have been called disconfirming responses, while communication that conveys a sense of valuing has been labeled confirming.

Communication climates are not a function of the setting or content of information exchanged. Rather, they are shaped by relational messages, both verbal and nonverbal. Confirming messages may involve recognition, acknowledgement, or endorsement of the other party. The most obvious disconfirming messages consist of verbal aggression or complaints. More subtle forms of disconfirmation include impervious, interrupting, irrelevant, tangential, impersonal, ambiguous, and incongruous responses. Whatever their nature, messages must be perceived as confirming or disconfirming in order to shape a relational climate.

Defensive communication can pollute a communication climate. Defensiveness can occur when individuals perceive their presenting self as being attacked by face-threatening acts. When confronted with such acts, individuals who act to save face may use a variety of defense mechanisms to attack the critic, distort critical information, or avoid dissonant messages.

Several communication behaviors can help create positive communication climates: acknowledging the other person, demonstrating an open-minded attitude, seeking common ground, using descriptive instead of evaluative communication, showing concern for the other person's interests, and communicating honestly.

When faced with criticism by others, there are two alternatives to responding defensively—seeking additional information from the critic, and agreeing with some aspect of the criticism. When performed sincerely, these approaches can transform an actual or potentially negative climate into a more positive one.

Activities

1. Explain the term "communication climate" and describe the types of confirming and disconfirming messages you offer to someone with whom you have a personal relationship. Then invite this person to do the following:

   a. Rate the quality of the communication climate in your relationship. Since climate is determined by the degree to which the participants believe they are valued, explore how much your partner views you as valuing him or her.

   b. Identify some recent examples of *confirming* messages you have expressed to your partner. What was the impact of these messages? How frequently do you convey confirming messages to your partner?

   c. Recall some recent examples of *disconfirming* messages you have expressed to your partner. What was the effect of these messages? How often do you convey these sorts of disconfirming messages to your partner?

2. Explore the dynamics of defensive communication in your life by recalling three recent times when you became defensive. If you have trouble remembering instances, invite someone who knows you well to help you recall them. For each instance, identify

   a. the behavior that triggered your defensiveness and the reaction (e.g., verbal aggression, rationalization, compensation).

   b. the part of your presenting self you were defending (e.g., "consistent," "fair," "generous").

   c. the relational consequences of your defensiveness. How was the communication climate affected by your reaction?

3. Review the list of communication behaviors on pages 339–343 that can help build a supportive climate. Describe how you could integrate these behaviors into one of your important relationships.

4. Develop your ability to communicate supportively instead of triggering defensive reactions in others. Restate each of the following "you" statements as "I" messages. Use details from your own personal relationships to create messages that are specific and personally relevant.

a. "You're only thinking of yourself."
b. "Don't be so touchy."
c. "Quit fooling around!"
d. "Stop beating around the bush and tell me the truth."
e. "You're a slob!"

5. Practice your skill at responding nondefensively to critical attacks by following these steps:
   a. Identify five criticisms you are likely to encounter from others in your day-to-day communication. If you have trouble thinking of criticisms, invite one or more people who know you well to supply some real, sincere gripes.
   b. For each criticism, write one or more nondefensive responses using the categories on pages 344–352. Be sure your responses are sincere, and that you can offer them without counterattacking your critic.
   c. Practice your responses, either by inviting a friend or classmate to play the role of your critics, or by approaching your critics directly and inviting them to share their gripes with you.

Readings

Adler, R. B. *Confidence in Communication: A Guide to Assertive and Social Skills.* New York: Holt, Rinehart and Winston, 1977.

Alberts, J. K. "A Descriptive Taxonomy of Couples' Complaint Interactions." *Southern Speech Communication Journal* 54 (1989): 125–43.

Alberts, J. K. "Perceived Effectiveness of Couples' Conversational Complaints." *Communication Studies* 40 (1990): 280–91.

Barbour, A., and A. A. Goldberg. *Interpersonal Communication: Teaching Strategies and Resources.* Annandale, VA: ERIC/RCS Speech Communication Module, 1974.

Buber, M. "Distance and Relation." *Psychiatry* 20 (1957): 97–104.

Burggraf, C., and A. L. Sillars. "A Critical Examination of Sex Differences in Marital Communication." *Communication Monographs* 54 (1987): 276–94.

*Cissna, K., and S. Keating. "Speech Communication Antecedents of Perceived Confirmation." *Western Journal of Speech Communication* 43 (1979): 48–60.

Cissna, K., and E. Seiberg. "Patterns of Interactional Confirmation and Disconfirmation." In *Rigor and Imagination: Essays from the Legacy of Gregory Bateson*, C. Wilder-Mott and J. H. Weakland, eds. New York: Praeger, 1981.

Clarke, F. P. *Interpersonal Communication Variables as Predictors of Marital Satisfaction-Dissatisfaction.* Doctoral dissertation, University of Denver, 1973.

deBono, E. *Lateral Thinking: Creativity Step by Step.* New York: Harper & Row, 1973.

Eadie, W. F. "Defensive Communication Revisited: A Critical Examination of Gibb's Theory." *Southern Speech Communication Journal* 47 (1982): 163–77.

Festinger, L. A. *Theory of Cognitive Dissonance.* Stanford, CA: Stanford University Press, 1957.

Gibb, J. R. "Defensive Communication." *Journal of Communication* 11 (September 1961): 141–48.

Gordon, R. D. "The Difference Between Feeling Defensive and Feeling Understood." *Journal of Business Communication* 25 (1988): 53–64.

Gordon, T. *T.E.T.: Teacher Effectiveness Training.* New York: David McKay, 1977.

Hays, E. R. "Ego-Threatening Classroom Communication: A Factor Analysis of Student Perceptions." *Speech Teacher* 19 (1970): 43–48.

Heineken, J. R. *Disconfirming Responses in Psychiatric Patients.* Doctoral dissertation, University of Denver, 1980.

Jacobs, M. R. *Levels of Confirmation and Disconfirmation in Interpersonal Communication.* Doctoral dissertation, University of Denver, 1973.

Leary, T. "The Theory and Measurement Methodology of Interpersonal Communication." *Psychiatry* 18 (1955): 147–61.

Lim, T. "Politeness Behavior in Social Influence Situations." In *Seeking Compliance: The Production of Interpersonal Influence Messages*, J. P. Dillard, ed. Scottsdale, AZ: Gorsuch Scarsbrick, 1990.

Mix, C. R. *Interpersonal Communication Patterns, Personal Values, and Predictive Accuracy: An Exploratory Study*. Doctoral dissertation, University of Denver, 1972.

Newton, D. A., and J. K. Burgoon, "The Use and Consequences of Verbal Strategies During Interpersonal Disagreements." *Human Communication Research* 16 (1990): 477–518.

Pearson, J. C. *Communication in the Family: Seeking Satisfaction in Changing Times*. New York: Harper & Row, 1989.

Powell, J. *Why Am I Afraid to Tell You Who I Am?* Chicago: Argus Communications, 1969.

Rosenfeld, L. B. "Communication Climate and Coping Mechanisms in the College Classroom." *Communication Education* 32 (1983): 167–74.

Rosenfeld, L. B., and M. W. Jarrard. "The Effects of Perceived Sexism in Female and Male College Professors on Students' Descriptions of Classroom Climate." *Communication Education* 34 (1985): 205–13.

Rosenfeld, L. B., and M. W. Jarrard. "Student Coping Mechanisms in Sexist and Nonsexist Professors' Classes." *Communication Education* 35 (1986): 157–62.

Shostrom, E. L. *Man, the Manipulator.* New York: Basic Books, 1960.

Sieburg, E. *Dysfunctional Communication and Interpersonal Responsiveness in Small Groups*. Doctoral dissertation, University of Denver, 1969.

*Sieburg, E. "Confirming and Disconfirming Organizational Communication." In *Communication in Organizations*, J. Owen, P. Page, and G. Zimmerman, eds. New York: West, 1976.

Sieburg, E., and C. Larson. "Dimensions of Interpersonal Response." Paper presented to the International Communication Association, Phoenix, AZ, 1971.

Smith, M. *When I Say No, I Feel Guilty.* New York: Bantam Books, 1975.

Straus, M., S. Sweet, and Y. M. Vissing. "Verbal Aggression Against Spouses and Children in a Nationally Representative Sample of American Families." Paper presented at the annual meeting of the Speech Communication Association convention, San Francisco, 1989.

Sundell, W. *The Operation of Confirming and Disconfirming Verbal Behavior in Selected Teacher-Student Interactions*. Doctoral dissertation, University of Denver, 1972.

Watzlawick, P., J. Beavin, and D. Jackson. *Pragmatics of Human Communication: A Study of Interactional Patterns, Pathologies, and Paradoxes*. New York: W. W. Norton, 1967.

*Wilmot, W. W. *Dyadic Communication*, 3d ed. New York: Random House, 1987.

*Items identified by an asterisk are recommended as especially useful follow-ups.

Managing Conflict

Chapter 11
Managing Conflict

After studying the material in this chapter

You should understand

1. The four elements of conflict.

2. That conflict is natural and inevitable.

3. The characteristics of functional and dysfunctional conflicts.

4. The differences between nonassertiveness, indirect communication, passive aggression, direct aggression, and assertiveness.

5. The ways individuals interact to create relational conflict systems.

6. The characteristics of win-lose, lose-lose, and win-win problem solving.

You should be able to

1. Recognize and accept the inevitability of conflicts in your life.

2. Identify the behaviors that characterize your dysfunctional conflicts and suggest more functional alternatives.

3. Identify the conflict styles you use most commonly and evaluate their appropriateness.

4. Use the assertive message format to express a message.

5. Describe the relational conflict system in one of your important relationships.

6. Use the win-win problem-solving approach to resolve an interpersonal conflict.

Key Terms

Assertion
Complementary conflict style
Conflict
Conflict ritual
Deescalatory spiral
Direct aggression

Dysfunctional conflict
Escalatory spiral
Functional conflict
Indirect communication
Lose-lose problem solving
Nonassertion

Parallel conflict style
Passive aggression
Relational conflict style
Symmetrical conflict style
Win-lose problem solving
Win-win problem solving

Once upon a time there was a world with no conflicts. The leaders of each nation recognized the need for cooperation and met regularly to solve any potential problems before they could grow. They never disagreed on areas needing attention or on ways to handle these areas, and so there were never any international tensions, and of course there was no war.

Within each nation things ran just as smoothly. The citizens always agreed on who their leaders should be, so elections were always unanimous. There was no social friction between various groups. Age, race, and educational differences did exist, but each group respected the others and all got along harmoniously.

Personal relationships were always perfect. Strangers were always kind and friendly to each other. Neighbors were considerate of each other's needs. Friendships were always mutual, and no disagreements ever spoiled people's enjoyment of one other. Once people fell in love—and everyone did—they stayed happy. Partners liked everything about each other and were able to satisfy each other's needs fully. Children and parents agreed on every aspect of family life and never were critical or hostile toward each other. Each day was better than the one before.

Of course, everybody lived happily ever after.

This story is obviously a fairy tale. Regardless of what we may wish for or dream about, a conflict-free world just doesn't exist. Even the best communicators, the luckiest people, are bound to wind up in situations when their needs don't match the needs of others. Money, time, power, sex, humor, aesthetic taste, as well as a thousand other issues, arise and keep us from living in a state of perpetual agreement.

For many people the inevitability of conflict is a depressing fact. They think that the existence of ongoing conflict means that there's little chance for happy relationships with others. Effective communicators know differently.

They realize that although it's impossible to *eliminate* conflict, there are ways to *manage* it effectively. Managing conflict skillfully can open the door to healthier, stronger, and more satisfying relationships.

What Is Conflict?

Stop reading and make a list of as many different conflicts as you can recall. Include both conflicts you've experienced personally and ones that only involved others.

What metaphors describe your conflicts? Do you think of them as a mess that needs to be cleaned up? As battles? Legalistic contests? Games? Follow the guidelines in Activity 1 on page 387 to find out.

The list will probably show you that conflict takes many forms. Sometimes there's angry shouting, as when parents yell at their children. In other cases, conflicts involve restrained discussion, as in labor-management negotiations or legal trials. Sometimes conflicts are carried on through hostile silence, as in the unspoken feuds of angry couples. Finally, conflicts may wind up in physical fighting between friends, enemies, or even total strangers.

Whatever forms they may take, all interpersonal conflicts share certain similarities. Joyce Hocker and William Wilmot (1991: 11–21) provide a thorough definition of conflict. They state that **conflict** is *an expressed struggle between at least two interdependent parties who perceive incompatible goals, scarce rewards, and interference from the other parties in achieving their goals.* Let's look at the various parts of this definition to develop a better understanding of conflicts in people's lives.

EXPRESSED STRUGGLE

Another way to describe an expressed struggle is to say that both individuals in a conflict know that some disagreement exists. For instance, you may be upset for months because a neighbor's loud stereo keeps you from getting to sleep at night, but no conflict exists between the two of you until the neighbor learns about your problem. Of course, the expressed struggle doesn't have to be verbal. You can show your displeasure with somebody without saying a word. A dirty look, the silent treatment, or avoiding the other person are all ways of expressing yourself. One way or another, both people must know that a problem exists before their conflict surfaces.

PERCEIVED INCOMPATIBLE GOALS

All conflicts look as if one person's gain would be another's loss. For instance, consider the neighbor whose stereo keeps you awake at night. Doesn't somebody have to lose? If the neighbor turns down the noise, then he loses the enjoyment of hearing the music at full volume; but if the neighbor keeps the volume up, then you're still awake and unhappy.

The goals in this situation really aren't completely incompatible—solutions do exist that allow both people to get what they want. For instance, you could achieve peace and quiet by closing your windows or getting the neighbor to close his. You might use a pair of earplugs, or perhaps the neighbor could get a set of earphones, allowing the music to play at full volume without bothering anyone. If any of these solutions prove workable, then the conflict disappears.

Unfortunately, people often fail to see mutually satisfying answers to their problems. As long as they *perceive* their goals to be mutually exclusive, then, although the conflict is unnecessary, it is still real.

PERCEIVED SCARCE REWARDS

Conflicts also exist when people believe there isn't enough of something to go around. The most obvious example of a scarce resource is money—a cause of many conflicts. If a worker asks for a raise in pay and the boss would rather keep the money or use it to expand the business, then the two people are in conflict.

Time is another scarce commodity. As authors, teachers, and family men, all three of us are constantly in the middle of struggles about how to use the limited time we have at home. Should we work on this book? Visit with our wives? Play with our children? Enjoy the luxury of being alone? With only twenty-four hours in a day, we're bound to wind up in conflicts with our families, editors, students, and friends—all of whom want more of our time than we have available to give.

INTERDEPENDENCE

However antagonistic they might feel, the people in a conflict are dependent upon each other. The welfare and satisfaction of one depends on the actions of another. If this were not true, then even in the face of scarce resources and incompatible goals there would be no need for conflict. Interdependence exists between conflicting nations, social groups, organizations, friends, and lovers. In each case, if the two people didn't need each other to solve the problem, they would go separate ways. In fact, many conflicts go unresolved because the people fail to understand their interdependence. One of the first steps toward resolving a conflict is to take the attitude that "we're all in this together."

Conflict Is Natural and Inevitable

Conflicts are bound to happen. Over time, every relationship will experience the incompatible goals and struggles over scarce resources that

characterize conflicts. College students who have kept diaries of their relationships report that they take part in about seven arguments per week. Most have argued with the other person before, often about the same topic (Benoit and Benoit 1987). When you consider that not all conflicts result in open arguments, this figure makes it clear that conflict is a fact of life for everyone.

Since it is impossible to *avoid* conflicts, the challenge is to handle them well when they do arise. Over twenty years of research shows that both happy and unhappy marriages have conflicts, but that they manage conflict in very different ways (see Adler and Towne 1990: 357; Hocker and Wilmot 1991: 37). Unhappy couples argue in ways cataloged in this book as destructive. They are more concerned with defending themselves than with being problem-oriented; they fail to listen carefully to one another, have little or no empathy for their partners, use evaluative "you" language, and ignore one another's relational messages.

Satisfied couples communicate far more effectively during their disagreements. While often arguing vigorously, they use perception-checking skills to find out what the other person is thinking, and they let one another know that they understand the other side of the dispute. They are willing to admit their defensiveness when it occurs, so that they can get back to the problem at hand.

Despite the fact that relationships can survive, and even prosper from constructive disagreements, most people view conflict as something to be avoided whenever possible. Some common metaphors reflect this attitude (Hocker and Wilmot 1991). It's common to talk about conflict as a kind of war: "He shot down my arguments"; "Okay, fire away"; "Don't try to defend yourself!" Another metaphor suggests conflict is explosive: "Don't blow up!"; I needed to let off steam"; "You've got a short fuse." Sometimes conflict seems like a kind of trial, in which one person accuses another: "Come on, admit you're guilty"; "Stop accusing me!"; "Just listen to my case." Language that suggests conflict is a mess is also common: "Let's not open this can of worms"; "That's a sticky situation"; "Don't make such a stink!" Even the metaphor of a game implies that one side has to defeat the other: "That was out of bounds"; "You're not playing fair"; "Okay, you win!"

Conflicts may not always be easy, but they *can* be constructive. We've already suggested that a more positive metaphor is to view conflict as a kind of dance in which partners work together to create something that would be impossible without their cooperation. You may have to persuade the other person to become your partner, and you may be clumsy together at first; but with enough practice and goodwill, you can work together instead of at cross purposes.

The attitude partners bring to their conflicts can make the difference between success and failure. One study by Sandra Metts and William Cupach (1990) revealed that college students in romantic relationships who believed that conflicts are destructive were most likely to neglect or leave the relationship and less likely to seek a solution than couples who had less negative attitudes. Of course, attitudes alone won't always guarantee satisfying solutions to conflicts. The kinds of skills you will learn in this chapter can help well intentioned partners handle their disagreements constructively. But without the right attitude, all the skills in the world will be little help.

Functional and Dysfunctional Conflicts

Some bacteria are "good," aiding digestion and cleaning up waste, whereas others are "bad," causing infection. There are helpful forest fires, which clean out dangerous accumulations of underbrush, and harmful ones, which threaten lives and property. In the same way, some conflicts can be beneficial. They provide a way for relationships to grow by solving the problem at hand and often improving other areas of interaction. Other conflicts can be harmful, causing pain and leaving a relationship weaker. Communication scholars usually describe harmful conflicts as *dysfunctional* and beneficial ones as *functional.*

What makes some conflicts functional and others dysfunctional? Usually the difference doesn't rest in the subject of the conflict, for it's possible to have good or poor results on almost any issue. Sometimes certain individual styles of communication are more productive than others. In other cases the success or failure of a conflict will depend on the method of resolution the parties choose. We'll talk more about types of conflict resolution later in this chapter. We want now to describe several symptoms that distinguish **functional** from **dysfunctional conflicts.**

What distinguishes your functional conflicts from dysfunctional ones? To answer this question, see Activity 2 on page 387.

INTEGRATION VS. POLARIZATION

In a dysfunctional conflict biases are rampant. Participants see themselves as "good" and the other person as "bad"; their actions as "protective" and the other's as "aggressive"; their behavior as "open and trustworthy" and the other's as "sneaky and deceitful." Researchers Robert Blake and Jane Mouton (1964) found that people engaged in this kind of polarization underestimate the commonalities shared with the other person, and so miss areas of agreement and goodwill.

By contrast, participants in a functional conflict realize that the other person's needs may be legitimate, too. A person who is allergic to cigarette smoke recognizes that smokers aren't necessarily evil people who delight in inflicting torment, while the smoker sympathizes with the other's need for cleaner air. In such issues, functional conflict is marked by mutual respect.

COOPERATION VS. ISOLATION

Participants in a dysfunctional conflict see each other as opponents and view the other's gain as their loss: "If you win, I lose" is the attitude. This belief keeps partners from looking for ways to

Student Reflection
Constructive and Destructive Conflicts

My fiancée and I have two kinds of arguments: "good" ones and "bad" ones. The bad ones really are nasty: We battle like two pit bulls, locked in combat until one is obviously beaten. It takes both—the loser and the winner—a few days to recover from these struggles. Our "good" fights feel very different. We still get mad at one another, but even when we're most angry it's clear that we care about each other and we're trying to figure out what's best for each of us.

I guess the biggest difference between good and bad fights is the goal. In bad ones we seem most concerned with putting down one another. In good fights we're struggling to find solutions that we both can live with.

agree or finding solutions that can satisfy them both. People rarely try to redefine the situation in more constructive ways, and seldom give in, even on noncritical issues.

A more functional approach recognizes that cooperation may bring about an answer that leaves everyone happy. Even nations basically hostile to each other often recognize the functional benefits of cooperating. For example, the United States and the Soviet Union have clearcut differences in certain areas, yet work together in fields such as disease control, halting air piracy, and disarmament. Such cooperation is also possible in interpersonal conflicts. We will have a great deal to say about cooperative problem solving later in this chapter.

AGREEMENT VS. COERCION

In destructive conflicts the participants rely heavily on power to get what they want. "Do it my way, or else" is a threat commonly stated or implied in dysfunctional conflicts. Money, favors, friendliness, sex, and sometimes even physical coercion become tools for forcing the other person to give in. Needless to say, victories won with such power plays don't do much for a relationship.

More enlightened communicators realize that power plays are usually a bad idea, not only on ethical grounds but because they can often backfire. Rarely is a party in a relationship

---

A quarrel between friends, when made up, adds a new tie to friendship, as experience shows that the callosity formed round a broken bone makes it stronger than before.

ST. FRANCIS DE SALES

---

totally powerless; it's often possible to win a battle only to lose a war. One classic case of the dysfunctional consequences of using power to resolve conflicts occurs in families where authoritarian parents make their children's requests into "unreasonable demands." It's easy enough to send five-year-olds out of a room for some real or imagined misbehavior, but when they grow into teenagers they acquire many ways of striking back.

DEESCALATION VS. ESCALATION

In destructive conflicts the problems seem to grow larger instead of smaller. As you read in Chapter 10, defensiveness is reciprocal: The person you attack is likely to strike back even harder. We've all seen a small incident get out of hand and cause damage out of proportion to its importance.

One clear sign of functional conflict is that in the long run the behaviors of the participants solve more problems than they create. We say "long run" because facing up to an issue instead of avoiding it frequently makes life more difficult for a while. In this respect handling conflicts functionally is rather like going to the dentist: You may find it a little (or even a lot!) painful for a while, but you're only making matters worse by not facing the problem.

FOCUSING VS. DRIFTING

In dysfunctional conflicts the partners often bring in issues having little or nothing to do with the original problem. Take for example a couple who are having trouble deciding whether to spend the holidays at his or her parents' home. As they begin to grow frustrated at their inability to solve the dilemma, their interaction sounds like this:

A: Your mother is always trying to latch onto us!
B: If you want to talk about latching on, what about your folks? Ever since they loaned us that money, they've been asking about every dime we spend.
A: Well, if you could ever finish with school and hold down a decent job, we wouldn't have to worry about money so much. You're always talking about wanting to be an equal partner, but I'm the one paying all the bills around here.

You can imagine how the conversation would go from here. Notice how the original issue became lost as the conflict expanded. Such open-ended hostility is unlikely to solve any of the problems it brings up, not to mention

---

Our marriage used to suffer from arguments that were too short. Now we argue long enough to find out what the argument is about.

HUGH PRATHER
Notes to Myself

---

its potential for creating problems that didn't even exist before.

One characteristic of communicators who handle conflict well is their ability to keep focused on one subject at a time. Unlike those dysfunctional battlers whom George Bach and Peter Wyden (1968) call "kitchen sink fighters," skillful communicators might say, "I'm willing to talk about how my parents have been acting since they made us that loan, but first let's settle the business of where to spend the holidays." In other words, for functional problem solving, the rule is "one problem at a time."

FORESIGHT VS. SHORTSIGHTEDNESS

Shortsightedness can produce dysfunctional conflicts even when partners do not lose sight of the original issue. One common type of shortsightedness occurs when disputants try to win a "battle" and wind up losing the "war." Friends might argue about who started a fight; but if you succeed in proving that you were "right" at the cost of the friendship, then the victory is a hollow one. In another type of shortsightedness, partners are so interested in defending their own solution to a problem that they overlook a different solution that would satisfy both their goals. A final type of shortsightedness occurs when one or both partners jump into a conflict without planning the necessary steps. We will have more to say about preventing these last two types of shortsightedness in a few pages.

POSITIVE VS. NEGATIVE RESULTS

So far we've looked at the differences between the *processes* of functional and dysfunctional conflicts. Now let's compare the *results* of these different styles.

Dysfunctional conflict typically has three consequences. First, no one is likely to get what was originally sought. In the short run it may

---

I'm lonesome; they are all dying; I have hardly a warm personal enemy left.

JAMES MCNEILL WHISTLER

---

look as if one person might win in a dispute while the other loses, but most often both people suffer in some way. For instance, an instructor might win by forcing an overly strict grading scale on students who clearly would lose out if they received grades lower than the ones they believed they deserved. However, in such situations, instructors also lose, for instead of trying to truly understand and master the material, the students most likely will become preoccupied with beating the system by simply memorizing facts, trying to "psych out" the forthcoming exams, or even cheating. Obviously this behavior prevents good learning, and the instructor has failed. In the long run, everyone has lost.

A second consequence of dysfunctional conflicts is that they threaten the future of the relationship. Let's return to the feuding couple. It's easy to imagine how the resentments of both partners would affect their behavior. For example, it's unlikely that either would feel affectionate after such an exchange, and so we might expect their home life to deteriorate: As their disappointment grows, they would probably be less willing to help each other in their usual ways. If this couple can't solve their original problems, it's likely that dissatisfaction with each other will grow like a cancer until it has poisoned almost every part of their relationship. This effect explains why it's important to deal successfully with seemingly inconsequential matters such as arriving on time for appointments or who takes out the trash, for every time partners don't resolve a small conflict they weaken their entire relationship.

Failure to resolve interpersonal problems is also personally destructive to each participant. We discussed the range of emotions in Chapter 4. Take a moment now to think about the feelings you've experienced when you were engaged in an unresolved conflict. It's likely that you felt (and still may feel) inadequate, foolish, unworthy, unlikable, or unlovable. Poorly managed conflicts have a strong effect on our self-esteem that can linger for years, threatening both our peace of mind and our future relationships with others.

In contrast to these dismal outcomes, functional conflicts have positive results. One benefit of skillfully handling issues is that interpersonal involvement increases. When we engage in a conflict productively, we get excited, motivated to act. In contrast to an apathetic person, the functional communicator is determined to do something to make the relationship better.

Skillfully handled conflict also promotes growth in a relationship. Along with restoring harmony, dealing with a conflict teaches people things about each other they didn't know before. They learn more about each other's needs and how such needs can be satisfied. Feelings are clarified. Backgrounds are shared. Of course growth can occur in nonconflict situations too; the point here is that dealing with problems can be an opportunity for getting to know each other better. Moreover, conflicts provide the opportunity for new kinds of sharing. We often fail to know where another person stands on an issue until that issue is confronted.

Constructive conflict also provides a safe outlet for the feelings of frustration and aggression that are bound to occur in any relationship. When people accept the inevitable fact that they'll occasionally disagree with each other, they can be willing to let their partners express that disagreement and in so doing defuse a great deal of it. Good interpersonal communicators allow each other to blow off steam without taking offense.

Finally, functional conflicts allow each person involved to establish a personal identity within the relationship. To see how important this individual identity is, think back to the early stages of your relationships. (Try to recall a wide variety: romantic, friendly, business, academic.) In many cases the earliest stages of relationships are marked by such a desire to promote harmony that the members behave unnaturally: They're so polite, so concerned with each other's happiness that they ignore their own needs and wants. In this effort to keep everything smooth, the members give up a bit of themselves. When conflicts finally do surface, each gives the other a chance to take a stand, to say, "I understand what you want, but let me tell you what's important to *me*." Conflicts handled skillfully allow the relationship to grow while at the same time letting each person remain an individual.

How would you describe your conflict style: Are you nonassertive? Directly or passively aggressive? Indirect? Assertive? Do others see you differently than you view yourself? You can find out by following the guidelines in Activity 3 on page 387.

Individual Conflict Styles

People have their individual styles of handling conflict—characteristic approaches they take when their needs appear incompatible with what others want. Sometimes a style is helpful and sometimes not. In either case, people should recognize their own styles so they can make the styles work for them.

What's your style of handling conflict? Find out by thinking about how two hypothetical characters—Sally and Ralph—manage a problem that you might find familiar.

Sally and Ralph have been friends for several years, ever since they moved into the same apartment building. They had always exchanged favors in a neighborly way, but lately Ralph has been depending more and more on Sally. He asks her to care for his cat and houseplants almost every other weekend while he travels, borrows food and cash without returning them, and drops in to talk about his unhappy love life at least once a week. Until lately, Sally hasn't minded much, but now she's getting tired of Ralph's behavior.

Read the four groups of responses below and rank them in the order you would be most likely to use them. Mark your most-likely response number 1; your next-most-likely, number 2; and so on.

_____ Steer clear of Ralph as much as possible. Pretend not to be home when he drops by. Make excuses for why you can't help him with his problems. *or* Do the favors for Ralph, hoping he'll stop imposing soon. After all, nobody's perfect, and it isn't worth making an issue.

_____ Hint to Ralph that you're not happy with his behavior. When he asks you to take care of his cat, hesitate and talk about your busy schedule. When he doesn't pay back his loans, mention that you're short of money and may need to borrow some from your friends and family. When he starts to talk about his romantic problems, mention that you need to study for an exam.

_____ Do the favors for Ralph, but let him know you aren't happy. Hint about the inconvenience of helping him. Sigh when he asks another favor. Make an occasional sarcastic remark about how much you enjoy being Ralph's housekeeper and psychotherapist. When he asks if you're upset with him, deny anything is wrong. Mention your unhappiness to some mutual friends, hoping they'll tell Ralph to back off.

―――― Ralph can't take a hint, so you tell him directly that you're fed up with his demands. Say you don't mind helping once in a while, but let him know he's taken advantage of your friendship. Warn him that continued impositions will threaten your friendship.

―――― Tell Ralph that you're beginning to feel uneasy about his requests. Let him know that you value his friendship, and want to keep feeling good about him.

Explain that's why you're telling him this, and ask him to work with you to find a way to solve his problems that's less of a strain for you.

Make sure you have ranked your responses before going on. Each of the choices above represents a different style of behavior in conflicts. These four styles are explained below and summarized in Table 11–1. As you read on, see which ones best describe the way you manage your own conflicts.

NONASSERTION

The inability or unwillingness to express thoughts or feelings in a conflict is called **nonassertion.** Sometimes nonassertion comes from a lack of confidence. In other cases, people lack the awareness or skill to use a more direct means of expression. Sometimes people know how to communicate in a straightforward way but choose to behave nonassertively.

Nonassertion can take a variety of forms. One is avoidance—either physical (steering clear of a friend after having an argument), or conversational (changing the topic, joking, or denying that a problem exists). People who avoid conflicts usually believe it's easier to put up with the status quo than to face the problem head-on and try to solve it. Accommodation is another type of nonassertive response. Accommodators deal with conflict by giving in, putting the other's needs ahead of their own.

Our example of Sally and Ralph illustrates the perils of nonassertion. Every time Sally hides from Ralph or changes the subject so he won't ask her for a favor, she becomes uncomfortable and probably leaves Ralph feeling the same way. After this avoidance goes on for a while, it's likely that whatever enjoyment Sally and Ralph had found together will be eclipsed by their new way of relating and the friend-

Table 11–1   Individual Styles of Conflict

	Nonassertive	Directly Aggressive	Passive Aggressive	Indirect	Assertive
Approach to Others	I'm not OK, you're OK.	I'm OK, you're not OK.	I'm OK, you're not OK. (But I'll let you think you are.)	I'm OK, you're not OK or I'm OK, you're not OK.	I'm OK. You're OK
Decision Making	Lets others choose	Chooses for others. They know it.	Chooses for others. They don't know it.	Chooses for others. They don't know it.	Chooses for self
Self-Sufficiency	Low	High or low	Looks high but usually low	High or low	Usually high
Behavior in Problem Situations	Flees; gives in	Outright attack	Concealed attack	Strategic, oblique	Direct confrontation
Response of Others	Disrespect, guilt, anger, frustration	Hurt, defensiveness, humiliation	Confusion, frustration, feelings of manipulation	Unknowing compliance or resistance	Mutual respect
Success Pattern	Succeeds by luck or charity of others	Beats out others	Wins by manipulation	Gains unwitting compliance of others	Attempts "win-win" solutions

Adapted with permission from Stanlee Phelps and Nancy Austin, *The Assertive Woman.* San Luis Obispo, CA: Impact, 1975, p. 11: and Gerald Piaget, American Orthopsychiatric Association, 1975. Further reproduction prohibited.

ship will degenerate into an awkward, polite charade.

Nonassertive behavior isn't always a bad idea. Avoidance may be the best course if a conflict is minor and short-lived. For example, you might let a friend's annoying grumpiness pass without saying anything, knowing that she is having one of her rare bad days. Likewise, you might not complain to a neighbor whose lawn sprinklers occasionally hit your newly washed car. You may also reasonably choose to keep quiet if the conflict occurs in an unimportant relationship, as with an acquaintance whose language you find offensive but whom you don't see often. Finally, you might choose to keep quiet if the risk of speaking up is too great: getting fired from a job you can't afford to lose, being humiliated in public, or even risking physical harm.

Like avoidance, accommodation can also be appropriate, especially in cases when the other person's needs may be more important than yours. For instance, if a friend wants to have a serious talk and you feel playful, you'd most likely honor your friend's request, particularly if that person is facing some kind of crisis and wants your help. In most cases, however, nonassertive accommodators fail to assert themselves either because they don't value themselves sufficiently, or because they don't know how to ask for what they want.

INDIRECT COMMUNICATION

Sometimes we choose to convey messages indirectly, hinting to others instead of expressing ourselves outright; this is **indirect communication.** Consider the case of Sally and Ralph. Rather than risk triggering a defensive reaction, Sally decides that she will try to change Ralph's bad habits with an indirect approach. If Ralph has the kind of sensitivity that characterizes most competent communicators, he may get Sally's message without forcing her to confront him.

As this example suggests, an indirect approach can save face for the other person. If your guests are staying too long at a party, it's probably kinder to yawn and hint about your big day tomorrow than bluntly to ask them to leave. Likewise, if you're not interested in going out with someone who has asked you for a date, it may be more compassionate to claim that you're busy than to say "I'm not interested in seeing you."

Sometimes indirect communication can be a form of self-protection. You might, for example, test the waters by hinting instead of directly asking the boss for a raise or letting your partner know you could use some affection instead of asking outright. At times like these an oblique approach may get the message across while minimizing the risk of a negative response.

The advantages of saving face for others and self-protection help explain why indirect com-

munication is the most common way people make requests (Jordan and Roloff 1990). The risk of an indirect message, of course, is that the other person will misunderstand you or fail to get the hint. There are also times when the importance of an idea is great enough that hinting lacks the necessary punch. When clarity and directness are your goals, the kind of assertive approach described on the following pages is in order.

PASSIVE AGGRESSION

When a communicator expresses dissatisfaction in a disguised manner, it is called **passive aggression.** Passive aggression can take the form of "crazymaking" (Bach and Wyden 1968).

This term takes its name from the effect such behavior usually has on its target. There are a number of crazymaking ways to deal with conflict indirectly. One is through guilt: "Never mind, I'll do all the work myself. Go ahead and have a good time. Don't worry about me." Hinting is another form of passive aggression: "When do you think you can get around to finishing the job?" Sometimes nonverbal behavior is a way to express aggression indirectly: a loud sigh, pained expression, or a disdainful laugh can get a message across. If the target of these messages asks about them, the passive aggressor can always deny the conflict exists. Even humor—especially sarcasm—can be used as passive aggression.

There are a number of risks to indirect approaches like these. First, they may not work. The other person might miss your message and continue with the undesirable behavior. On the other hand, the target of your indirect message might understand your message clearly but refuse to comply, possibly out of irritation at your underhanded style of communicating. Even when passive aggression proves successful in the short run, it can have unpleasant consequences over a longer period of time. You

The test of a man or woman's breeding is how they behave in a quarrel.

GEORGE BERNARD SHAW

---

might get immediate compliance ("All right, I'll help you with the damn thing"), but create a resentful climate that will harm the relationship in the future.

DIRECT AGGRESSION

Where the nonasserter underreacts, a directly aggressive communicator overreacts, lashing out to attack the source of displeasure. Common consequences of **direct aggression** are anger and defensiveness on the one hand, and hurt and humiliation on the other. In either case, aggressive communicators build themselves up at the expense of others. A directly aggressive attack can often lead to an equally combative reaction, starting a destructive spiral that can expand beyond the original dispute and damage the entire relationship (Wilmot 1987).

ASSERTION

In **assertion,** a speaker's statement expresses thoughts and feelings clearly. Unlike an aggressive message, it does not attack the other person (Infante and Wigley 1986). One format for an assertive message consists of five elements (Miller et al. 1975):

1. *A description of the observable behavior that prompted your message.*   The key here is to describe the behavior objectively, without blaming or name calling. Notice how each of the following statements just describes the facts: "When you didn't call me after you said

Get it yourself.

you would . . . ," "Last week you asked me to buy the tickets, and now you tell me you don't want them. . . . "

2. *Your interpretation of the behavior.*   Be sure to label the interpretation as subjective, not as a matter of fact. For example, "I get the idea you're mad at me" is a better statement than "Why are you mad at me?"

3. *The feelings that arise from your interpretation.*   Notice the difference between saying "I get the idea you're mad at me" and the more complete description "I get the idea you're mad at me *and I feel hurt* (or *defensive, confused,* or *sorry*)." Review Chapter 4 for suggestions on how to express emotions clearly.

Assertion may sound fine in theory, but how would it work in real life? You can begin to answer this question by turning to Activity 4 on page 387.

---

4. *The consequences of the information you have shared so far.*   Consequences can describe what happens to *you,* the speaker ("When you tease me, I avoid you"), what happens to the *target of the message* ("When you drink too

---

Student Reflection

Flexibility in Conflict Styles

My roommate <u>thinks</u> he's assertive, but most of his friends would call him an aggressive creep. He won't compromise on anything: what to cook for dinner, what TV show to watch, or when it's time to party or study. He justifies his arguments by saying "I'm just telling the truth" and "I'd be a hypocrite if I didn't say what I was thinking."

He may be honest, but he sure can be mean! I wish this guy would realize that not every issue needs to be a conflict. There's a time to stand up for yourself, but there's also a time to give in.

---

much, you start to drive dangerously"), or what happens to *others* ("When you play the radio so loud, it wakes up the baby").

5. *An intention statement.* Some intention statements are requests ("I hope you'll come again"). Others describe *how you plan to act* ("Unless we can work out some sort of studying arrangement, I may have to find a new place to live").

Sally could have used this format to express herself assertively to Ralph: "Ralph, I've been bothered by some things lately and I'd like to talk them over with you. (She identifies the problem as hers, and not Ralph's.) When you ask me to take care of your apartment two or three times a month and borrow food and cash without returning them (behavior), I don't think you realize the inconveniences I face (interpretation). I didn't mind until recently—that's why I

haven't said anything before—but I'm starting to feel resentful (feeling), and I'm afraid it might spoil our friendship (consequence). I don't want that to happen (intention), so I'd like to figure out some way I can help you when you really need it, but without it being quite so much of a burden on me (another intention)."

This sort of assertive message gets results, especially in our most important interpersonal relationships. While less direct forms may work in nonintimate situations, directness is more effective at getting compliance in intimate relationships (Jordan and Roloff 1990). When the issue is important and the commitment between partners is high, speaking from the heart instead of beating around the bush seems to be the best approach.

Besides boosting your chances of getting what you want, an assertive approach maintains the self-respect of both people. As a result, people who manage their conflicts assertively usually feel better about themselves and each other afterward—not always the case with other styles.

WHICH STYLE TO USE?

Although communicating assertively might seem like the most attractive alternative to the other styles described in this chapter, it's an oversimplification to imagine that there is a single "best" way to respond to conflicts (Canary and Cupach 1988; Canary and Spitzberg 1987). Generally speaking, assertive tactics like asking for information and considering alternatives are preferable to aggressive tactics like shouting or blaming. But we've already seen that there are times when aggression or even nonassertion are appropriate. Occasionally you may have to shout to get the other person's attention, and other times the smartest approach may be to swallow the other person's abuse instead of responding.

If I am not for myself, who will be?
If I am only for myself, what am I?

RABBI HILLEL

A personal conflict style isn't a personality "trait" that carries across all situations. Hocker and Wilmot (1991: 128) suggest that roughly 50 percent of the population changes their style from one situation to another. As you learned in Chapter 1, this sort of behavioral flexibility is a characteristic of competent communicators. Several factors can govern which style to use (Putnam and Wilson 1982).

The Situation   When someone clearly has more power than you, nonassertion may be the best approach. If the boss tells you to fill that order *now!* you probably ought to do it without comment. A more assertive response ("When you use that tone of voice, I feel defensive") might be clearer, but it could also cost you your job. Likewise, an aggressive message is sometimes most appropriate. At one time or another, it will probably be necessary to raise your voice to show that you mean business.

The Other Person   Although assertiveness has the best chance of success with many people, some receivers respond better to other approaches. You probably know some communicators who are so sensitive or defensive that an assertive approach would be too much for them to handle. Others are so insensitive that aggressiveness is necessary, at least to get their attention.

The decision about which conflict style to use also depends on the cultural background of the other person. For example, the kind of assertiveness that is valued in the United States would be considered offensive in Japan (Okabe

1987). Even a simple request like "Close the door" would be too straightforward in that culture. A more indirect statement like "It is somewhat cold today" would be more appropriate. To take a more important example, the Japanese are reluctant to say "No" to a request. A more likely answer would be "Let me think about it for a while," which anyone familiar with Japanese culture would recognize as refusal. When indirect communication is a cultural norm, it is unreasonable to expect more straightforward approaches to succeed.

Your Goals   When you want to solve a problem, assertiveness is probably the best approach. But there are other reasons for communicating in a conflict. Sometimes your overriding concern is to calm down an enraged or upset communicator. Tolerating an outburst from your crotchety and sick neighbor, for example, is probably better than standing up for yourself and triggering a stroke. Likewise, you might choose to sit quietly through the nagging of a family member rather than ruin Thanksgiving dinner. In other cases, your moral principles might compel an aggressive statement even though it might not get you what you originally sought: "I've had enough of your racist jokes. I've tried to explain why they're so offensive, but you obviously haven't listened. I'm leaving!"

Conflict in Relational Systems

So far we have been describing individual conflict styles. Even though the style you choose in a conflict is important, your approach isn't the only factor that will determine how a conflict unfolds. In reality, conflict is *relational:* Its character usually is determined by the way the people interact (Hocker and Wilmot 1991; Knapp et al. 1988). You might, for example, be determined to handle a conflict with your

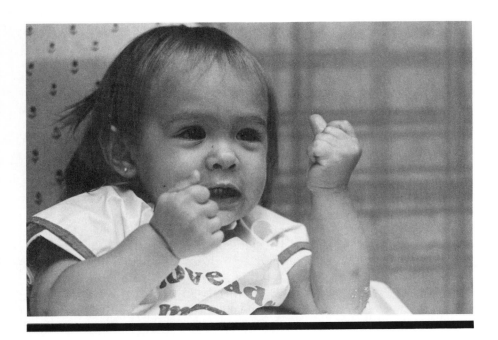

neighbors assertively, only to be driven to aggression by their uncooperative nature . . . or even to nonassertion by their physical threats. Likewise, you might plan to hint to a professor that you are bothered by his apparent indifference, but wind up discussing the matter in an open, assertive way in reaction to his constructive reaction. Examples like these suggest that conflict isn't a just matter of individual choice. Rather, it depends on how the partners interact.

When two or more people are in a long-term relationship they develop their own **relational conflict style**—a pattern of managing disagreements that repeats itself over time. The mutual influence parties have on one another is so powerful that it can overcome our disposition to handle conflicts in the manner that comes most easily to one or the other (Burggraf and Sillars 1987; Newton and Burgoon 1990). As we will soon see, some relational conflict styles are constructive, while others can make life miserable and threaten relationships.

How would you characterize the conflict system in one of your important relationships? You can begin to answer this important question by following the guidelines in Activity 5 on page 387.

COMPLEMENTARY, SYMMETRICAL, AND PARALLEL STYLES

Partners in interpersonal relationships—and impersonal ones too—can use one of three styles to manage their conflicts. In relationships with a **complementary conflict style** the partners use different but mutually reinforcing behaviors. In a **symmetrical conflict style,** both parties use the same tactics. Some relationships are characterized by a **parallel con-**

flict style, which shifts between complementary and symmetrical patterns from one issue to another. Table 11–2 illustrates how the same conflict can unfold in very different ways, depending on whether the partners' communication is symmetrical or complementary. A parallel style would alternate between these two forms, depending on the situation.

Research shows that a complementary "fight-flight" style is common in many unhappy marriages. One partner—most commonly the wife—addresses the conflict directly, while the other—usually the husband—withdraws (Gottman and Krokoff 1989; Pike and Sillars 1985). It's easy to see how this pattern can lead to a cycle of increasing hostility and isolation, since each partner punctuates the conflict differently, blaming the other for making matters worse. "I withdraw because she's so critical," a husband might say. The wife wouldn't organize the sequence in the same way, however. "I criticize because he withdraws," would be her perception.

Complementary styles aren't the only ones that can lead to problems. Some distressed relationships suffer from destructively symmetrical communication. If both partners treat one another with matching hostility, one threat and insult leads to another in an **escalatory spiral.** If the partners both withdraw from one another instead of facing their problems, a complementary **deescalatory spiral** results, in which the satisfaction and vitality ebb from the relationship, leaving it a shell of its former self.

As Table 11–2 shows, both complementary and symmetrical behavior can produce "good" results as well as "bad" ones. If the complementary behaviors are positive, then a positive spiral results and the conflict stands a good chance of being resolved. This is the case in the second example in Table 11–2, in which the boss is open to hearing the employee's concerns, listening willingly as the employee talks. Here, a complementary talk-listen pattern works well.

Student Reflection

Conflict Is Shaped by Relationships

I'm like three people when it comes to conflict. I'm almost always assertive with my husband. It may take a while, but sooner or later I bring up any problems and we talk them over until we work out an answer. With my daughter I'm usually an aggressive Hyde instead of a rational Jekyll. She and I may start out calmly, but soon we're screaming at one another. With my parents I avoid conflicts altogether. They still think of me as a child, and they won't take my ideas seriously, so there's no point in talking to them.

I can see now that my conflict style isn't just a matter of what I choose. How I behave depends on how the other person treats me. Communication theory might say that we can control our behavior, but in real life it isn't that simple.

Symmetrical styles can also be beneficial, as another look at the boss-employee example shows. Many women have found that giving insensitive men a taste of their own sexist medicine is an effective way to end harassment without provoking an argument. The clearest example of a constructive symmetry occurs when both people communicate assertively, listening to one another's concerns and working together to resolve them. The potential for this sort of solution occurs in the parent-teenager conflict in Table 11–2. With enough mutual respect and careful listening, both the parents and their

Table 11–2   Complementary and Symmetrical Conflict Styles

Situation	Complementary Styles	Symmetrical Styles
Wife upset because husband is spending little time at home.	Wife complains; husband withdraws, spending even less time at home.	Wife complains. Husband responds angrily and defensively.
Female employee offended when boss calls her "sweetie."	Employee objects to boss, explaining her reasons for being offended. Boss apologizes for his unintentional insult.	Employee tries to make boss understand how she feels by calling *him* "cutie." The boss gets the hint and stops using the term.
Parents uncomfortable about teenager's new friends.	Parents express concerns. Child dismisses them, saying "There's nothing to worry about."	Teen expresses concern that parents are being too protective.

teenager can understand one another's concerns, and possibly find a way to give everyone what they want.

INTIMATE AND AGGRESSIVE STYLES

Another way to look at conflict styles is to examine the interaction between intimacy and aggression. The following scheme was originally used to describe communication between couples, but it also works well for other types of relationships.

■ *Nonintimate-Aggressive:* Partners fight, but are unsuccessful at satisfying important content and relational goals. In some relationships aggression is expressed directly: "Forget it. I'm not going to another stupid party with your friends. All they do is gossip and eat." In other relationships, indirect aggression is the norm: (Sarcastically): "Sure I'd *love* to go to another party with your friends." Neither of these approaches is satisfying, since there are few rewards to justify the costs of the unpleasantness.

■ *Nonintimate-Nonaggressive* The partners avoid conflicts—and one another—instead of facing issues head-on: "You won't be coming home for the holidays? Oh well, I guess that's okay...." Relationships of this sort can be quite stable, but because this pattern of communication doesn't confront and resolve problems, the vitality and satisfaction can decline over time.

■ *Intimate-Aggressive* This pattern combines aggression and intimacy in a manner that might seem upsetting to outsiders, but which can work well in some relationships. Lovers may fight like cats and dogs, but then make up just as intensely. Coworkers might argue about how to get the job done, but cherish their association.

■ *Intimate-Nonaggressive* This sort of relationship has a low amount of attacking or blaming. Partners may confront one another directly or indirectly, but one way or another they manage to prevent issues from interfering with their relationship.

The pattern partners choose may reveal a great deal about the kind of relationship they have chosen. Mary Ann Fitzpatrick (1977) identified three types of couples: separates, independents, and traditionals. Further research revealed that partners in each type of relationship approached conflict in a different manner (Fitzpatrick et al. 1982). Separates took a nonintimate-nonaggressive approach (and were the least satisfied of all subjects studied). They maintained a neutral emotional climate and kept their discussion of conflict to a minimum. Successful independents were best described as intimate-aggressives. They expressed negative emotions frequently, but also sought and revealed a large amount of personal information. Satisfied traditional couples fit the intimate-nonaggressive pattern, communicating more positive and less negative information than independents.

Information like this suggests that there's no single "best" relational conflict style. Some families or couples may fight intensely but love one another just as strongly. Others might handle issues more rationally and calmly. Even a non-intimate-nonagressive style can work well when there's no desire to have an interpersonal relationship. You might, for example, be willing to accommodate the demands of an eccentric professor for a semester, since rolling with the punches gets you the education you are seeking without provoking a confrontation that could be upsetting and costly.

Student Reflection

A Destructive Conflict Ritual

My parents have a very unhealthy conflict ritual. When my Mom wants something (like spending the holidays at her family's or a new car) that my dad doesn't agree with, she gets very quiet. She's very proper, and will talk to him if he asks her anything, but she doesn't crack a smile or go an inch out of her way to help him or (as nearly as I can tell) give him any affection.

After about three days of this, my dad starts acting very sweet to her. He'll suggest they go out for dinner or do favors around the house that he usually avoids. But my mom holds out until my dad will give in on the original issue, which he presents as if it was his decision: "I've been thinking, honey, maybe it would be nice to visit your sister for Christmas."

Since my dad sees compromising as a sign of weakness, this may be the best my mom can do—but it still seems pretty sick to me.

CONFLICT RITUALS

When people have been in a relationship for some time, their communication often develops into **conflict rituals**—unacknowledged but very real repeating patterns of interlocking behavior (Hocker and Wilmot 1991: 142). Consider a few common rituals:

A young child interrupts his parents, demanding to be included in their conversation. At first the parents tell the child to wait, but he whines and cries until the parents find it easier to listen than to ignore the fussing.

A couple fights. One partner leaves. The other accepts blame for the problem and begs forgiveness. The first partner returns, and a happy reunion takes place. Soon they fight again.

One friend is unhappy with the other. He or she withdraws until the other asks what's wrong.

"Nothing," the first replies. The questioning persists until the problem is finally out in the open. The friends then solve the issue and continue happily until the next problem arises, when the pattern repeats itself.

There's nothing inherently wrong with the interaction in many rituals. Consider the examples above. In the first, the child's whining may be the only way he can get the parents' attention. In the second, both partners might use the fighting as a way to blow off steam, and both might find that the joy of a reunion is worth the grief of the separation. The third ritual might

work well when one friend is more assertive than the other.

Rituals can cause problems, though, when they become the *only* way relational partners handle their conflicts. As you learned in Chapter 1, competent communicators have a large repertoire of behaviors, and they are able to choose the most effective response for a given situation. Relying on one pattern to handle all conflicts is no more effective than using a screwdriver to handle every home repair or putting the same seasoning in every dish you cook: What works in one situation isn't likely to succeed in many others. Conflict rituals may be familiar and comfortable, but they aren't the best way to solve the variety of conflicts that are part of any relationship.

Methods of Conflict Resolution

Whatever the style, every conflict is a struggle to have one's goals met. Sometimes that struggle succeeds, and in other cases it fails. In the remainder of this chapter we'll look at various approaches to resolving conflicts and see which ones are most promising.

WIN-LOSE

In **win-lose problem solving,** one person gets satisfaction while the other comes up short. People resort to this method of resolving disputes when they perceive a situation as being an "either-or" one: Either I get my way, or you get your way. The most clear-cut examples of win-lose situations are certain games, such as baseball or poker, in which the rules require a winner and a loser. Some interpersonal issues seem to fit into this win-lose framework: two co-workers seeking a promotion to the same job, say, or a couple arguing over how to spend their limited money.

Power is the distinguishing characteristic in win-lose problem solving, for it's necessary to defeat an opponent to get what you want. The most obvious kind of power is physical. Some parents threaten their children with warnings such as "Stop misbehaving or I'll send you to your room." Adults who use physical power to deal with each other usually aren't so blunt, but the threat often exists nonetheless. For instance, behind the legal system is the implied threat "Follow the rules or we'll lock you up."

Real or implied force isn't the only kind of power used in conflicts. People who rely on authority of many types engage in win-lose methods without ever threatening physical coercion. In most jobs supervisors have the potential to use authority in the assignment of working hours, job promotions, desirable or undesirable tasks, and of course in the power to fire an unsatisfactory employee. Teachers can use the power of grades to coerce students to act in desired ways.

Intellectual or mental power can also be a tool for conquering an opponent. Everyone is familiar with stories of how a seemingly weak hero defeats a stronger enemy through cleverness, showing that brains can triumph over brawn. In a less admirable way, crazymakers can defeat their partners in effective, if destructive, ways: by inducing guilt, avoiding issues, withholding desired behaviors, false accommodating, and so on.

Even the usually admired democratic principle of majority rule is a win-lose method of resolving conflicts. However fair it may be, the system results in one group getting its way and another being unsatisfied.

The win-lose method may sometimes be necessary, as when there are truly scarce resources, and when only one party can achieve satisfaction. For instance, if two suitors want to marry the same person, only one can succeed. To return to an earlier example, it's often true that

THE FAR SIDE By GARY LARSON

© 1988 Universal Press Syndicate

9·8

"I tell you I've *had* it! ... I'm not climbing into that getup one more time until you tell me why I'm always the back end."

only one applicant can be hired for a job. Still, don't be too willing to assume that your conflicts are necessarily win-lose. Many situations seeming to require a loser can be resolved to everyone's satisfaction.

There is a second kind of situation where win-lose is the best method of conflict. Even when cooperation is possible, if the other person insists on defeating you, then the most logical response might be to defend yourself by fighting back. "It takes two to tango," the cliché goes, and it takes two to cooperate. Some people are so resistant to constructive problem solving that it may be fruitless to try that approach. In one study, employees identified by their managers as "difficult" consistently refused to cooperate in collaborative problem-solving approaches (Monroe et al. 1989). Instead, they responded with passive-aggressive strategies, refusing to accept managers' feedback, excuses, and avoidance. When faced with this sort of absolute refusal to cooperate, it may be self-defeating to hang on to a collaborative approach.

A final and much-less-frequent justification for trying to defeat another person occurs when the other person is clearly behaving in a wrongful manner, and when defeating that person is the only way to stop the wrongful behavior. Few people would deny the importance of restraining a person who is deliberately harming others, even if the belligerent person's freedom is sacrificed in the process. It seems justifiable to coerce others into behaving as we think they should only in the most extreme circumstances.

LOSE-LOSE

In **lose-lose problem solving** neither side is satisfied with the outcome. Although the name of this approach is so discouraging that it's hard to imagine how anyone could willingly use it, lose-lose is a fairly common approach to handling conflicts.

Compromise is the most respectable form of lose-lose conflict resolution. In compromising, all the partners are willing to settle for less than they want because they believe that partial satisfaction is the best result they can hope for. In *Interpersonal Conflict Resolution*, Alan Filley (1975) makes an interesting observation about our attitudes toward this method. Why is it, he asks, that if someone says, "I will compromise my values," we view the action unfavorably; yet we talk admiringly about people in a conflict who compromise to reach a solution? Although compromises may be the best obtainable result in some conflicts, it's important to realize that both people in a dispute can often work together to find much better solutions. In such cases "compromise" is often a negative concept.

Most of us are surrounded by the results of bad compromises. Consider a common example, the conflict between one person's desire to smoke cigarettes and another's need for clean air. The win-lose outcomes on this issue are obvious: Either the smoker abstains or the non-smoker gets polluted lungs. Neither solution is mutually satisfying. A compromise whereby the smoker only gets to enjoy a rare cigarette or must retreat outdoors to smoke, and the non-smoker still must inhale some fumes or feel like an ogre, is hardly better. Both sides still have lost considerable comfort and good will.

The costs involved in still other compromises are even greater. For example, if a divorced couple compromises on child care by haggling over custody and then, finally, grudgingly splits the time with their youngsters, it's hard to say that anybody has won.

Compromises aren't the only lose-lose solutions or even the worst ones. There are many instances in which the partners both strive to be winners, but as a result of the struggle both wind up losers. On the international scene, many wars illustrate this sad point. A nation that gains military victory at the cost of thousands of lives, large amounts of resources, and a damaged national conscience hasn't truly won much. On the interpersonal level the same principle holds true. Most of us have seen battles of pride in which both people strike out and both suffer. There should be a better alternative, and fortunately, there often is.

WIN-WIN

As its name suggests, the outcome of a **win-win problem-solving** style is different than one in a win-lose conflict. Results that satisfy everyone are no accident: They usually result from an approach that is very different from those we've discussed so far (see Table 11–3).

In win-win problem solving, the goal is to find a solution that satisfies the needs of every-

Table 11–3 Differences Between Win-Lose and Win-Win Problem Solving	
Win-Lose	Win-Win
Conflicting interests	Shared interests
Negotiations based on power	Negotiations based on trust
Low self-disclosure	High self-disclosure
Concern only for self	Concern for self and other

one involved. Not only do the partners avoid trying to win at each other's expense, but there's a belief that working together can provide a solution in which all reach their goals without needing to compromise.

One way to understand how no-lose problem solving works is to look at a few examples.

A boss and her employees get into a conflict over scheduling. The employees often want to shift the hours they're scheduled to work in order to accommodate personal needs, whereas the boss needs to be sure that the operation is fully staffed at all times. After some discussion they arrive at a solution that satisfies everyone: The boss works up a monthly master schedule indicating the hours during which each employee is responsible for being on the job. Employees are free to trade hours between themselves, as long as the operation is fully staffed at all times.

A conflict about testing arises in a college class. Due to sickness or other reasons, a certain number of students need to take exams on a makeup basis. The instructor doesn't want to give these students any advantage over their peers, and doesn't want to go through the task of making up a brand-new test for just a few people. After working on the problem together, instructor and students arrive at a no-lose solution. The instructor will hand out a list of twenty possible exam questions in advance of the test day. At examination time five of these questions are randomly drawn for the class to answer. Students who take makeups will draw from the same pool of questions at the time of their test. In this way, makeup students are taking a fresh test without the instructor having to create a new exam.

The win-win approach sounds too good to be true. Can it work in real life? The best way to answer this question is to try it out for yourself. *See Activity 6 on page 387 for directions.*

A newly married husband and wife found themselves arguing frequently over their budget. The husband enjoyed buying impractical and enjoyable items for himself and the house, whereas the wife feared that such purchases would ruin their carefully constructed budget. Their solution was to set aside a small amount of money each month for "fun" purchases. The amount was small enough to be affordable, yet gave the husband a chance to escape from their Spartan life-style. Additionally, the wife was satisfied with the arrangement, because the luxury money was now a budget category by itself, which got rid of the "out of control" feeling that came when her husband made unex-

Student Reflection

Real-World Problem Solving

The win-win approach does work, but only if (and it's a big "if") the other person cares about the relationship and is interested in helping you as well as himself. I can almost always come up with win-win solutions with some people (my parents, my girlfriend, a few friends), because we want to help each other as well as ourselves. There are other people (like my boss and my roommates), though, who only care about themselves. With them I have to look out for number one or else I'd be a sucker. The win-win method is great—but not with everybody.

pected purchases. The plan worked so well that the couple continued to use it even after their income rose, by increasing the amount devoted to luxuries.

Although such solutions might seem obvious when you read them here, a moment's reflection will show you that such cooperative problem solving is all too rare. People faced with these types of conflicts often resort to such dysfunctional styles of communicating as withdrawing, avoiding, or competing, and wind up handling the issues in a manner resulting in either a win-lose or lose-lose outcome. As we said earlier, it's a shame to see one or both partners in a conflict come away unsatisfied when they could both get what they're seeking by communicating in a no-lose manner.

Win-win problem solving works best when it follows a seven-step approach, based on a plan developed by Deborah Weider-Hatfield (1981).

1. **Define your needs**   Begin by deciding what you want or need. Sometimes the answer is obvious, as in our earlier example of the neighbor whose loud stereo music kept others awake. In other instances, however, the apparent problem masks a more fundamental one. Consider an example: After dating for a few months, Beverly started to call Jim after they parted for the evening—a "goodnight call." Although the calling was fine with Jim at the beginning, he began to find it irritating after several weeks.

   At first Jim thought his aggravation focused on the nuisance of talking late at night when he was ready for sleep. More self-examination showed that his irritation centered on the relational message he thought Beverly's calls implied: that she was either snooping on Jim or was so insecure she needed constant assurances of his love. Once he recognized the true sources of his irritation, Jim's needs became clear: (1) to have Beverly's trust and (2) to be free of her insecurities.

   Because your needs won't always be clear, it's often necessary to think about a problem alone, before approaching the other person involved. Sometimes talking to a third person can help you sort out your thoughts. In either case, you should explore both the apparent content of your dissatisfaction and the relational issues that may lurk behind it.

2. **Share your needs with the other person**   Once you've defined your needs, it's time to share them with the other person. Two guidelines are important here: First, be sure to choose a time and place that is suitable. Unloading on a tired or busy partner lowers the odds your concerns will be well received. Likewise, be sure you are at your best: Don't bring an issue up when your anger may cause you to say things you'll later

Don't fight a battle if you don't gain anything by winning.

GENERAL GEORGE S. PATTON, JR.

regret, when your discouragement blows the problem out of proportion, or when you're distracted by other business. Making a date to discuss the problem—after dinner, over a cup of coffee, or even a day in advance—can often boost the odds of a successful outcome.

The second guideline for sharing a problem is to use the descriptive "I" language outlined in Chapter 10 and the assertive message format on page 371. Rather than implying blame, messages worded in this way convey how your partner's behavior affects you. Notice how Jim's use of the assertive message format conveys a descriptive, nonjudgmental attitude as he shares his concern with Beverly: "When you call me after every date (sense data), I begin to wonder whether you're checking up on me (interpretation of Beverly's behavior). I've also started to think that you're feeling insecure about whether I care about you, and that you need lots of reassurance (more interpretation). I'm starting to feel closed in by the calls (feeling), and I feel myself pulling back from you (consequence). I don't like the way we're headed, and I don't think it's necessary. I'd like to know whether you are feeling insecure, and to find a way that we can feel sure about each other's feelings without needing so much reassurance (intentions)."

3. **Listen to the other person's needs**   Once your own wants and needs are clear, it's time to find out what the other person wants and needs. (Now the listening skills described in Chapter 7 and the supportive behaviors described in Chapter 10 become most important.) When Jim began to talk to Beverly about her telephoning,

he learned some interesting things. In his haste to hang up the phone the first few times she called, he had given her the impression that he didn't care about her once the date was over. Feeling insecure about his love, she called as a way of getting attention and expressions of love from him.

Once Jim realized this fact, it became clear that he needed to find a solution that would leave Beverly feeling secure and at the same time allow him to feel unpressured.

Arriving at a shared definition of the problem requires skills associated with creating a supportive and confirming climate. The ability to be nonjudgmental, descriptive, and empathic are important support-producing behaviors. Both Jim and Beverly needed to engage in paraphrasing to discover all the details of the conflict.

When they're really communicating effectively, partners can help each other clarify what they're seeking. Truly believing that their happiness depends on each other's satisfaction, they actively try to analyze what obstacles need to be overcome.

4. **Generate possible solutions**   In the next step, the partners try to think of as many ways to satisfy both of their needs as possible. They can best do so by "brainstorming"—inventing as many potential solutions as they can. The key to success in brainstorming is to seek quantity without worrying about quality. The rule is to prohibit criticism of all ideas, no matter how outlandish they may sound. An idea seeming farfetched can sometimes lead to a more workable one. Another rule of brainstorming is that ideas aren't personal property. If one person makes a suggestion, the other should feel free to suggest another solution that builds upon or modifies the original one. The original solution and its offshoots are all solutions that will be considered later. Once partners get over their possessiveness about ideas, the level of defen-

---

The first fight is a ritual, a test of the relationship. Very often it will be provoked deliberately, usually over a false issue (I know a couple who fell out forever, after a very promising start, over whether the Marx Brothers were greater than W. C. Fields), just to see what happens. Do they really care? How do they both feel? How deeply? Of course, all it really proves is that they can survive until the next fight.

JANE O'REILLY

---

siveness drops and both people can work together to find the best solution without worrying about whose idea it is.

All of the supportive and confirming behaviors discussed in Chapter 10 are important during this step. Two, however, stand out as crucial: the ability to communicate provisionalism rather than certainty, and the ability to refrain from premature evaluations of any solution. The aim of this step is to generate *all* the possible solutions—whether immediately reasonable or not. By behaving provisionally and avoiding any evaluation until all the solutions are generated, creative and spontaneous behavior is encouraged. The final result is a long list of solutions that most likely contains the best solution, one that might not have been expressed if the communication climate were defensive.

Jim and Beverly used brainstorming to generate solutions to their telephone problem. Their list consisted of continuing the calling but limiting the time spent on the phone; limiting the calls to a "once in a while" basis; Beverly's keeping a journal that could serve as a substitute for calling; Jim's calling Beverly on a "once in a while" basis; cutting out all calling;

moving in together to eliminate the necessity for calling; getting married; and breaking up. Although some of these solutions were clearly unacceptable to both of them, they listed all the ideas they could think of, preparing themselves for the next step in no-lose problem solving.

5. Evaluate the possible solutions and choose the best one   The time to evaluate the solutions is after they have all been generated, after the partners feel they have exhausted all the possibilities. In this step, the possible solutions generated during the previous step are evaluated for their ability to satisfy the mutually shared goal. How does each solution stand up against the individual and mutual goals? Which solution satisfies the most goals? Partners need to work cooperatively in examining each solution and in finally selecting the best one.

It is important during this step to react spontaneously rather than in a strategic fashion. Selecting a particular solution because the other person finds it satisfactory, while seemingly a "nice" thing to do, is as manipulative a strategy as getting the other person to accept a solution satisfactory only to you. Respond as you feel as solutions are evaluated, and encourage your partner to do the same. Any solution agreed upon as "best" has little chance of satisfying both partners' needs if it was strategically manipulated to the top of the list.

The solution Beverly and Jim selected as satisfying her need to feel secure, his need to be undisturbed before turning in, and their mutual goal of maintaining their relationship at a highly intimate level was to limit both the frequency and length of the calls. Also, Jim agreed to share in the calling.

6. Implement the solution   Now the time comes to try out the idea selected to see if it does, indeed, satisfy everyone's needs. The key questions to answer are *who* does *what* to *whom*, and *when?*

Before Jim and Beverly tried out their solution, they went over the agreement to make sure it was clear. This step proved to be important, for a potential misunderstanding existed. When will the solution be implemented? Should Beverly wait a few weeks before calling? Should Jim begin the calling? They agreed that Jim would call after their next date.

Another problem concerned their different definitions of length. How long is too long? They decided that more than a few minutes would be too long.

The solution was implemented after they discussed the solution and came to mutual agreement about its particulars. This process may seem awkward and time-consuming, but both Beverly and Jim decided that without a clear understanding of the solution, they were opening the door to future conflicts.

Interestingly, the discussion concerning their mutual needs and how the solution satisfied them was an important part of their relationship development. Jim learned that Beverly felt insecure about his love (sometimes); Beverly learned that Jim needed time to himself, and that this need did not reflect on his love for her. Soon after implementing the solution, they found that the problem ceased to exist. Jim no longer felt the calls were invading his privacy, and Beverly, after talks with Jim, felt more secure about his love.

7. Follow up the solution   To stop after selecting and implementing a particular solution assumes any solution is forever, that time does not change things, that people remain constant, and that events never alter circumstances. Of course this assumption is not the case: As people and circumstances change, a particular solution may lose or increase its effectiveness. Regardless, it remains for a follow-up evaluation to take place.

After you've tested your solution for a short time, it's a good idea to *plan* a meeting to talk

I will not play at tug o' war.
I'd rather play at hug o' war.
Where everyone hugs
Instead of tugs,
Where everyone giggles
And rolls on the rug,
Where everyone kisses,
And everyone grins,
And everyone cuddles,
And everyone wins.

SHEL SILVERSTEIN

about how things are going. You may find that you need to make some changes or even rethink the whole problem.

Reviewing the effects of your solution does not mean that something is wrong and must be corrected. Indeed, everything may point to the conclusion that the solution is still working to satisfy the individuals' needs and the mutually shared goal, and that the mutually shared goal is still important to you.

It is important at this stage in the no-lose problem-solving process to be honest with yourself as well as the other person. It may be difficult for you to say, "We need to talk about this again," yet it could be essential if the problem is to remain resolved. Planning a follow-up talk at the same time the solution is first implemented is important.

Beverly and Jim decided to wait one month before discussing the effects of their solution. Their talk was short, because both felt the problem no longer existed. Also, their discussions helped their relationship grow: They learned more about each other, felt closer, and developed a way to handle their conflicts constructively.

The win-win approach seems too good to be true. Reassuringly enough, research shows that seeking mutual benefit is not only desirable—it works. In fact, it works far better than a win-lose approach.

Robert Axelrod (1984) presented subjects with a bargaining situation called "prisoner's dilemma," in which they could choose either to cooperate or betray a confederate. There are three types of outcomes in prisoner's dilemma: One partner can win big by betraying a confederate, both can win by cooperating, or both can lose by betraying each other.

Although cynics may assume that the most effective strategy is to betray a partner (a win-lose approach), Axelrod demonstrates that cooperation is actually the best hard-nosed choice. He staged a tournament in which participants played against a computer that was programmed to represent several negotiating strategies. The winning strategy was one called "Tit-for-Tat." It starts out by cooperating and continues to cooperate until the other person betrays it. After that, the program always does what the other player did on the previous move. It never punishes an opponent more than once for a betrayal, and it will always cooperate if the other player does.

A win-win Tit-for-Tat strategy succeeds for several reasons (Kinsley 1984). First, it isn't a sucker. It responds quickly to betrayal, discouraging others from taking unfair advantage. At the same time, it is quick to forgive. It doesn't hold a grudge: As soon as the other person cooperates, it does too. Finally, it isn't too sneaky. By making its behavior obvious and predictable, Tit-for-Tat creates an atmosphere of trust.

There are certainly some conflicts that can't be resolved with win-win outcomes. Only one suitor can marry the prince or princess, and only one person can be hired for the advertised job. Most of the time, however, good intentions and creative thinking can lead to outcomes that satisfy everyone's needs.

Summary

Despite wishes and cultural myths to the contrary, conflict is a natural and unavoidable part of any relationship. Since conflict can't be escaped, the challenge is how to deal with it effectively, so that it strengthens a relationship rather than weakening it.

All conflicts possess the same characteristics: expressed struggle, perceived incompatible goals, perceived scarce rewards, and interdependence. Functional conflicts cope with these characteristics in very different ways from dysfunctional ones. Partners strive to cooperate instead of compete; to focus on rather than avoid the issues in dispute; and to seek positive, long-term solutions that meet one another's needs.

Individuals can respond to conflicts in a variety of ways: nonassertively, indirectly, with direct or passive aggression, and assertively. Each of these approaches can be justified in certain circumstances. The way a conflict is handled isn't always the choice of a single person, since the parties influence one another as they develop a relational conflict style. Out of this style can come three possible outcomes to a particular conflict: lose-lose, win-lose, and win-win. In most circumstances a win-win outcome is most desirable, and it can be achieved by following the guidelines outlined in this chapter.

Activities

1. Even the best relationships have conflicts. Using the criteria on pages 359–361, describe at least five conflicts in one of your important relationships. Then answer the following questions:
   a. Which conflicts involve content issues? Which involve relational issues?
   b. Which conflicts were one-time affairs, and which recur?

2. From your recent experience recall two conflict incidents: one functional and one dysfunctional. Then answer the following questions:
   a. What distinguished these two conflicts?
   b. What were the consequences of each?
   c. How might the dysfunctional conflict have turned out differently if it had been handled in a more functional manner?
   d. How could you have communicated differently to make the conflict more functional?

3. Interview someone who knows you well. Ask your informant which personal conflict styles (nonassertive, indirect, etc.) you use most often, and the effect each of these styles has on the relationship. Based on your findings, discuss whether different behavior might produce more productive results.

4. With the help of a classmate, construct an assertive message you *could* deliver to someone in your life: a boss, professor, friend, family member, neighbor, and so on. Once you have rehearsed the message, consider the risks and benefits of delivering it. Based on your deliberations, decide whether the assertive approach is justified in this case.

5. This activity will be most productive if you consult with the other person or people in the relationship as you answer the following questions.
   a. Is your relational style of handling conflict complementary, symmetrical, or parallel? What are the consequences of this style?
   b. What combination of intimacy and aggressiveness characterizes your approach to conflict? Are you satisfied with this approach?
   c. What conflict rituals do you follow in this relationship? Are these rituals functional or dysfunctional? What might be better alternatives?

6. To explore how the win-win approach might work in your life, try one of the following alternatives:
   a. Use the steps on pages 382–386 to describe how you could manage a conflict following the win-win approach. How could you try this approach in your personal life? What difference might such an approach make?
   b. Try the win-win approach with a relational partner. What parts prove most helpful? Which are most difficult? How can you improve your relationship by using some or all of the win-win approach in future conflicts?

Readings

Adler, R., and N. Towne. *Looking Out/Looking In*. Fort Worth, TX: Holt, Rinehart and Winston, 1990.

Axelrod, R. *The Evolution of Cooperation*. New York: Basic Books, 1984.

*Bach, G. R., and P. Wyden. *The Intimate Enemy*. New York: Avon, 1968.

Benoit, W. L., and P. J. Benoit. "Everyday Argument Practices of Naive Social Actors." In *Argument and Critical Practices* J. Wenzel, ed. Annandale, VA: Speech Communication Association, 1987.

Blake, R. R., and J. S. Mouton. *The Managerial Grid*. Houston: Gulf Publishing Co., 1964.

Burggraf, C. S. "A Critical Examination of Sex Differences in Marital Communication." Paper presented at the Speech Communication Association conference, Chicago, 1986.

Burggraf, C. S., and A. L. Sillars. "A Critical Examination of Sex Differences in Marital Communication." *Communication Monographs* 54 (1987): 276–94.

Canary, D. J., and W. R. Cupach. "Relational and Episodic Characteristics Associated with Conflict Tactics." *Journal of Social and Personal Relationships* 5 (1988): 305–25.

Canary, D. J., and B. H. Spitzberg. "Appropriateness and Effectiveness Perceptions of Conflict Strategies." *Human Communication Research* 15 (1987): 93–118.

Ellis, D. G., and B. A. Fisher. "Phases of Conflict in Small Group Development." *Human Communication Research* 1 (1975): 195–212.

Fahs, M. L. "The Effects of Self-Disclosing Communication and Attitude Similarity on the Reduction of Interpersonal Conflict." *Western Journal of Speech Communication* 45 (1981): 38–50.

Filley, A. C. *Interpersonal Conflict Resolution*. Glenview, IL: Scott, Foresman, 1975.

*Fisher, R., and W. Ury. *Getting to Yes: Negotiating Agreement Without Giving In*. Boston: Houghton Mifflin, 1981.

Fitzpatrick, M. A. "A Typological Approach to Communication in Relationships." In *Communication Yearbook 1* B. Rubin, ed. New Brunswick, NJ: Transaction Books, 1977.

Fitzpatrick, M. A., S. Fallis, and L. Vance. "Multifunctional Coding of Conflict Resolution Strategies in Marital Dyads." *Family Relations* 21 (1982): 61–71.

*Hocker, J. L., and W. W. Wilmot. *Interpersonal Conflict*, 3d ed. Dubuque, IA: Wm. C. Brown, 1991.

Infante, D. A., and C. J. Wigley III. "Verbal Aggressiveness: An Interpersonal Model and Measure." *Communication Monographs* 53 (1986): 61–69.

Jandt, F. E. *Conflict Resolution Through Communication*. New York: Harper & Row, 1973.

Jordan, J., and M. E. Roloff. "Acquiring Assistance from Others: The Effect of Indirect Requests and Relational Intimacy on Verbal Compliance." *Human Communication Research* 16 (1990): 519–55.

Kinsley, M. "It Pays to Be Nice." *Science* 222 (1984): 162.

Knapp, M. L., L. L. Putnam, and L. J. Davis. "Measuring Interpersonal Conflict in Organizations: Where Do We Go From Here?" *Management Communication Quarterly* 1 (1988): 414–429.

Metts, S., and W. Cupach. "The Influence of Relationship Beliefs and Problem-Solving Responses on Satisfaction in Romantic Relationships." *Human Communication Research* 17 (1990): 170–85.

Miller, S., E. W. Nunnally, and D. B. Wackman. *Alive and Aware: How to Improve Your Relationships Through Better Communication*. Minneapolis: Interpersonal Communication Programs, 1975.

Monroe, C., M. G. Borzi, V. S. DiSalvo. "Conflict Behaviors of Difficult Subordinates." *Southern Communication Journal* 34 (1989): 311–29.

Okabe, K. "Indirect Speech Acts of the Japanese." In *Communication Theory: Eastern and Western Perspectives*, D. L. Kincaid, ed. San Diego: Academic Press, 1987.

Pearson, J. C. *Gender and Communication*, 3d ed. Dubuque, IA: Wm. C. Brown, 1991.

Putnam L., and C. Wilson "Communicative Strategies in Organizational Conflicts: Reliability and Validity of a Measurement Scale." *Communication Yearbook 6*, edited by M. Burgoon, Beverly Hills Calif. Sage 1982.

Rands, M., G. Levinger, and G. D. Mellinger. "Patterns of Conflict Resolution and Marital Satisfaction." *Journal of Family Issues* 2 (September 1981): 297–321.

Simons, H. "Persuasion in Social Conflicts: A Critique of Prevailing Conceptions and a Framework for Future Research." *Speech Monographs* 39 (1972): 227–47.

*Thomas, K. "Conflict and Conflict Management." In *Handbook of Industrial and Organizational Psychology*, M. D. Dunnette, ed. Chicago: Rand McNally, 1976.

*Weider-Hatfield, D. "A Unit in Conflict Management Skills." *Communication Education* 30 (1981): 265–73.

*Wilmot, W. *Dyadic Communication*. New York: McGraw-Hill, 1987.

*Items identified by an asterisk are recommended as especially useful follow-ups.

Glossary

Abstraction ladder   A range of more-to-less abstract terms describing an event or object.

Accenting   Nonverbal behaviors that emphasize part of a verbal message.

Active listening   *See* Reflecting.

Advising response   A helping response in which the receiver offers suggestions about how the speaker should deal with a problem.

Affinity   The degree to which persons like or appreciate one another.

Agape   Altruistic, compassionate form of love given without ulterior motives or expectations of anything in return.

Ambiguous response   A disconfirming response with more than one meaning, leaving the other person unsure of the responder's position.

Ambushing   A style in which the receiver listens carefully in order to gather information to use in an attack on the speaker.

Analyzing statement   A helping style in which the listener offers an interpretation of a speaker's message.

Androgynous   Possessing both masculine and feminine traits.

Apathy   A defense mechanism in which a person avoids admitting emotional pain by pretending not to care about an event. *See also* Emotional insulation.

Assertion   A direct expression of the sender's needs, thoughts, or feelings, delivered in a way that does not attack the receiver's dignity.

Assimilation to prior input   The tendency to interpret a message in terms of similar messages remembered from the past.

Attending   A phase of the listening process in which the communicator focuses on a message, excluding other messages.

Avoiding   A relational stage immediately prior to terminating in which the partners minimize contact with one another.

Behavioral description   An account that refers only to observable phenomena.

Bonding   A stage of relational development in which the partners make symbolic public gestures to show that their relationship exists.

"But" statement   A statement in which the second half cancels the meaning of the first, e.g., "I'd like to help you, *but* I have to go or I'll miss my bus."

Channel   The medium through which a message passes from sender to receiver.

Circumscribing   A relational stage in which partners begin to reduce the scope of their contact and commitment to one another.

Cognitive complexity   The ability to construct a variety of frameworks for viewing an issue.

Cognitive conservatism   The tendency to seek out information that conforms to an existing self-concept and ignore information that contradicts it.

Communication   A continuous, irreversible, transactive process involving communicators who occupy different but overlapping environments and are simultaneously senders and receivers of messages, many of which are distorted by physical and psychological noise.

Communication climate   The emotional tone of a relationship between two or more individuals.

Communication competence   The ability to accomplish one's personal goals in a manner that maintains a relationship on terms that are acceptable to all.

Compensation   A defense mechanism in which a person stresses a strength in one area to camouflage a shortcoming in some other area.

Complementary relational structure   One in which the distribution of power is unequal, with one person occupying a "one-up" and the other a "one-down" position.

Complementing   Nonverbal behavior that reinforces a verbal message.

Compliance gaining strategy   A tactic used to persuade others to think or behave in a desired way.

Confirming response   A message that expresses caring or respect for another person.

Conflict   An expressed struggle between at least two interdependent people who perceive incompatible goals, scarce rewards, and interference from the other person in achieving their goals.

Content message   A message that communicates information about the subject being discussed. *See also* Relational message.

Contradicting   Nonverbal behavior that is inconsistent with a verbal message.

Control   The social need to influence others.

Debilitative emotions   Emotions that prevent a person from functioning effectively.

Deception cues Nonverbal behaviors that signal the untruthfulness of a verbal message.

Decoding The process in which a receiver attaches meaning to a message. Synonymous with *interpreting.*

Deescalatory spiral A reciprocal communication pattern in which one person's nonthreatening behavior leads to reduced hostility by the other, with the level of hostility steadily decreasing.

Defense mechanism A psychological device used to maintain a presenting self-image that an individual believes is threatened.

Defensive listening A response style in which the receiver perceives a speaker's comments as an attack.

Defensiveness The attempt to protect a presenting image a person believes is being attacked.

Descriptive communication Messages that describe the speaker's position without evaluating others. Synonymous with "I" language.

Desired self The person we would like to be. It may be identical to or different from the perceived and presenting selves.

Differentiating A relational stage in which the partners reestablish their individual identities after having bonded together.

Direct aggression An expression of the sender's thoughts and/or feelings that attacks the position and dignity of the receiver.

Direct request A compliance gaining strategy in which the communicator directly asks another person to meet his or her needs.

Disclaimer A phrase that disqualifies the value of the following statement, e.g., *"You probably won't believe this ..."*

Disconfirming response A message that expresses a lack of caring or respect for another person.

Disfluency A nonlinguistic verbalization, for example, *um, er, ah.*

Dissonance An inconsistency between two conflicting pieces of information, attitudes, or behavior. Communicators strive to reduce dissonance, often through defense mechanisms that maintain an idealized presenting image.

Double message Contradiction between a verbal message and one or more nonverbal cues.

Emblems Deliberate nonverbal behaviors with precise meanings, known to virtually all members of a cultural group.

Emotive language Language that conveys the sender's attitude rather than simply offering an objective description.

Empathy The ability to project oneself into another person's point of view so as to experience the other's thoughts and feelings.

Encoding The process of putting thoughts into symbols, most commonly words.

Environment Both the physical setting in which communication occurs and the personal perspectives of the people involved.

Equivocal language Ambiguous language that has two or more equally plausible meanings.

Eros An intense form of love, based on physical and psychological attraction.

Escalatory spiral A reciprocal communication pattern in which one person's attack leads to a counterattack by the other, with the level of hostility steadily increasing.

Euphemism A pleasant term substituted for a blunt one in order to soften the impact of unpleasant information.

Evaluative language Messages in which the sender judges the receiver in some way, usually resulting in a defensive response.

Exchange theory The theory that people seek relationships in which the benefits they gain equal or exceed the costs they incur.

Experimenting An early stage in relational development, consisting of a search for common ground. If the experimentation is successful, the relationship will progress to intensifying. If not, it may go no further.

External noise Factors outside the receiver that interfere with the accurate reception of a message.

Face The image an individual wants to project to the world. *See also* Presenting self.

Face maintenance strategy Strategies that lead others to act in ways that reinforce the communicator's presenting self.

Face threatening act Behavior by another that is perceived as attacking an individual's presenting image, or face.

Facework The degree to which people act to preserve their own presenting image and the image of others.

Facilitative emotions Emotions that contribute to effective functioning.

Fallacy of approval The irrational belief that it is vital to win the approval of virtually every person a communicator deals with.

Fallacy of catastrophic expectations   The irrational belief that the worst possible outcome will probably occur.

Fallacy of causation   The irrational belief that emotions are caused by others and not by the person who has them.

Fallacy of helplessness   The irrational belief that satisfaction in life is determined by forces beyond one's control.

Fallacy of overgeneralization   Irrational beliefs in which (1) conclusions (usually negative) are based on limited evidence or (2) communicators exaggerate their shortcomings.

Fallacy of perfection   The irrational belief that a worthwhile communicator should be able to handle every situation with complete confidence and skill.

Fallacy of shoulds   The irrational belief that people should behave in the most desirable way.

Feedback   The discernible response of a receiver to a sender's message.

Hearing   The first stage in the listening process, in which sound waves are received by a communicator.

Hedge   Words or phrases that soften the impact of a statement, e.g., "I *guess* I'm *a little bit* disappointed . . ."

Hesitations   Filler words that add no meaning to a statement, e.g., "*Uh*, I'd like to talk to you about . . . *um* . . . what happened at the party last night."

"I" language   A statement that describes the speaker's reaction to another person's behavior without making judgments about its worth. *See also* "You" language.

Illustrators   Nonverbal behaviors that accompany and support verbal messages.

Impersonal communication   Behavior that treats others as objects rather than individuals. *See* Interpersonal communication.

Impersonal response   A disconfirming response that is superficial or trite.

Impervious response   A disconfirming response that ignores another person's attempt to communicate.

Inclusion   The social need to feel a sense of belonging in some relationship with others.

Incongruous response   A disconfirming response in which two messages, one of which is usually nonverbal, contradict one another.

Indirect appeal   A compliance-gaining strategy based on the hope that the other party will infer or assume the communicator's unexpressed intent.

Indirect communication   Hinting at a message instead of expressing thoughts and feelings directly. *See also* Passive aggression and Assertion.

Inference   A statement based on interpretation of sense data.

Initiating   The first stage in relational development, in which the parties express interest in one another.

Insensitive listening   Failure to recognize the thoughts or feelings that are not directly expressed by a speaker; instead, accepting the speaker's words at face value.

Insulated listening   A style in which the receiver ignores undesirable information.

Integrating   A relational stage in which the parties begin to take on a single identity.

Intensifiers   Adjectives and adverbs that intensify the noun or verb being described, e.g., a *very* bad idea, a *really* good time.

Intensifying   A relational stage following integrating, in which the parties move toward integration by increasing the amount of contact and the breadth and depth of self-disclosure.

Interactive communication model   A characterization of communication as a two-way event in which sender and receiver exchange messages in response to one another.

Interpersonal communication   Communication in which the individuals consider one another as unique individuals rather than as objects. It is characterized by minimal use of stereotyped labels; unique, idiosyncratic social rules; and a high degree of information exchange.

Interpersonal relationship   An association in which the people meet each other's social needs to a greater or lesser degree.

Interpretation   The process of attaching meaning to sense data. Synonymous with *Decoding.*

Interrupting response   A disconfirming response in which one communicator interrupts another.

Intimacy   Intellectual, emotional, and/or physical closeness.

Intimate distance   One of Hall's four distance zones, ranging from skin contact to eighteen inches.

Irrelevant response   A disconfirming response in which one communicator's comments bear no relationship to the previous speaker's ideas.

Johari Window   A model that describes the relationship between self-disclosure and self-awareness.

Judging response   A reaction in which the receiver evaluates the sender's message either favorably or unfavorably.

Kinesics The study of body motion.

Leakage Nonverbal behaviors that reveal information a communicator does not disclose verbally.

Lie A deliberate act of deception.

Linear communication model A characterization of communication as a one-way event in which a message flows from sender to receiver.

Listening The process of hearing, attending, understanding, remembering, and responding to messages.

Lose-lose problem solving An approach to conflict resolution in which neither party achieves its goals. Sometimes lose-lose outcomes result from both partners seeking a win-lose victory over one another. In other cases, the partners settle for a lose-lose outcome (for example, compromise) because they cannot find any better alternative.

Ludus A game-like form of love, pleasant but lacking strong feeling and commitment.

Manipulators Movements in which one part of the body grooms, massages, rubs, holds, fidgets, pinches, picks, or otherwise manipulates another part.

Mania A romantic form of love, intensive, obsessive, and painful. It is characterized by a lack of control by the lover.

Message Information sent from a sender to a receiver.

Metacommunication Messages (usually relational) that refer to other messages: communication about communication.

Microexpressions Brief facial expressions.

Mixed emotions Emotions that are combinations of primary emotions. Some mixed emotions can be expressed in single words (that is, *awe, remorse*) whereas others require more than one term (that is, *embarrassed and angry, relieved and grateful*).

Negotiation A process in which two or more people discuss specific proposals in order to find a mutually acceptable agreement.

Neutrality A defense-arousing behavior described by Gibb in which the sender expresses indifference toward a receiver.

Noise External, physiological, and psychological distractions that interfere with the accurate transmission and reception of a message.

Nonassertion The inability to express one's thoughts or feelings when necessary. Nonassertion may be due to a lack of confidence, communication skill, or both.

Nonverbal communication Messages expressed by other than linguistic means.

Norm of reciprocity A social convention that obligates one communicator to return the favors extended by others.

One-way communication Communication in which a receiver provides no feedback to a sender.

Organization The stage in the perception process that involves arranging data in a meaningful way.

Paralanguage Nonlinguistic means of vocal expression: rate, pitch, tone, and so on.

Parallel relational structure One in which the balance of power shifts from one person to the other, according to the situation.

Paraphrasing Restating a speaker's thoughts and feelings in the listener's own words.

Passive aggression An indirect expression of aggression, delivered in a way that allows the sender to maintain a façade of kindness.

Perceived self The person we believe ourselves to be in moments of candor. It may be identical with or different from the present and desired selves.

Perception checking A three-part method for verifying the accuracy of interpretations, including a description of the sense data, two possible interpretations, and a request for confirmation of the interpretations.

Personal distance One of Hall's four distance zones, ranging from eighteen inches to four feet.

Personality A relatively consistent set of traits exhibited by a person across a variety of situations.

Physiological noise Biological factors in the receiver that interfere with accurate reception of a message.

Polite language forms Overly polite terms that weaken the power of a statement, e.g., *"Excuse me, please,* I'd like to talk to you for a minute, *sir."*

Powerless speech mannerisms Forms of speech that communicate a lack of power to others: hedges, hesitations, intensifiers, and so on.

Pragma A form of love in which the primary goal is contentment and avoidance of pain.

Pragmatic rules Rules that govern interpretation of language in terms of its social context. *See also* Semantic rules, Syntactic rules.

Presenting self The image a person presents to others. It may be identical with or different from the perceived and desired selves.

Primary emotions   Basic emotions. Some researchers have identified eight primary emotions: joy, acceptance, fear, surprise, sadness, disgust, anger, and anticipation.

Problem orientation   A supportive style of communication described by Gibb in which the communicators focus on working together to solve their problems instead of trying to impose their own solutions on one another.

Proxemics   The study of how people and animals use space.

Pseudolistening   An imitation of true listening in which the receiver's mind is elsewhere.

Psychological noise   Forces within a communicator that interfere with the ability to express or understand a message accurately.

Public distance   One of Hall's four distance zones, extending outward from twelve feet.

Punctuation   The process of determining the causal order of events.

Questioning   A style of helping in which the receiver seeks additional information from the sender. Some questioning responses are really disguised advice.

Rationalization   A defense mechanism in which logical but untrue explanations maintain an unrealistic desired or presenting self-image.

Receiver   One who notices and attends to a message.

Reference groups   Groups against which we compare ourselves, thereby influencing our self-concept and self-esteem.

Reflected appraisal   The theory that a person's self-concept matches the way the person believes others regard him or her.

Reflecting   A style of listening to help another, consisting of paraphrasing both the speaker's thoughts and feelings.

Regression   A defense mechanism in which a person avoids assuming responsibility by pretending that he or she is unable to do something instead of admitting to being simply unwilling.

Regulating   Nonverbal behaviors that control the flow of verbal messages in a conversation.

Regulative rules   Rules that govern what interpretation of a message is appropriate in a given context.

Relational appeal   Compliance gaining strategies that rely on the target's relationship with the person making the request.

Relational message   A message that expresses the social relationship between two or more individuals.

Relationship   *See* Interpersonal relationship.

Relative language   Words that gain their meaning by comparison.

Remembering   A phase of the listening process in which a message is recalled.

Repeating   Nonverbal behaviors that duplicate the content of a verbal message.

Repression   A defense mechanism in which a person avoids facing an unpleasant situation or fact by denying its existence.

Respect   The social need to be held in esteem by others.

Responding   A phase of the listening process in which feedback occurs, offering evidence that the message has been received.

Selection   A phase of the perception process in which a communicator attends to a stimulus from the environment.

Selective listening   A listening style in which the receiver responds only to messages that interest him or her.

Self-concept   The relatively stable set of perceptions each individual holds of himself or herself.

Self-disclosure   The process of deliberately revealing information about oneself that is significant and that would not normally be known by others.

Self-fulfilling prophecy   A prediction or expectation of an event that makes the outcome more likely to occur than would otherwise have been the case.

Self-monitoring   The process of attending to one's behavior and using these observations to shape the way one behaves.

Self-talk   The nonvocal process of thinking. On some level, self-talk occurs as a person interprets another's behavior.

Semantic rules   Rules that govern the meaning of language, as opposed to its structure. *See also* Syntactic rules.

Sender   The creator of a message.

Sex role   The social orientation that governs behavior, rather than biological gender.

Significant other   A person whose opinion is important enough to affect one's self-concept strongly.

Social comparison   Evaluating oneself in terms of or by comparison to others.

Social distance   One of Hall's distance zones, ranging from four to twelve feet.

Social penetration model A model that describes relationships in terms of their breadth and depth.

Spiral A reciprocal communication pattern in which messages reinforce one another. *See also* Escalatory spiral, Deescalatory spiral.

Spontaneity A supportive communication behavior described by Gibb in which the sender expresses a message without any attempt to manipulate the receiver.

Stage hogging A listening style in which the receiver is more concerned with making his or her own point than in understanding the speaker.

Stagnation A relational stage characterized by declining enthusiasm and standardized forms of behavior.

Static evaluation Treating people or objects as if they were unchanging.

Storge A form of love that is an extension of friendship, comfortable but lacking in intensity.

Substituting Nonverbal behavior that takes the place of a verbal message.

Superiority A defense-arousing style of communication described by Gibb in which the sender states or implies that the receiver is not worthy of respect.

Supporting A response style in which the receiver reassures, comforts, or distracts the person seeking help.

Symmetrical relationship Communication in which the power is distributed evenly between the individuals.

Sympathy Compassion for another's situation. *See also* Empathy.

Syntactic rules Rules that govern the ways symbols can be arranged, as opposed to the meanings of those symbols. *See also* Semantic rules.

Tag questions Questions that follow a declarative statement and relate to it, e.g., "Let's get going, *okay?*"

Tangential response A disconfirming response that uses the speaker's remark as a starting point for a shift to a new topic.

Terminating The conclusion of a relationship, characterized by the acknowledgement of one or both partners that the relationship is over.

Territory A stationary area claimed by an individual.

Transactional communication model A characterization of communication as the simultaneous sending and receiving of messages in an ongoing, irreversible process.

Understanding A stage in the listening process in which the receiver attaches meaning to a message.

Verbal aggression A defense mechanism in which a person avoids facing unpleasant information by verbally attacking the confronting source.

"We" statement A statement in which the speaker diffuses responsibility for the message by using the first person plural instead of the singular, e.g., *"We* have a problem here . . ."

White lie A deliberate hiding or misrepresentation of the truth, intended to help or not to harm the receiver.

Win-lose problem solving An approach to conflict resolution in which one person reaches her or his goal at the expense of the other.

Win-win problem solving An approach to conflict resolution in which people work together to satisfy all their goals.

"You" language A statement that expresses or implies a judgment of the other person. *See also* Evaluative language, "I" language.

PHOTO CREDITS

1 Photograph, *Struss Family on a Picnic,* from the Karl Struss Collection. Courtesy, Amon Carter Museum, Fort Worth (83.25/1346). **3** © Owen Franken, Stock, Boston. **18** © Alan Carey/The Image Works. **24** © Mimi Forsyth, Monkmeyer Press Photo Service. **31** Photograph, *Eastman Co./Woman with Camera in Grass Field,* from Karl Struss Collection. Courtesy Amon Carter Museum, Fort Worth (83.25/3455). **33** © Marla Murphy, amwest. **40** © Joan Liftin. **46** © David Wells, The Image Works. **51** © R. M. Collins, III, The Image Works. **63** © Mark Chester, Photo 20–20. **75** © Spencer Grant, Monkmeyer Press Photo Service. **79** © Steven M. Stone, The Picture Cube. **85** © Mark Chester, Photo 20–20. **93** © J. Moore, The Image Works. **102** © Joan Liftin, Actuality, Inc. **112** © Joan Liftin, Actuality, Inc. **117** © Frank Siteman, Monkmeyer Press Photo Service. **123** Photograph, *Delaware Water Gap (Group of People on Porch Visiting),* from Karl Struss Collection. Courtesy Amon Carter Museum, Fort Worth, Texas (83.25/3467). **125** © Charles Gatewood, The Image Works. **128** © Mark Chester, Photo 20–20. **131** © Mark Chester, Photo 20–20. **133** © Mark Antman, The Image Works. **143** © Charles Gatewood, The Image Works. **161** © Bob Kalman, The Image Works. **168** © The Bergen Evening Record Corp., Hackensack, N.J. **171** © Bob Daemmrich, The Image Works. **172** © Brian W. Smith, The Picture Cube. **178** © Gratie H. Sandlin, amwest. **182** © Toni Michaels, The Image Works. **192** © Randy Matusow, Monkmeyer Press Photo Service. **197** © Charles Gatewood, The Image Works. **207** © David S. Strickler, The Picture Cube. **212** © Spencer Grant, The Picture Cube. **227** © Joan Liftin, Actuality, Inc. **230** © Mac Donald, The Picture Cube. **239** Photograph, *Barbara & Family,* from the Karl Struss Collection. Courtesy Amon Carter Museum, Fort Worth, Texas (83.25/1410) **241** © Elizabeth Crews, The Image Works. **247** © Charles Gatewood, The Image Works. **253** © Jack Spratt, The Image Works. **259** © Mark Chester, Photo 20–20. **264** © Sarah Putnam, The Picture Cube. **267** © Bobbi Carrey, The Picture Cube. **270** © Charles Gatewood, The Image Works. **275** © Polly Brown, Actuality. **289** © Mark Chester, Photo 20–20. **300** © Horst Schafer, amwest. **318** © Charles Harbutt. **325** © Yvona Mamatiuk, amwest. **329** © Bob Kalman, The Image Works. **334** © Steve Takatsuno, The Picture Cube. **340** © Stanley Rowin, The Picture Cube. **343** © David S. Strickler, The Picture Cube. **357** © Frank Siteman, The Picture Cube. **360** © Alan Dorow, Actuality, Inc. **364** © Joan Liftin, Actuality, Inc. **368** © David S. Strickler, The Image Works. **374** © Mimi Forsyth, Monkmeyer Press Photo Service. **378** © Mac Donald, The Picture Cube.

LITERARY CREDITS

9 Drawing by Weber; © 1989 The New Yorker Magazine, Inc. **13** Reprinted by permission of Chronicle Features, San Francisco. **19** Drawing by Stevenson; © 1983 The New Yorker Magazine, Inc. **38** ZIGGY; © 1986 Universal Press Syndicate Reprinted by permission. All rights reserved. **47** Drawing by Bernard Schoenbaum; © 1990 The New Yorker Magazine, Inc. **55** Reprinted from The Saturday Evening Post © 1973. **59** © Gahan Wilson. **71** Reprinted with special permission of North American Syndicate, Inc. **73** CATHY; © 1986 Universal Press Syndicate. Reprinted by permission. All rights reserved. **76** "Coming and Going" from *Dragonflies, Codfish & Frogs* by Ric Masten. Reprinted by permission of the poet. Sunflower Ink, Palo Colorado Road, Carmel, CA 93923. **77** © 1984 by Sidney Harris—*American Scientist Magazine.* **84** Drawing by M. Stevens; © 1990 The New Yorker Magazine, Inc. **96** Drawing by Weber; © 1981 The New Yorker Magazine, Inc. **108** Excerpt from *Benchley Beside Himself* by Robert Benchley. © 1921, 1922, 1925, 1927, 1928, 1943 by Harper & Row, Publishers, Inc. Reprinted by permission of Harper-Collins Publishers. **109** ZIGGY; © 1974 Universal Press Syndicate. Reprinted by permission. All rights reserved. **114** CATHY; © 1988 Universal Press Syndicate. Reprinted by permission. All rights reserved. **129** © 1984 by Sidney Harris—*Phi Delta Kappan.* **132** Excerpt from *Conversations and Communication* by J. A. M. Meerloo, © International Universities Press, Inc. Used by permission. **136** Reprinted with special permission of King Features Syndicate, Inc. **138** CATHY; © 1983 Universal Press Syndicate. Reprinted by permission. All rights reserved. **139** Excerpt from *Miss Manners' Guide to Excruciatingly Correct Behavior* by Judith Martin. © 1982 Warner Books Inc. **148** Excerpt from *I And Thou: Here And Now: Contributions of Gestalt Therapy.* Reprinted courtesy of the author, Dr. Claudio Naranjo. **151** By Herbert Goldberg; © 1970 by Saturday Review, Inc. **166** Used by permission of the estate of Michael ffolkes. **173** From "The Ring of Untruth" by Jack Rosenthal. Copyright © 1987 by The New York Times Company. Reprinted by permission. **174** "Nothing" from *Love Poems for the Very Married* by Lois Wyse. © 1967 by Lois Wyse. Reprinted by permission of Harper & Row Publishers, Inc. **176** Drawing by Maslin; © 1990 The New Yorker Magazine, Inc. **180** Drawing by James Thurber. © 1943 James Thurber. © 1971 Helen Thurber and Rosemary A. Thurber. From *Men, Women and Dogs* published by Harcourt Brace Jovanovich, Inc. **186** Reproduced from Carol A. Valentine and Banisa Saint Damian, "Communicative Power: Gender and Culture as Determinants of the Ideal Voice" in *Women and Commu-*

COVER CREDIT